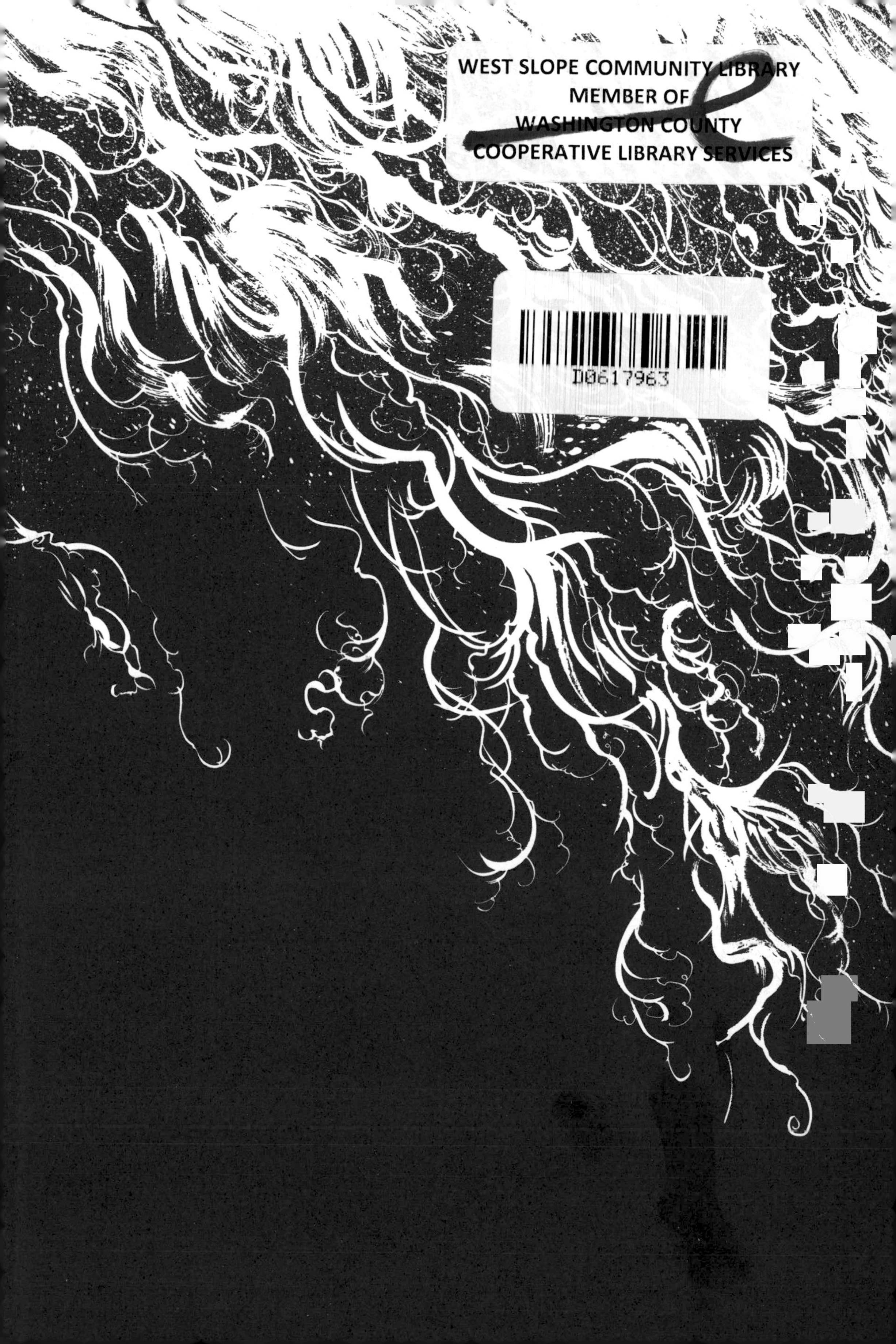

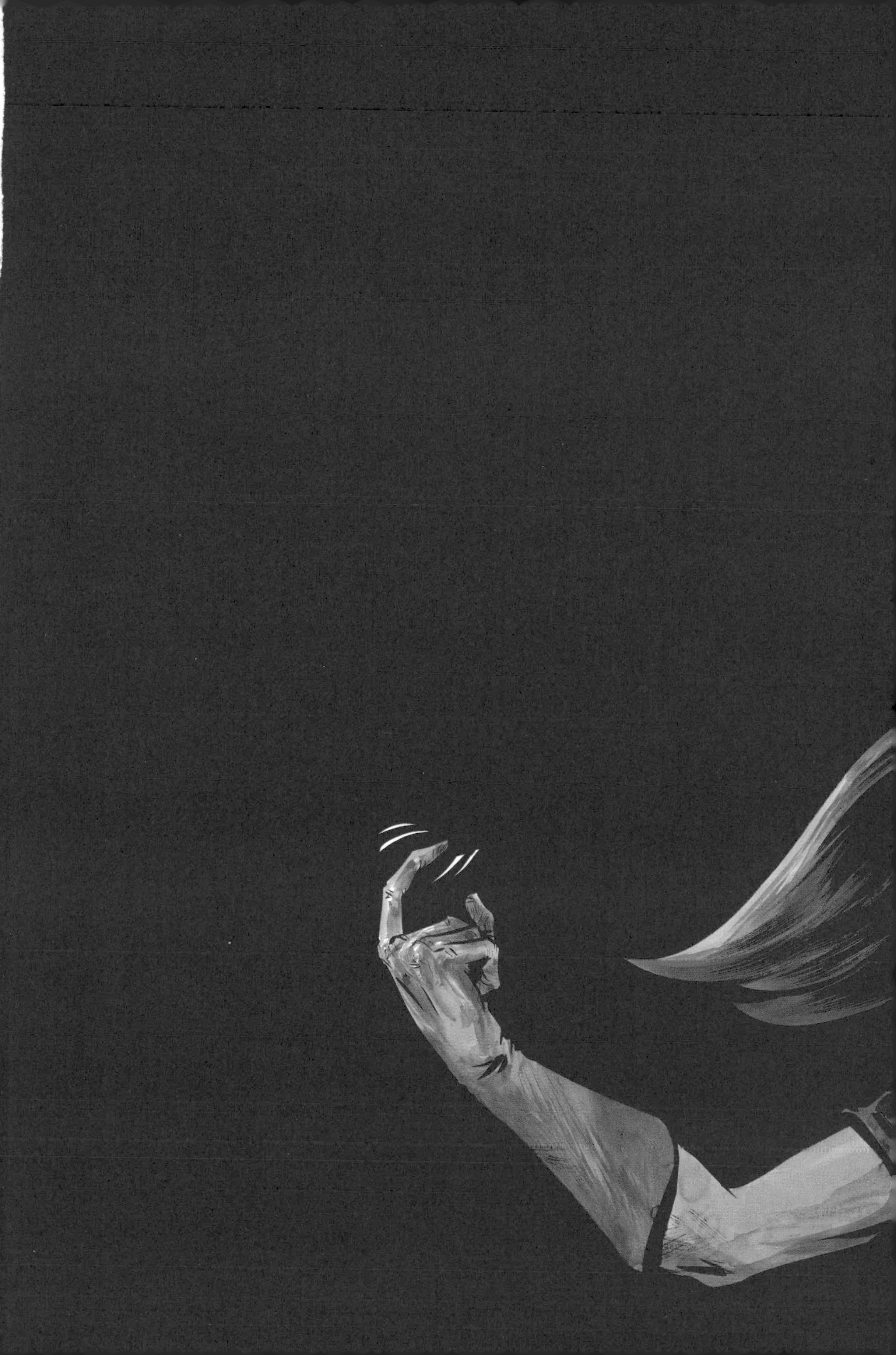

— TO LIGHTS WE'VE SEEN —

Come Again © 2018 Nate Powell.

Editor-In-Chief: Chris Staros.

Edited by Chris Staros + Leigh Walton.

Designed by Nate Powell + Chris Ross.

Published by Top Shelf Productions, PO Box 1282, Marietta, GA 30061-1282, USA.
Top Shelf Productions is an imprint of IDW Publishing, a division of Idea
and Design Works, LLC. Offices: 2765 Truxtun Road, San Diego, CA 92106.
Top Shelf Productions ®, the Top Shelf logo, Idea and Design Works ®, and the
IDW logo are registered trademarks of Idea and Design Works, LLC.
All Rights Reserved. With the exception of small excerpts of artwork used
for review purposes, none of the contents of this publication may be
reprinted without the permission of IDW Publishing. IDW does not read
or accept unsolicited submissions of ideas, stories, or artwork.

Visit our online catalog at www.topshelfcomix.com.

ISBN 978-1-60309-428-3

Printed in Korea.

22 21 20 19 18   1 2 3 4 5

COME AGAIN

NATE POWELL

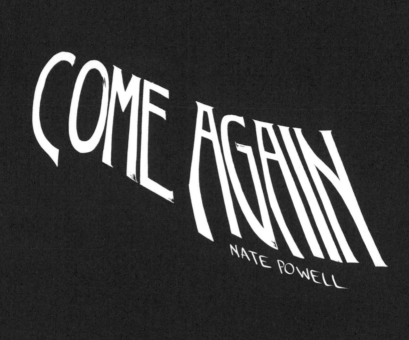

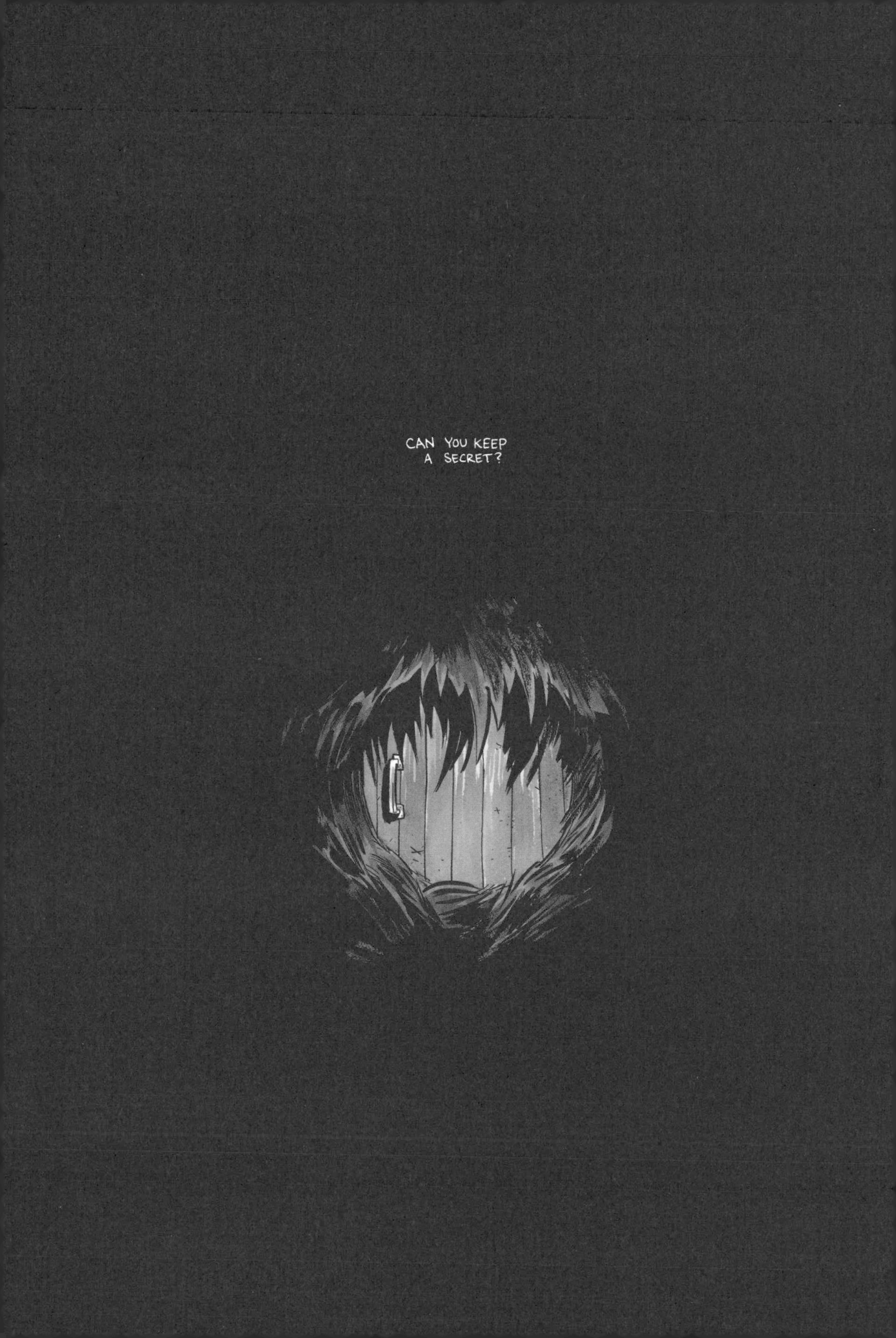
CAN YOU KEEP A SECRET?

HOW LONG WAS
IT HELD?

come
closer.

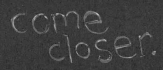

crawl inside.

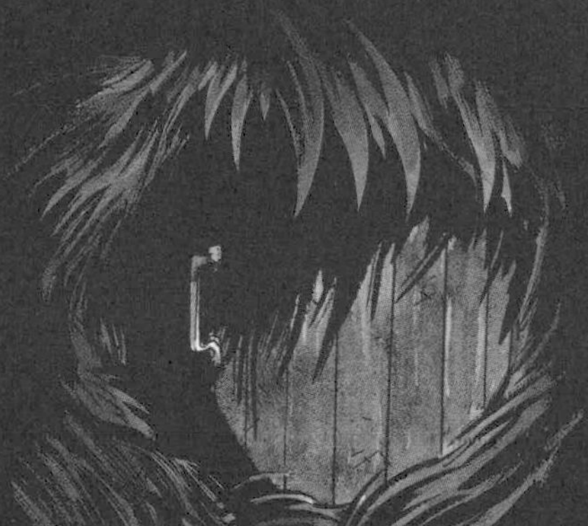

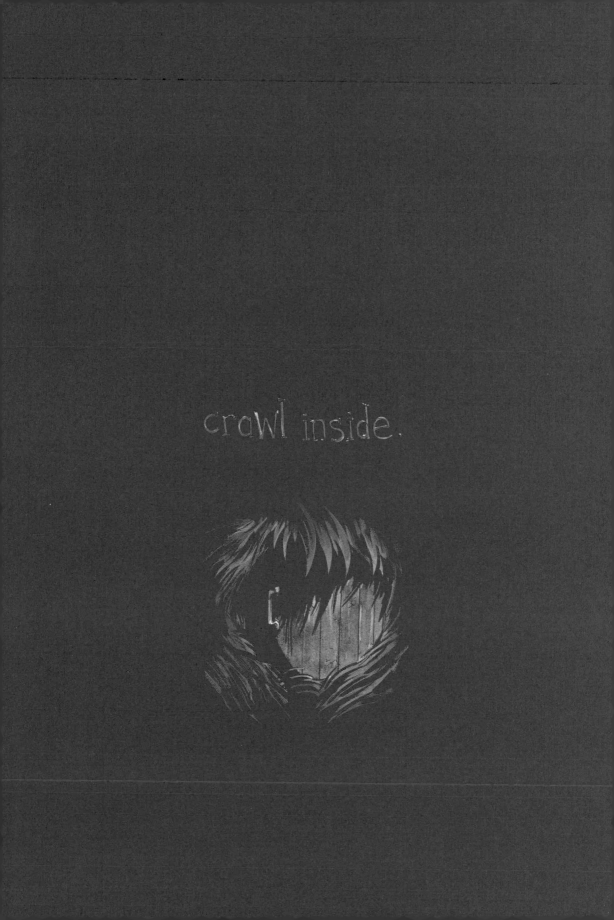

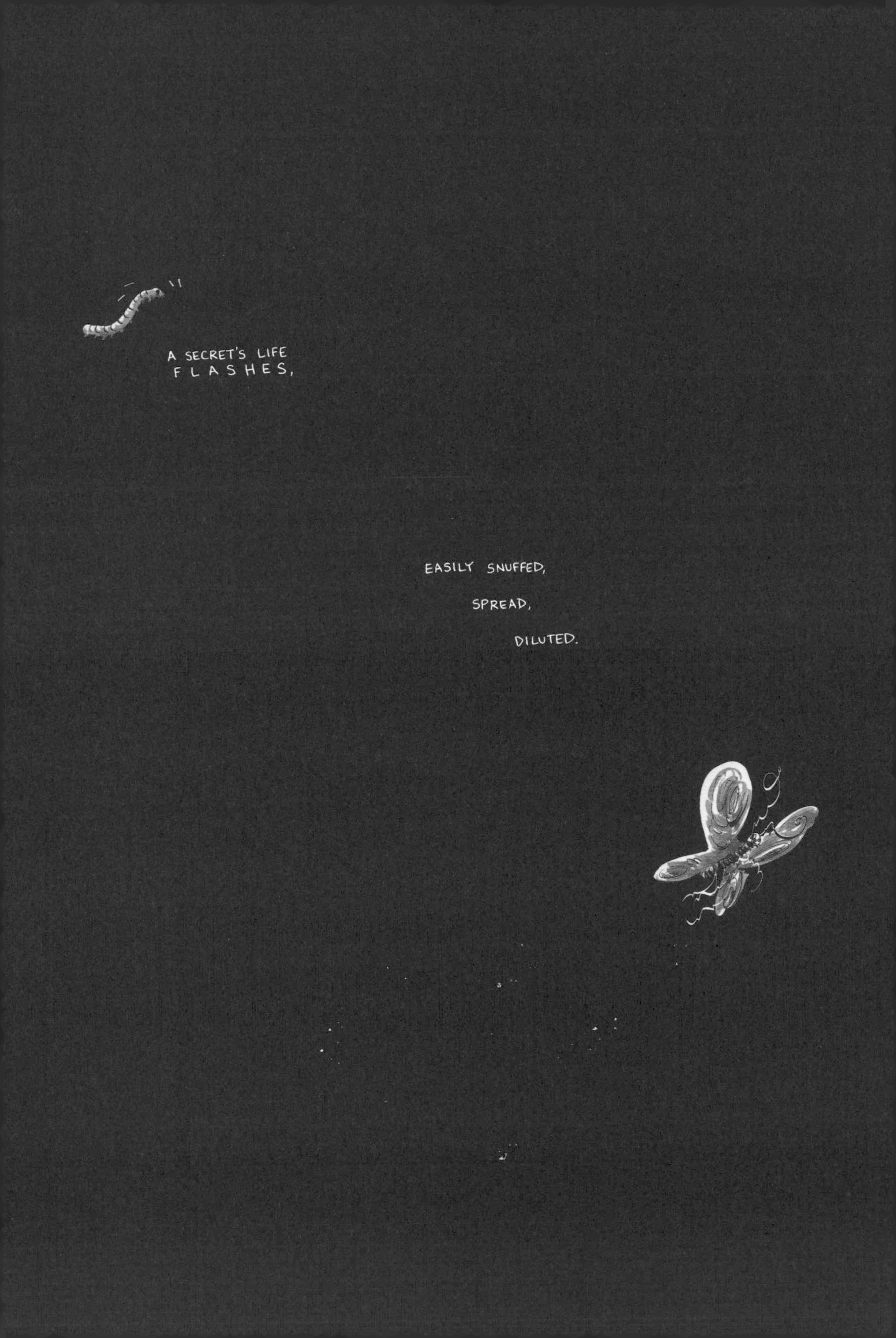
A SECRET'S LIFE
F L A S H E S,
EASILY SNUFFED,
SPREAD,
DILUTED.

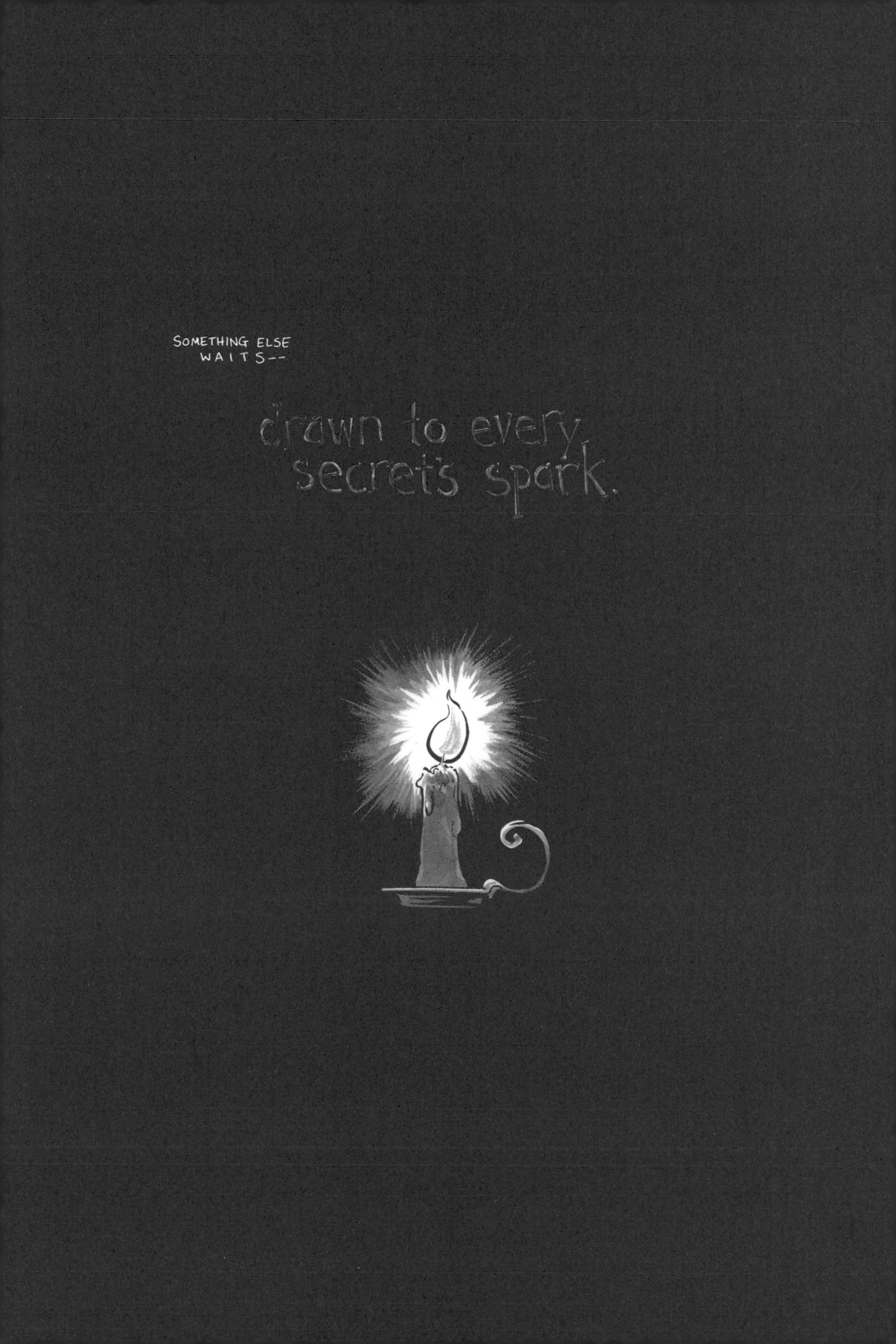
SOMETHING ELSE WAITS--
drawn to every secret's spark.

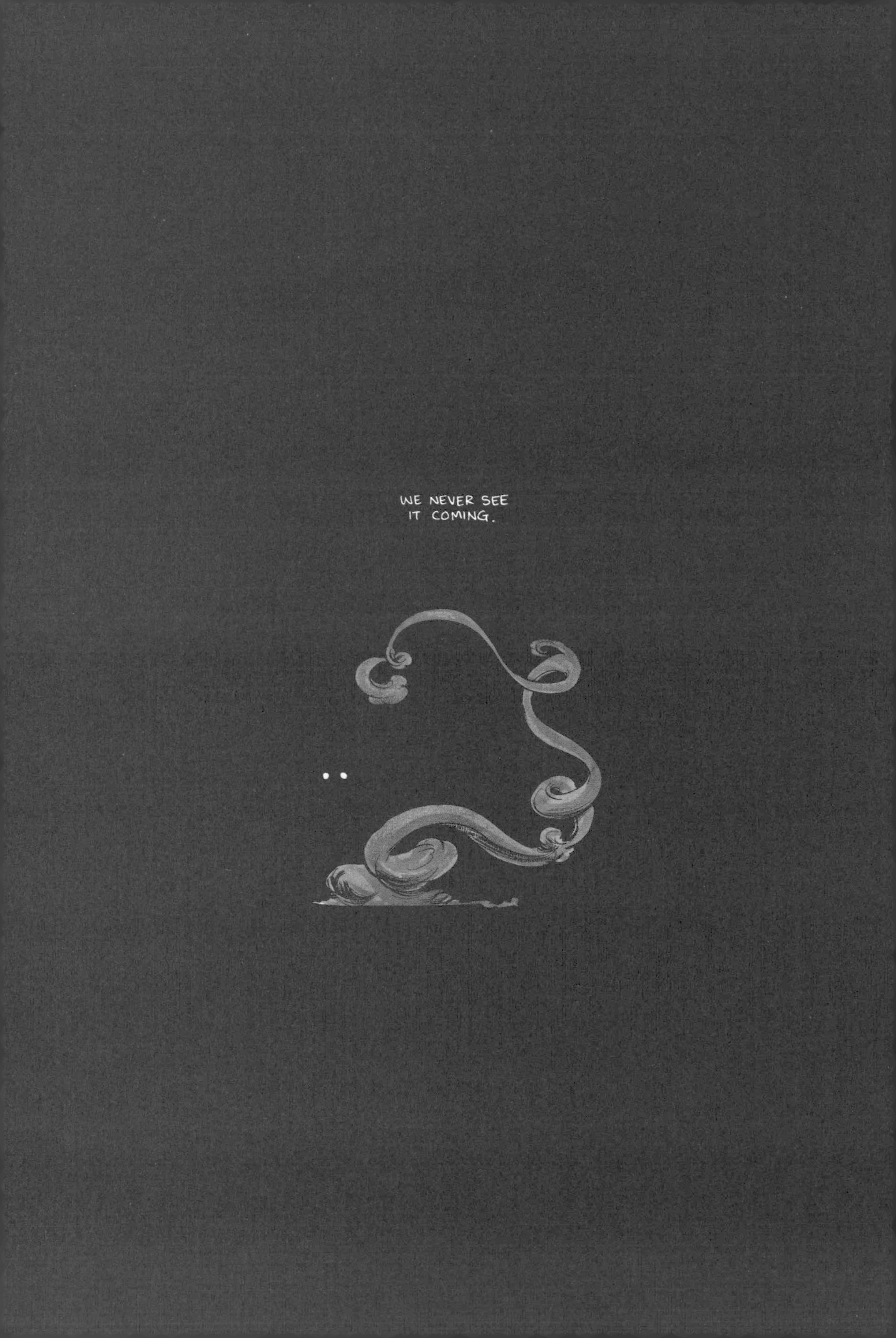
WE NEVER SEE IT COMING.

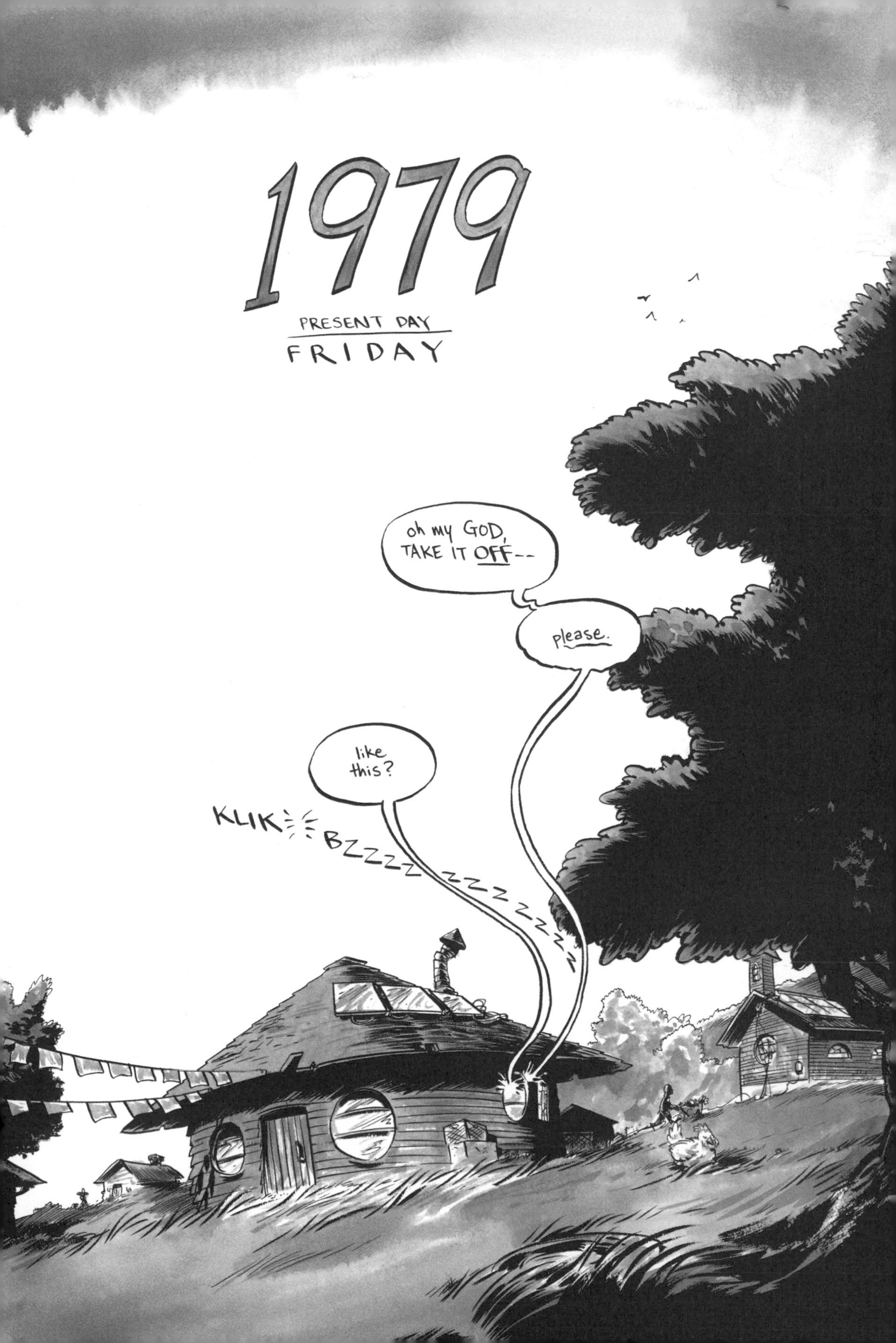
1979
PRESENT DAY
FRIDAY
oh my GOD, TAKE IT OFF--
please.
like this?
KLIK
BZZZZZZZZZZZZZ

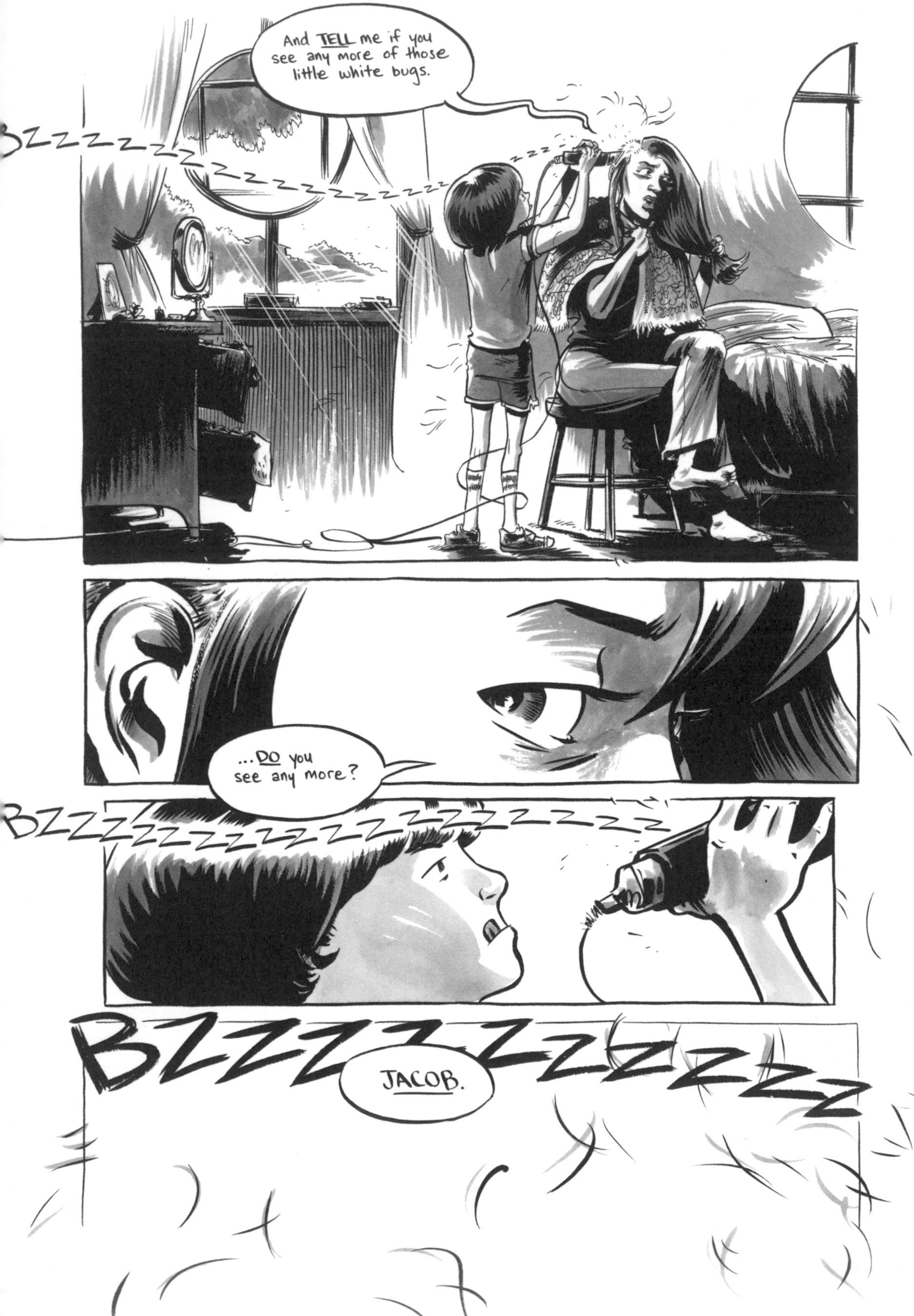
And TELL me if you see any more of those little white bugs.
BZZZZZZZZZZZZZZZZZZZZZZZ
...DO you see any more?
BZZZZZZZZZZZZZZZZZZZZZZZZZZZZZZZZ
BZZZZZZZZZZZZZ
JACOB.

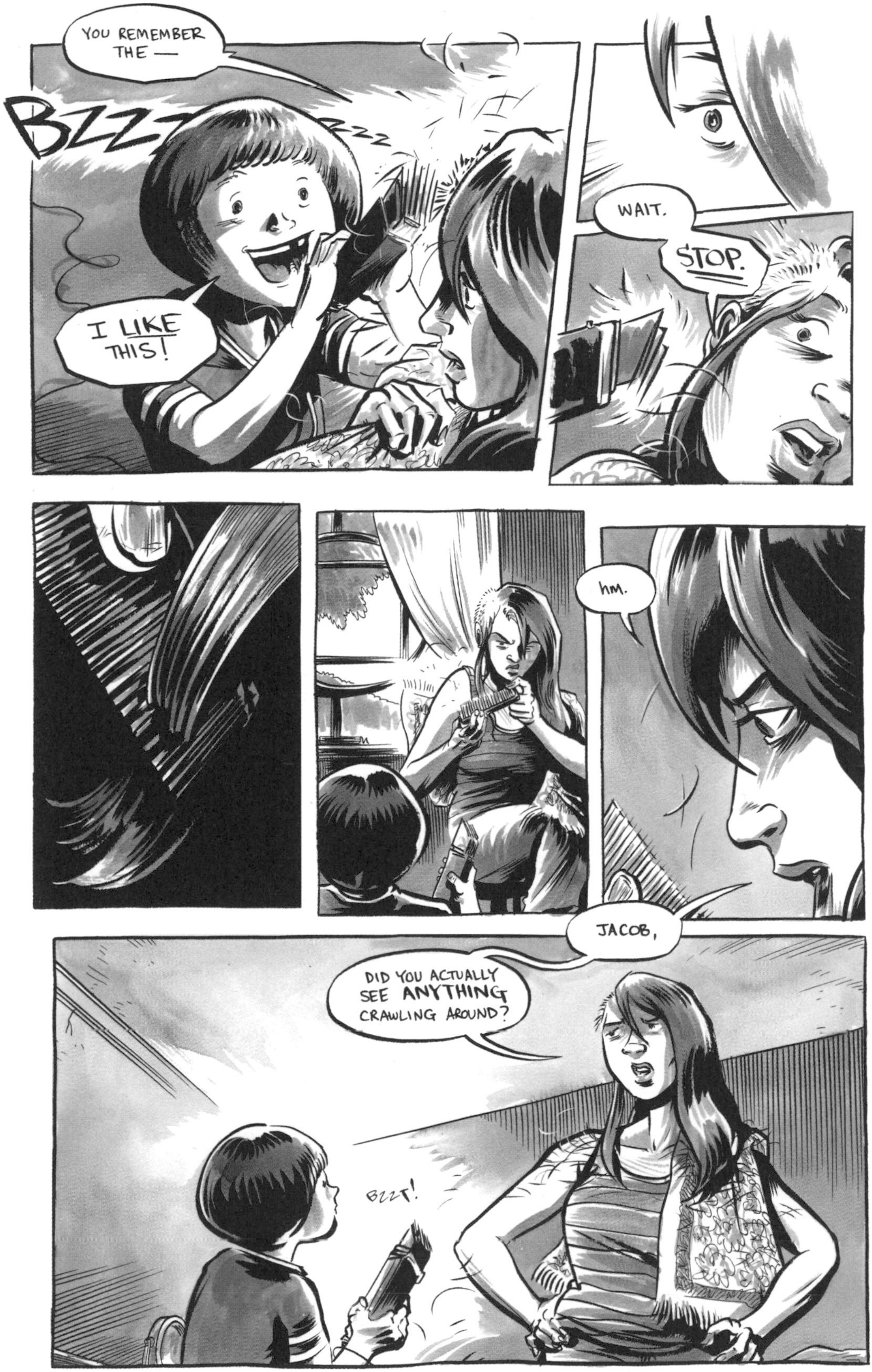
YOU REMEMBER THE —
BZZZZZZZ
I LIKE THIS!
WAIT.
STOP.
hm.
JACOB,
DID YOU ACTUALLY SEE ANYTHING CRAWLING AROUND?
BZZT!

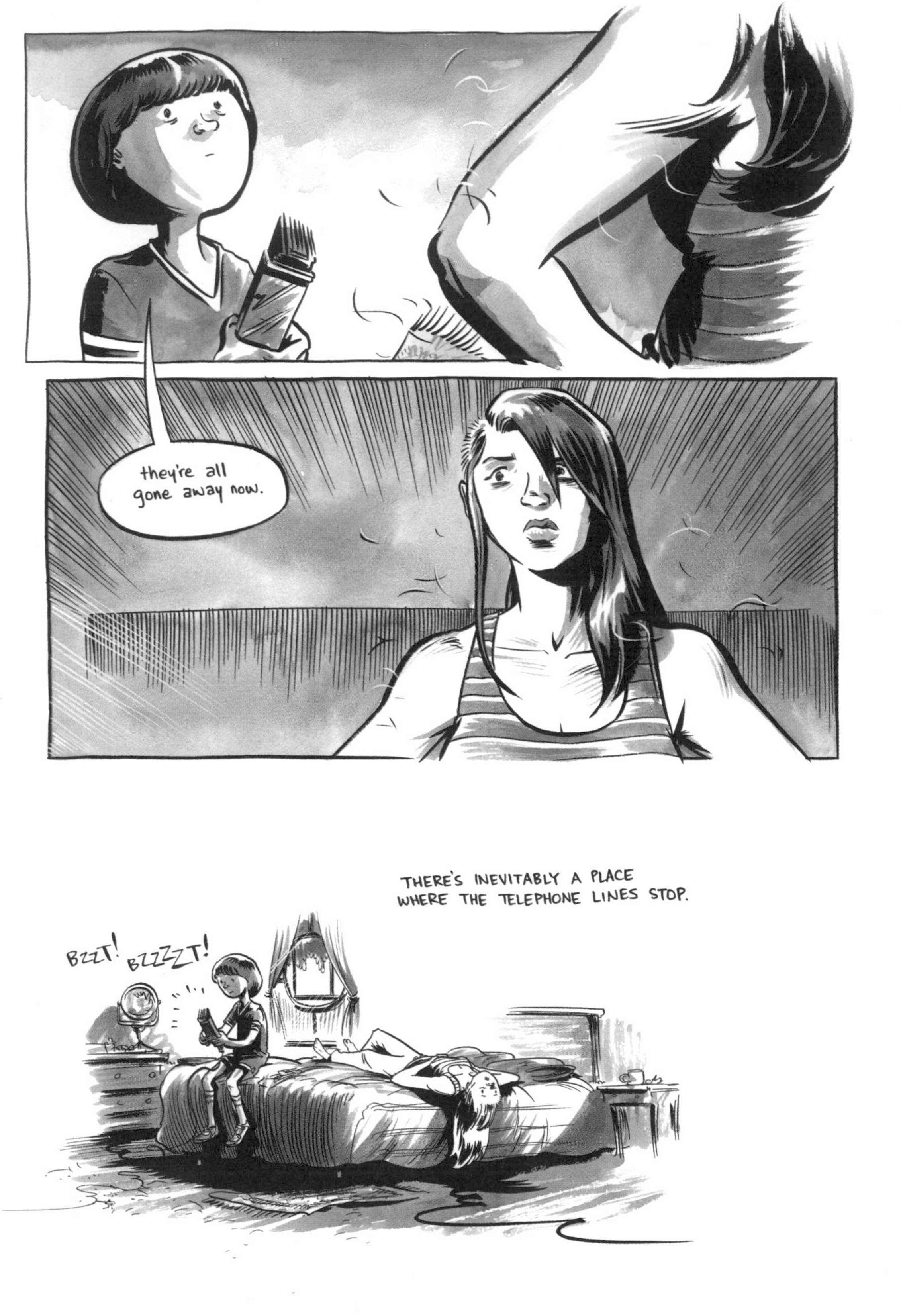
they're all gone away now.
THERE'S INEVITABLY A PLACE WHERE THE TELEPHONE LINES STOP.
BZZT!
BZZZZT!

FOLKS ALREADY THINK OF THE SOUTH
LIKE IT'S ANOTHER COUNTRY.

BUT EVEN TO ARKANSANS,
THE OZARKS ARE REMOTE.

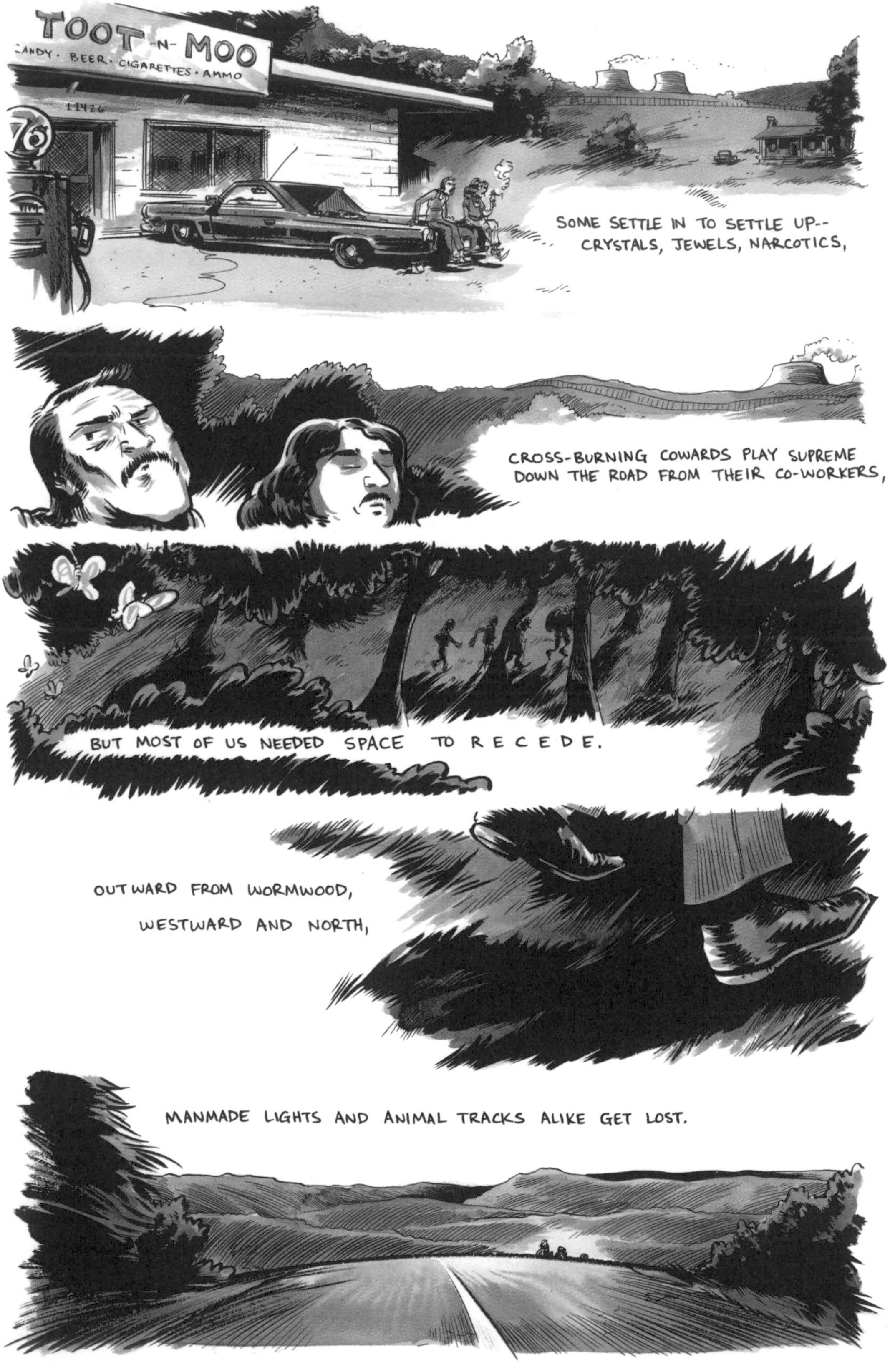
TOOT-N-MOO
CANDY · BEER · CIGARETTES · AMMO
11426
76
SOME SETTLE IN TO SETTLE UP--
CRYSTALS, JEWELS, NARCOTICS,
CROSS-BURNING COWARDS PLAY SUPREME
DOWN THE ROAD FROM THEIR CO-WORKERS,
BUT MOST OF US NEEDED SPACE TO R E C E D E.
OUTWARD FROM WORMWOOD,
WESTWARD AND NORTH,
MANMADE LIGHTS AND ANIMAL TRACKS ALIKE GET LOST.

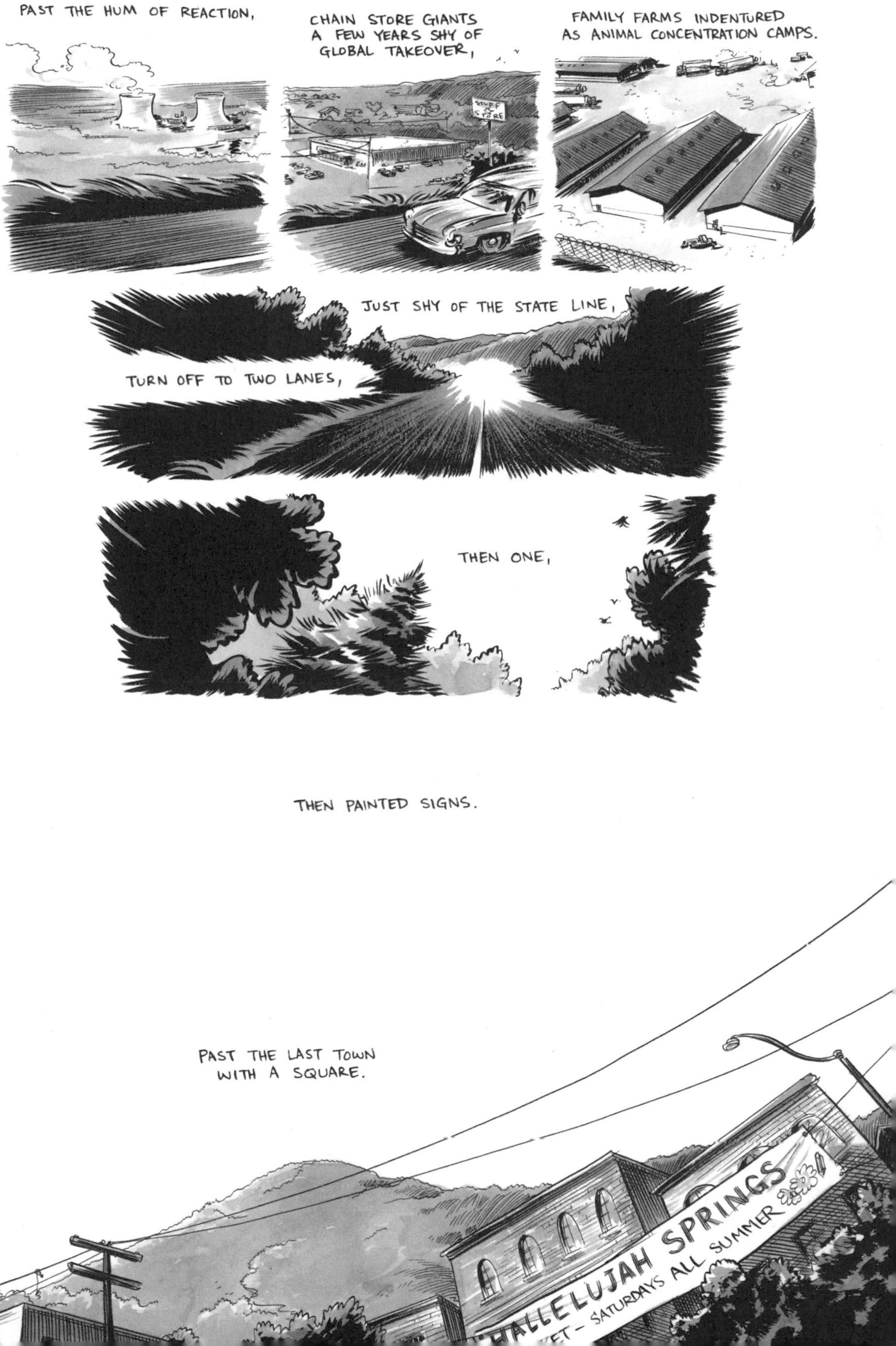
PAST THE HUM OF REACTION,
CHAIN STORE GIANTS A FEW YEARS SHY OF GLOBAL TAKEOVER,
STUFF STORE
FAMILY FARMS INDENTURED AS ANIMAL CONCENTRATION CAMPS.
JUST SHY OF THE STATE LINE,
TURN OFF TO TWO LANES,
THEN ONE,
THEN PAINTED SIGNS.
PAST THE LAST TOWN WITH A SQUARE.
HALLELUJAH SPRINGS
SATURDAYS ALL SUMMER

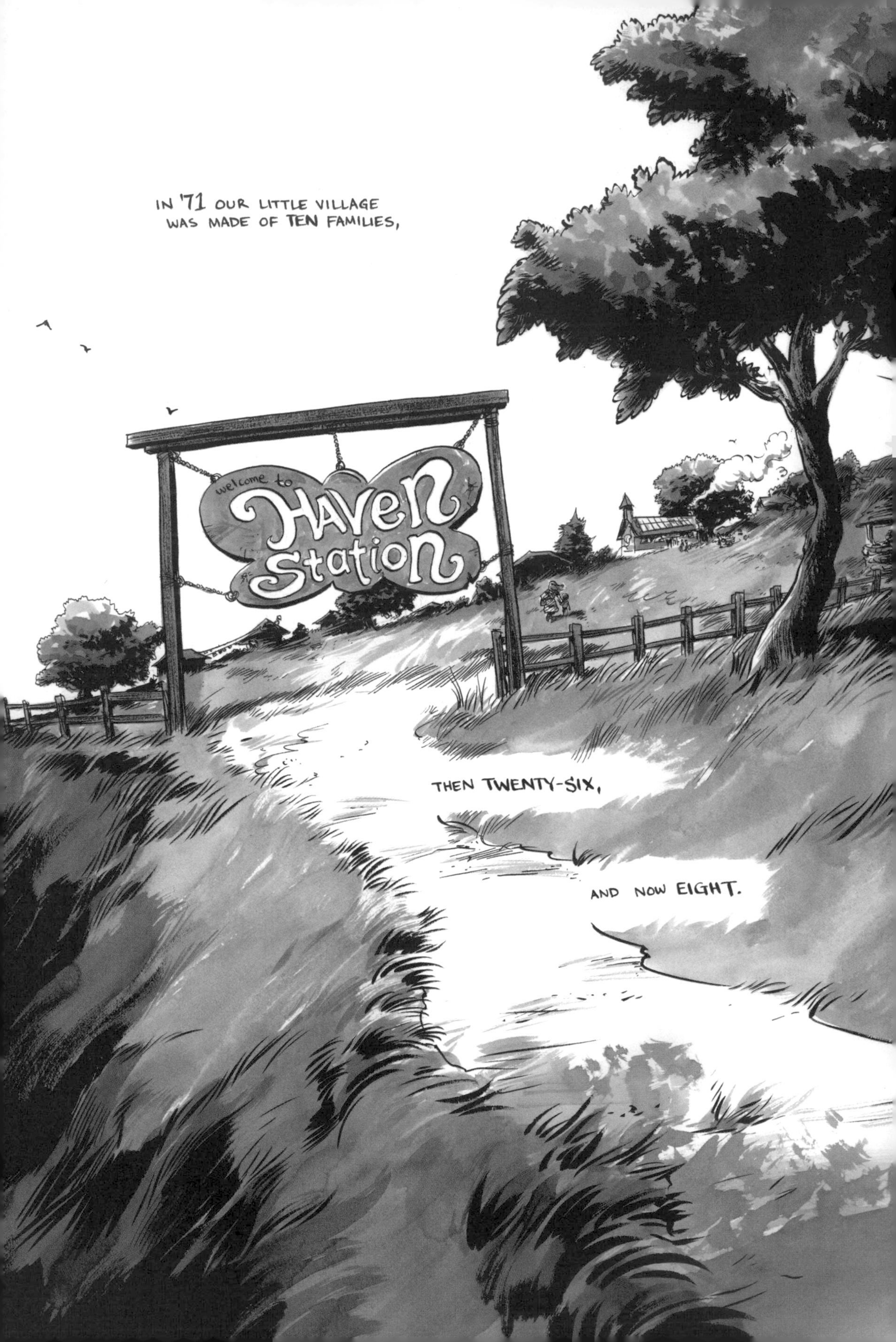
IN '71 OUR LITTLE VILLAGE WAS MADE OF TEN FAMILIES,
welcome to Haven Station
THEN TWENTY-SIX,
AND NOW EIGHT.

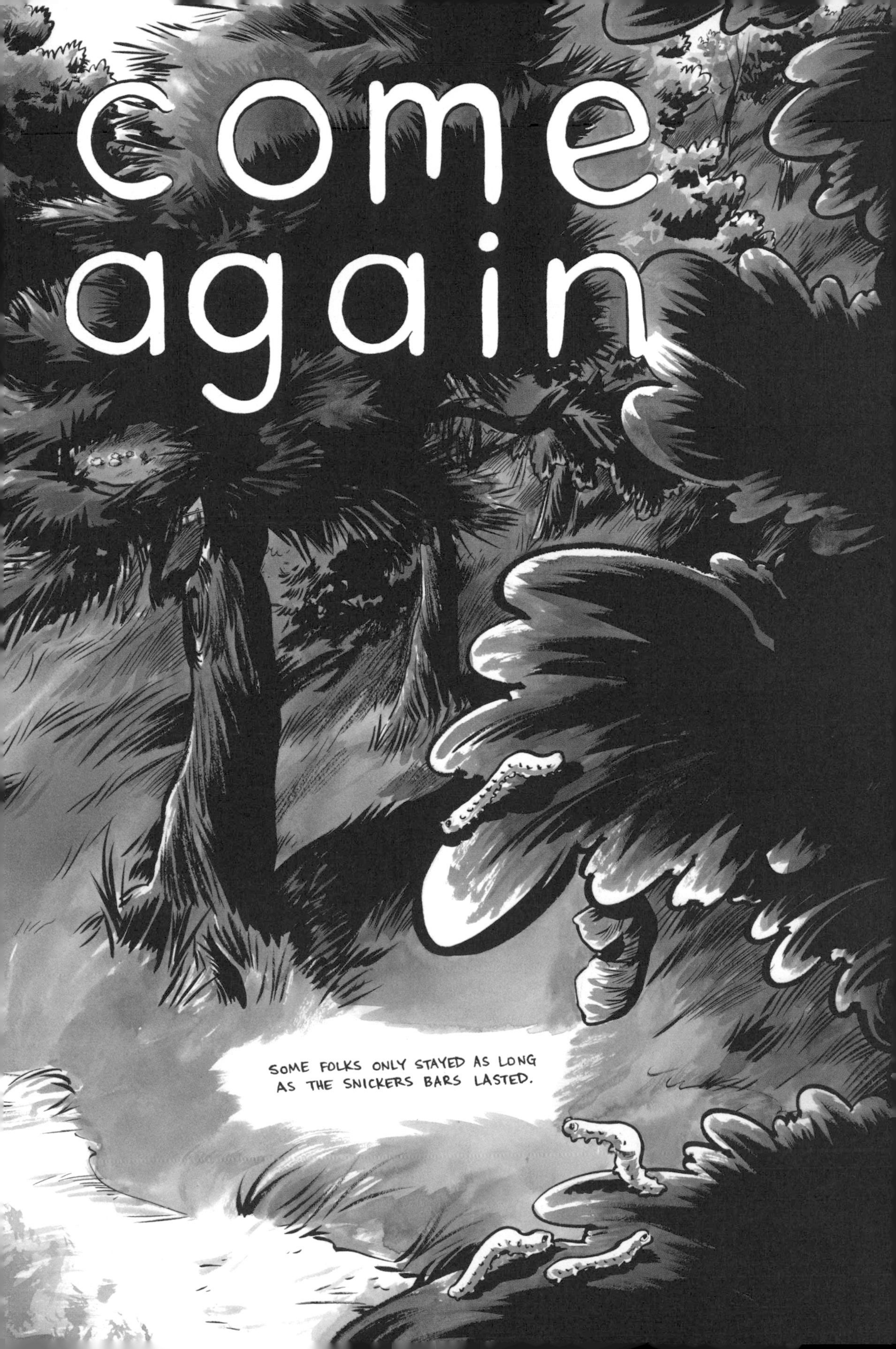
come again
SOME FOLKS ONLY STAYED AS LONG AS THE SNICKERS BARS LASTED.

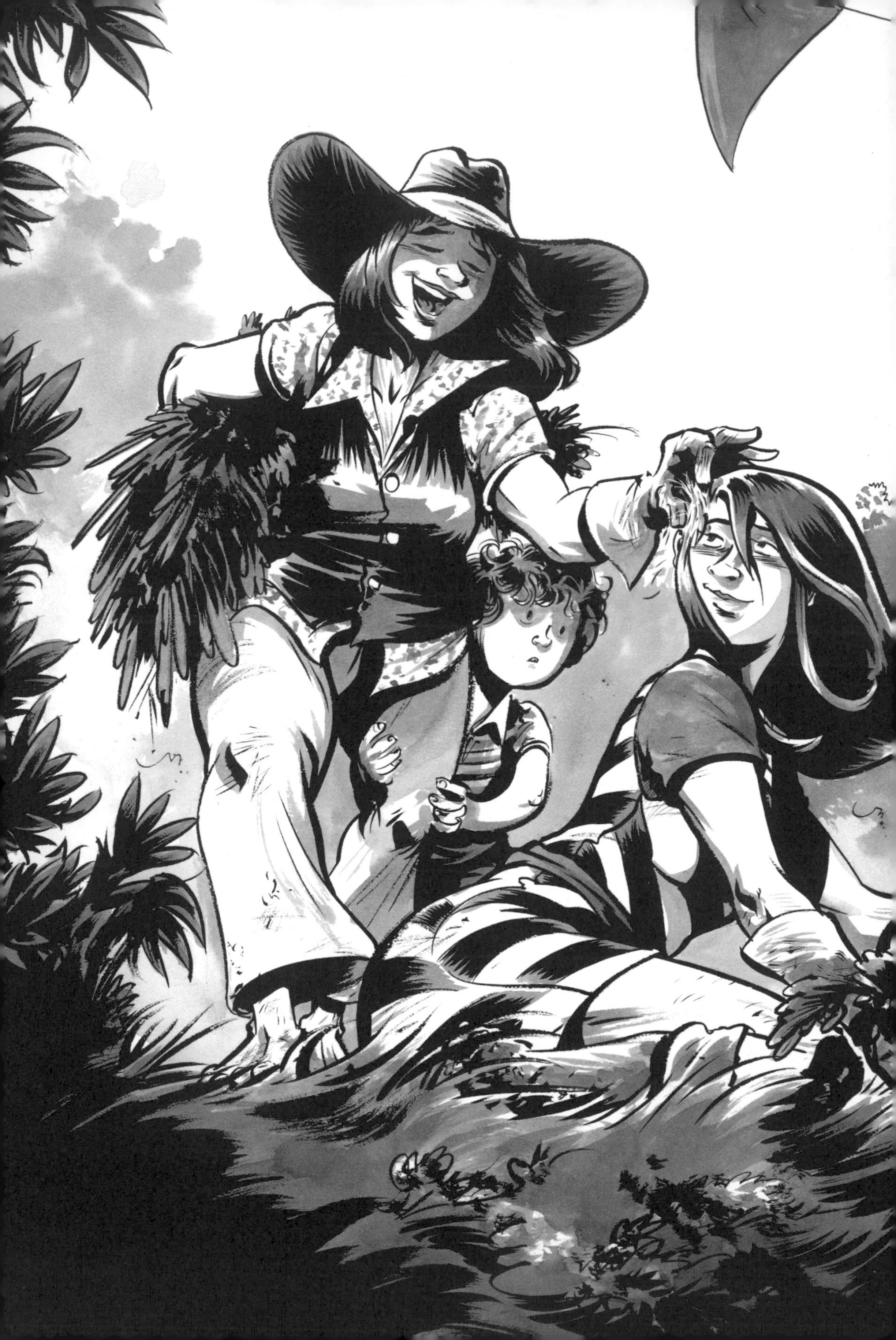

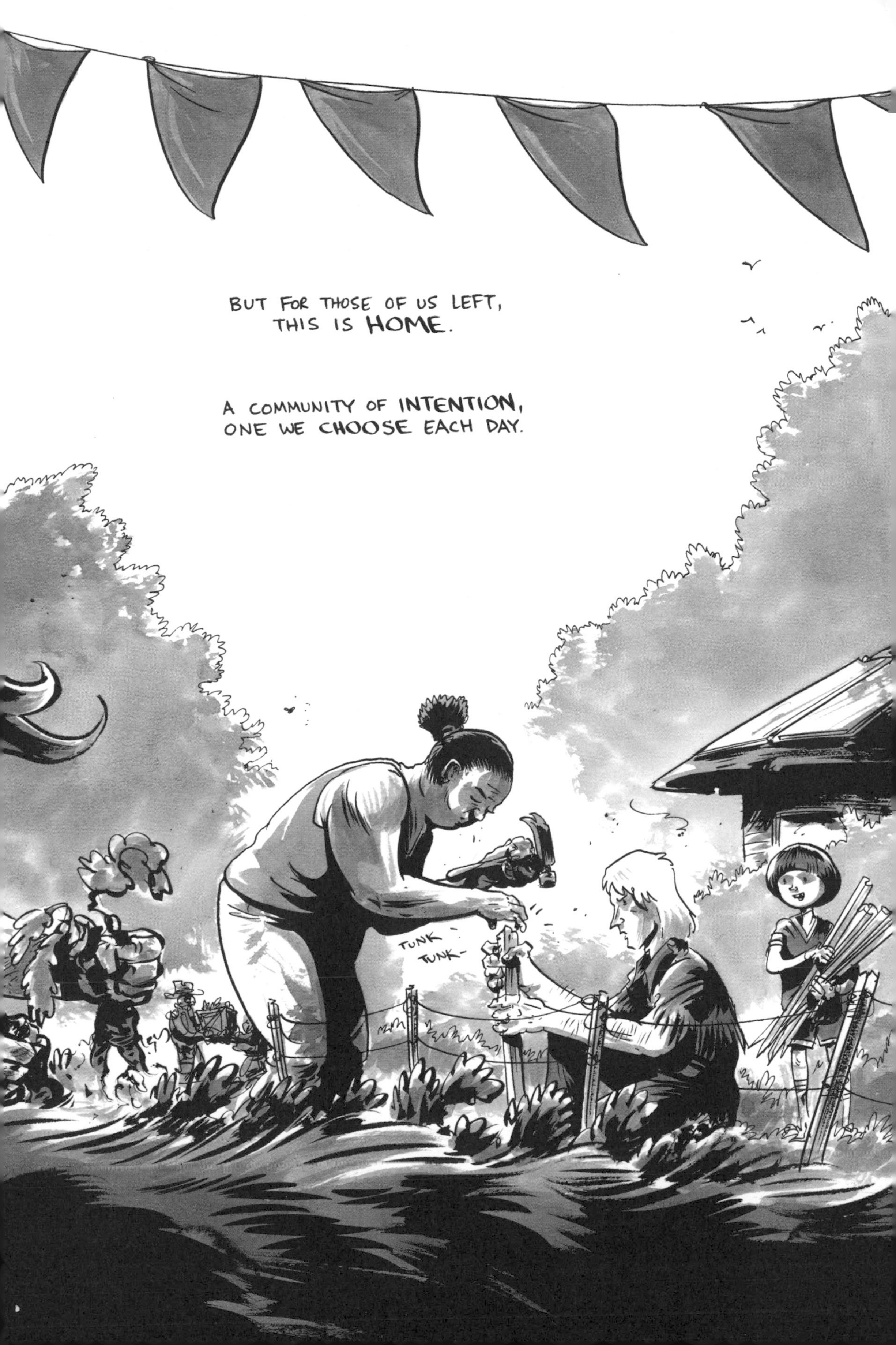
BUT FOR THOSE OF US LEFT, THIS IS HOME.
A COMMUNITY OF INTENTION, ONE WE CHOOSE EACH DAY.
TUNK
TUNK

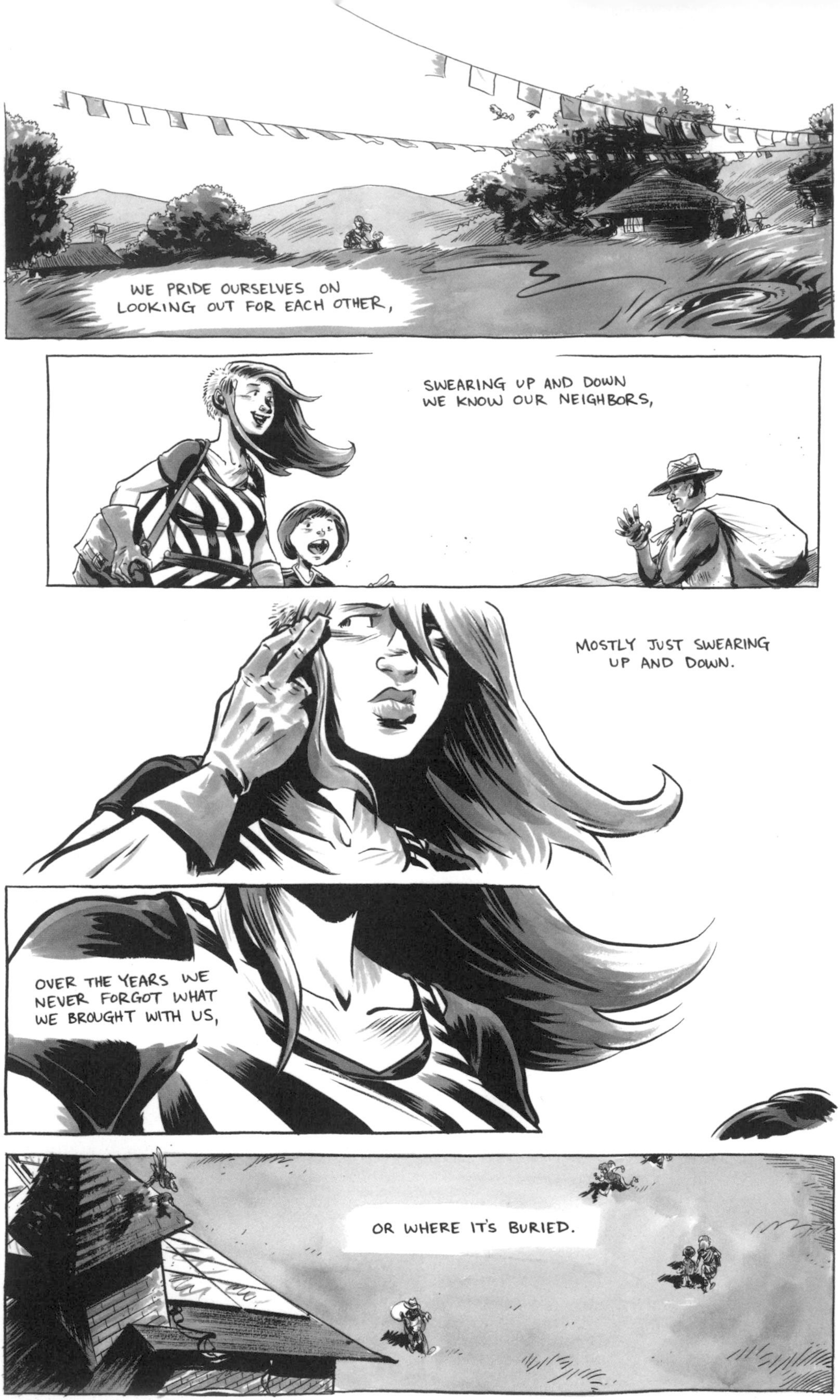
WE PRIDE OURSELVES ON LOOKING OUT FOR EACH OTHER,
SWEARING UP AND DOWN WE KNOW OUR NEIGHBORS,
MOSTLY JUST SWEARING UP AND DOWN.
OVER THE YEARS WE NEVER FORGOT WHAT WE BROUGHT WITH US,
OR WHERE IT'S BURIED.

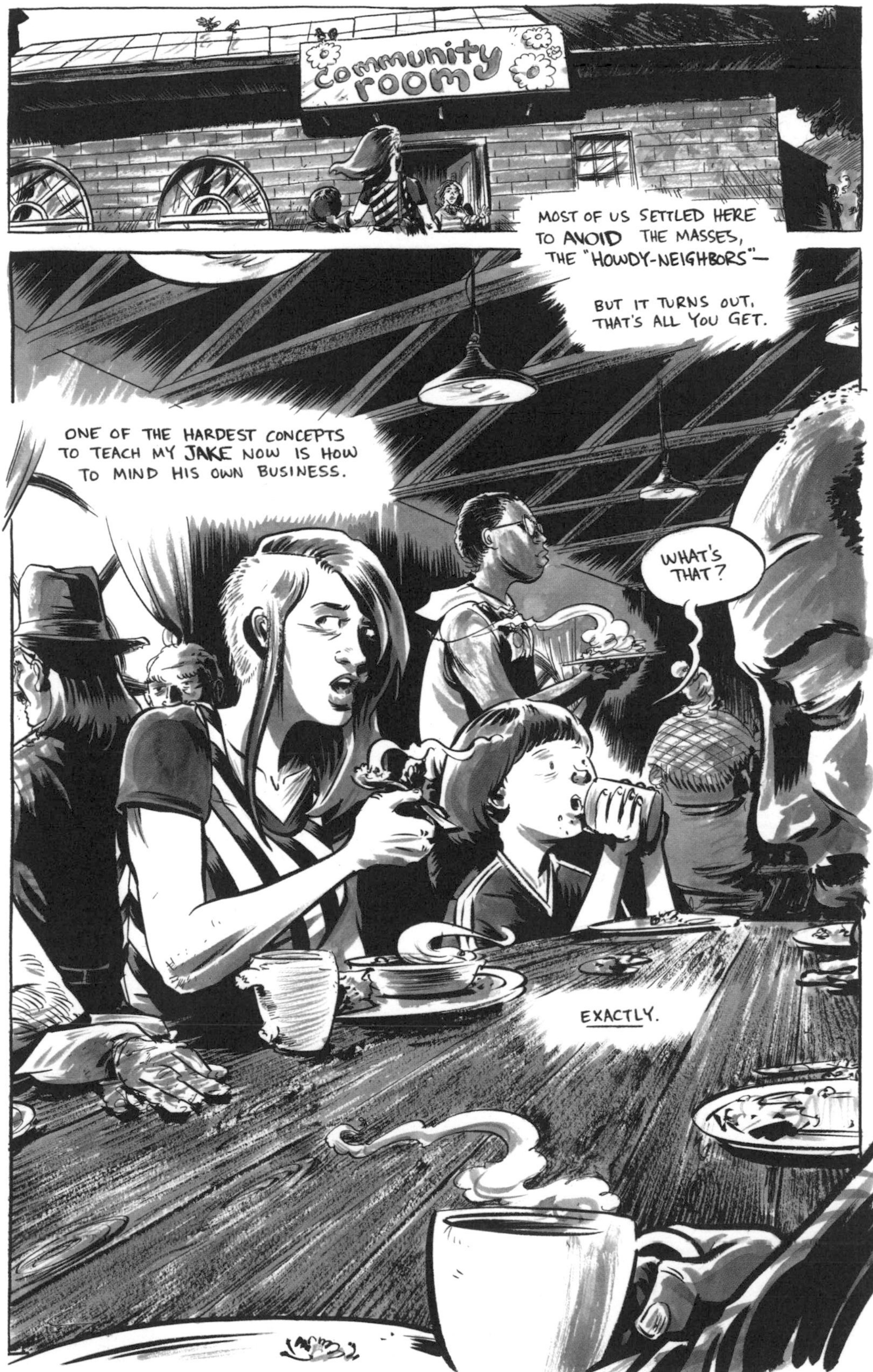

community room
MOST OF US SETTLED HERE TO AVOID THE MASSES, THE "HOWDY-NEIGHBORS"—
BUT IT TURNS OUT, THAT'S ALL YOU GET.
ONE OF THE HARDEST CONCEPTS TO TEACH MY JAKE NOW IS HOW TO MIND HIS OWN BUSINESS.
WHAT'S THAT?
EXACTLY.

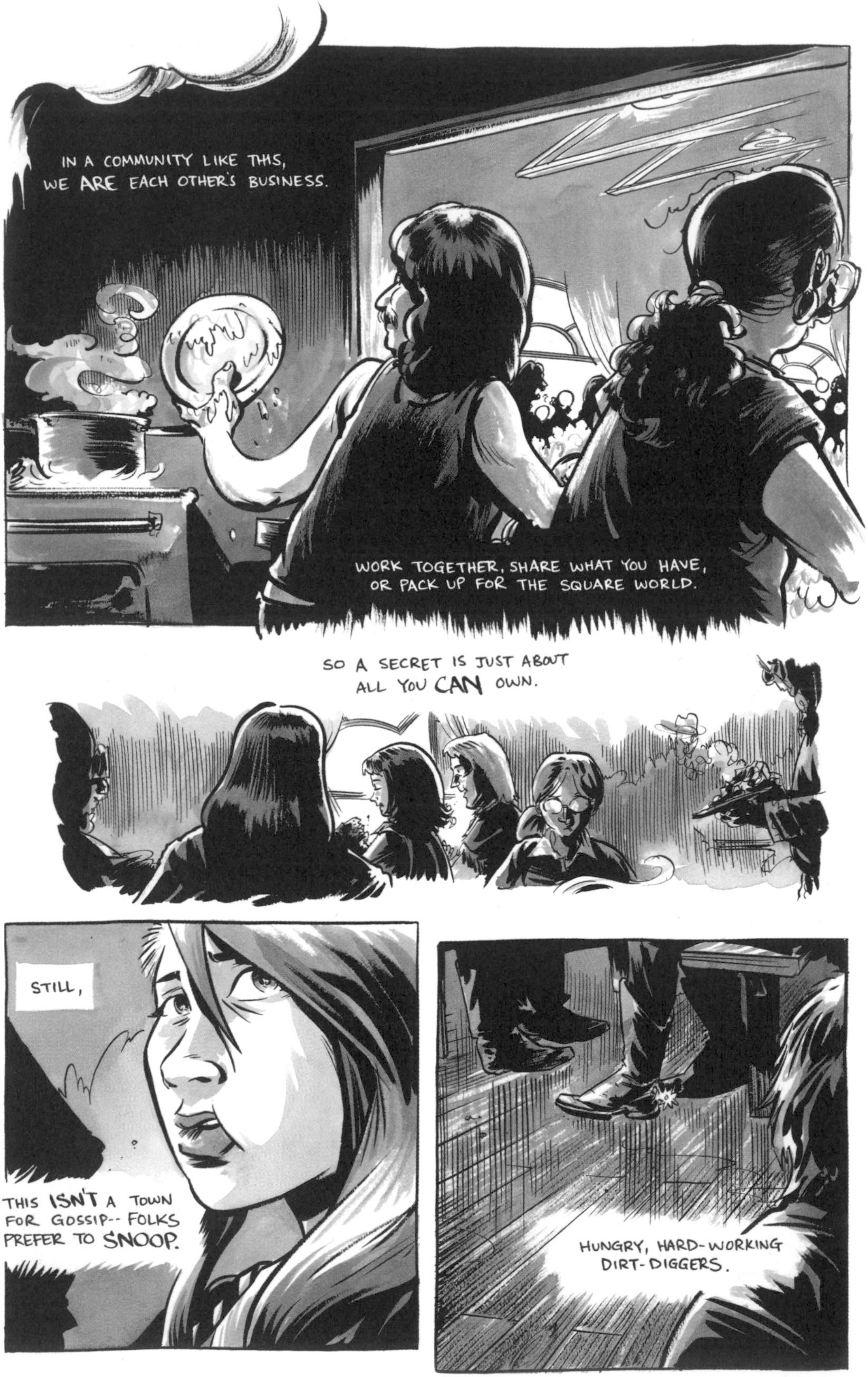
IN A COMMUNITY LIKE THIS, WE ARE EACH OTHER'S BUSINESS.
WORK TOGETHER, SHARE WHAT YOU HAVE, OR PACK UP FOR THE SQUARE WORLD.
SO A SECRET IS JUST ABOUT ALL YOU CAN OWN.
STILL,
THIS ISN'T A TOWN FOR GOSSIP-- FOLKS PREFER TO SNOOP.
HUNGRY, HARD-WORKING DIRT-DIGGERS.

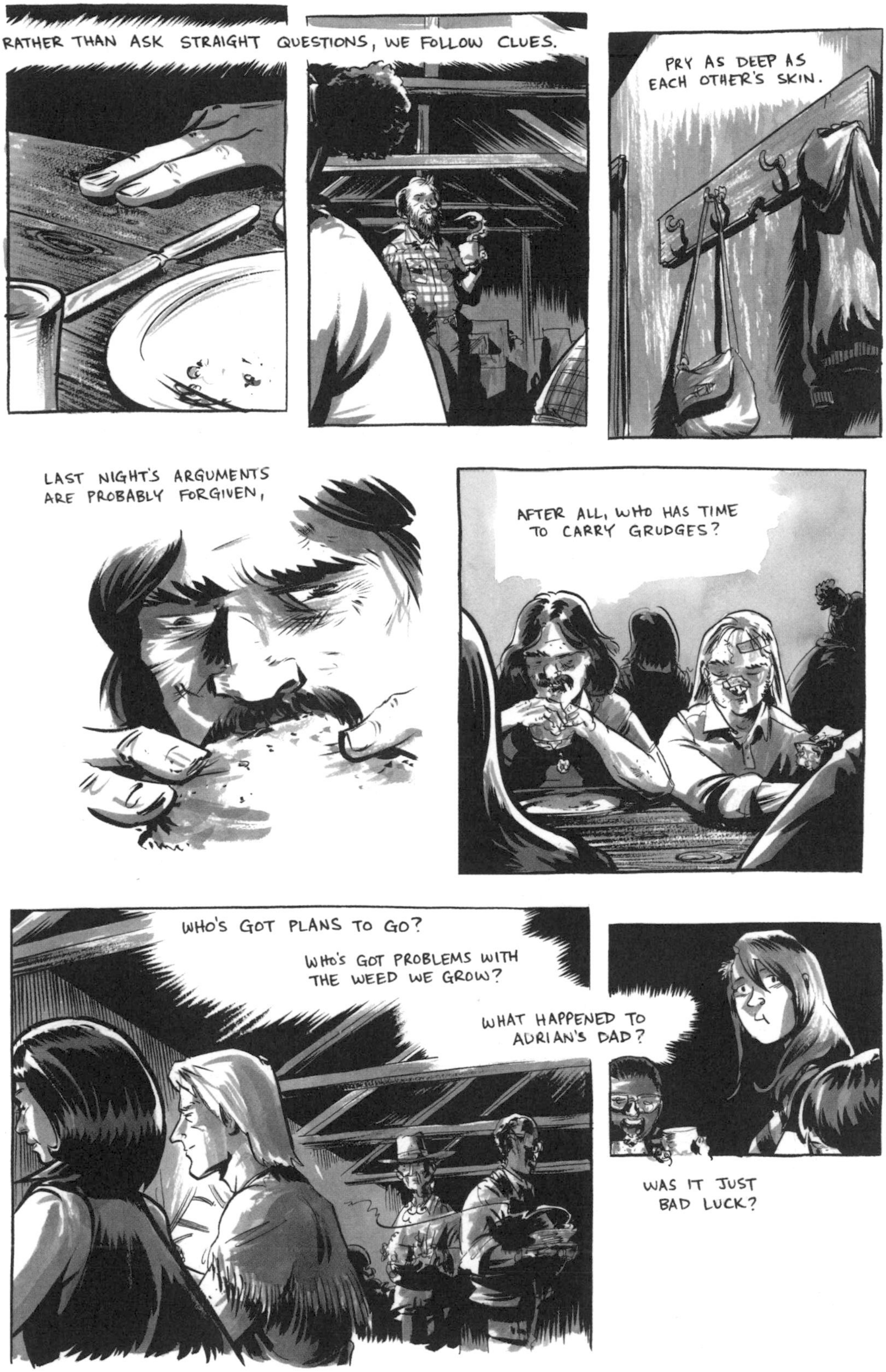
RATHER THAN ASK STRAIGHT QUESTIONS, WE FOLLOW CLUES.
PRY AS DEEP AS EACH OTHER'S SKIN.
LAST NIGHT'S ARGUMENTS ARE PROBABLY FORGIVEN,
AFTER ALL, WHO HAS TIME TO CARRY GRUDGES?
WHO'S GOT PLANS TO GO?
WHO'S GOT PROBLEMS WITH THE WEED WE GROW?
WHAT HAPPENED TO ADRIAN'S DAD?
WAS IT JUST BAD LUCK?

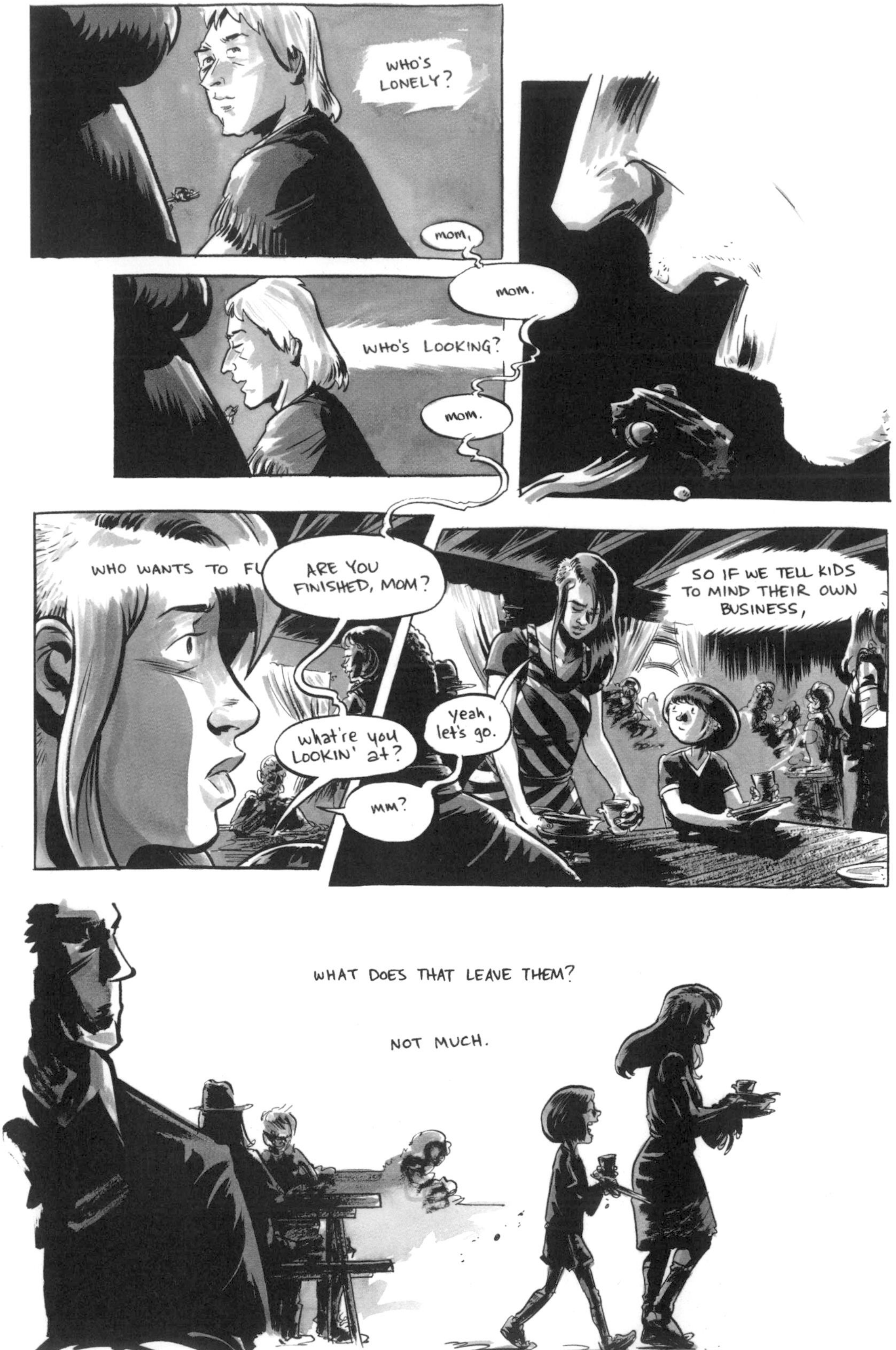
WHO'S LONELY?
mom,
mom.
WHO'S LOOKING?
mom.
WHO WANTS TO F
ARE YOU FINISHED, MOM?
what're you LOOKIN' at?
yeah, let's go.
mm?
SO IF WE TELL KIDS TO MIND THEIR OWN BUSINESS,
WHAT DOES THAT LEAVE THEM?
NOT MUCH.

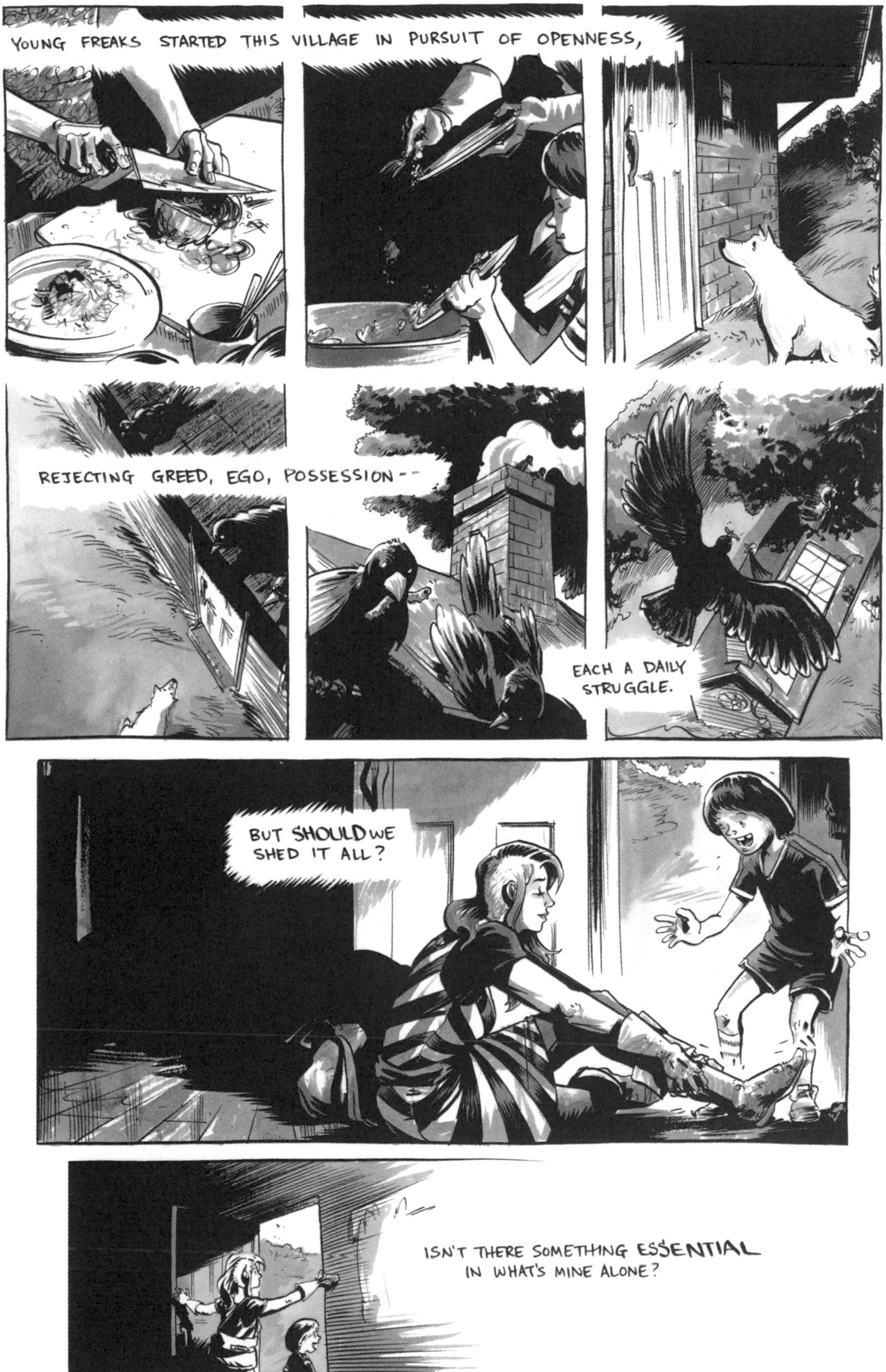
YOUNG FREAKS STARTED THIS VILLAGE IN PURSUIT OF OPENNESS,
REJECTING GREED, EGO, POSSESSION--
EACH A DAILY STRUGGLE.
BUT SHOULD WE SHED IT ALL?
ISN'T THERE SOMETHING ESSENTIAL IN WHAT'S MINE ALONE?

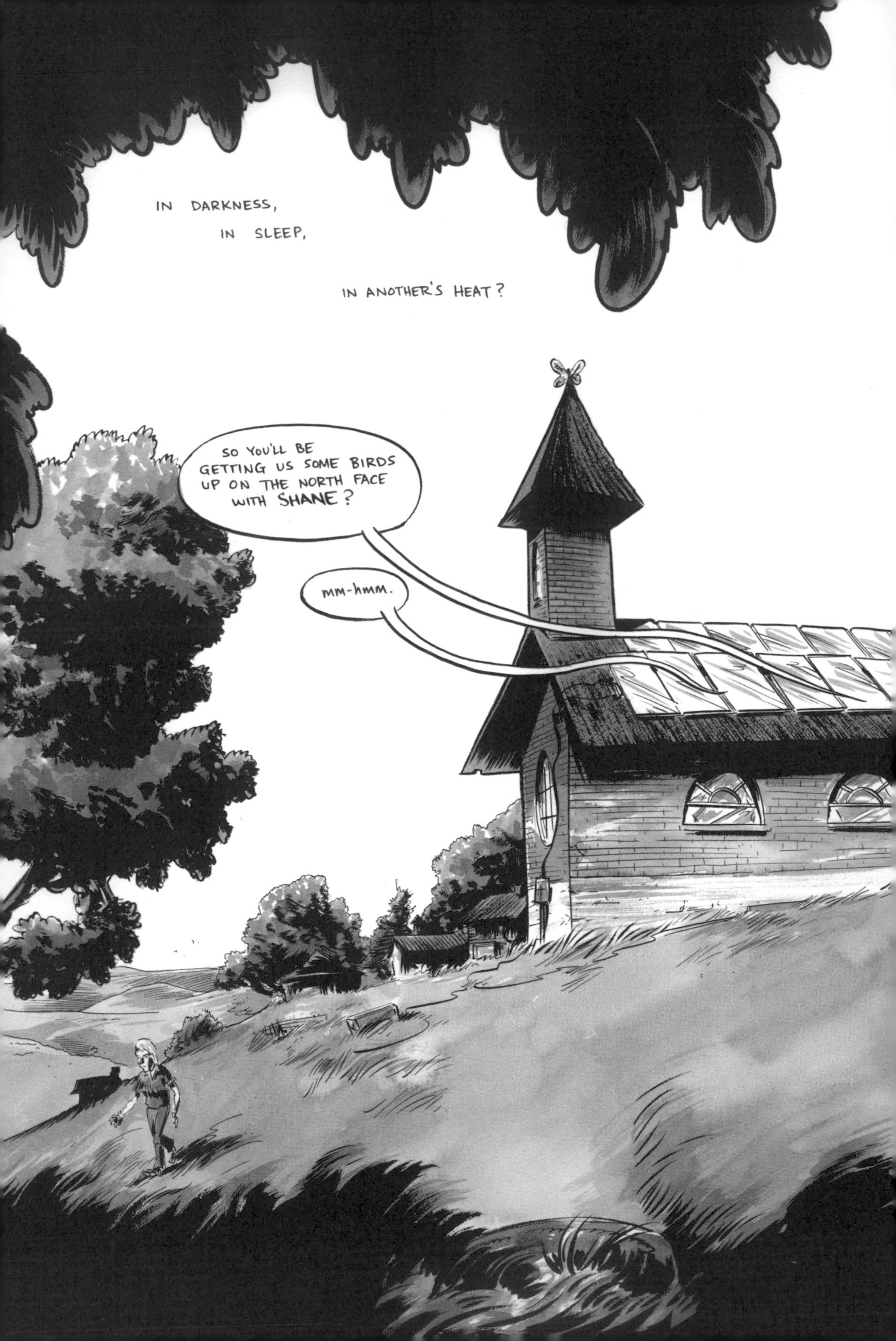
IN DARKNESS,
IN SLEEP,
IN ANOTHER'S HEAT?
SO YOU'LL BE GETTING US SOME BIRDS UP ON THE NORTH FACE WITH SHANE?
mm-hmm.

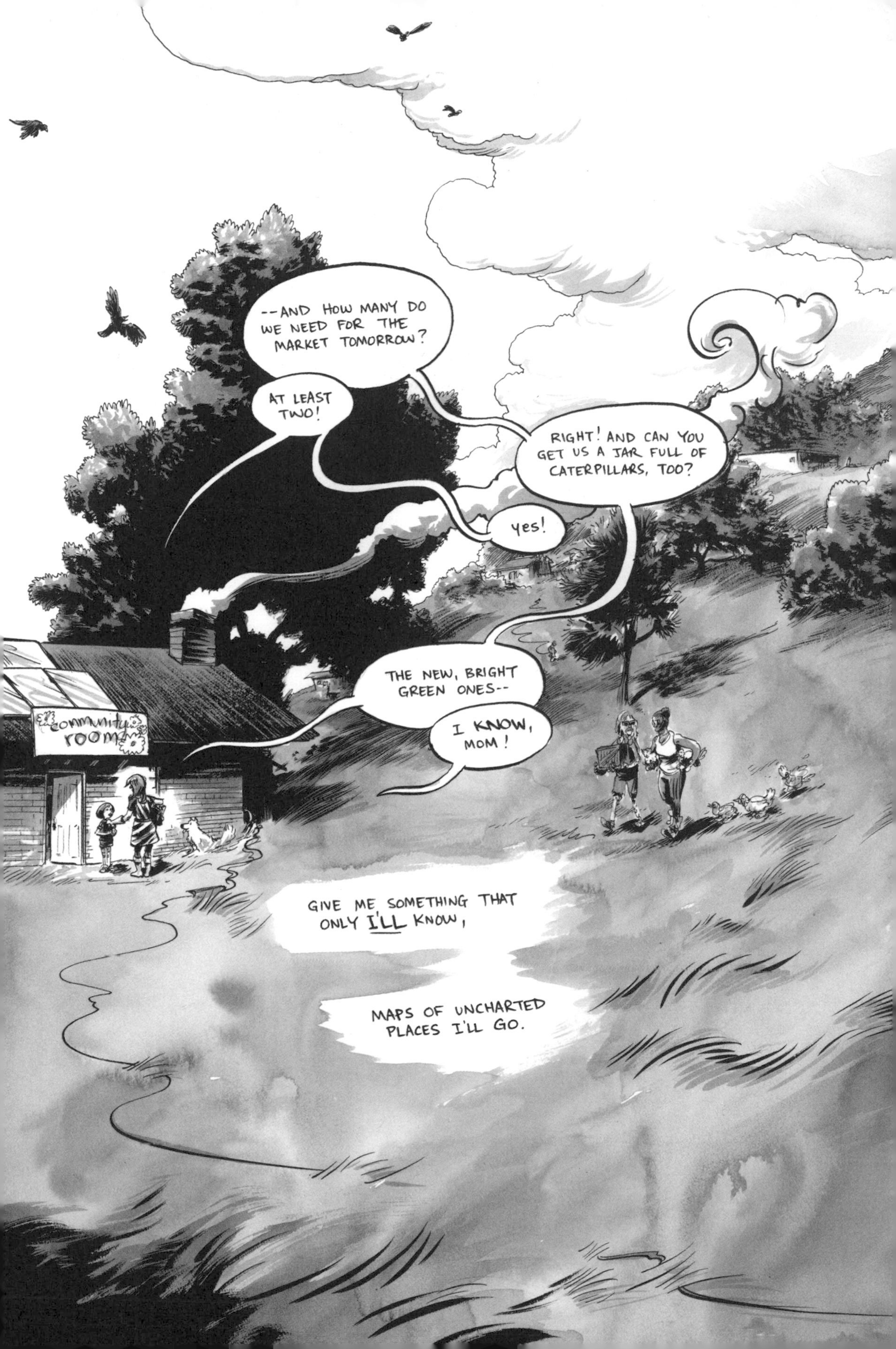
--AND HOW MANY DO WE NEED FOR THE MARKET TOMORROW?
AT LEAST TWO!
RIGHT! AND CAN YOU GET US A JAR FULL OF CATERPILLARS, TOO?
yes!
THE NEW, BRIGHT GREEN ONES--
I KNOW, MOM!
community room
GIVE ME SOMETHING THAT ONLY I'LL KNOW,
MAPS OF UNCHARTED PLACES I'LL GO.

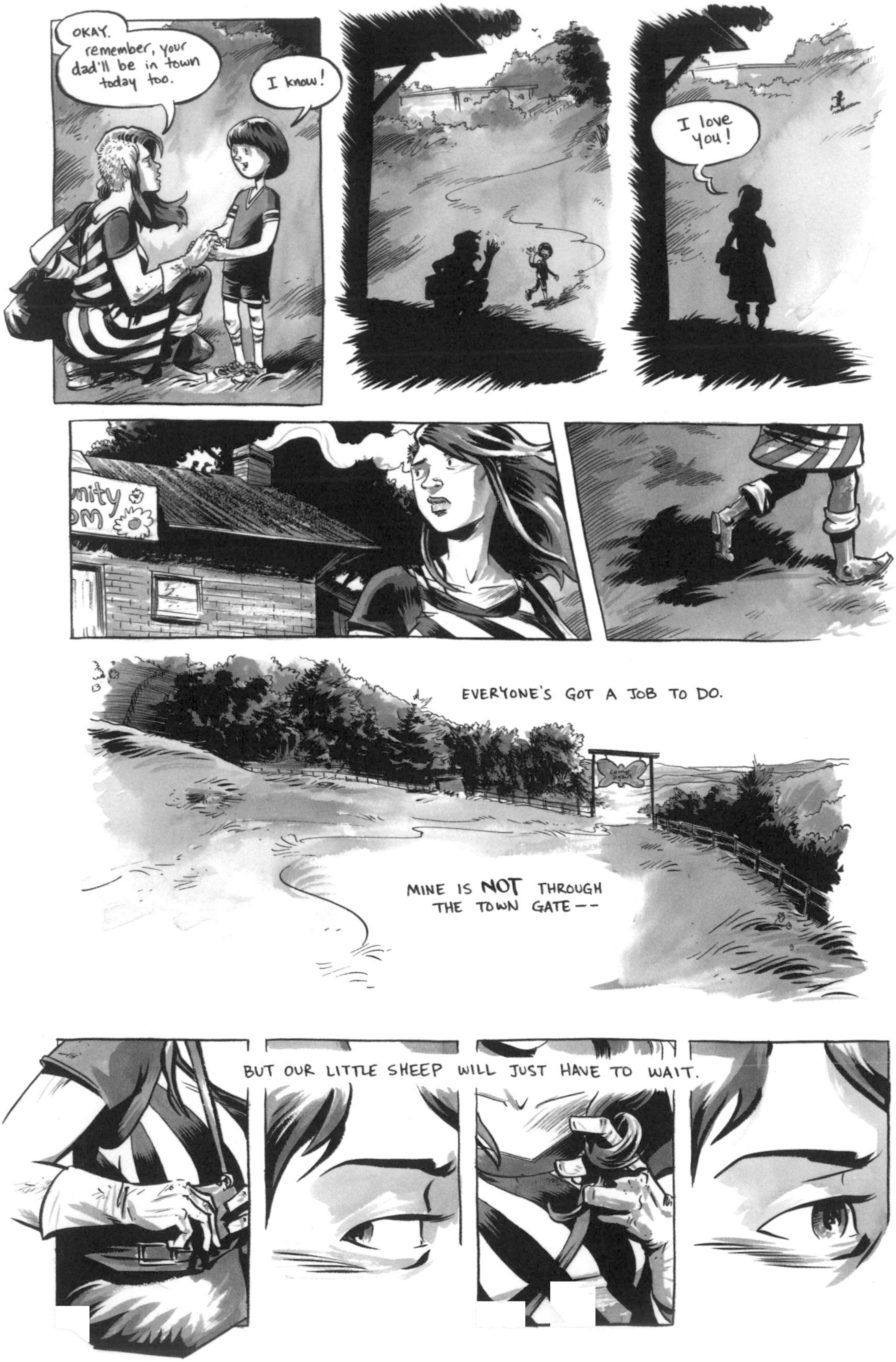
OKAY. remember, your dad'll be in town today too.
I know!
I love you!
EVERYONE'S GOT A JOB TO DO.
MINE IS NOT THROUGH THE TOWN GATE--
BUT OUR LITTLE SHEEP WILL JUST HAVE TO WAIT.

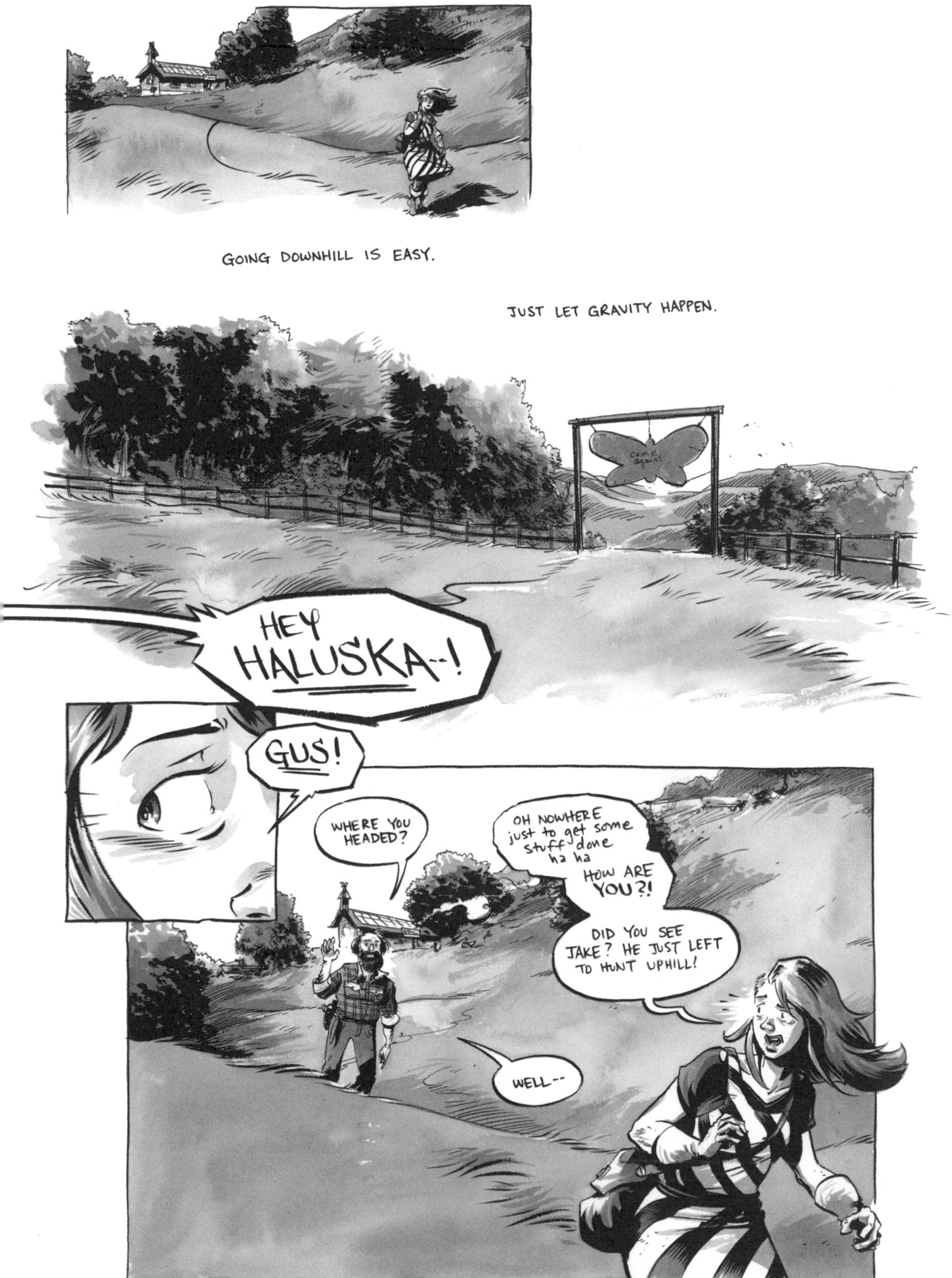
GOING DOWNHILL IS EASY.
JUST LET GRAVITY HAPPEN.
come again!
HEY HALUSKA--!
GUS!
WHERE YOU HEADED?
OH NOWHERE just to get some stuff done ha ha
HOW ARE YOU?!
DID YOU SEE JAKE? HE JUST LEFT TO HUNT UPHILL!
WELL--

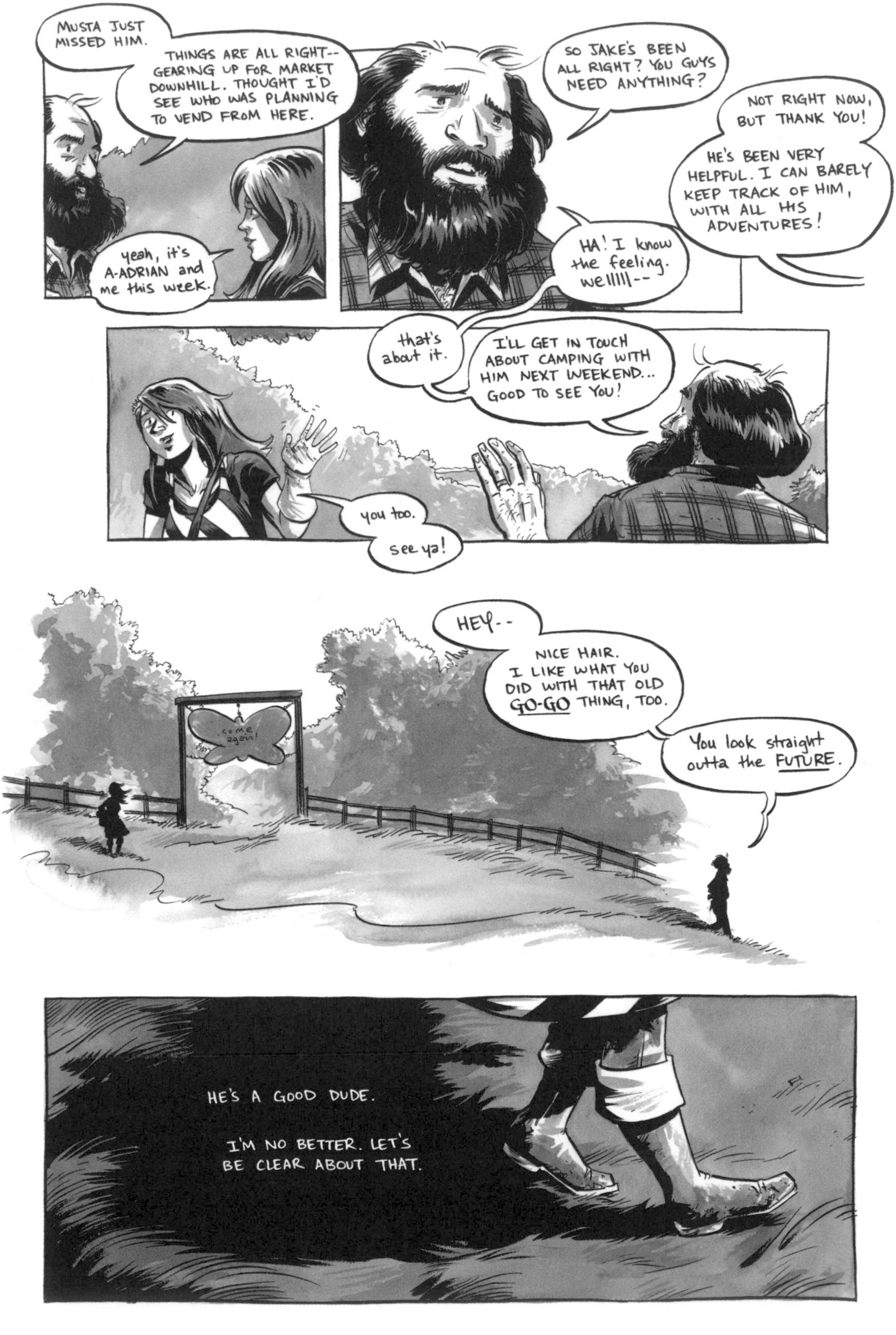
MUSTA JUST MISSED HIM.
THINGS ARE ALL RIGHT-- GEARING UP FOR MARKET DOWNHILL. THOUGHT I'D SEE WHO WAS PLANNING TO VEND FROM HERE.
yeah, it's A-ADRIAN and me this week.
SO JAKE'S BEEN ALL RIGHT? YOU GUYS NEED ANYTHING?
NOT RIGHT NOW, BUT THANK YOU!
HE'S BEEN VERY HELPFUL. I CAN BARELY KEEP TRACK OF HIM, WITH ALL HIS ADVENTURES!
HA! I know the feeling. wellll--
that's about it.
I'LL GET IN TOUCH ABOUT CAMPING WITH HIM NEXT WEEKEND... GOOD TO SEE YOU!
you too.
see ya!
HEY--
NICE HAIR. I LIKE WHAT YOU DID WITH THAT OLD GO-GO THING, TOO.
You look straight outta the FUTURE.
come again!
HE'S A GOOD DUDE.
I'M NO BETTER. LET'S BE CLEAR ABOUT THAT.

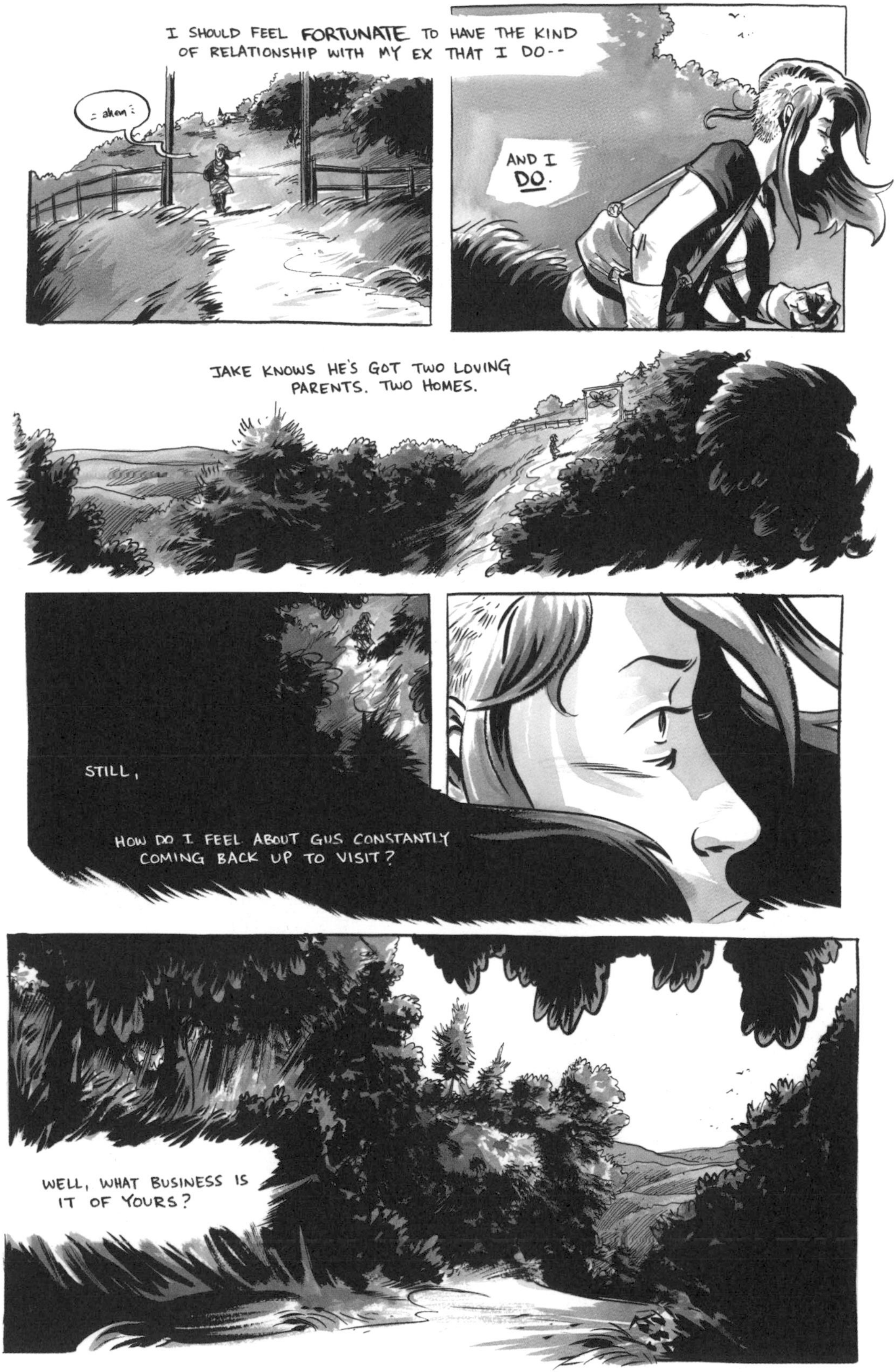
I SHOULD FEEL FORTUNATE TO HAVE THE KIND OF RELATIONSHIP WITH MY EX THAT I DO--
ahem
AND I DO.
JAKE KNOWS HE'S GOT TWO LOVING PARENTS. TWO HOMES.
STILL,
HOW DO I FEEL ABOUT GUS CONSTANTLY COMING BACK UP TO VISIT?
WELL, WHAT BUSINESS IS IT OF YOURS?

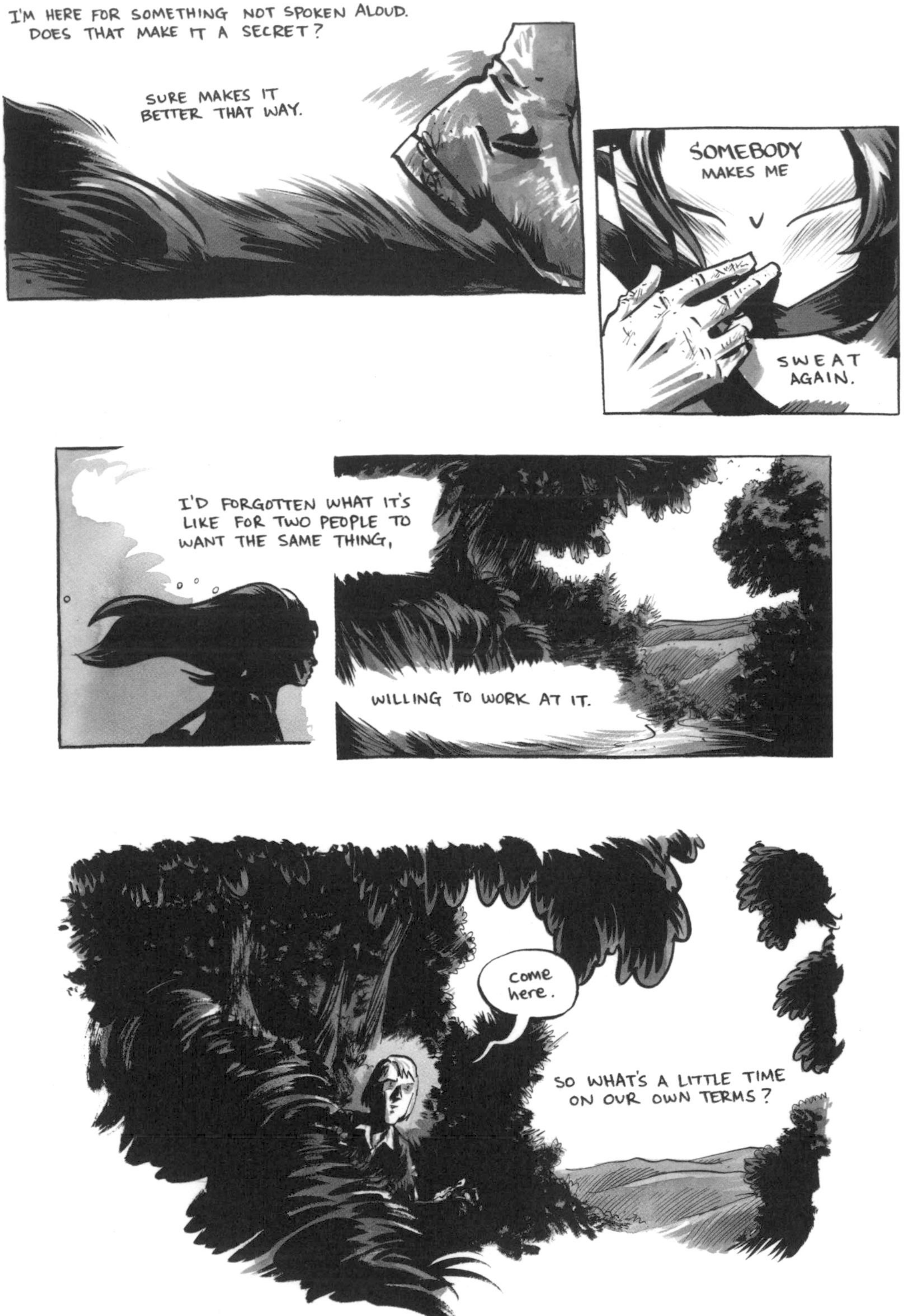
I'M HERE FOR SOMETHING NOT SPOKEN ALOUD.
DOES THAT MAKE IT A SECRET?
SURE MAKES IT BETTER THAT WAY.
SOMEBODY MAKES ME
SWEAT AGAIN.
I'D FORGOTTEN WHAT IT'S LIKE FOR TWO PEOPLE TO WANT THE SAME THING,
WILLING TO WORK AT IT.
come here.
SO WHAT'S A LITTLE TIME ON OUR OWN TERMS?

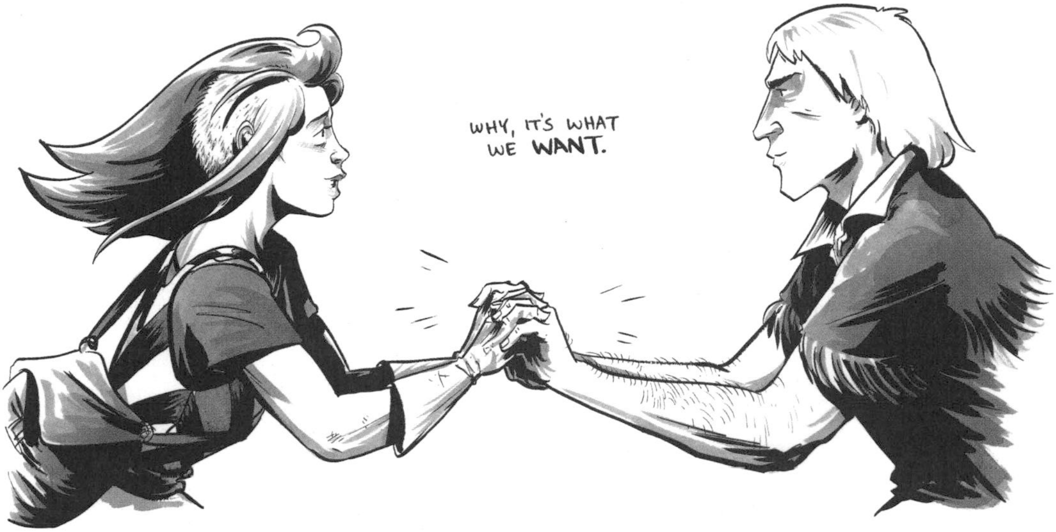
WHY, IT'S WHAT WE WANT.
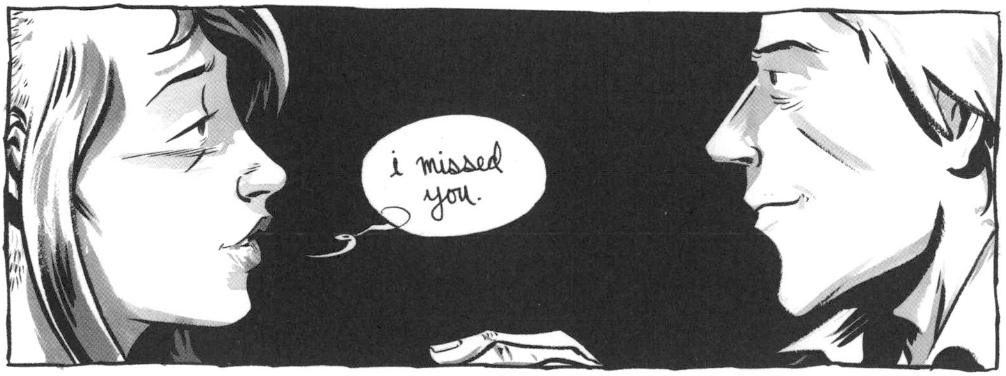
i missed you.
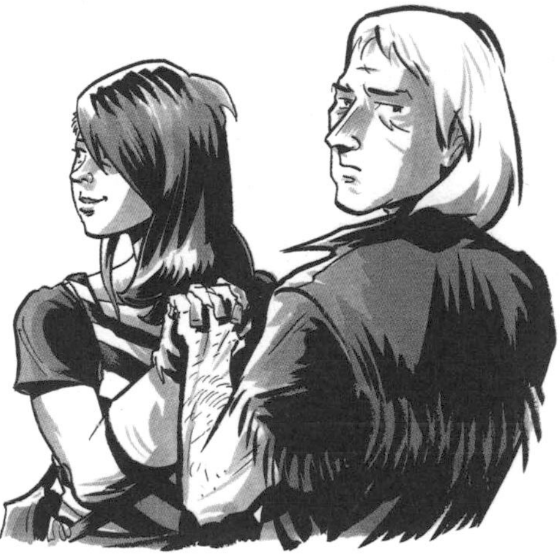

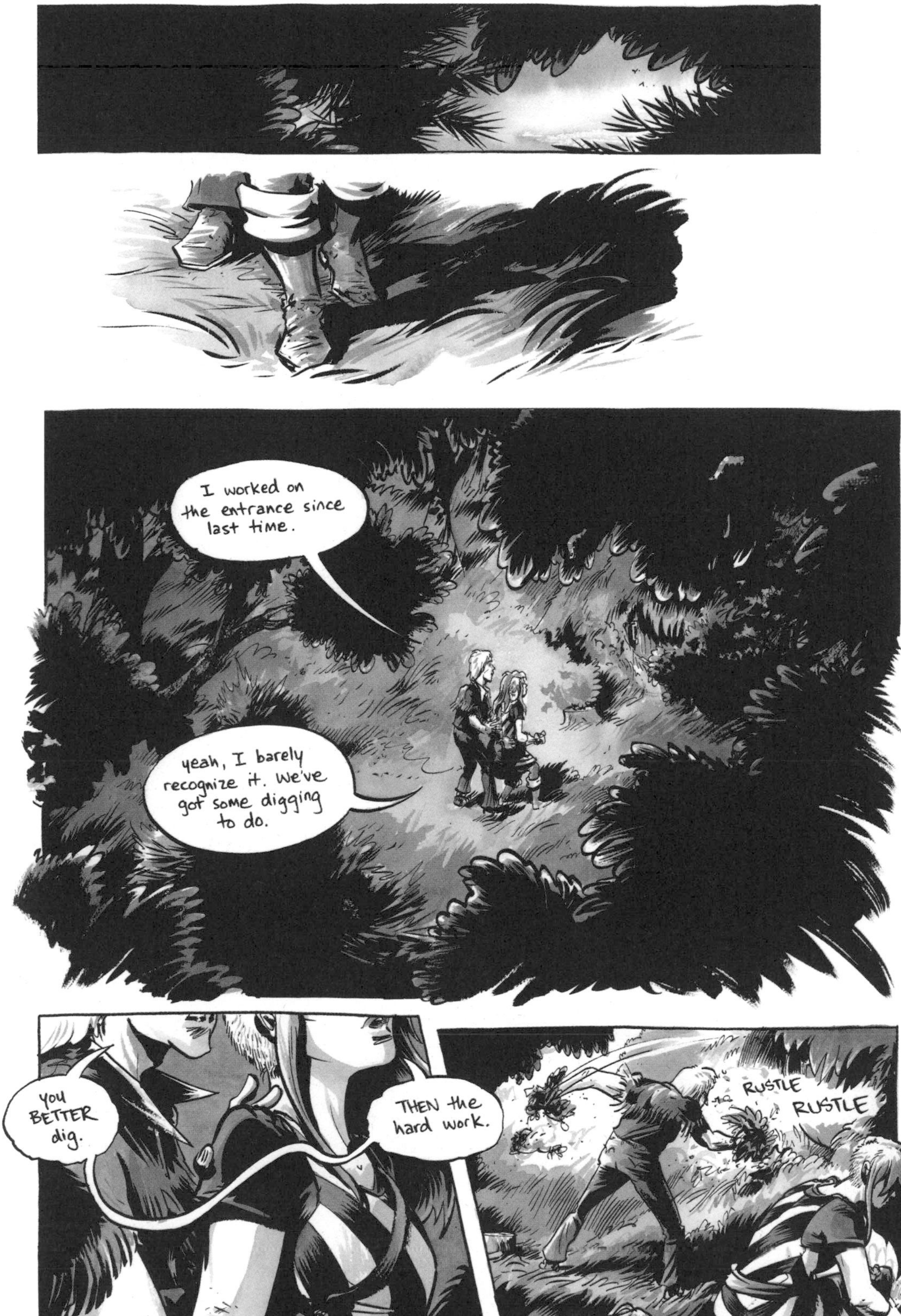
I worked on the entrance since last time.
yeah, I barely recognize it. We've got some digging to do.
you BETTER dig.
THEN the hard work.
RUSTLE
RUSTLE

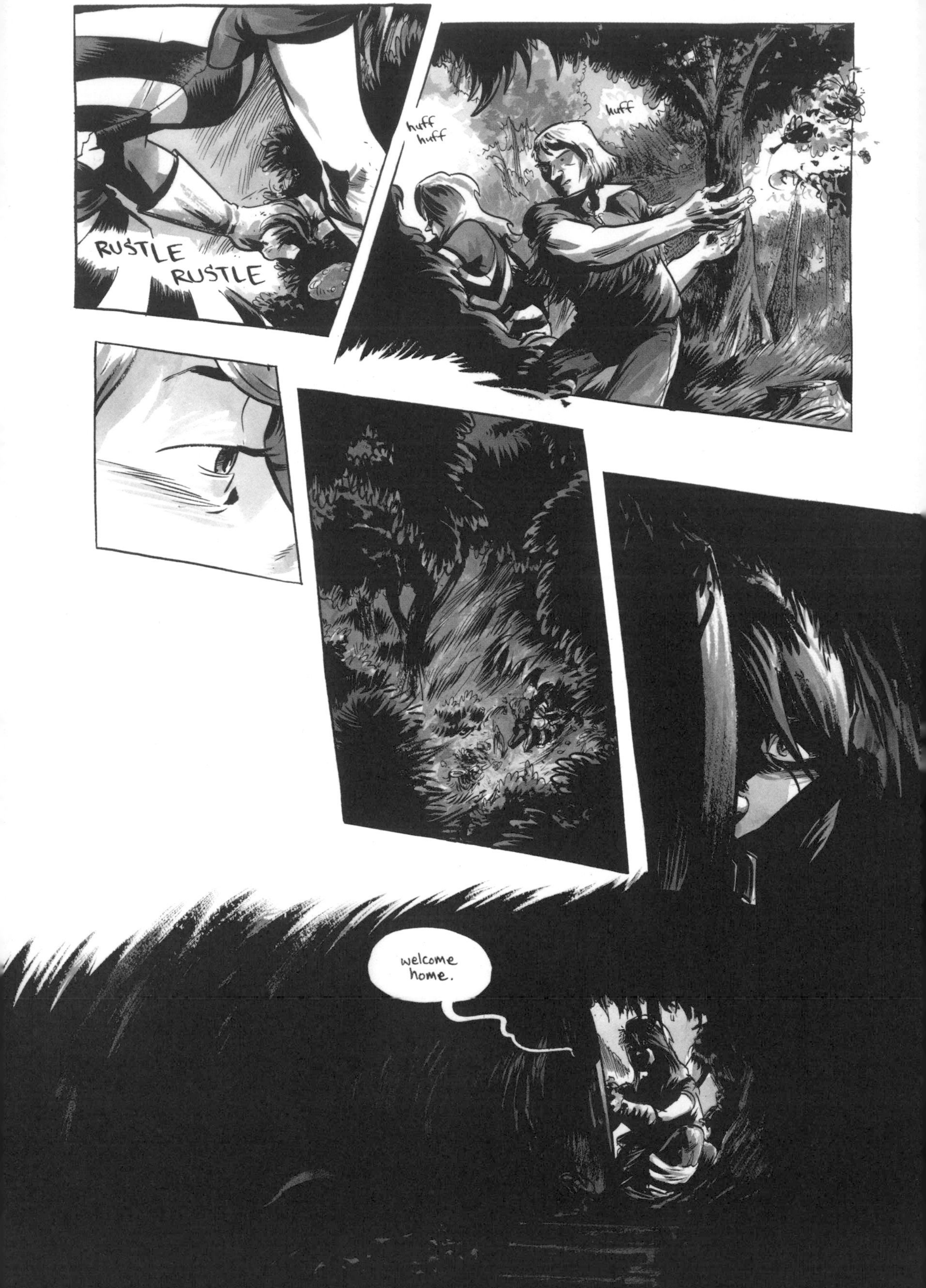
RUSTLE
RUSTLE
huff
huff
huff
welcome home.

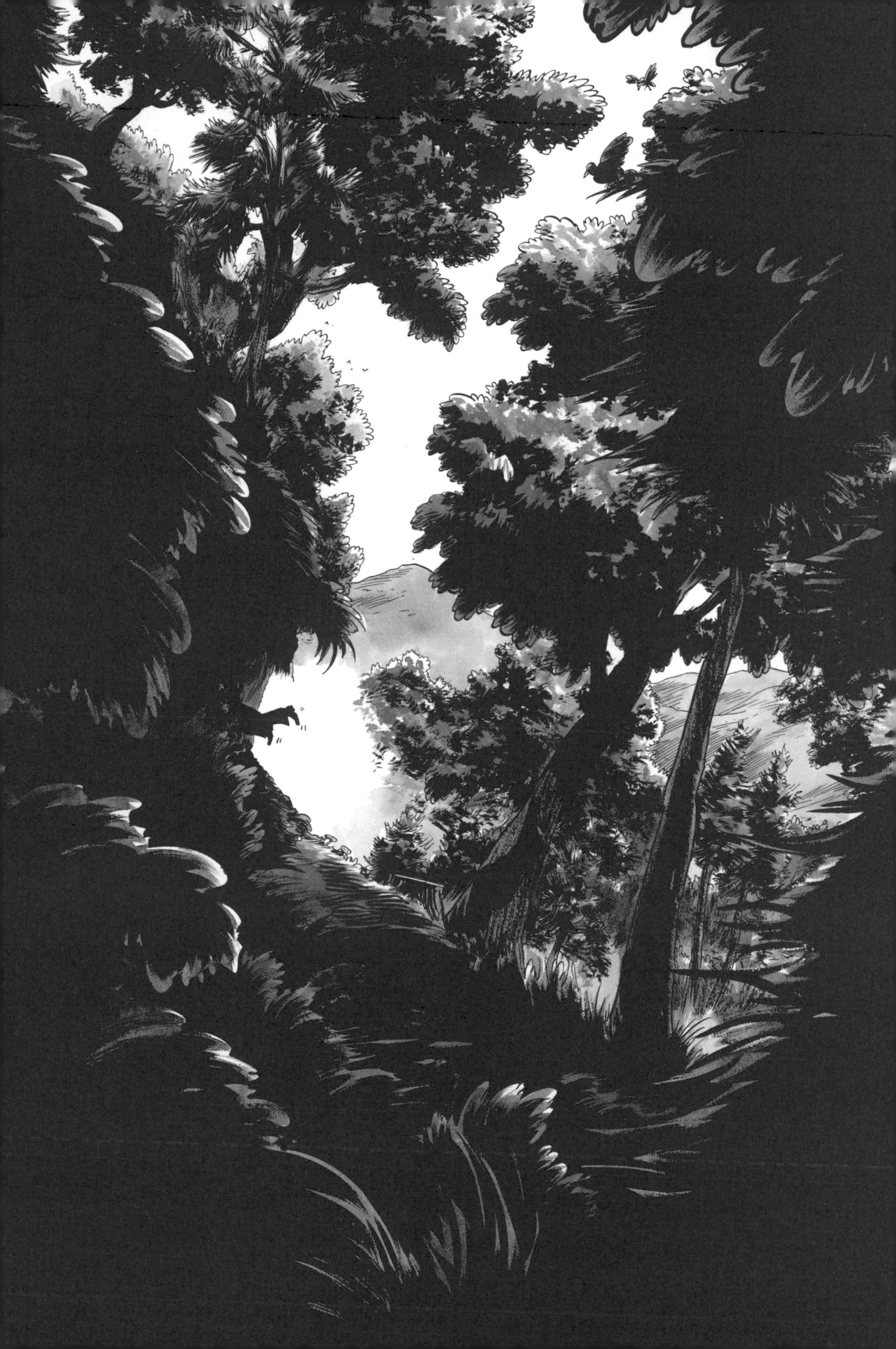

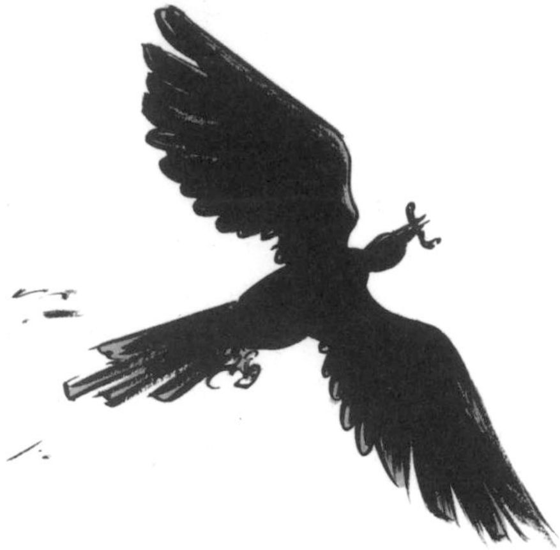
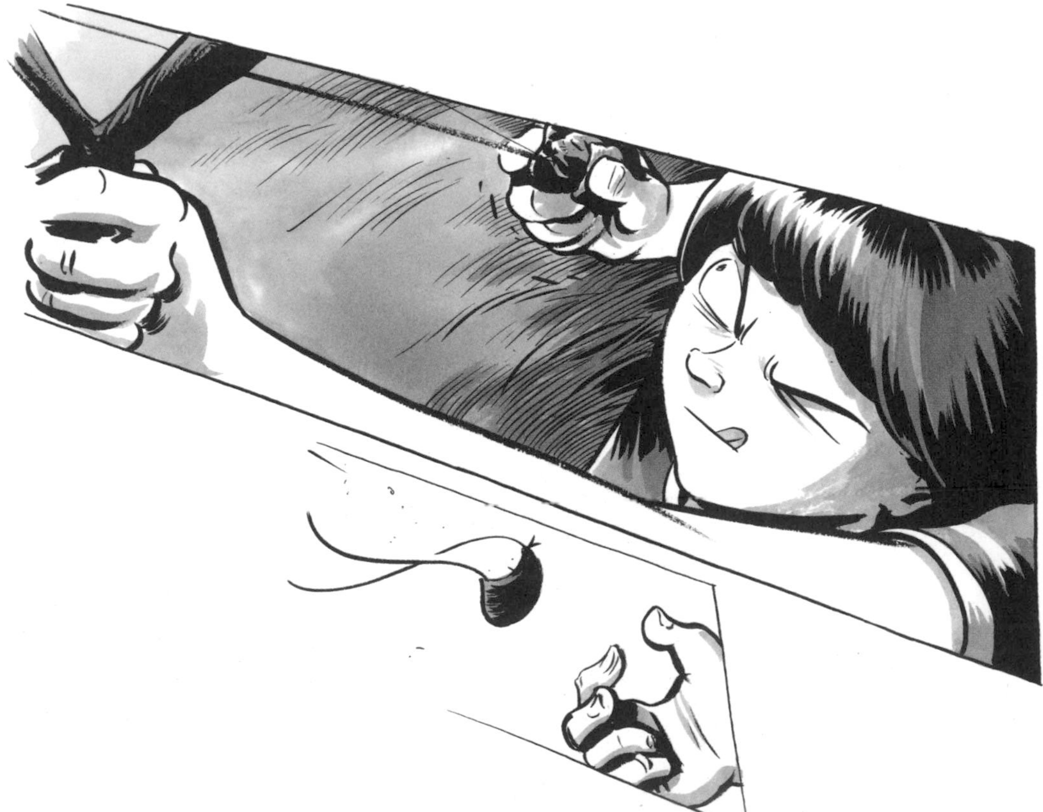

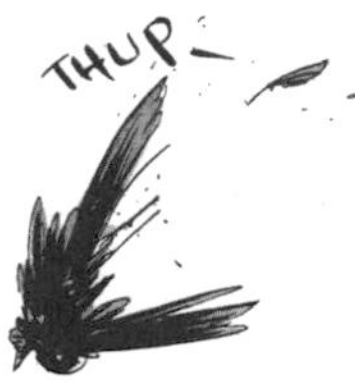
THUP

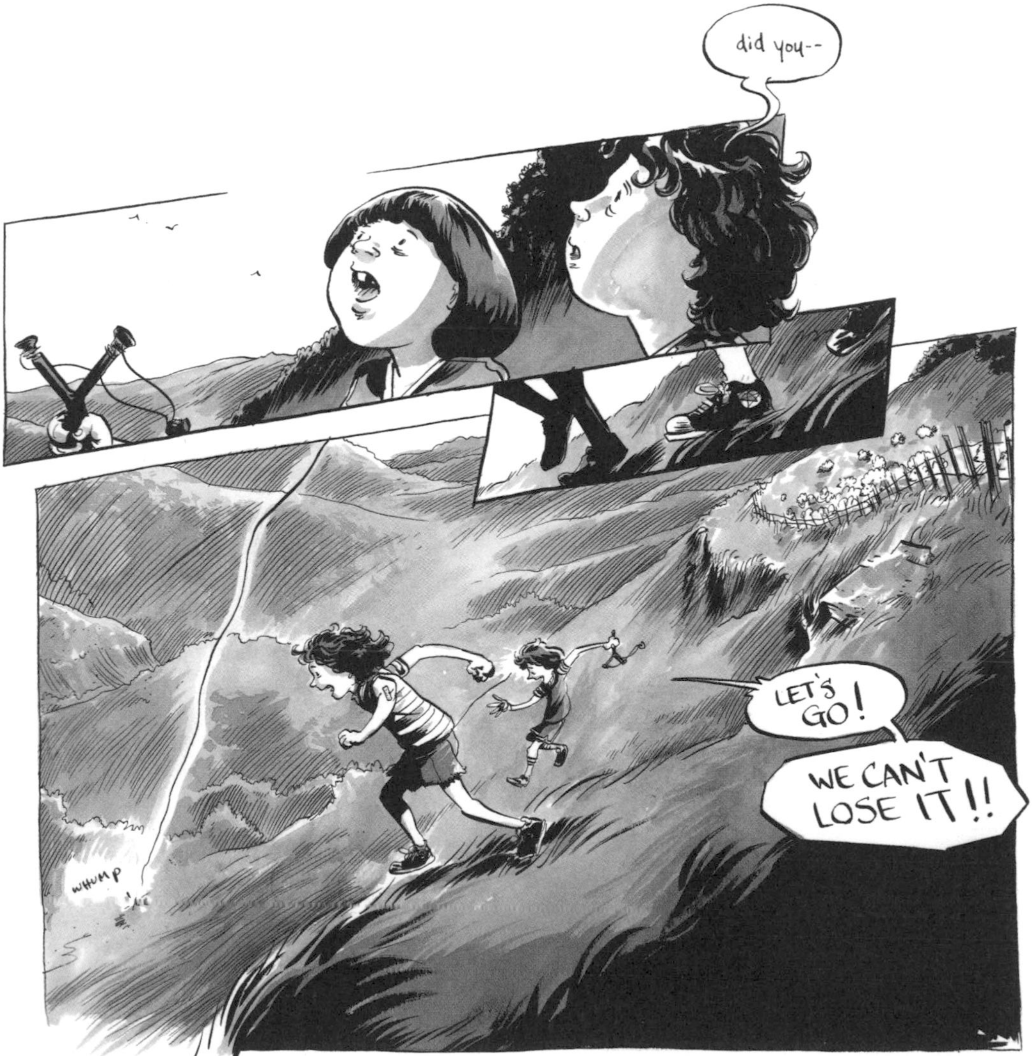
did you--
LET'S GO!
WE CAN'T LOSE IT!!
whump

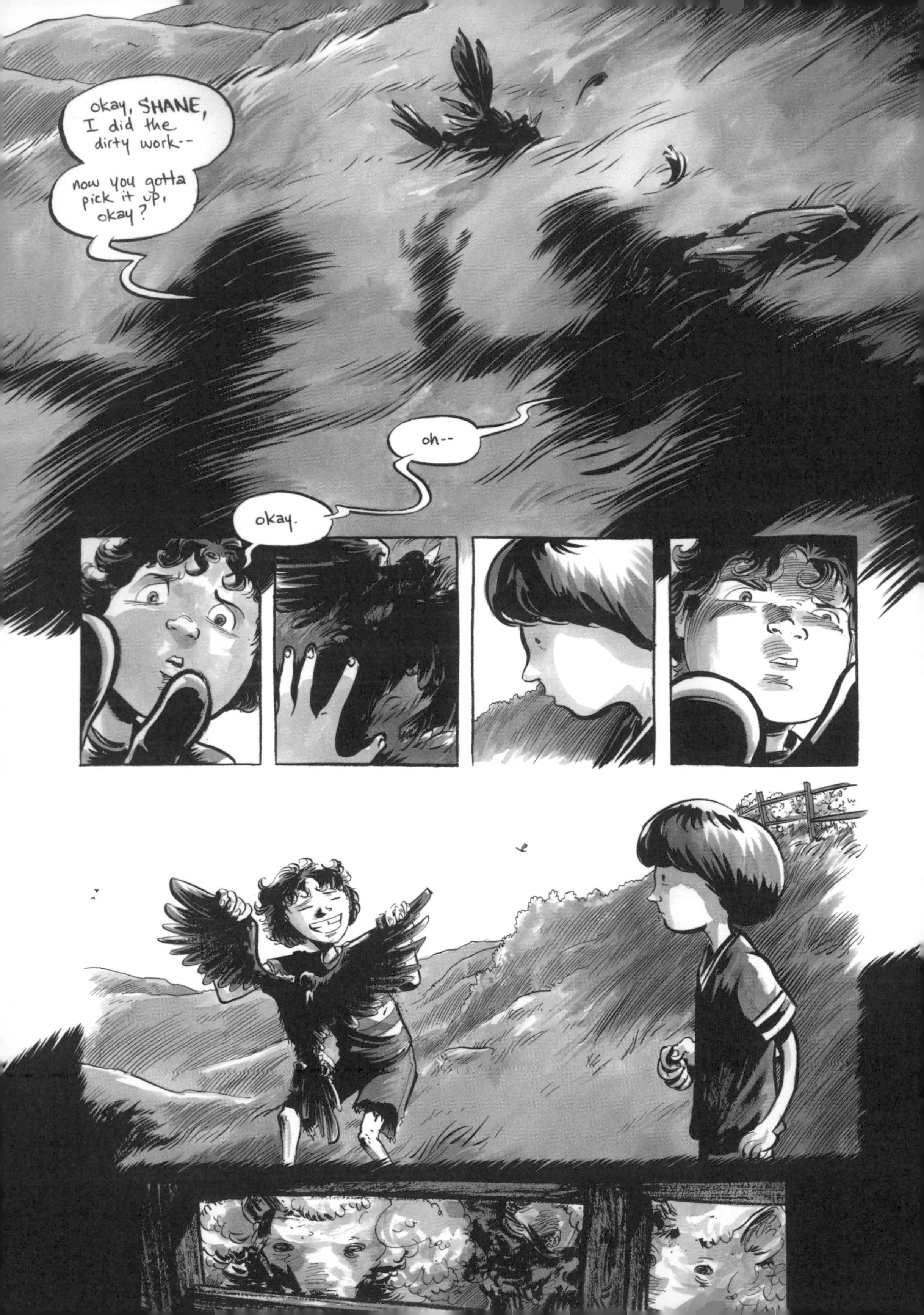
okay, SHANE, I did the dirty work--
now you gotta pick it up, okay?
oh--
okay.

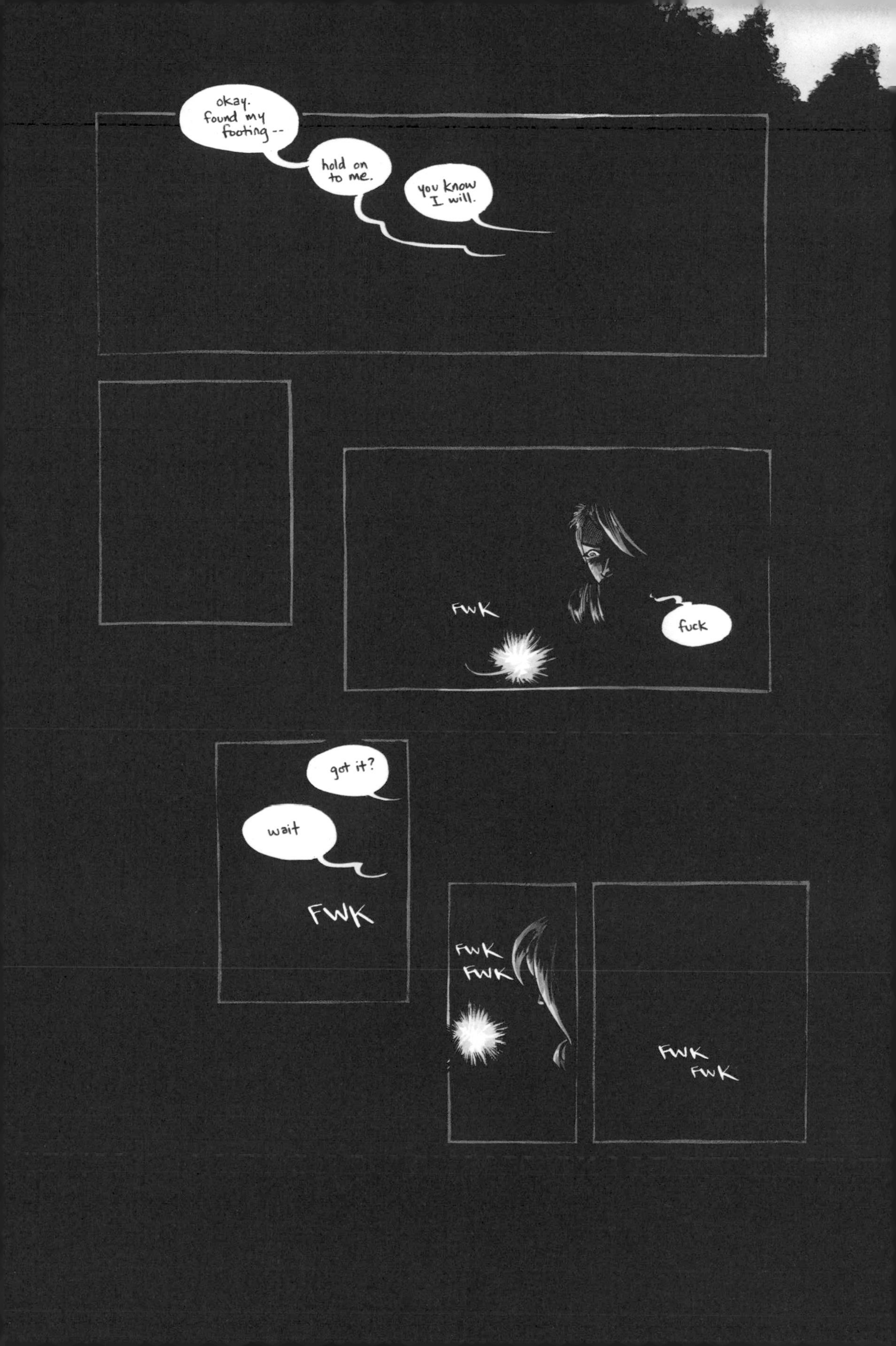
okay. found my footing --
hold on to me.
you know I will.
FWK
fuck
got it?
wait
FWK
FWK
FWK
FWK
FWK

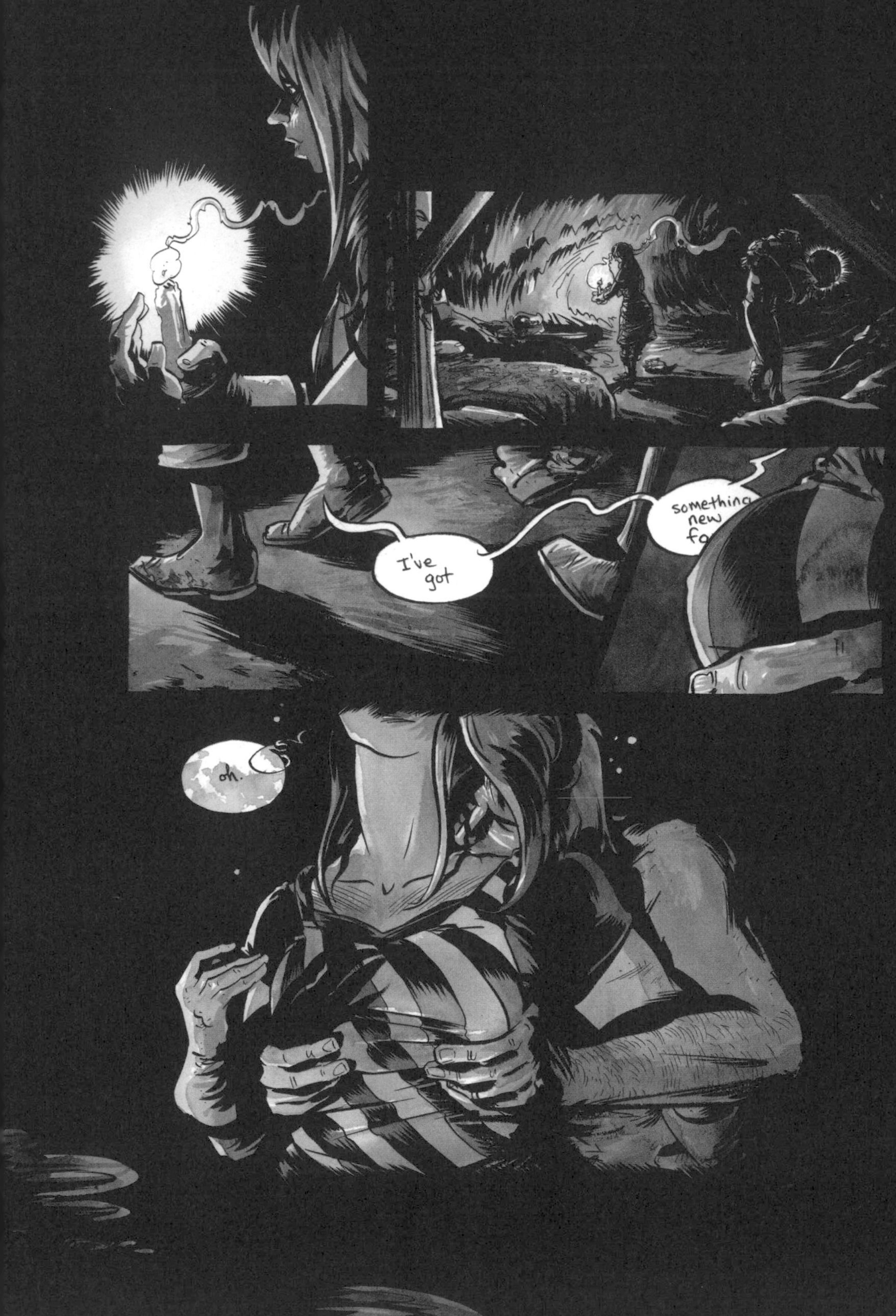
I've got
something new fo
oh.

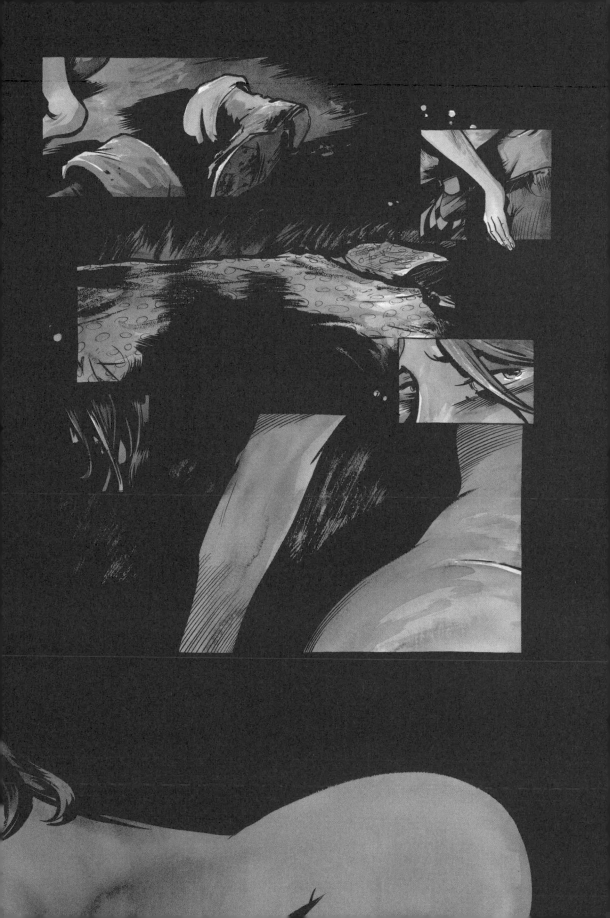

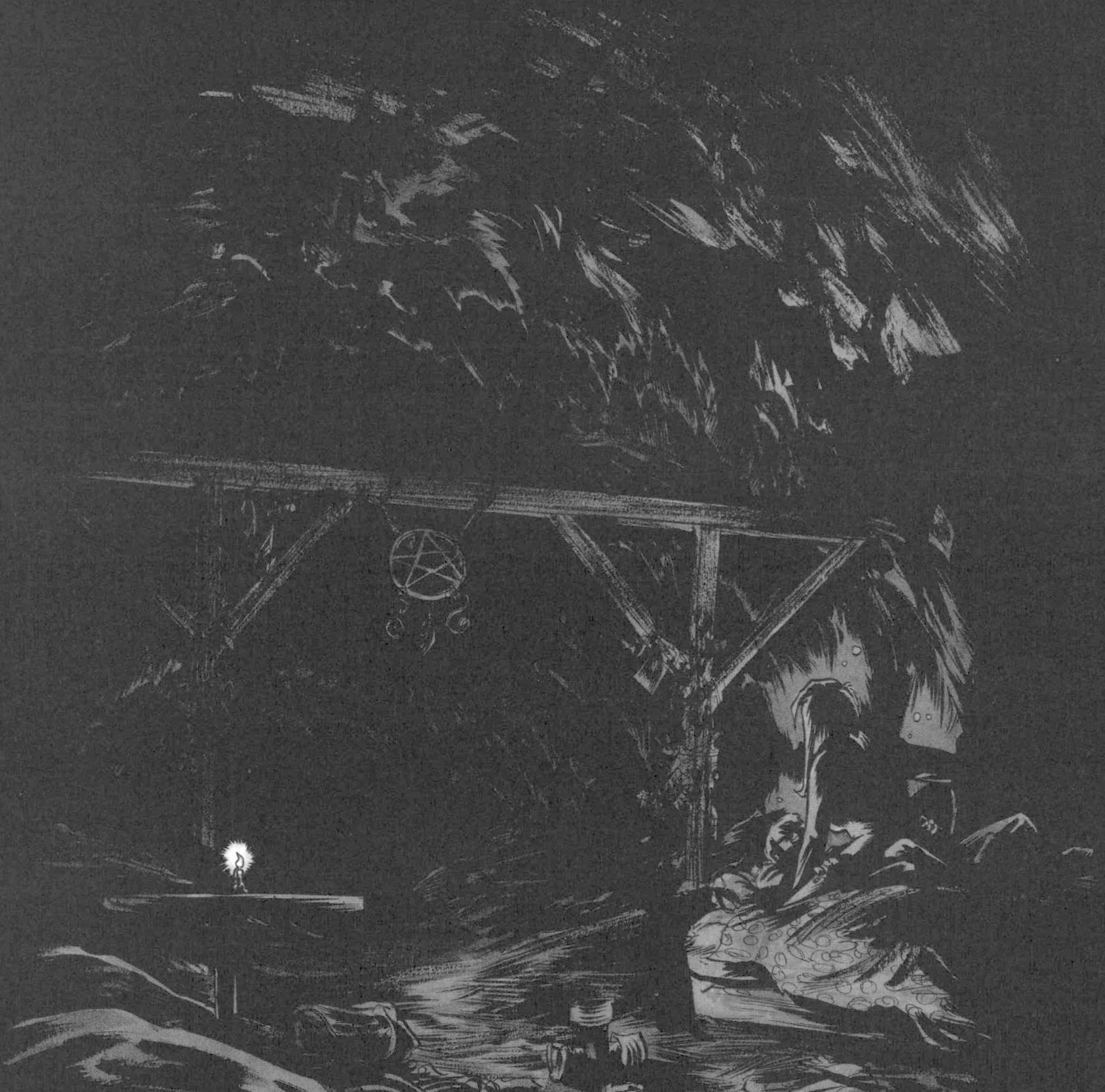

no, I'm serious!
come ON!
you're bad.
oh, look--

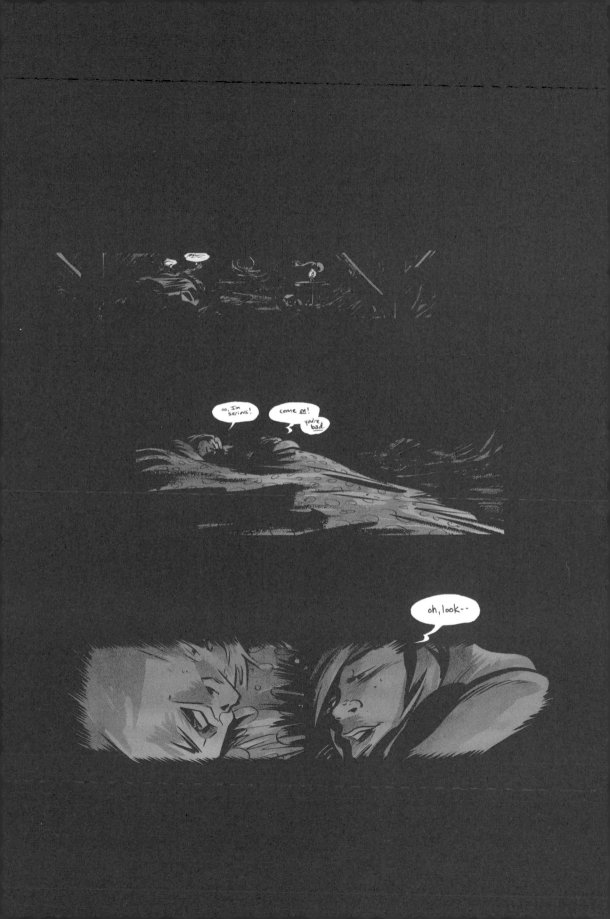

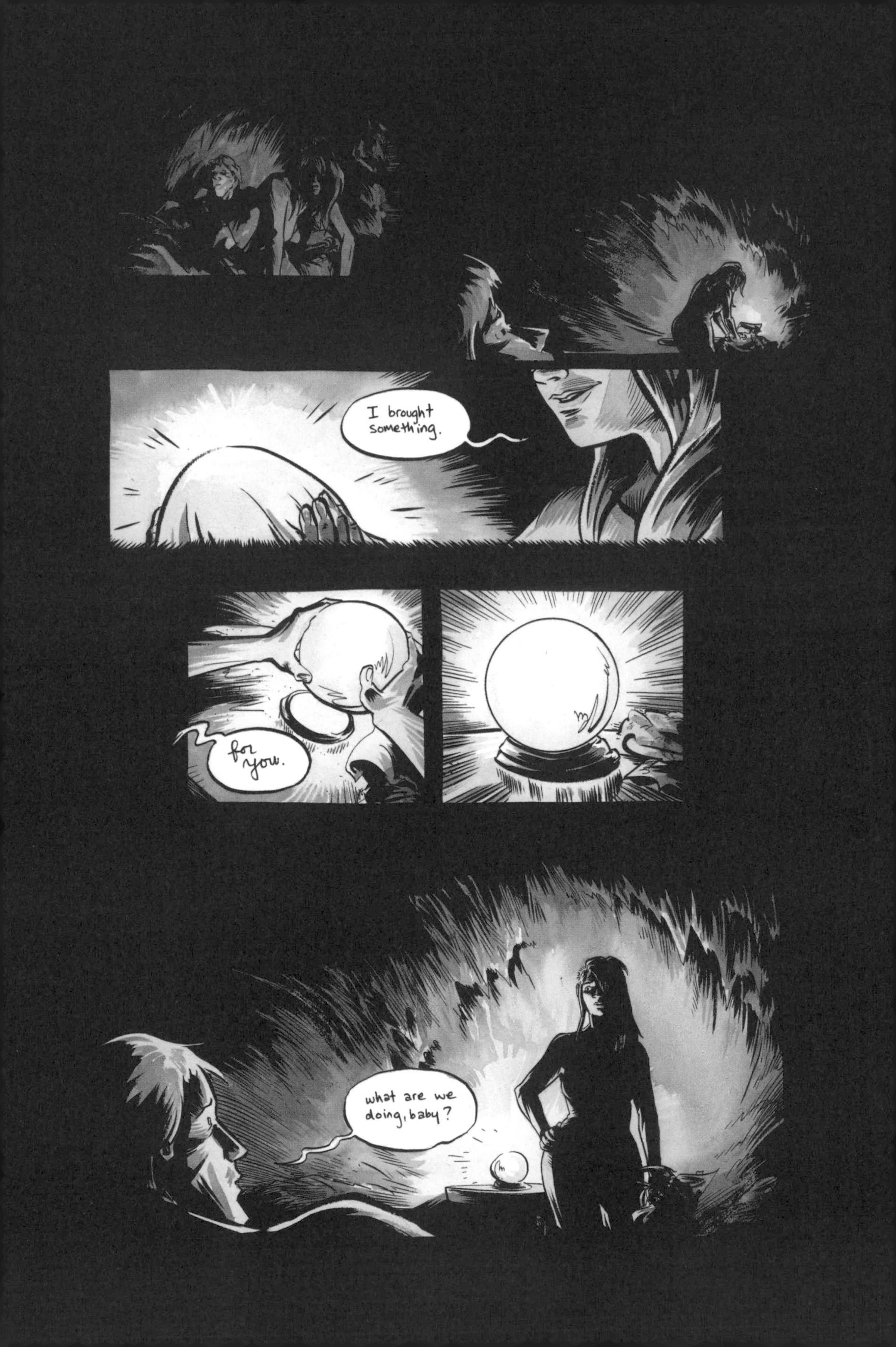
I brought something.
for you.
what are we doing, baby?

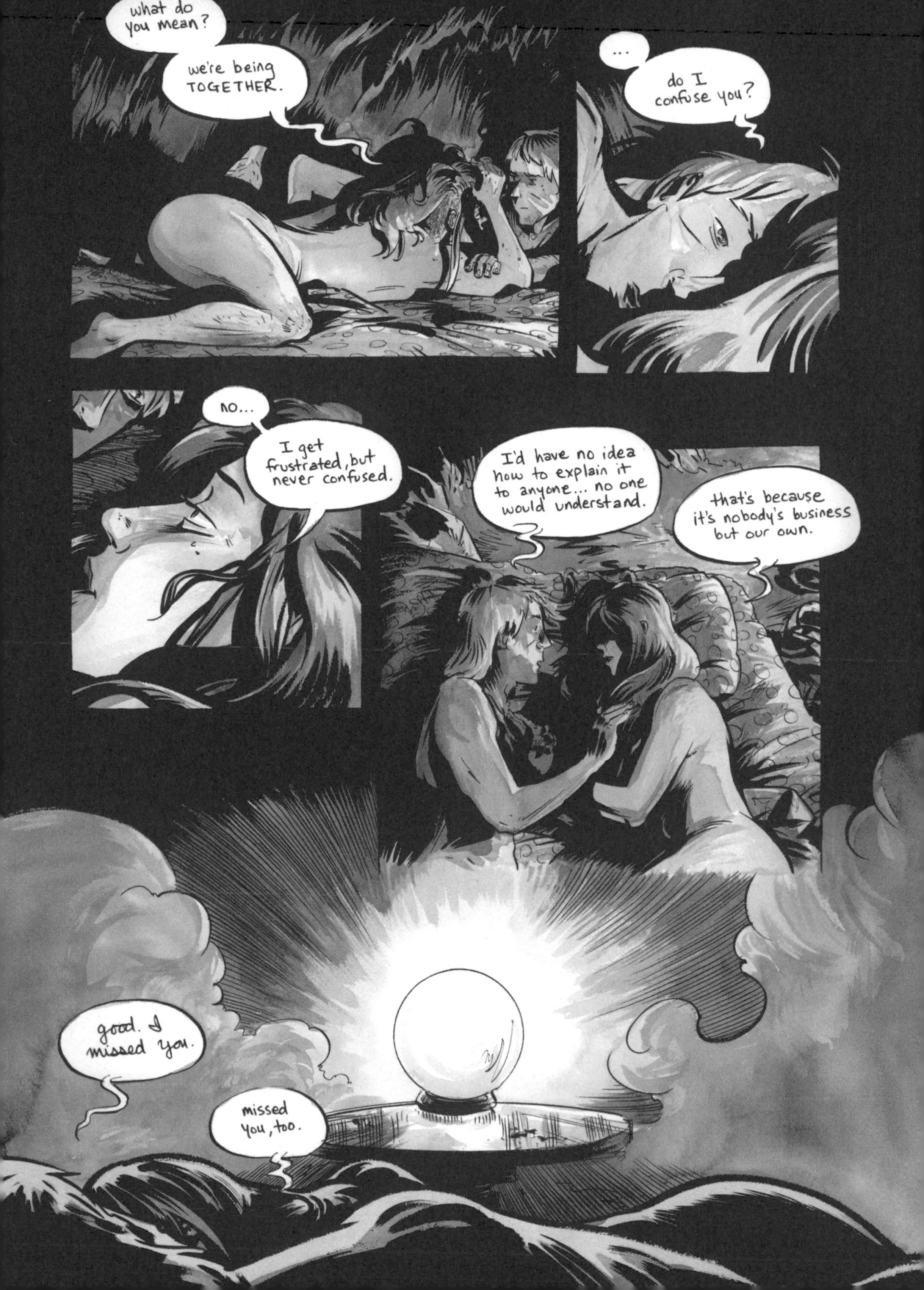
what do you mean?
we're being TOGETHER.
...
do I confuse you?
no...
I get frustrated, but never confused.
I'd have no idea how to explain it to anyone... no one would understand.
that's because it's nobody's business but our own.
good. I missed you.
missed you, too.

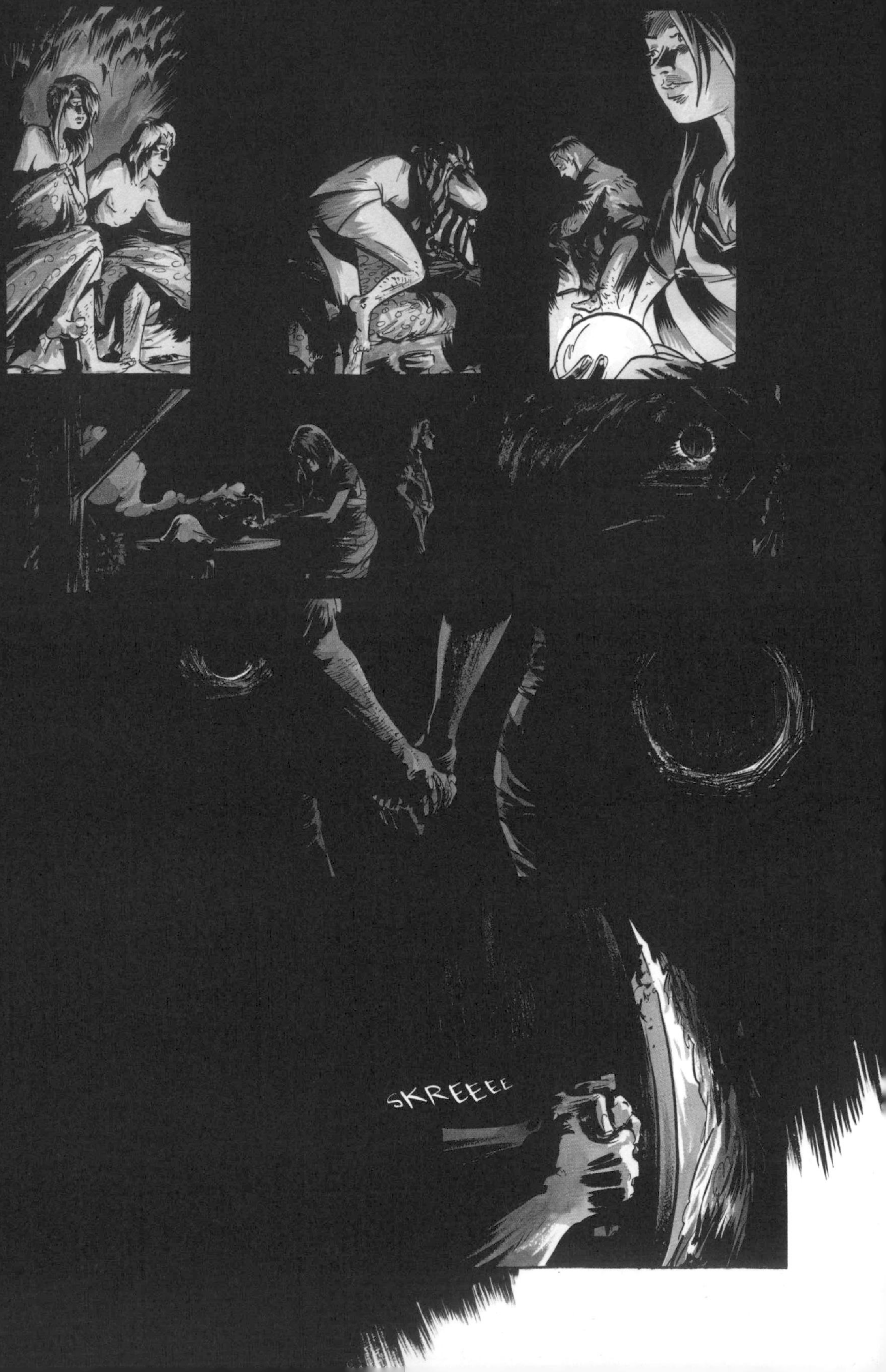
SKREEEE

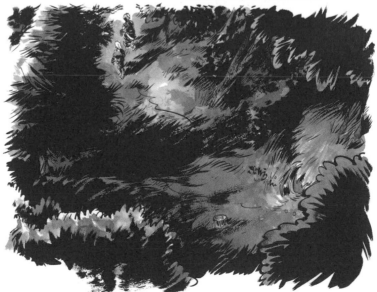

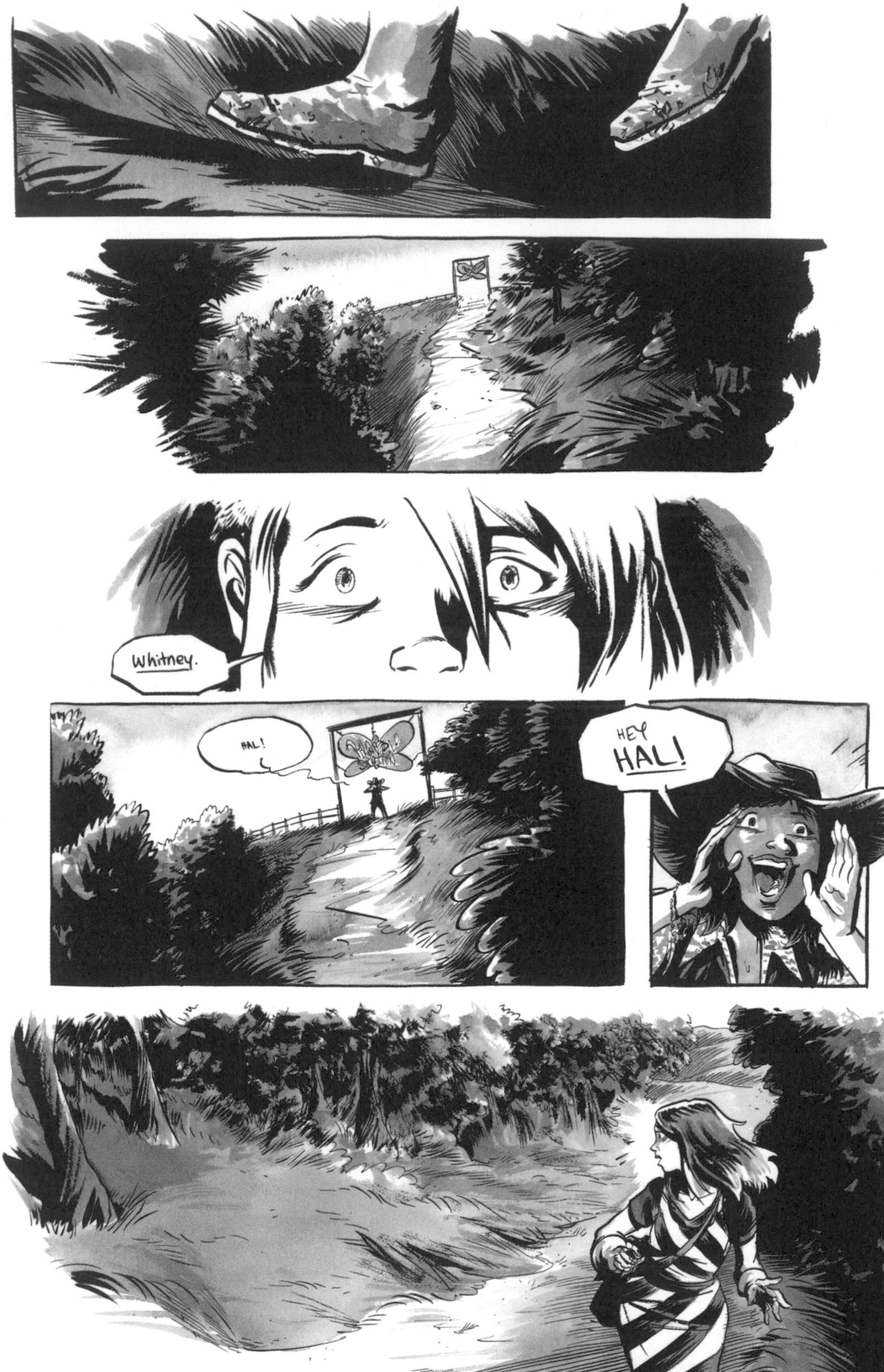
Whitney.
HAL!
HEY HAL!

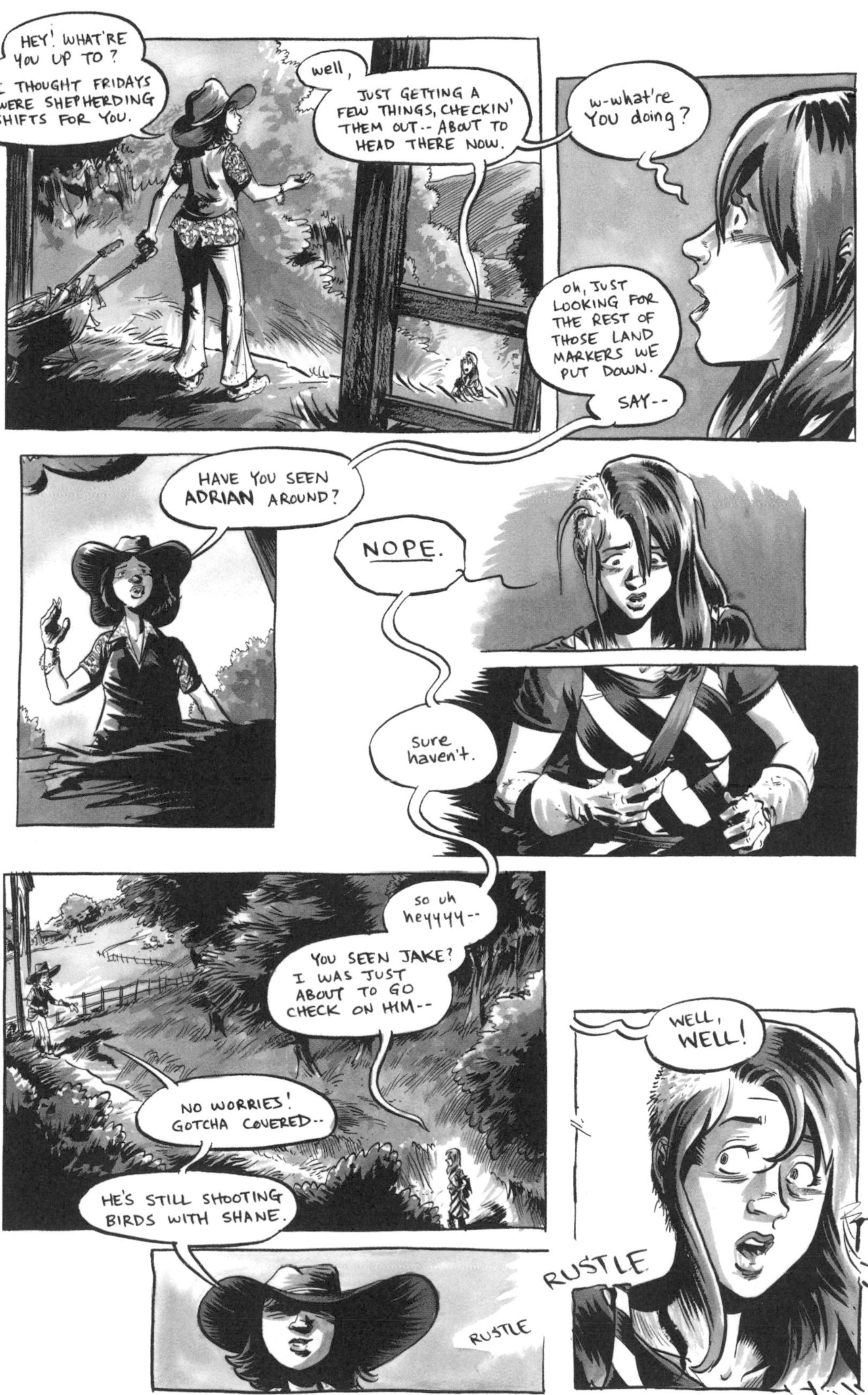
HEY! WHAT'RE YOU UP TO?
I THOUGHT FRIDAYS WERE SHEPHERDING SHIFTS FOR YOU.
well,
JUST GETTING A FEW THINGS, CHECKIN' THEM OUT-- ABOUT TO HEAD THERE NOW.
w-what're you doing?
oh, JUST LOOKING FOR THE REST OF THOSE LAND MARKERS WE PUT DOWN.
SAY--
HAVE YOU SEEN ADRIAN AROUND?
NOPE.
sure haven't.
so uh heyyyy--
YOU SEEN JAKE? I WAS JUST ABOUT TO GO CHECK ON HIM--
NO WORRIES! GOTCHA COVERED--
HE'S STILL SHOOTING BIRDS WITH SHANE.
WELL, WELL!
RUSTLE
RUSTLE

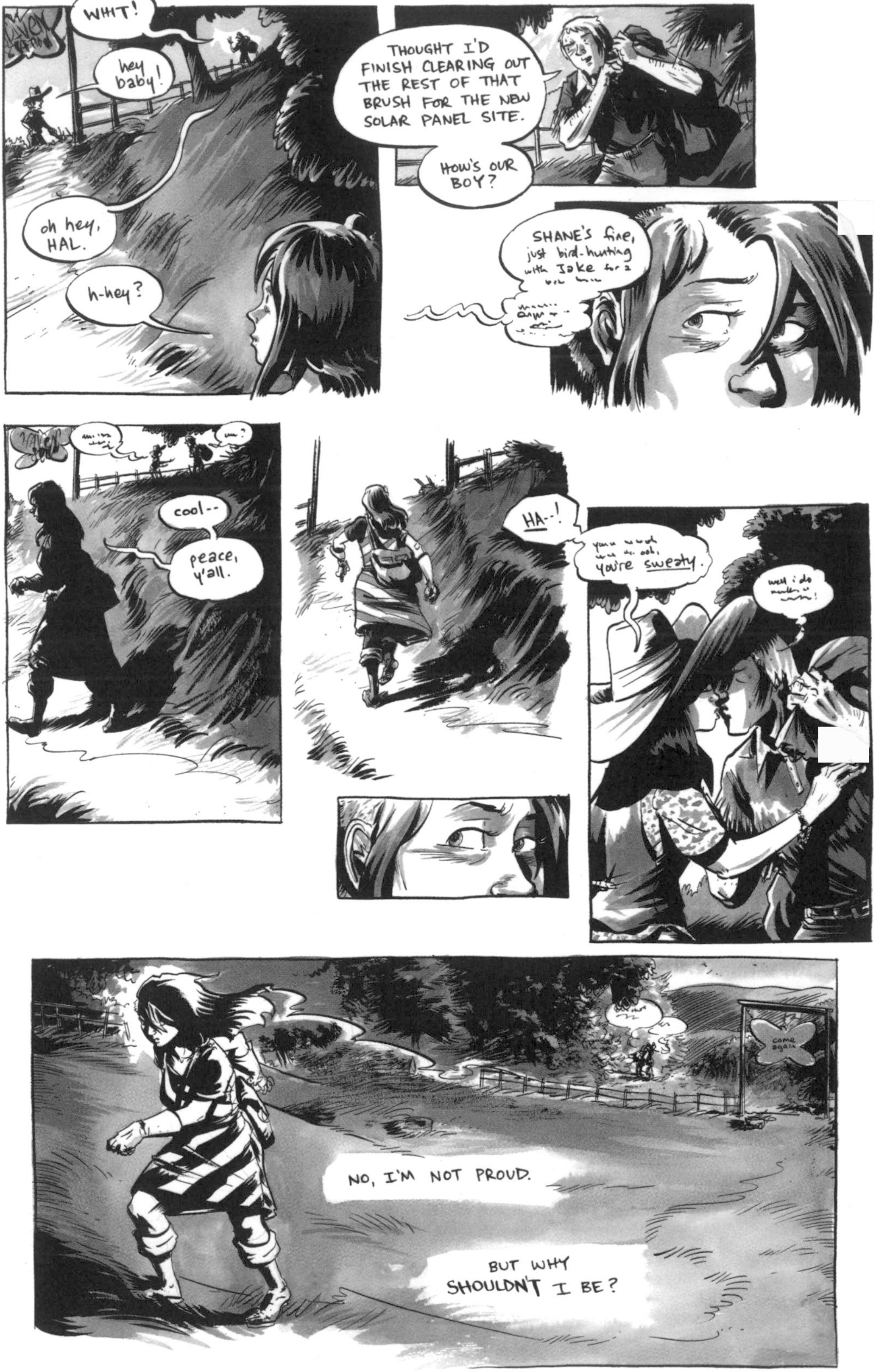
WHIT!
hey baby!
oh hey, HAL.
h-hey?
THOUGHT I'D FINISH CLEARING OUT THE REST OF THAT BRUSH FOR THE NEW SOLAR PANEL SITE.
HOW'S OUR BOY?
SHANE'S fine, just bird-hunting with Jake for a
cool--
peace, y'all.
HA--!
you're sweaty.
NO, I'M NOT PROUD.
BUT WHY SHOULDN'T I BE?

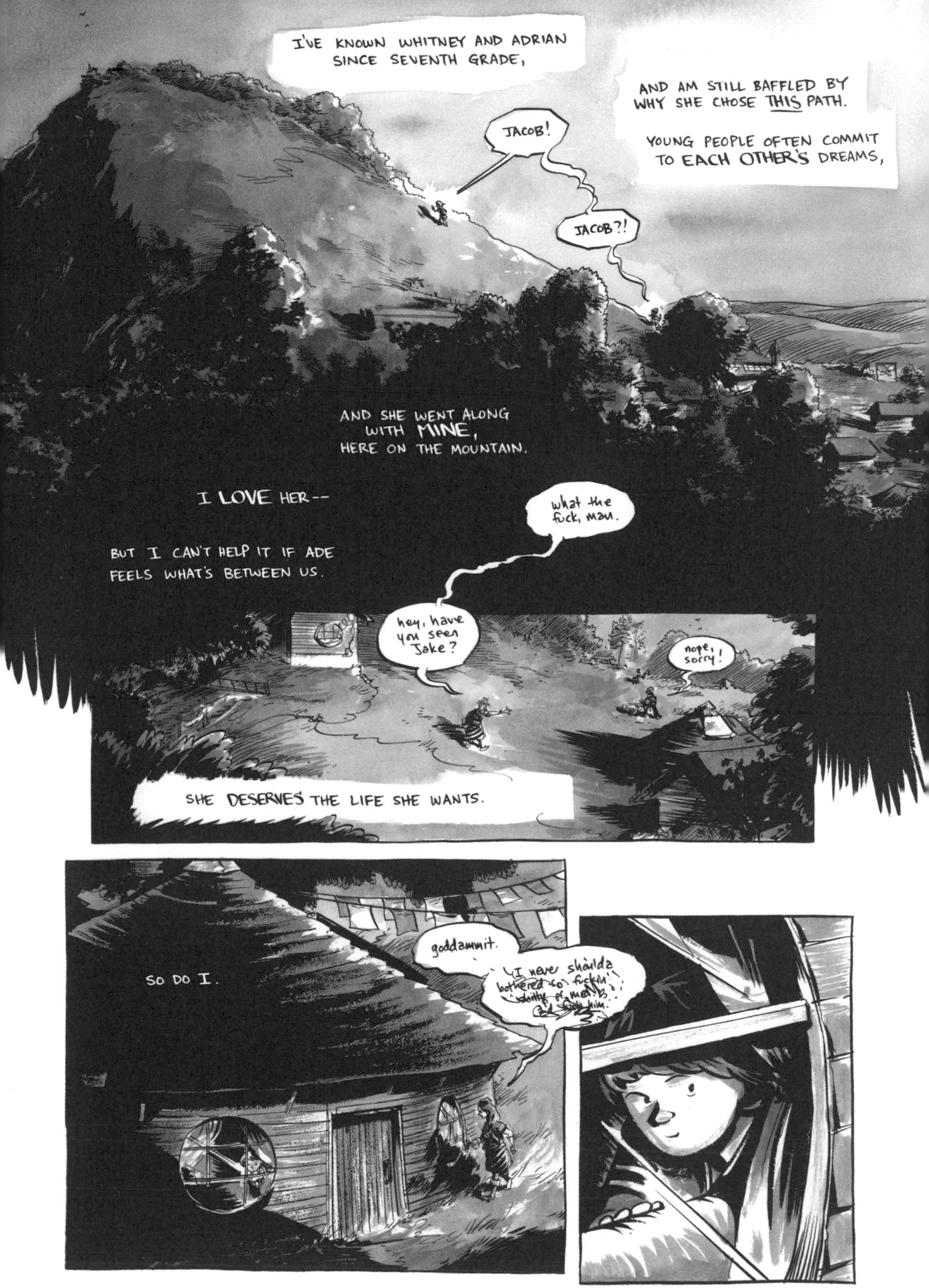
I'VE KNOWN WHITNEY AND ADRIAN SINCE SEVENTH GRADE,
AND AM STILL BAFFLED BY WHY SHE CHOSE THIS PATH.
YOUNG PEOPLE OFTEN COMMIT TO EACH OTHER'S DREAMS,
JACOB!
JACOB?!
AND SHE WENT ALONG WITH MINE, HERE ON THE MOUNTAIN.
I LOVE HER--
BUT I CAN'T HELP IT IF ADE FEELS WHAT'S BETWEEN US.
what the fuck, man.
hey, have you seen Jake?
nope, sorry!
SHE DESERVES THE LIFE SHE WANTS.
SO DO I.
goddammit.
I never shoulda bothered so fuckin' shitty of me him.

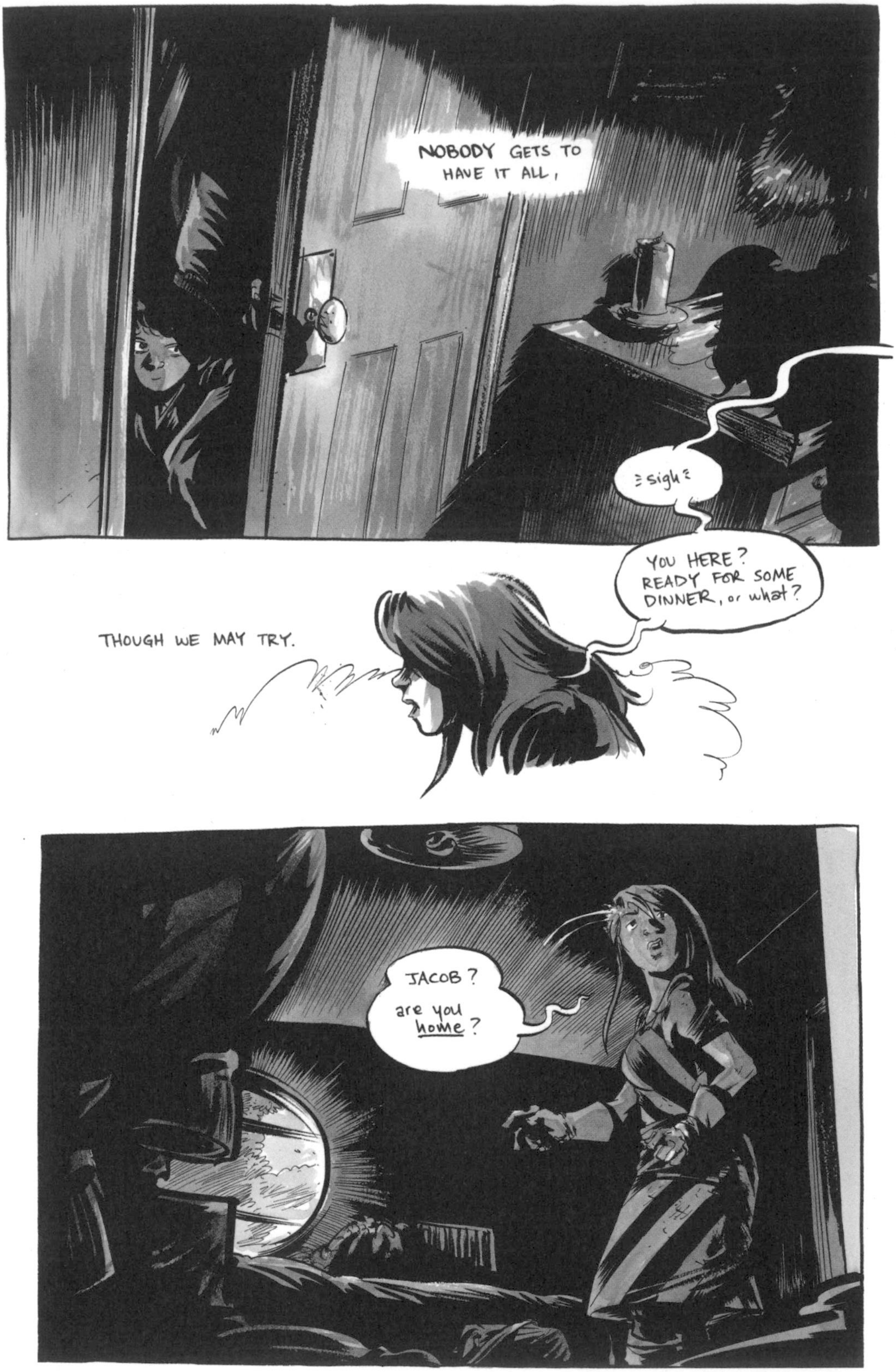
NOBODY GETS TO HAVE IT ALL,
≡ sigh ≡
YOU HERE? READY FOR SOME DINNER, or what?
THOUGH WE MAY TRY.
JACOB?
are you home?

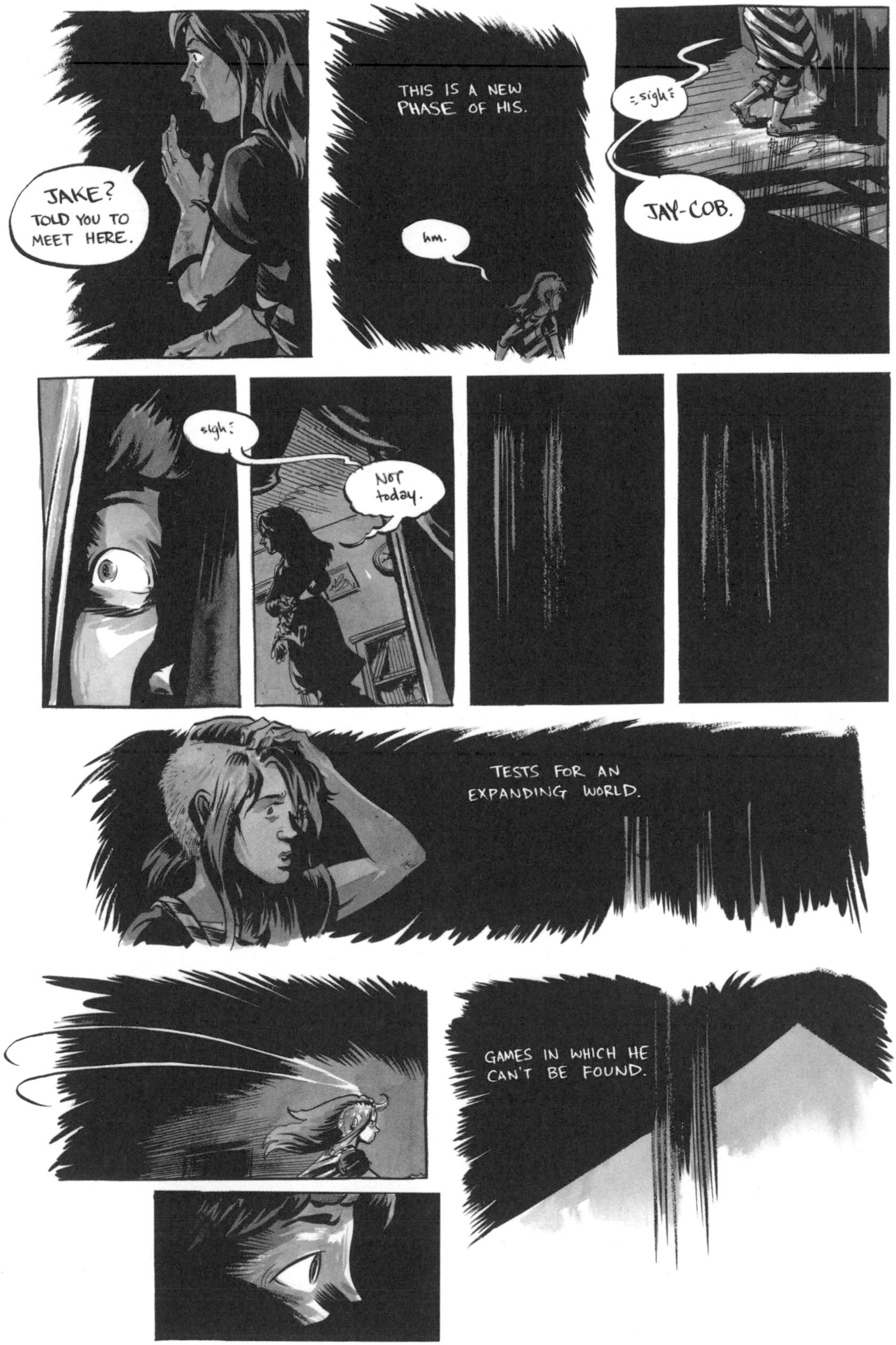
JAKE? TOLD YOU TO MEET HERE.
THIS IS A NEW PHASE OF HIS.
hm.
sigh
JAY-COB.
sigh
Not today.
TESTS FOR AN EXPANDING WORLD.
GAMES IN WHICH HE CAN'T BE FOUND.

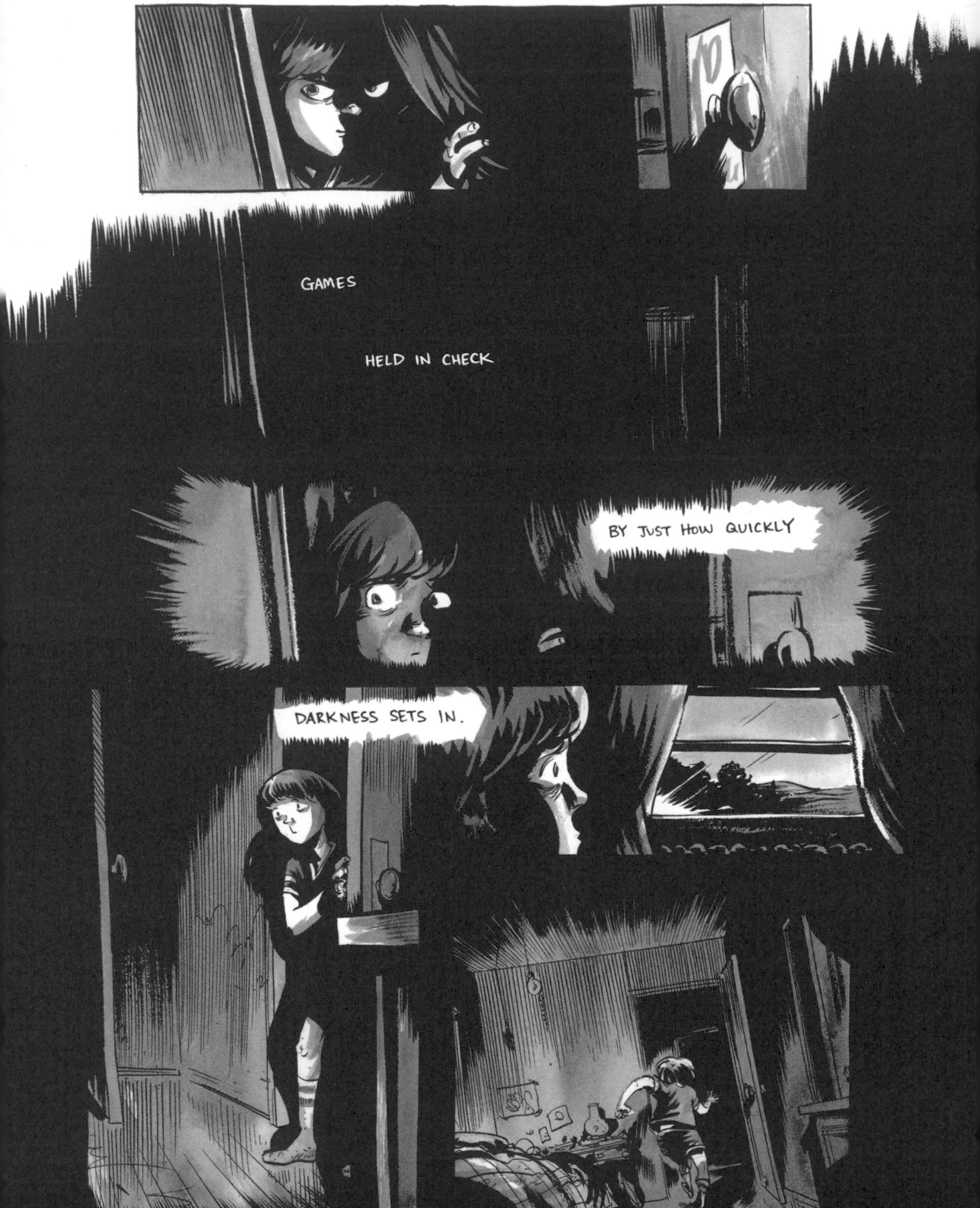
GAMES
HELD IN CHECK
BY JUST HOW QUICKLY
DARKNESS SETS IN.

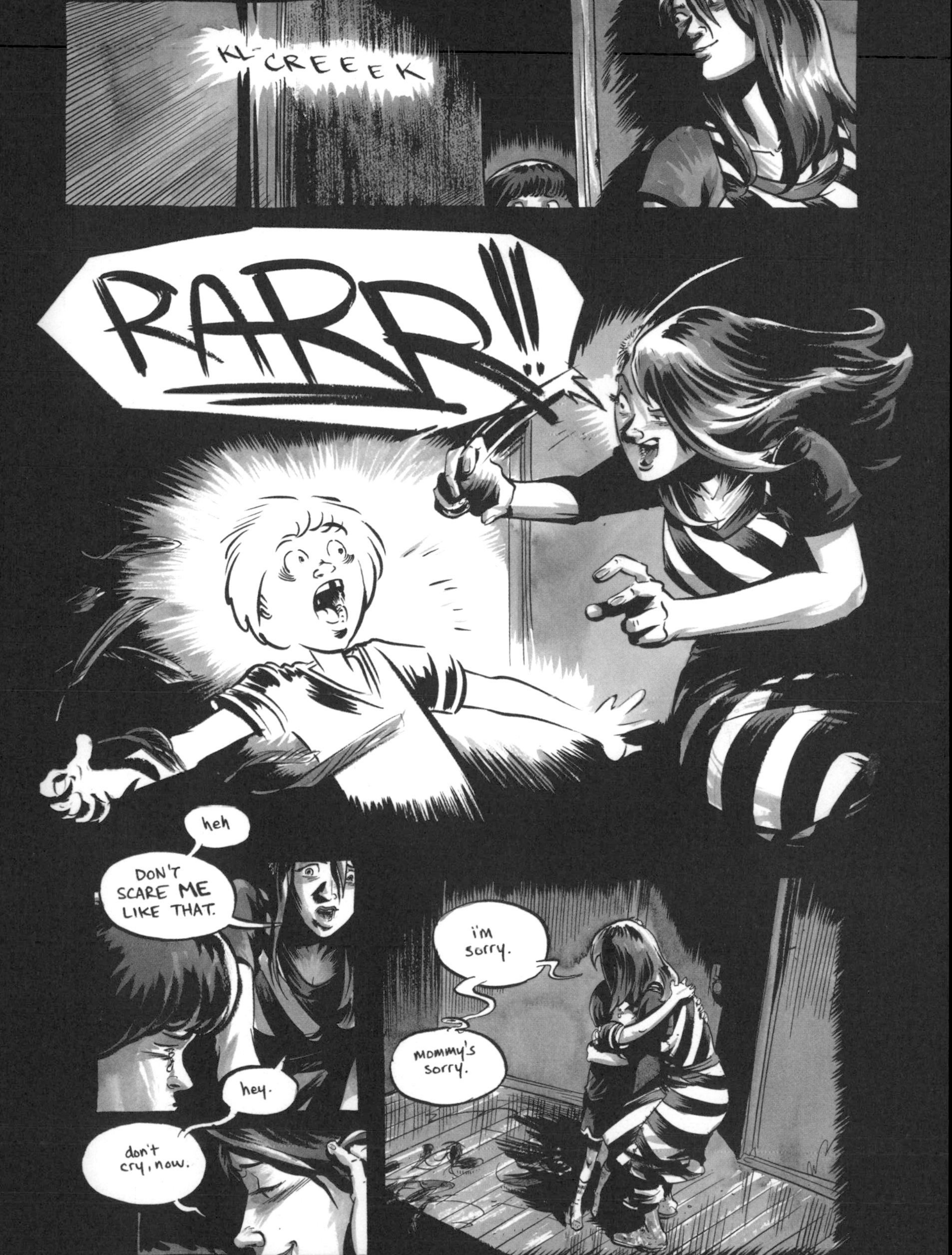
KL-CREEEK
RARR!!
heh
DON'T SCARE ME LIKE THAT.
hey.
don't cry, now.
i'm sorry.
mommy's sorry.

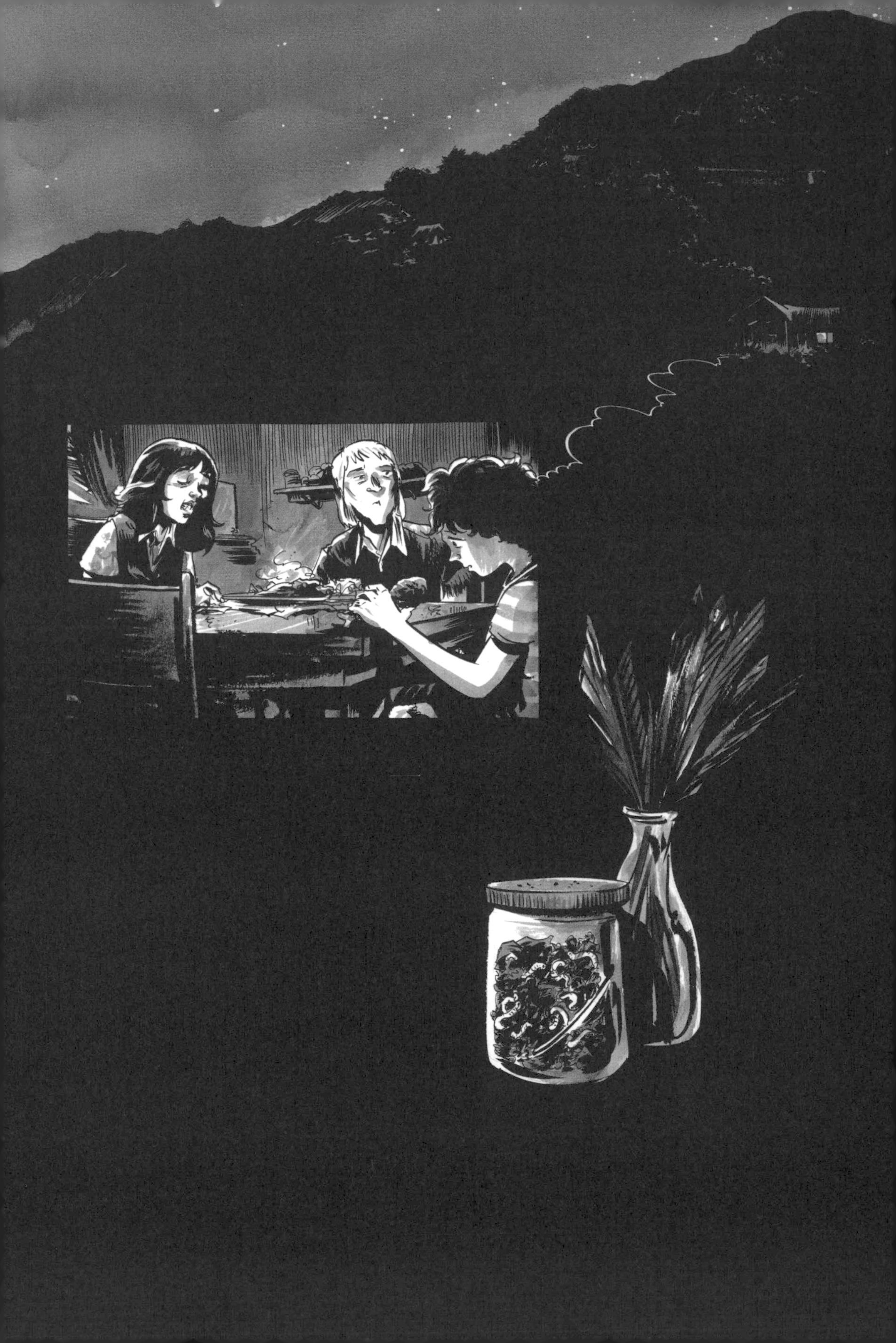

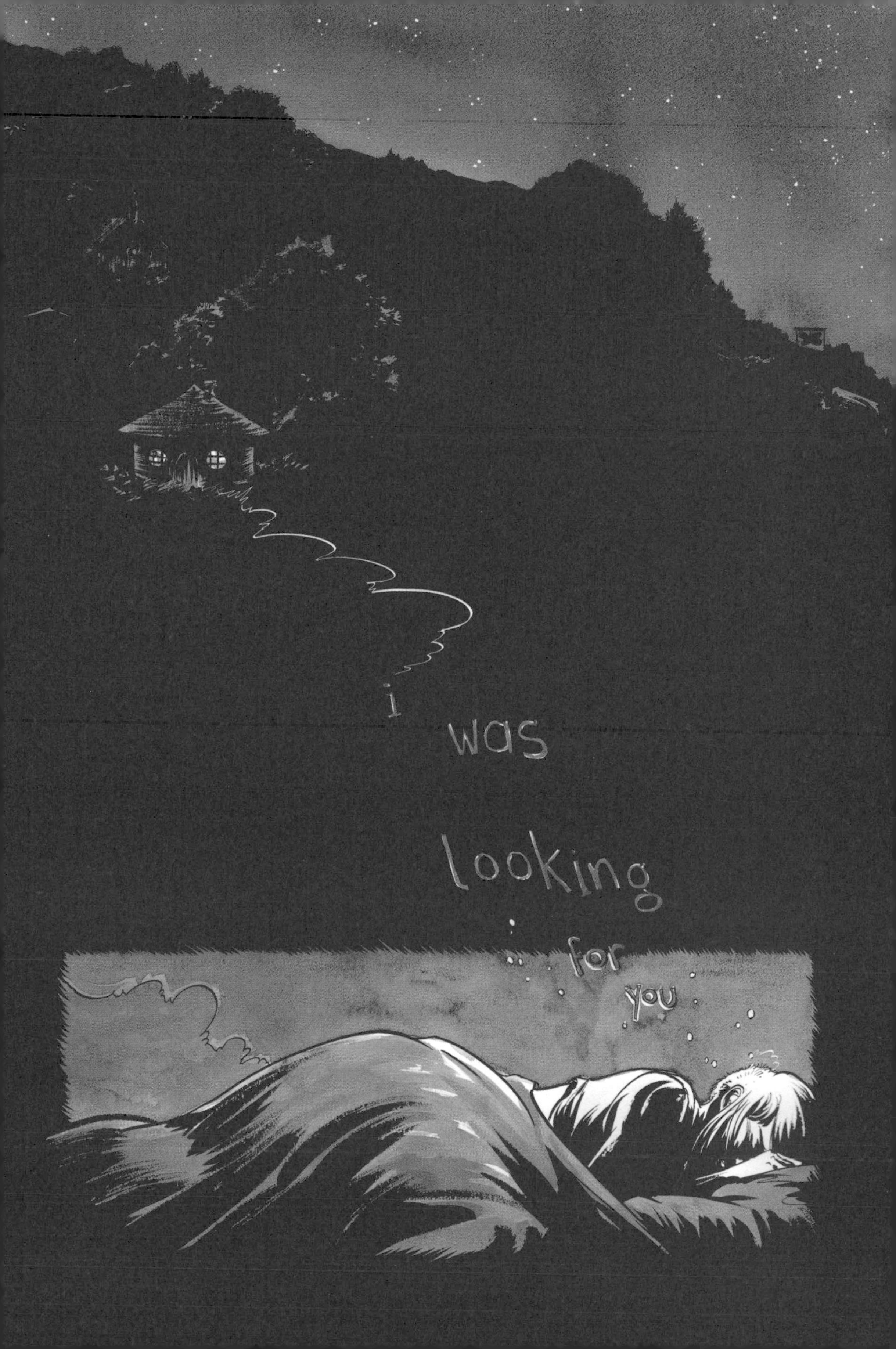
i was looking for you

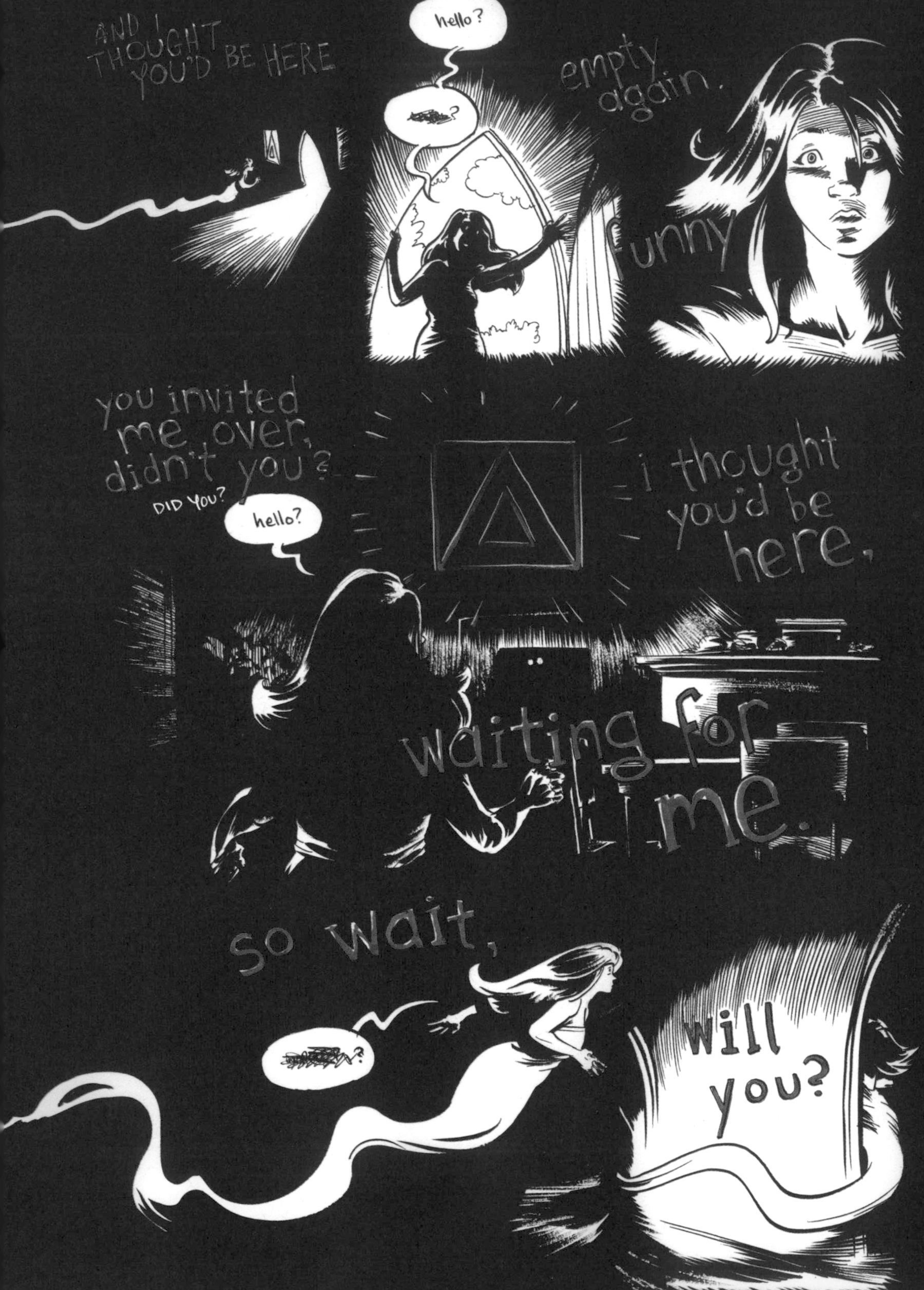
AND I THOUGHT YOU'D BE HERE
hello?
empty again.
funny
you invited me over, didn't you?
DID YOU?
hello?
i thought you'd be here.
waiting for me.
so wait,
will you?

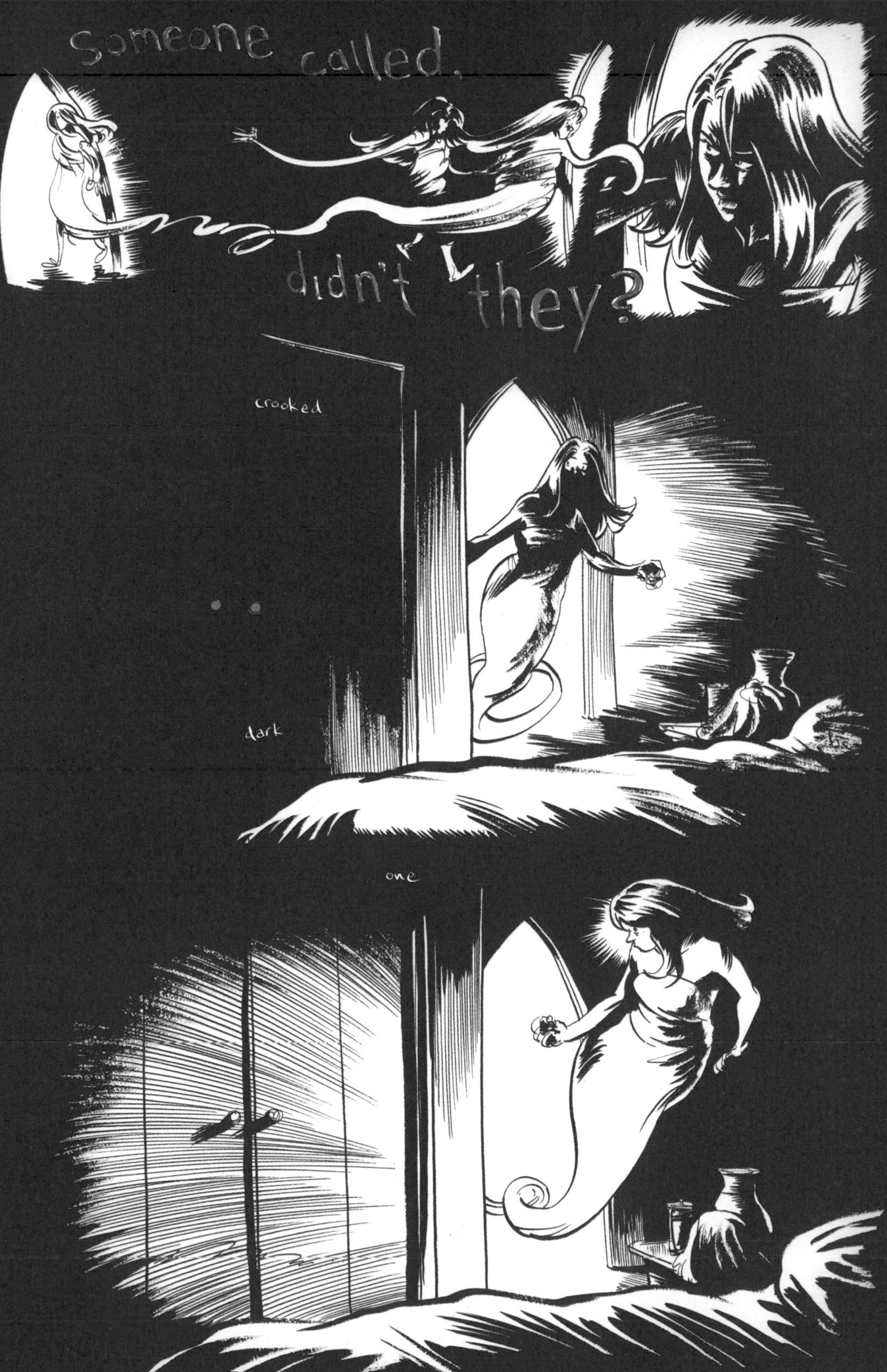
Someone called, didn't they?
crooked
. .
dark
one

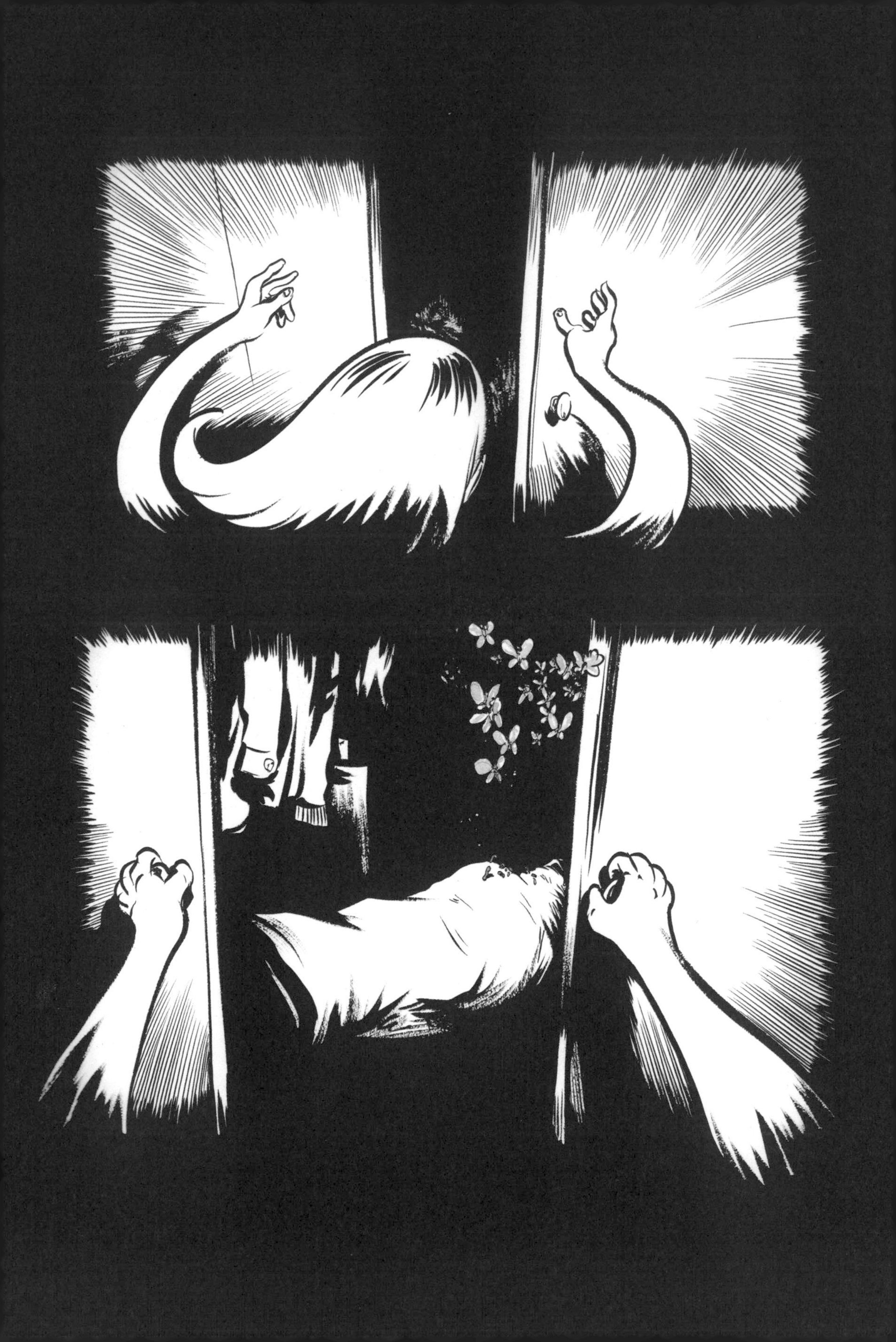

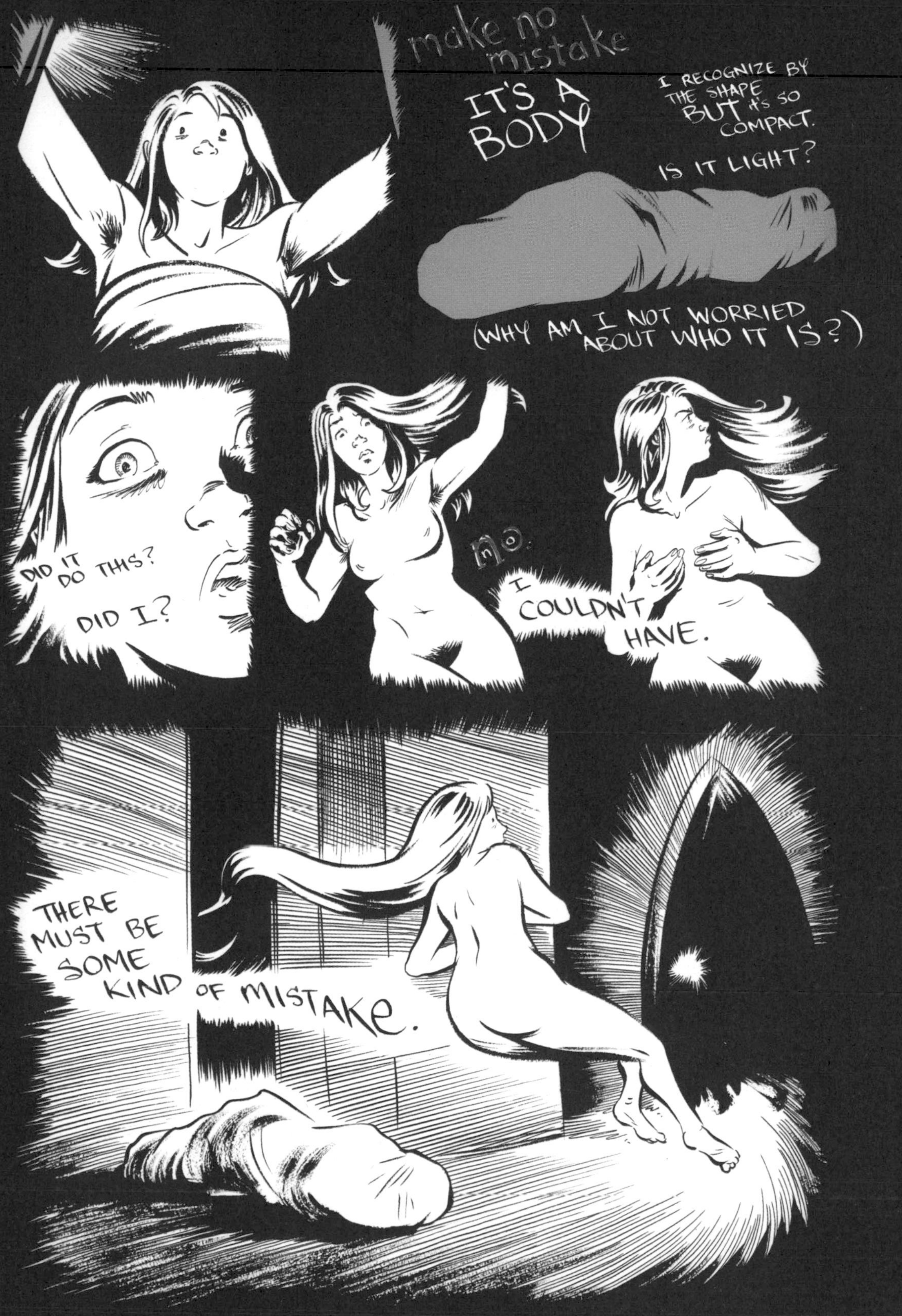
make no mistake
IT'S A BODY
I RECOGNIZE BY THE SHAPE BUT it's so COMPACT.
IS IT LIGHT?
(WHY AM I NOT WORRIED ABOUT WHO IT IS?)
DID IT DO THIS?
DID I?
no.
I COULDN'T HAVE.
THERE MUST BE SOME KIND OF MISTAKE.

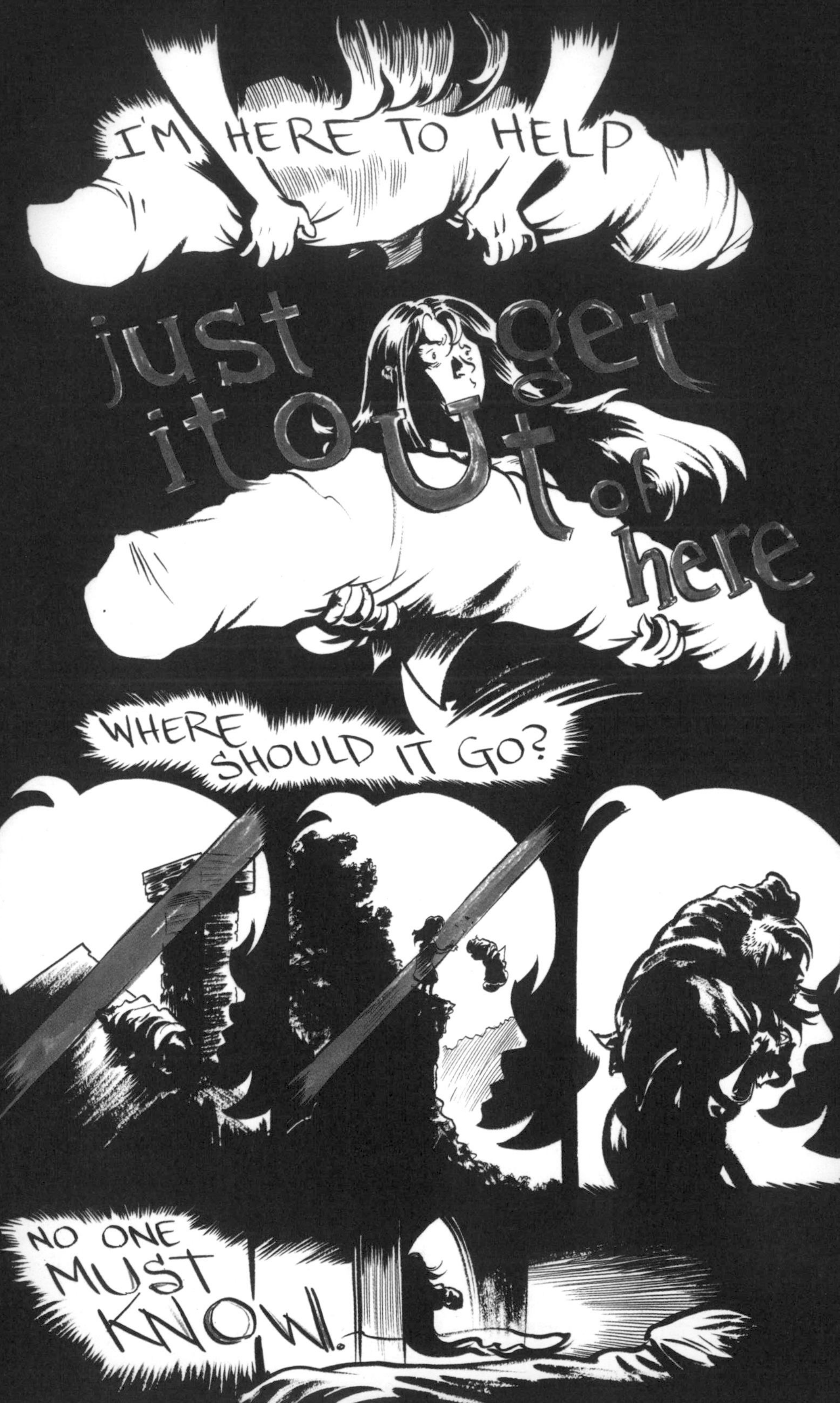
I'M HERE TO HELP
just get it out of here
WHERE SHOULD IT GO?
NO ONE MUST KNOW.

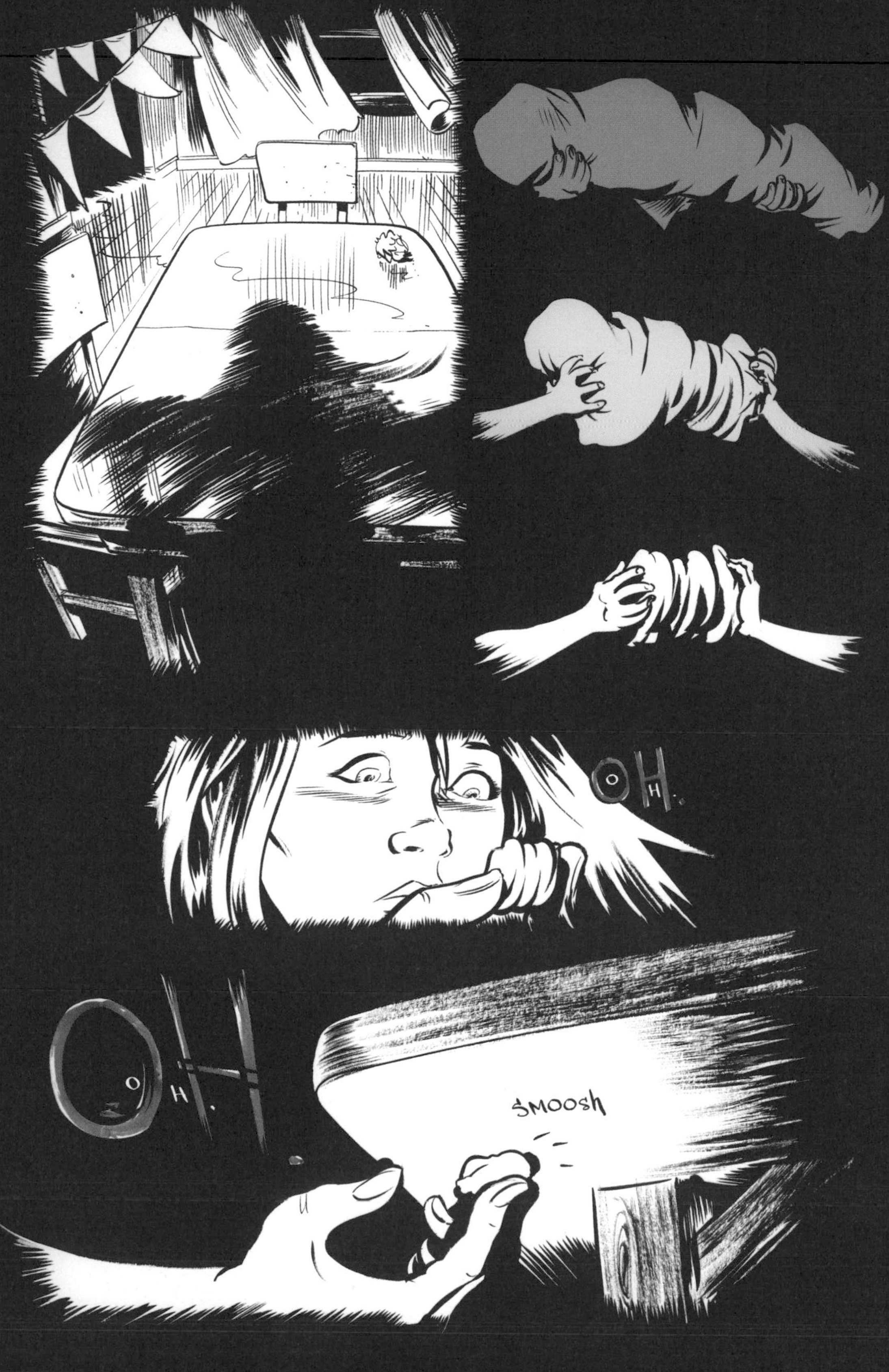
OH.
OH.
OH.
SMOOSH

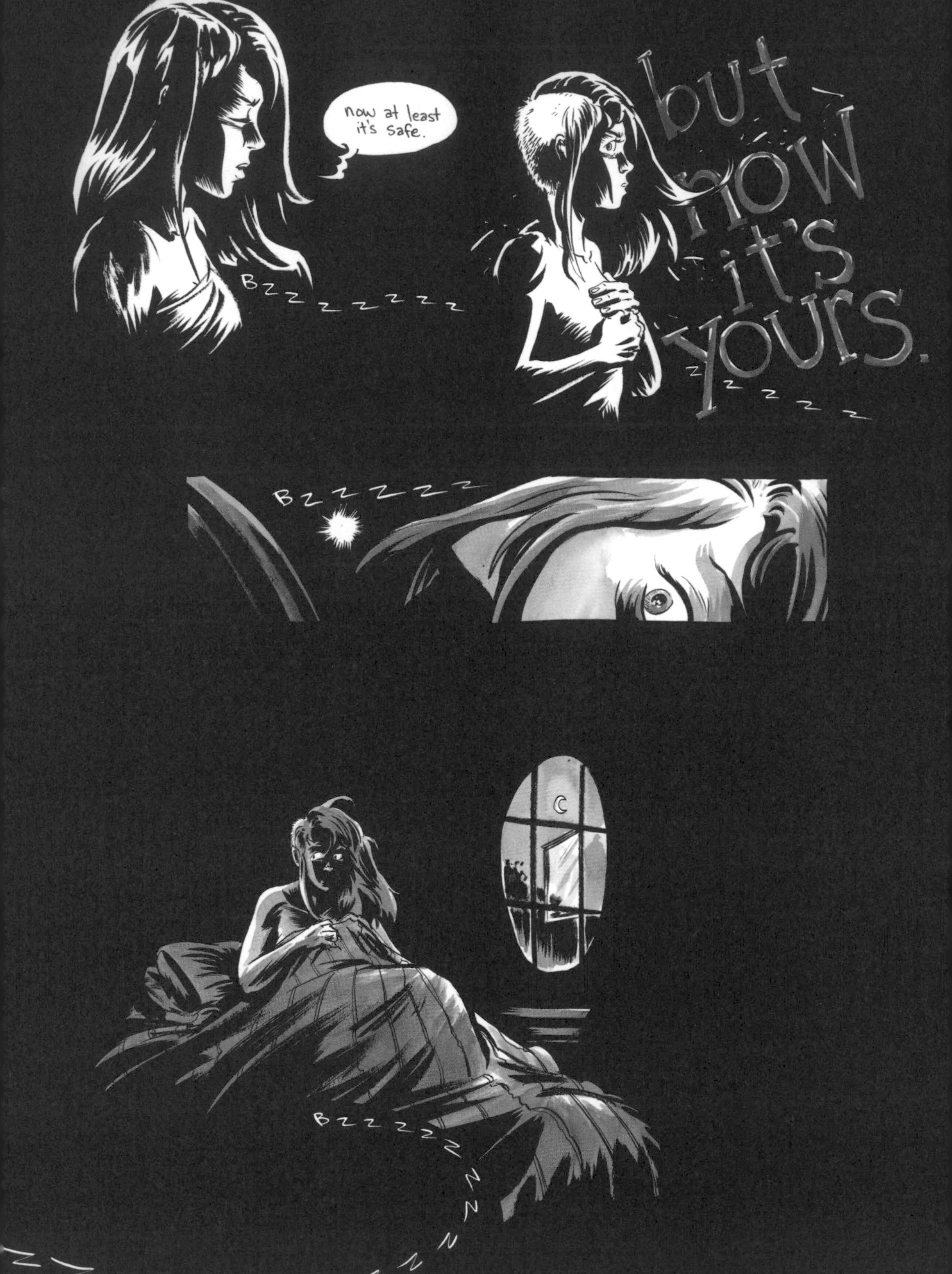
now at least it's safe.
Bzzzzzzzzz
but now it's yours.
zzzzz
Bzzzzzzz
Bzzzzzzzzzz
zzzzzzzzzzzzzz

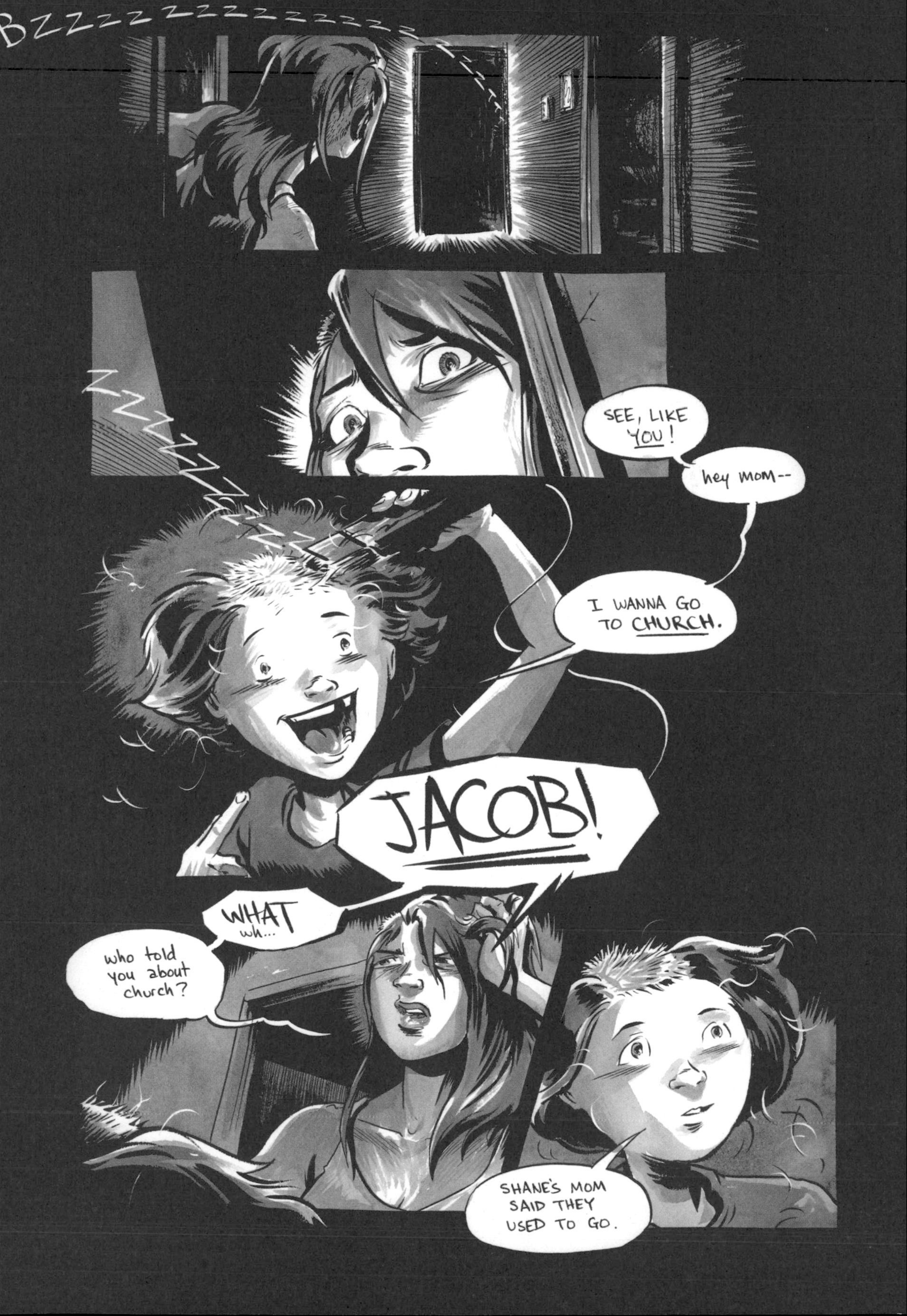
BZZZZZZZZZZZZZZZ
ZZZZZZZZZZZ
SEE, LIKE YOU!
hey mom--
I WANNA GO TO CHURCH.
JACOB!
WHAT wh...
who told you about church?
SHANE'S MOM SAID THEY USED TO GO.

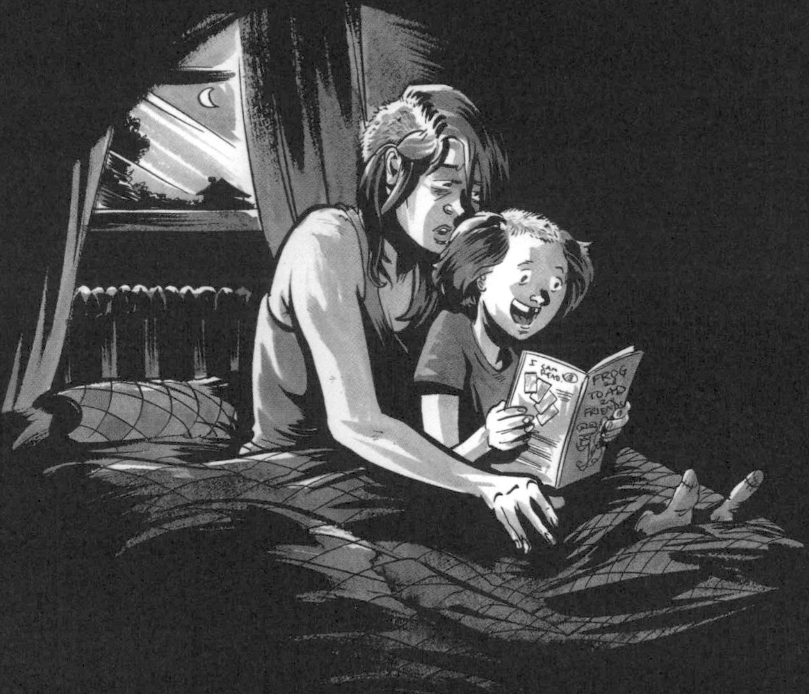
I CAN READ
FROG
TOAD

STRANGE THINGS HAPPEN
ALL THE TIME.

1971

IT'S NOT A QUESTION OF BELIEVING

AS COLD HANDS BRUSH YOUR NECK
ON A STAIRCASE,

AS A PALE LIGHT FORCES YOU OFF-ROAD.

WE CALLED IT THE SECRET EATER.

OR SOMEBODY DID.

AT FIRST, JUST SLUMBER-PARTY TALK,
STORIES WAVED AWAY BY SQUARES:

there's a spirit underneath,

a lonesome glow to
drag the young away---

inching closer with
each secret held.

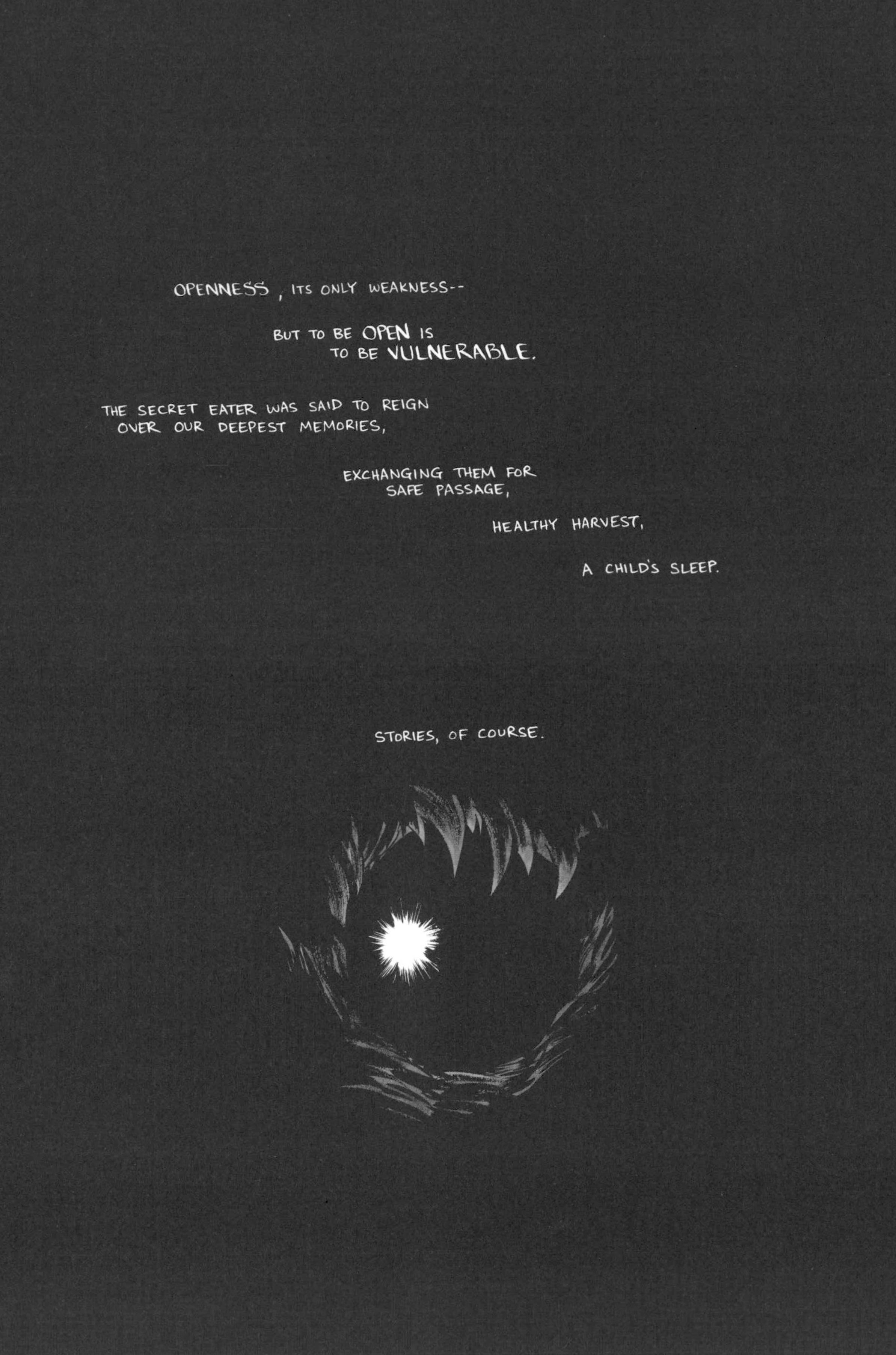
OPENNESS, ITS ONLY WEAKNESS--
BUT TO BE OPEN IS TO BE VULNERABLE.
THE SECRET EATER WAS SAID TO REIGN OVER OUR DEEPEST MEMORIES,
EXCHANGING THEM FOR SAFE PASSAGE,
HEALTHY HARVEST,
A CHILD'S SLEEP.
STORIES, OF COURSE.

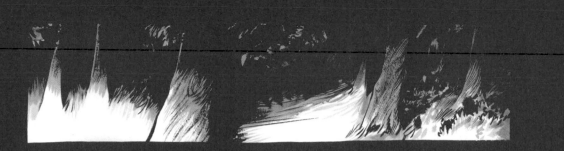

WHITNEY TOOK US FIRST.

WE SAW NOTHING
ON THE DRIVE,

SETTING SAIL INTO DARKNESS.

UNDER COVER,

CHANGING TUNE
AND TOUCH.

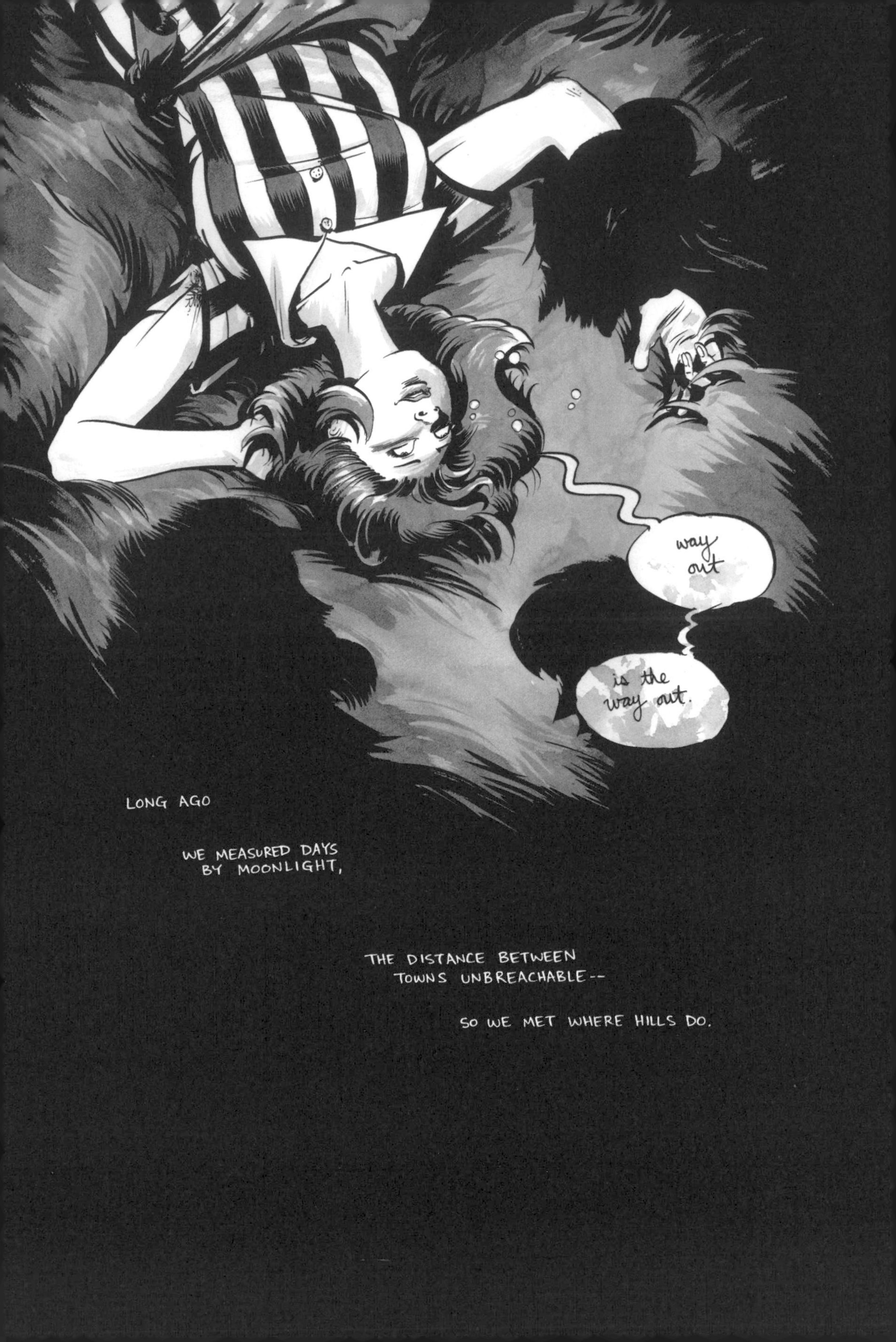
way out
is the way out.
LONG AGO
WE MEASURED DAYS BY MOONLIGHT,
THE DISTANCE BETWEEN TOWNS UNBREACHABLE--
SO WE MET WHERE HILLS DO.

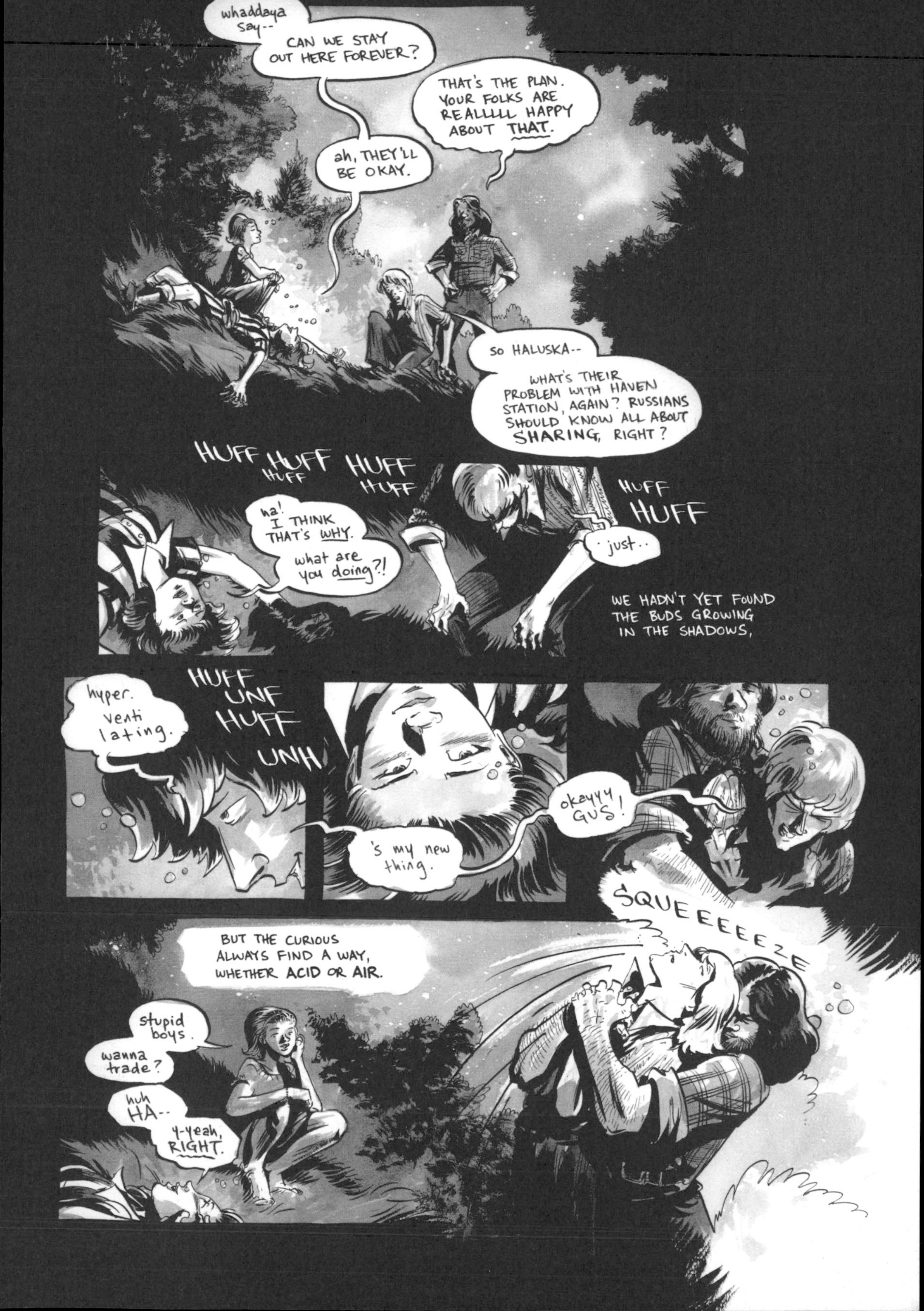
whaddaya say--
CAN WE STAY OUT HERE FOREVER?
THAT'S THE PLAN. YOUR FOLKS ARE REALLLLL HAPPY ABOUT THAT.
ah, THEY'LL BE OKAY.
SO HALUSKA--
WHAT'S THEIR PROBLEM WITH HAVEN STATION, AGAIN? RUSSIANS SHOULD KNOW ALL ABOUT SHARING, RIGHT?
HUFF HUFF HUFF HUFF HUFF HUFF
ha! I THINK THAT'S WHY.
what are you doing?!
HUFF HUFF
..just..
WE HADN'T YET FOUND THE BUDS GROWING IN THE SHADOWS,
hyper. venti lating.
HUFF UNF HUFF UNH
's my new thing.
okayyy GUS!
SQUEEEEEEZE
BUT THE CURIOUS ALWAYS FIND A WAY, WHETHER ACID OR AIR.
stupid boys.
wanna trade?
huh HA--
y-yeah, RIGHT.

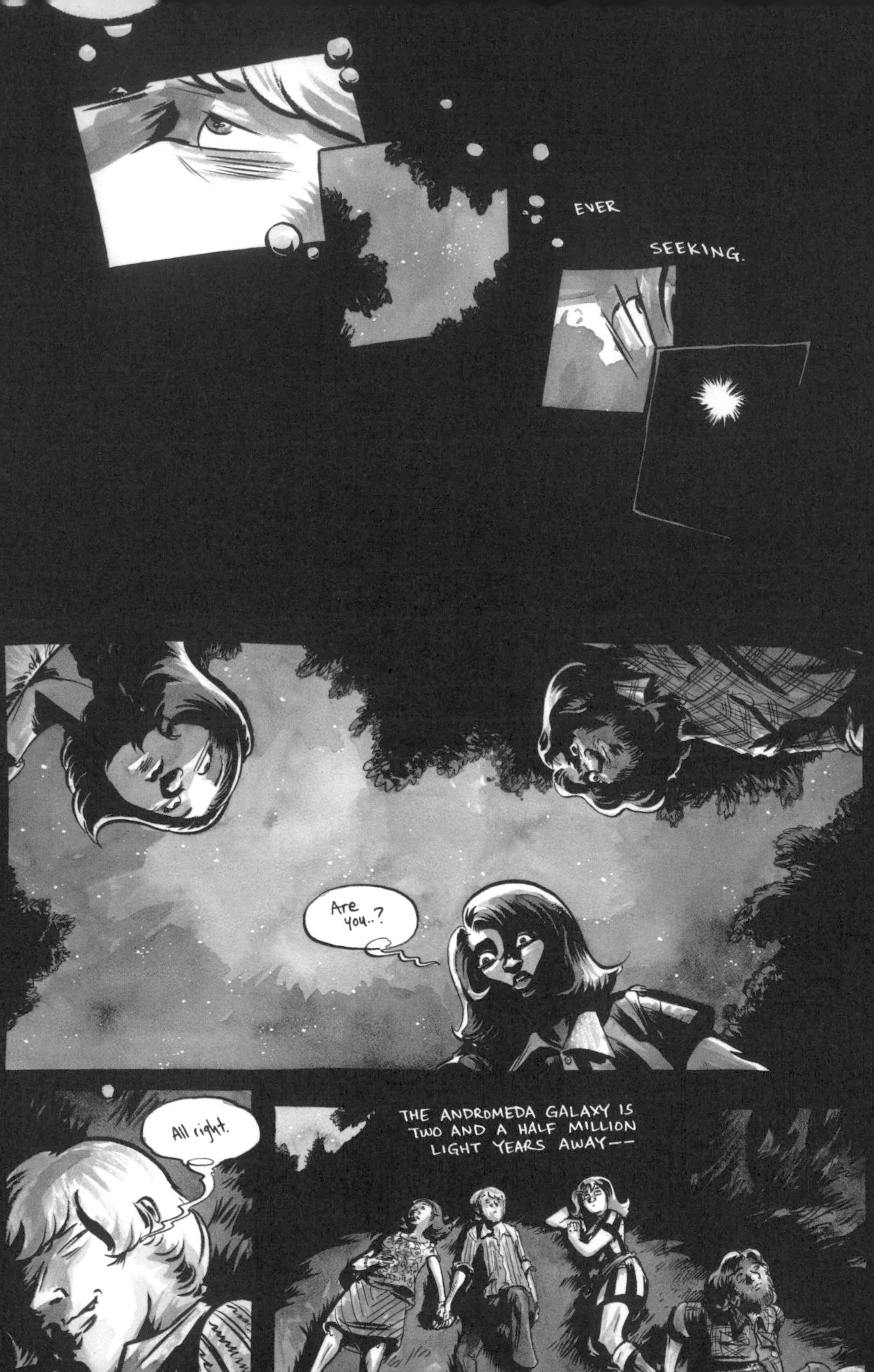
EVER
SEEKING.
Are you..?
All right.
THE ANDROMEDA GALAXY IS TWO AND A HALF MILLION LIGHT YEARS AWAY--

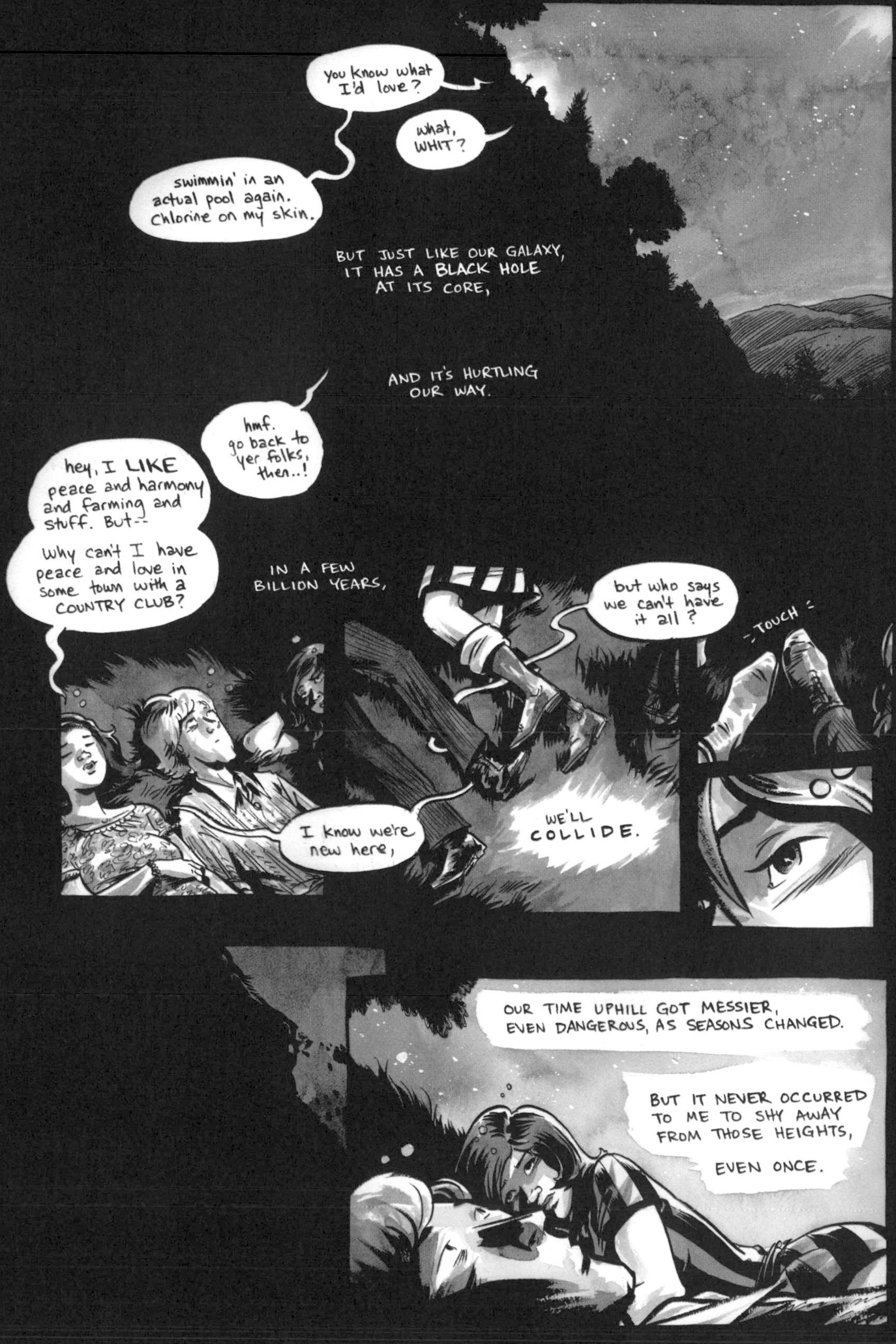
you know what I'd love?
what, WHIT?
swimmin' in an actual pool again. Chlorine on my skin.
BUT JUST LIKE OUR GALAXY, IT HAS A BLACK HOLE AT ITS CORE,
AND IT'S HURTLING OUR WAY.
hmf. go back to yer folks, then..!
hey, I LIKE peace and harmony and farming and stuff. But--
Why can't I have peace and love in some town with a COUNTRY CLUB?
IN A FEW BILLION YEARS,
I know we're new here,
but who says we can't have it all?
WE'LL COLLIDE.
TOUCH
OUR TIME UPHILL GOT MESSIER, EVEN DANGEROUS, AS SEASONS CHANGED.
BUT IT NEVER OCCURRED TO ME TO SHY AWAY FROM THOSE HEIGHTS,
EVEN ONCE.

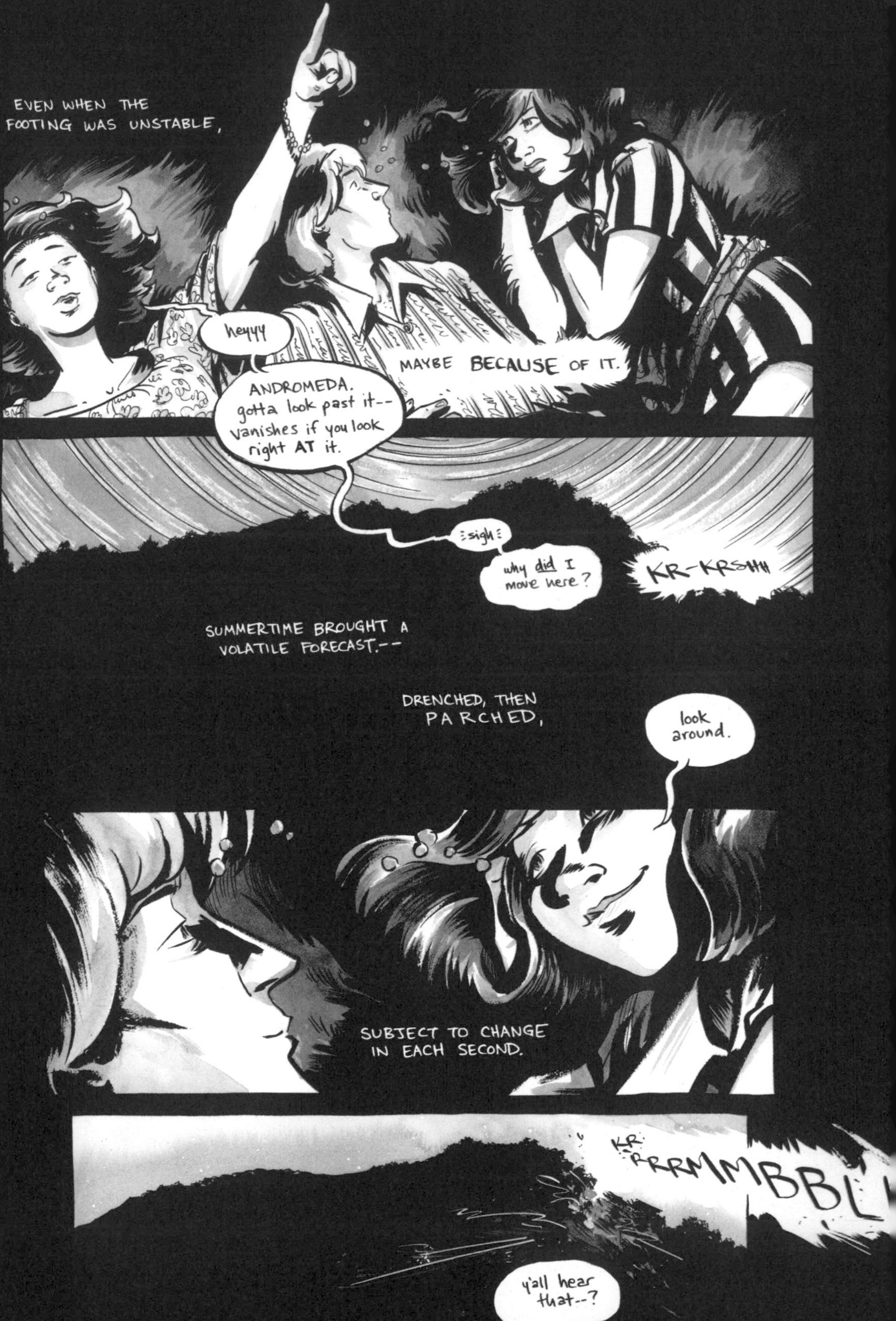
EVEN WHEN THE FOOTING WAS UNSTABLE,
heyyy
ANDROMEDA. gotta look past it-- vanishes if you look right AT it.
MAYBE BECAUSE OF IT.
sigh
why did I move here?
KR-KRSHH
SUMMERTIME BROUGHT A VOLATILE FORECAST.--
DRENCHED, THEN PARCHED,
look around.
SUBJECT TO CHANGE IN EACH SECOND.
KR-RRRMMBBL
y'all hear that--?

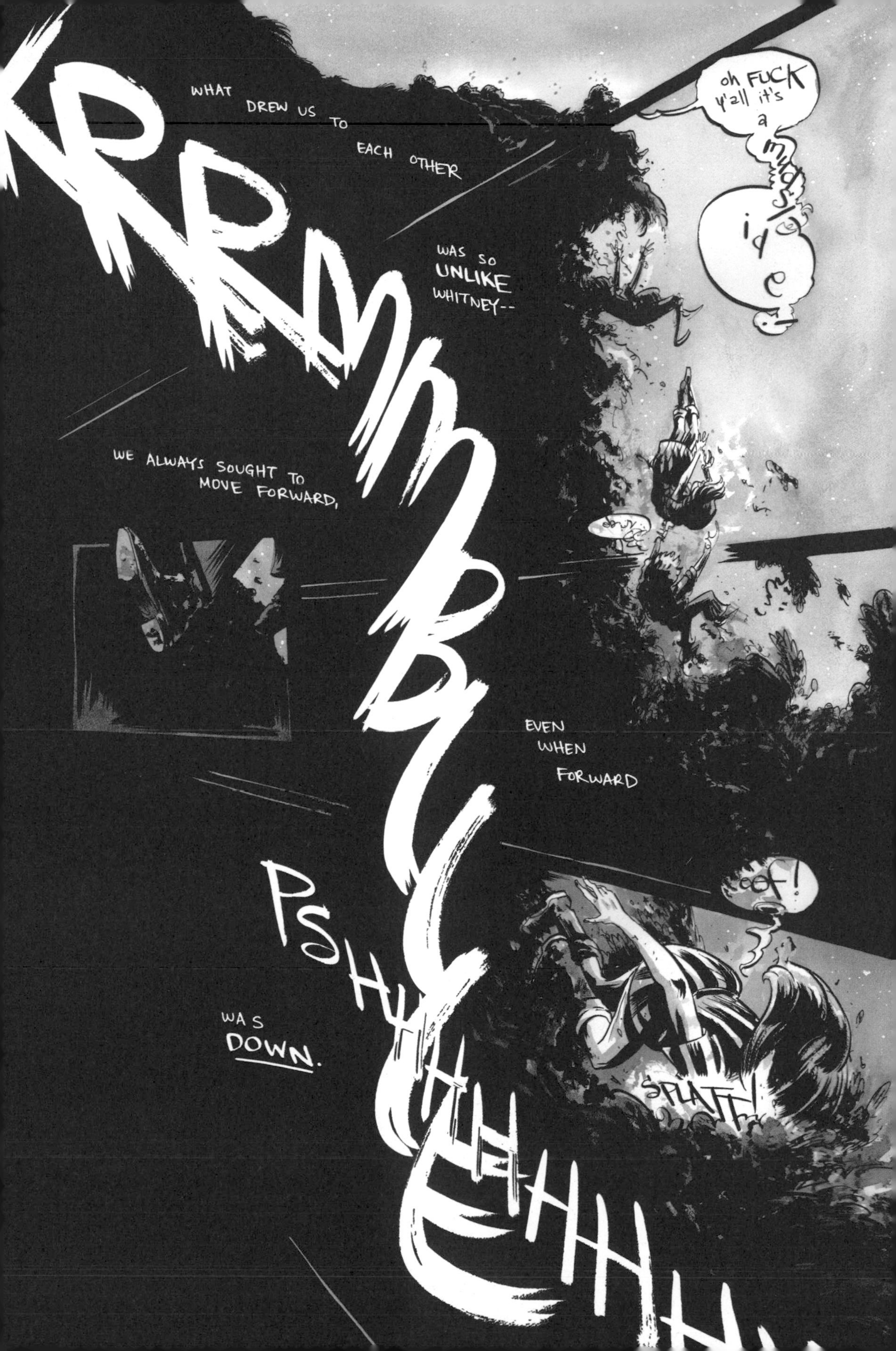
WHAT DREW US TO EACH OTHER
oh FUCK y'all it's a mudslide!
WAS SO UNLIKE WHITNEY--
WE ALWAYS SOUGHT TO MOVE FORWARD,
EVEN WHEN FORWARD
oof!
WAS DOWN.
PSHHHHHHH
SPLATT!

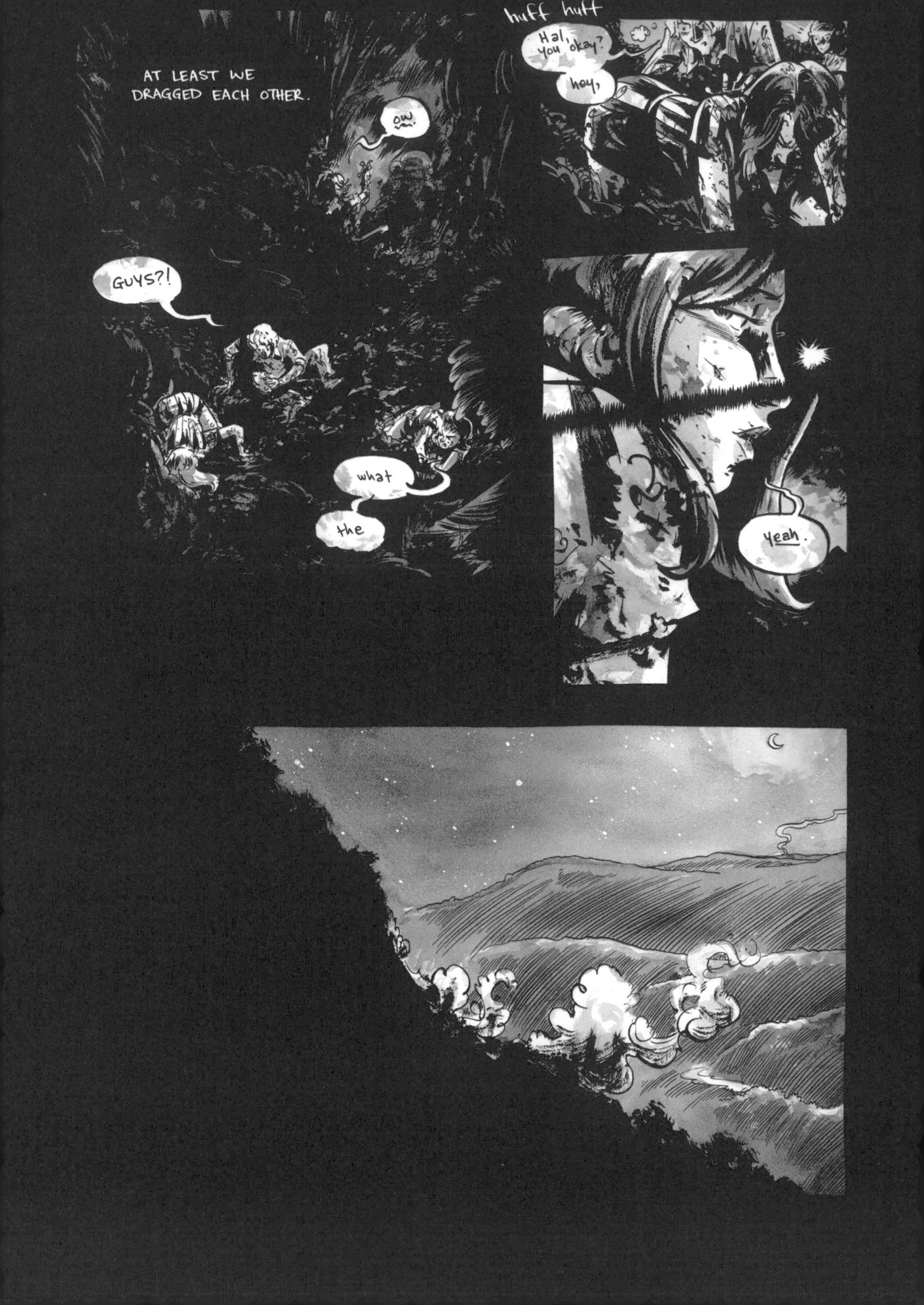
AT LEAST WE DRAGGED EACH OTHER.
ow
huff huff
Hal, you okay?
hey,
GUYS?!
what
the
yeah.

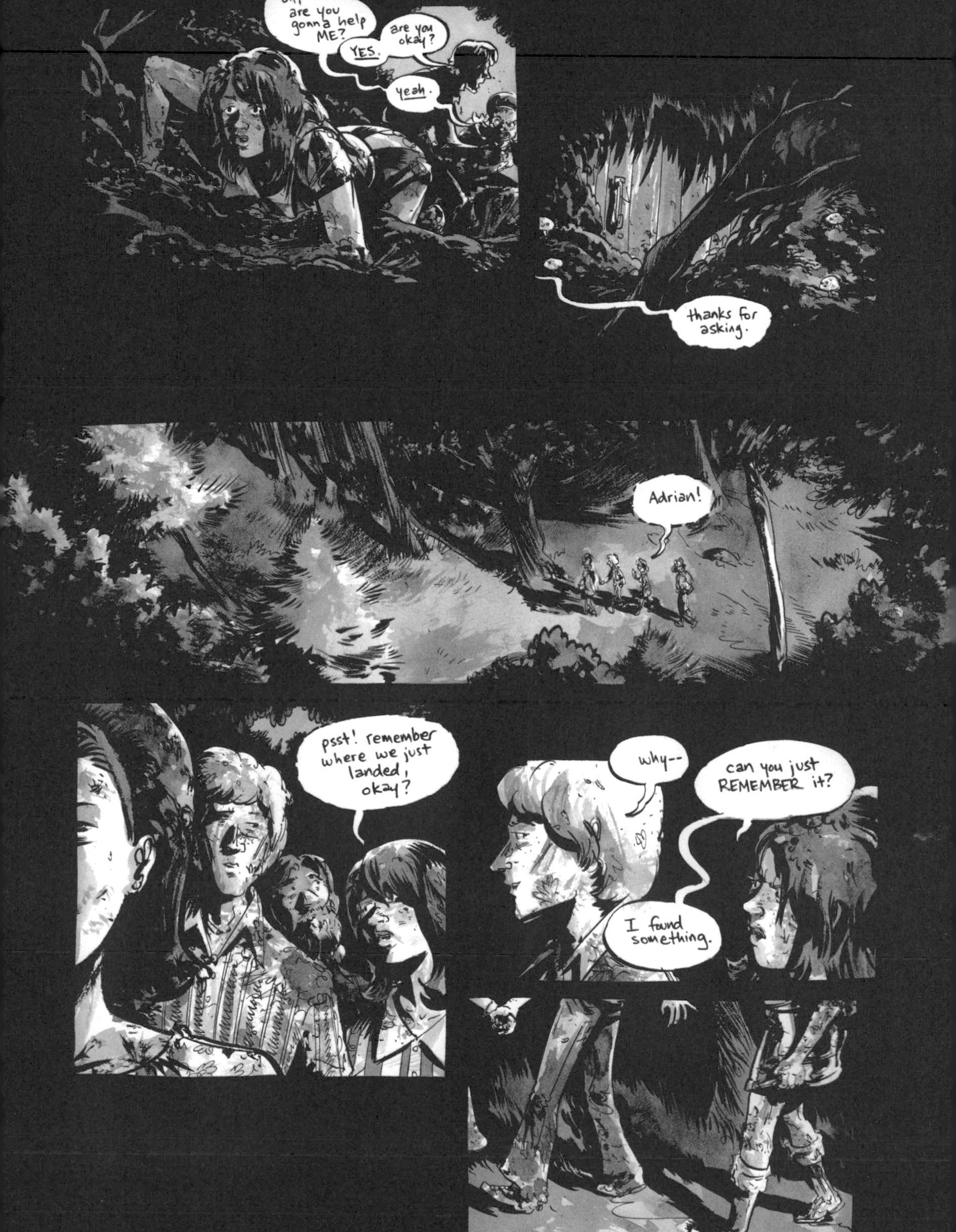
uh, are you gonna help ME?
are you okay?
YES.
yeah.
thanks for asking.
Adrian!
psst! remember where we just landed, okay?
why--
can you just REMEMBER it?
I found something.

ITS ORIGIN DEFIES,

MOTHERLESS.

AS SECRECY GROWS

SO DOES ITS
APPETITE.

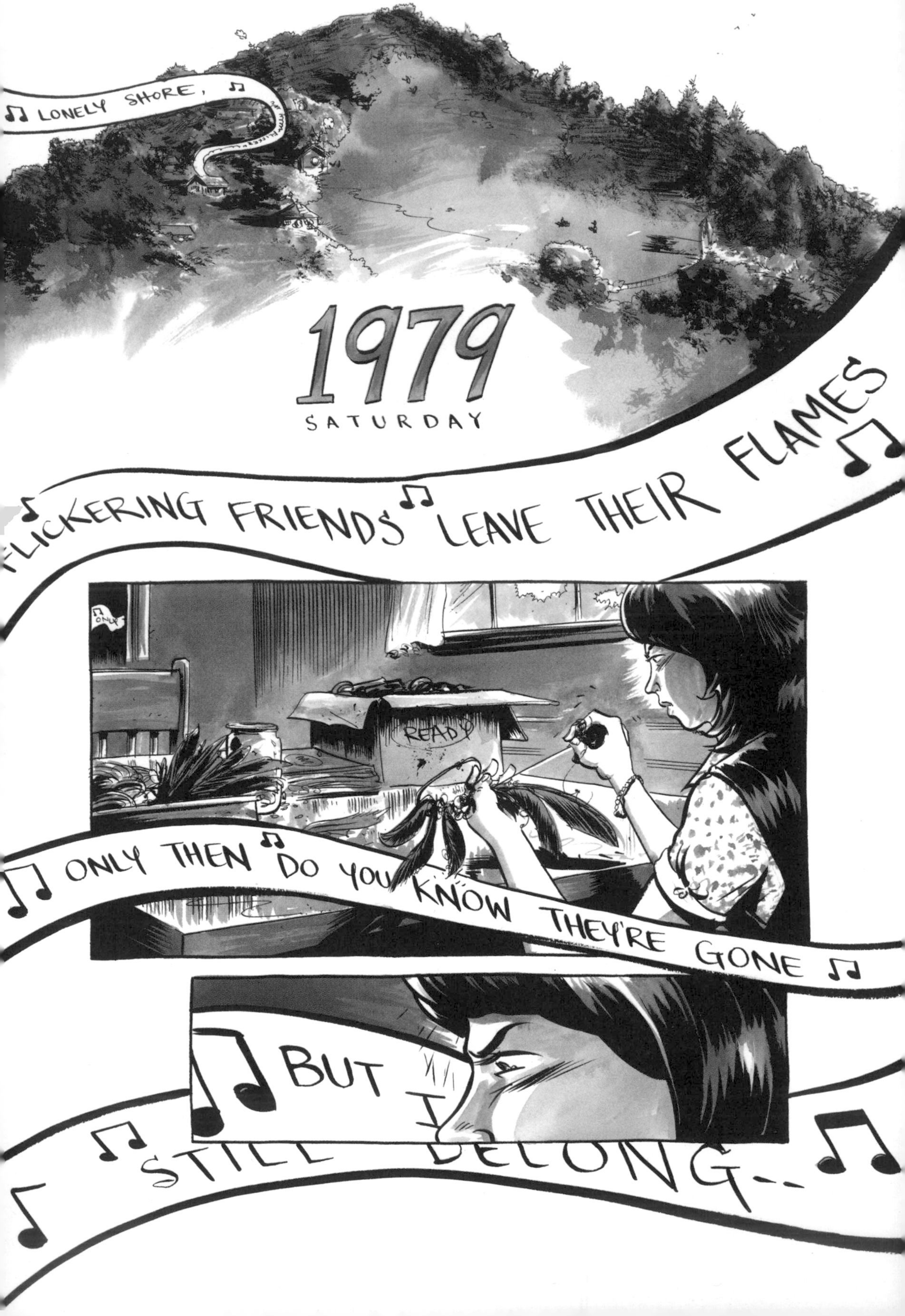
♫ LONELY SHORE, ♫
1979
SATURDAY
♫ FLICKERING FRIENDS ♫ LEAVE THEIR FLAMES ♫
READY
♫ ONLY THEN ♫ DO YOU KNOW THEY'RE GONE ♫
♫ BUT I
♫ ♫ STILL BELONG-- ♫

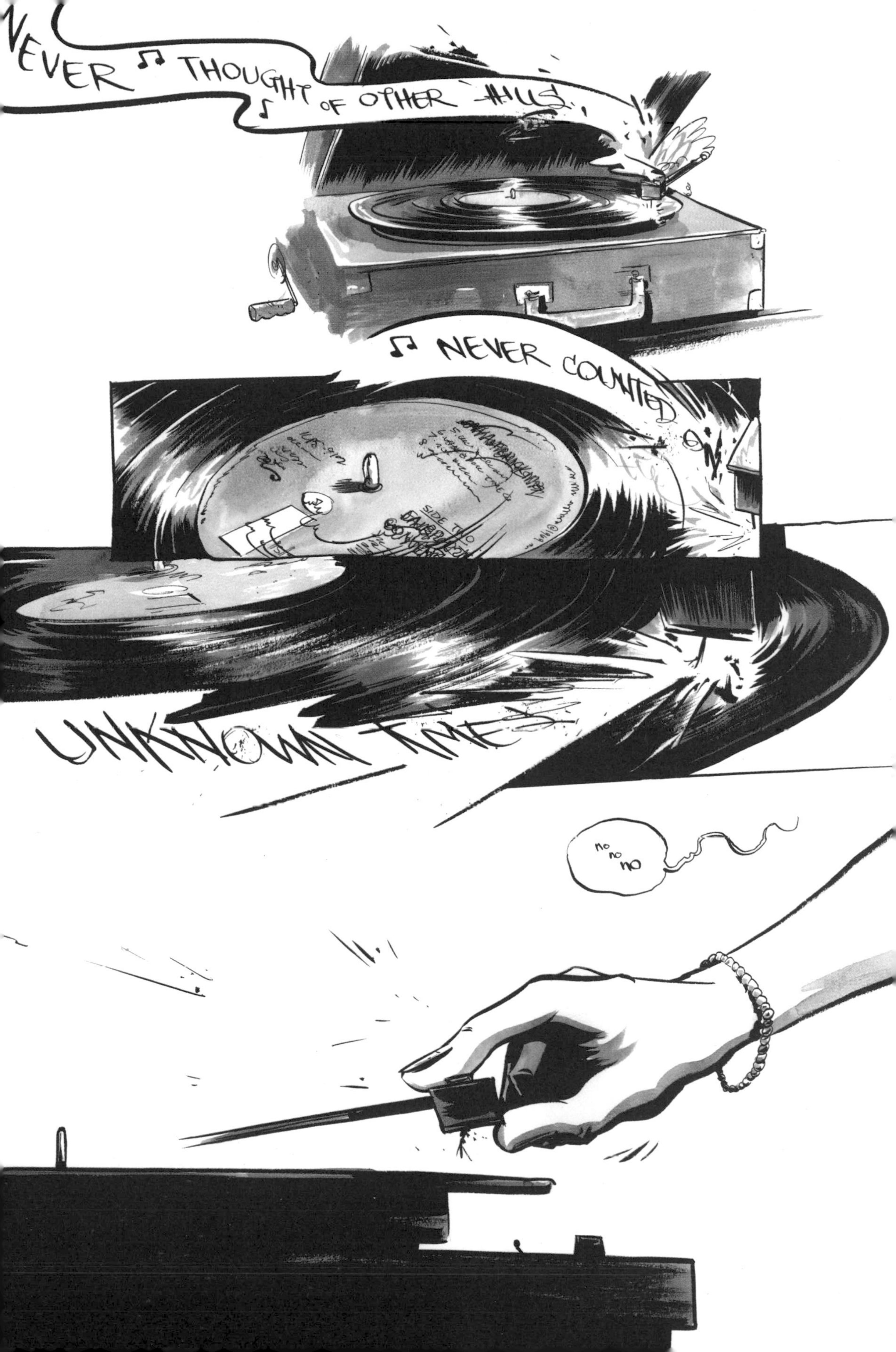
NEVER ♫ THOUGHT OF OTHER HILLS ♫
♫ NEVER COUNTED ON
UNKNOWN TIMES
no no no

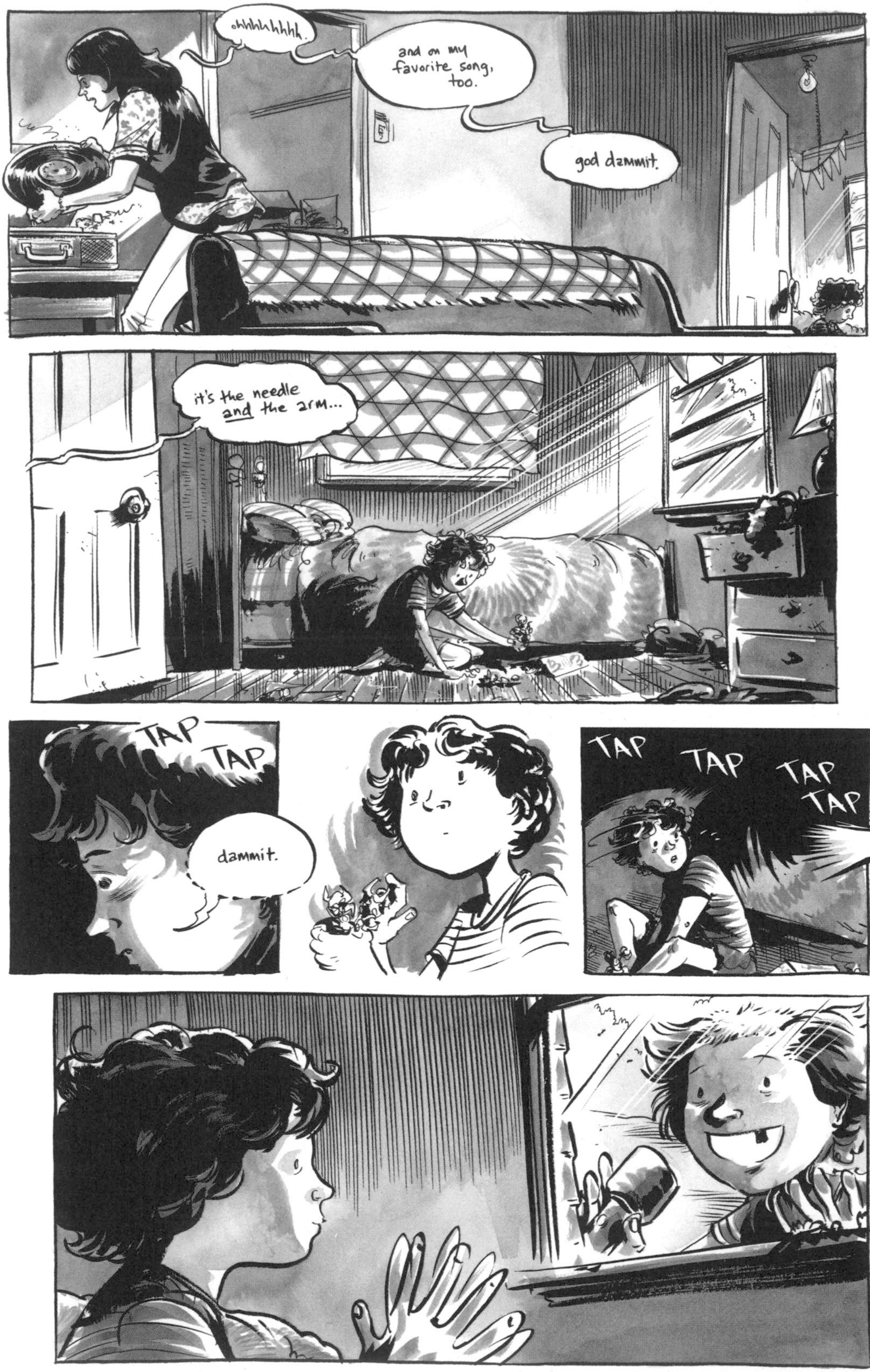
ohhhhhhh.
and on my favorite song, too.
god dammit.
it's the needle and the arm...
TAP TAP
dammit.
TAP TAP TAP TAP

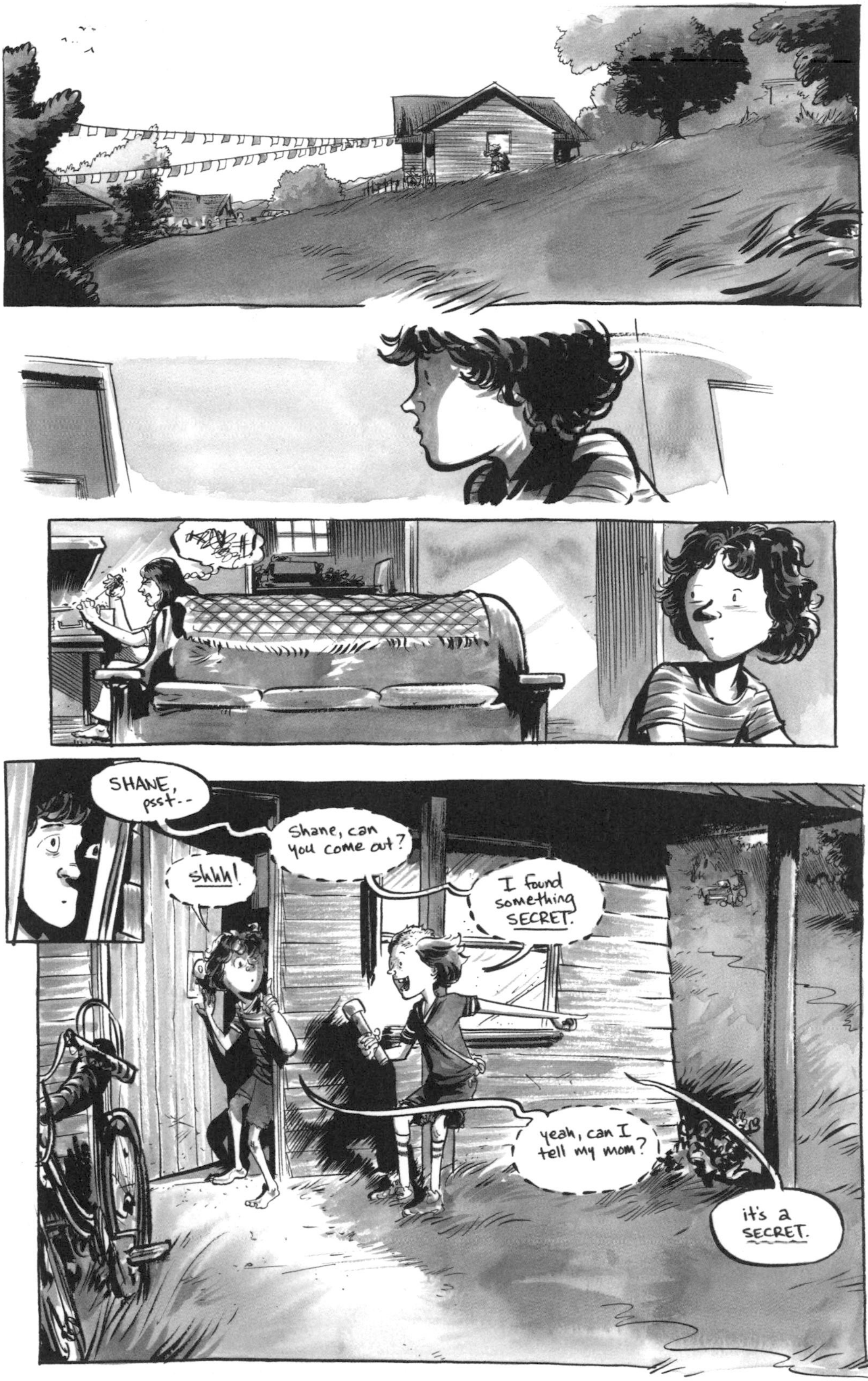
SHANE, psst-.
Shane, can you come out?
shhh!
I found something SECRET.
yeah, can I tell my mom?
it's a SECRET.

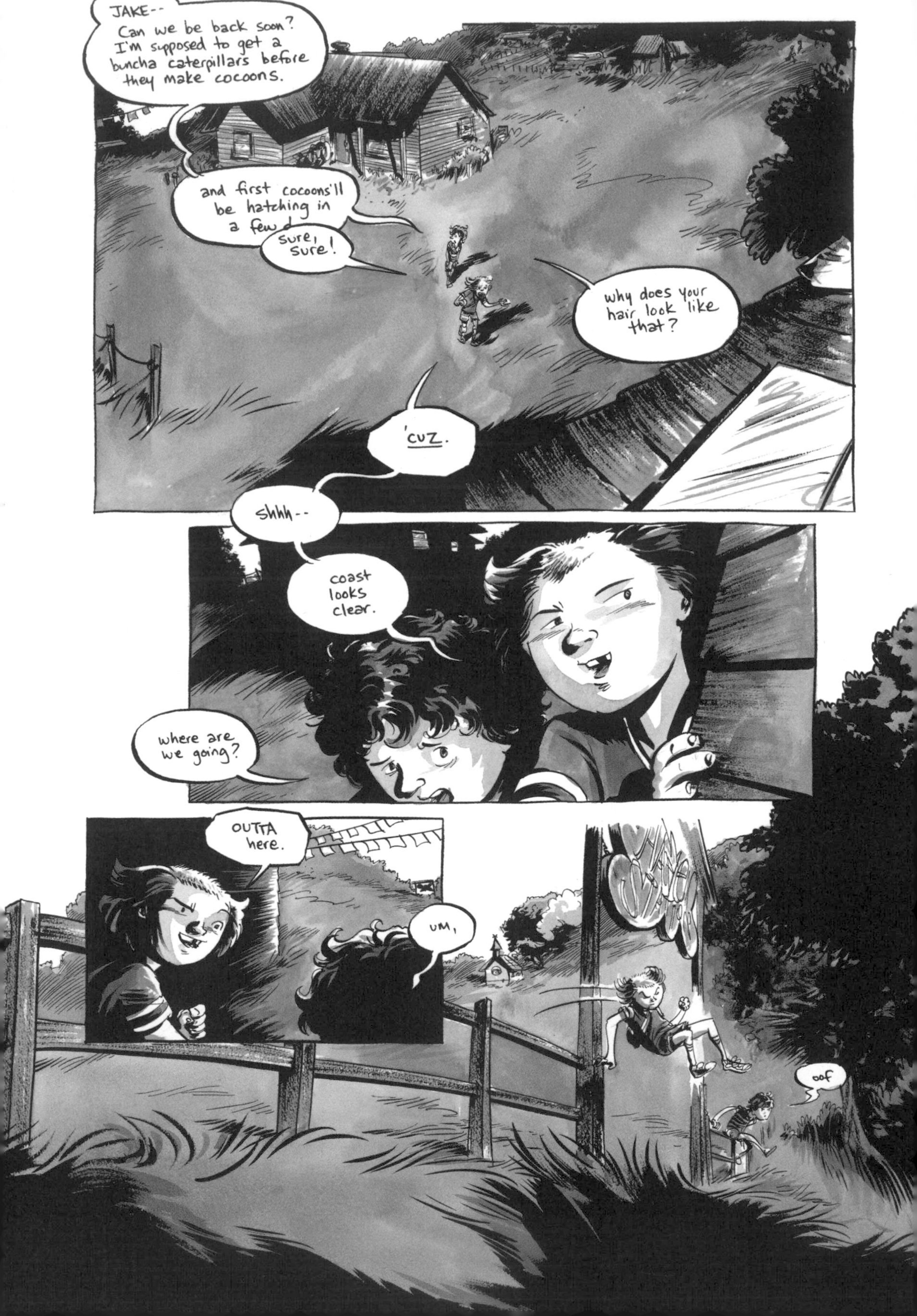
JAKE--
Can we be back soon? I'm supposed to get a buncha caterpillars before they make cocoons.
and first cocoons'll be hatching in a few d
sure, sure!
why does your hair look like that?
'CUZ.
shhh--
coast looks clear.
where are we going?
OUTTA here.
um,
oof

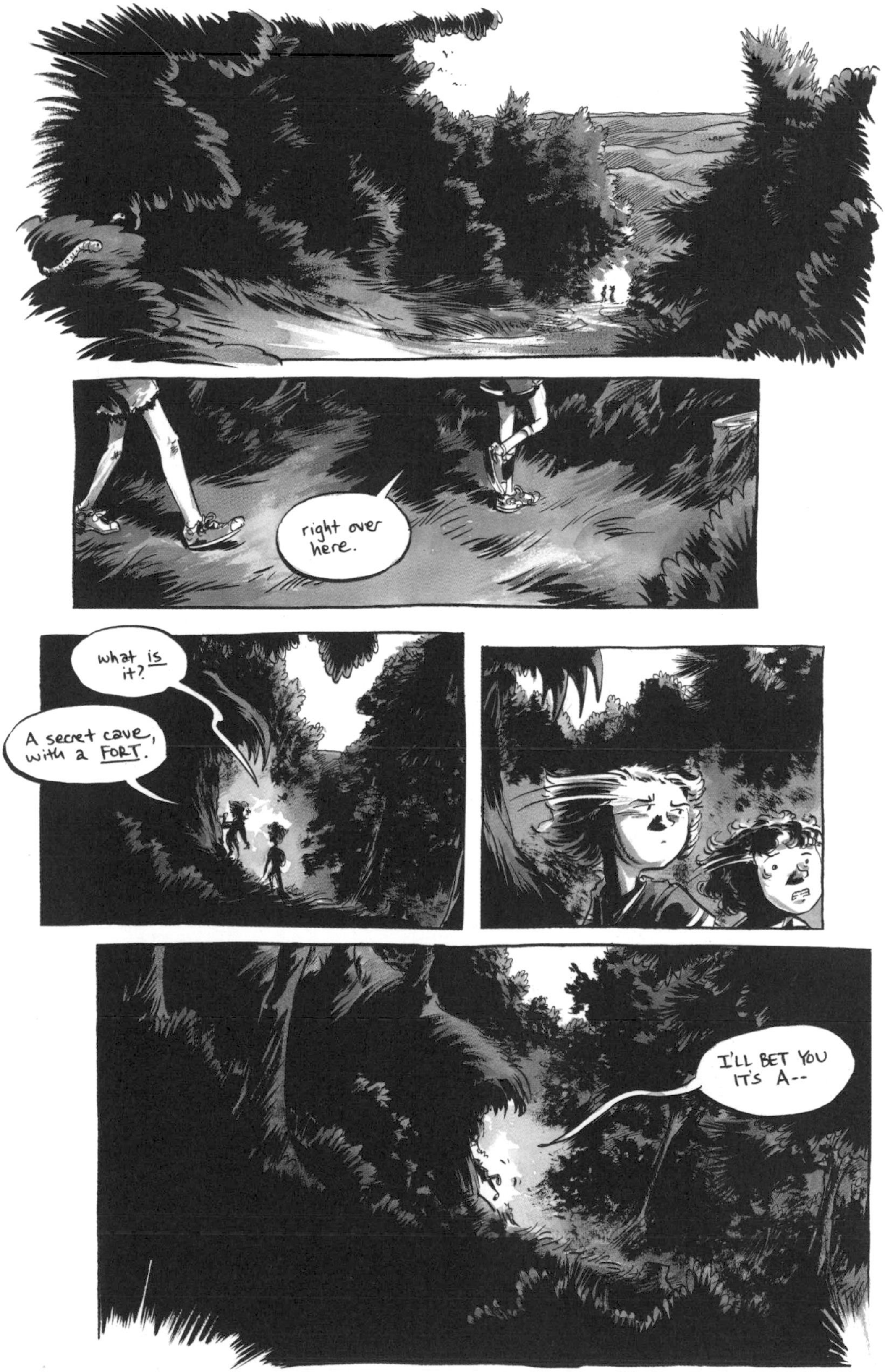
right over here.
what IS it?
A secret cave, with a FORT.
I'LL BET YOU IT'S A--

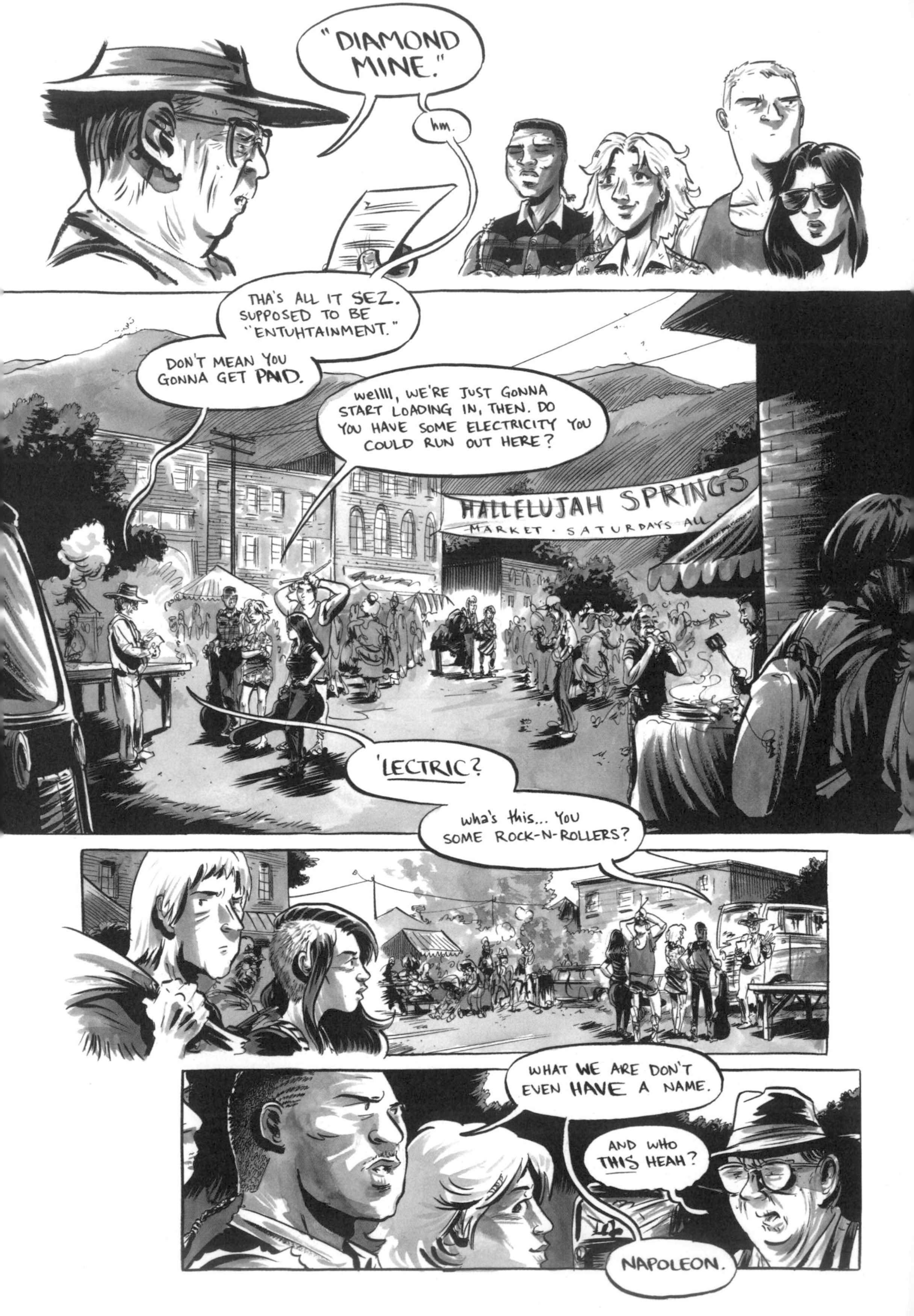
"DIAMOND MINE."
hm.
THA'S ALL IT SEZ. SUPPOSED TO BE "ENTUHTAINMENT."
DON'T MEAN YOU GONNA GET PAID.
welllll, WE'RE JUST GONNA START LOADING IN, THEN. DO YOU HAVE SOME ELECTRICITY YOU COULD RUN OUT HERE?
HALLELUJAH SPRINGS
MARKET · SATURDAYS ALL
'LECTRIC?
wha's this... YOU SOME ROCK-N-ROLLERS?
WHAT WE ARE DON'T EVEN HAVE A NAME.
AND WHO THIS HEAH?
NAPOLEON.

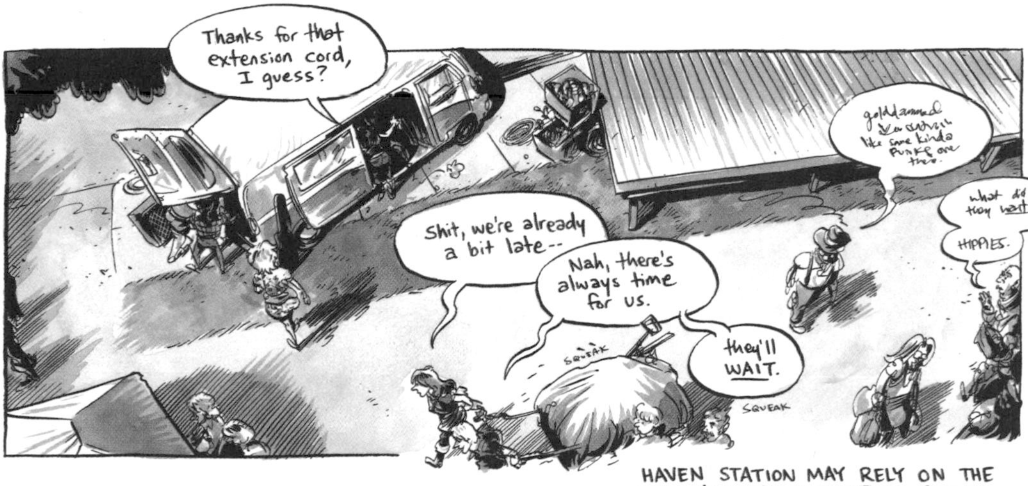
Thanks for that extension cord, I guess?
Shit, we're already a bit late--
Nah, there's always time for us.
they'll WAIT.
what did they want?
HIPPIES.
SQUEAK
SQUEAK

HAVEN STATION MAY RELY ON THE FARMER'S MARKET TRADE TO GET BY,

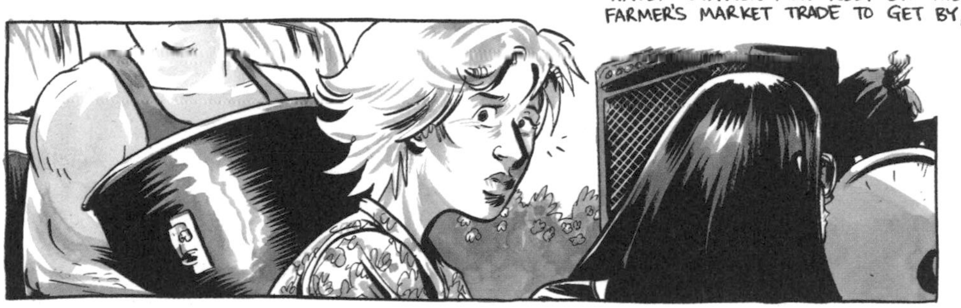

BUT IF I MAY BE SO BOLD--

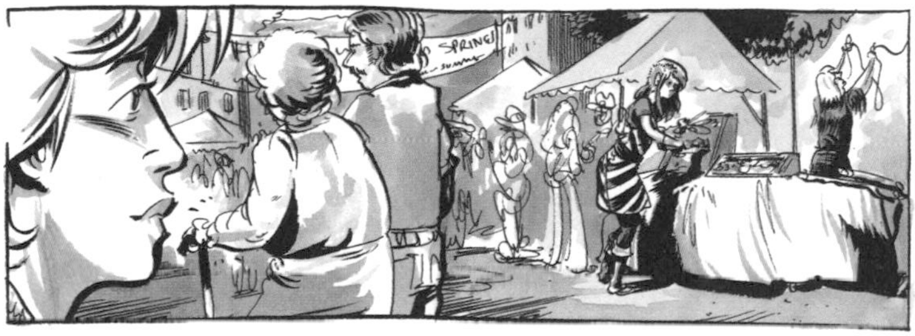

FOLKS DOWN HERE RELY JUST AS MUCH ON WHAT WE BRING DOWN.

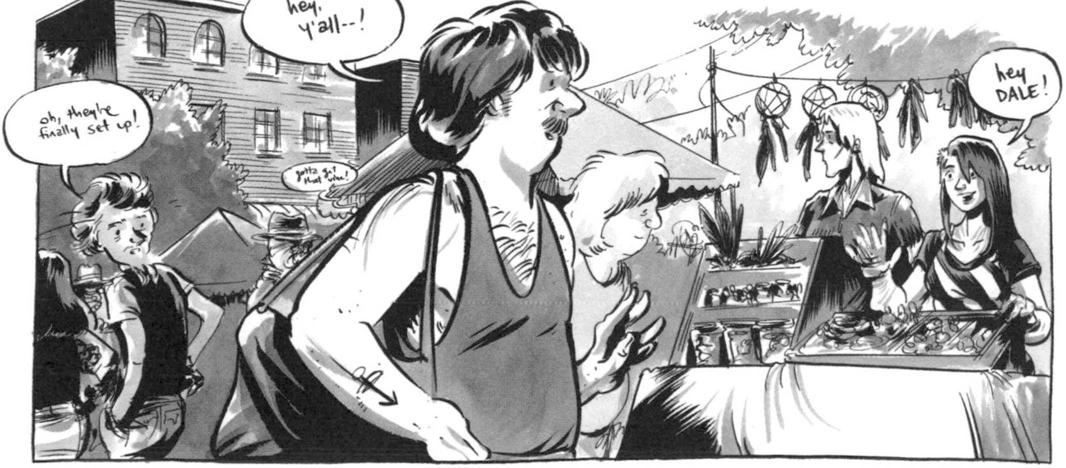
hey, y'all--!
oh, they're finally set up!
gotta get that vibe!
hey DALE!

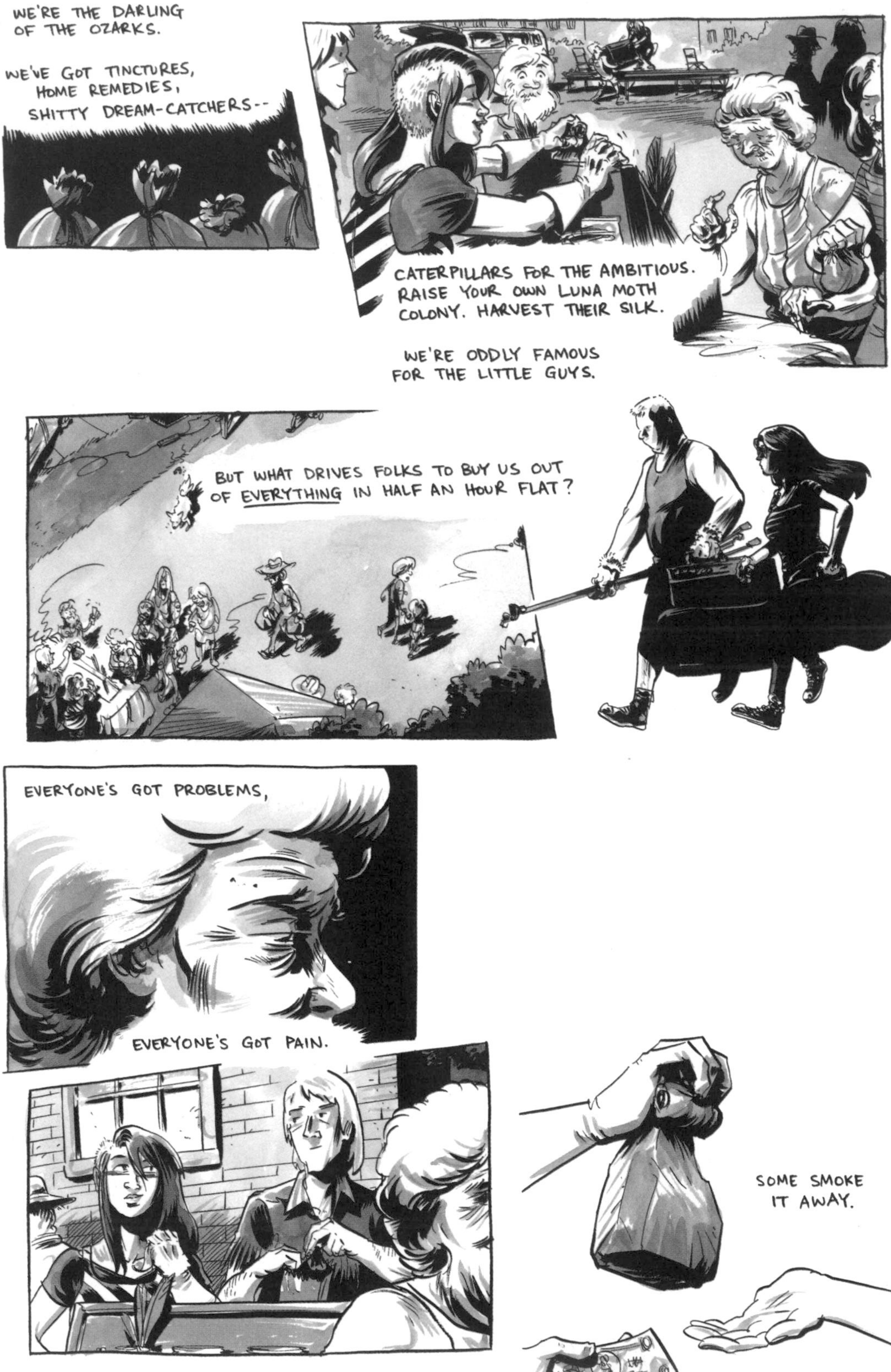
WE'RE THE DARLING OF THE OZARKS.
WE'VE GOT TINCTURES, HOME REMEDIES, SHITTY DREAM-CATCHERS--
CATERPILLARS FOR THE AMBITIOUS. RAISE YOUR OWN LUNA MOTH COLONY. HARVEST THEIR SILK.
WE'RE ODDLY FAMOUS FOR THE LITTLE GUYS.
BUT WHAT DRIVES FOLKS TO BUY US OUT OF EVERYTHING IN HALF AN HOUR FLAT?
EVERYONE'S GOT PROBLEMS,
EVERYONE'S GOT PAIN.
SOME SMOKE IT AWAY.

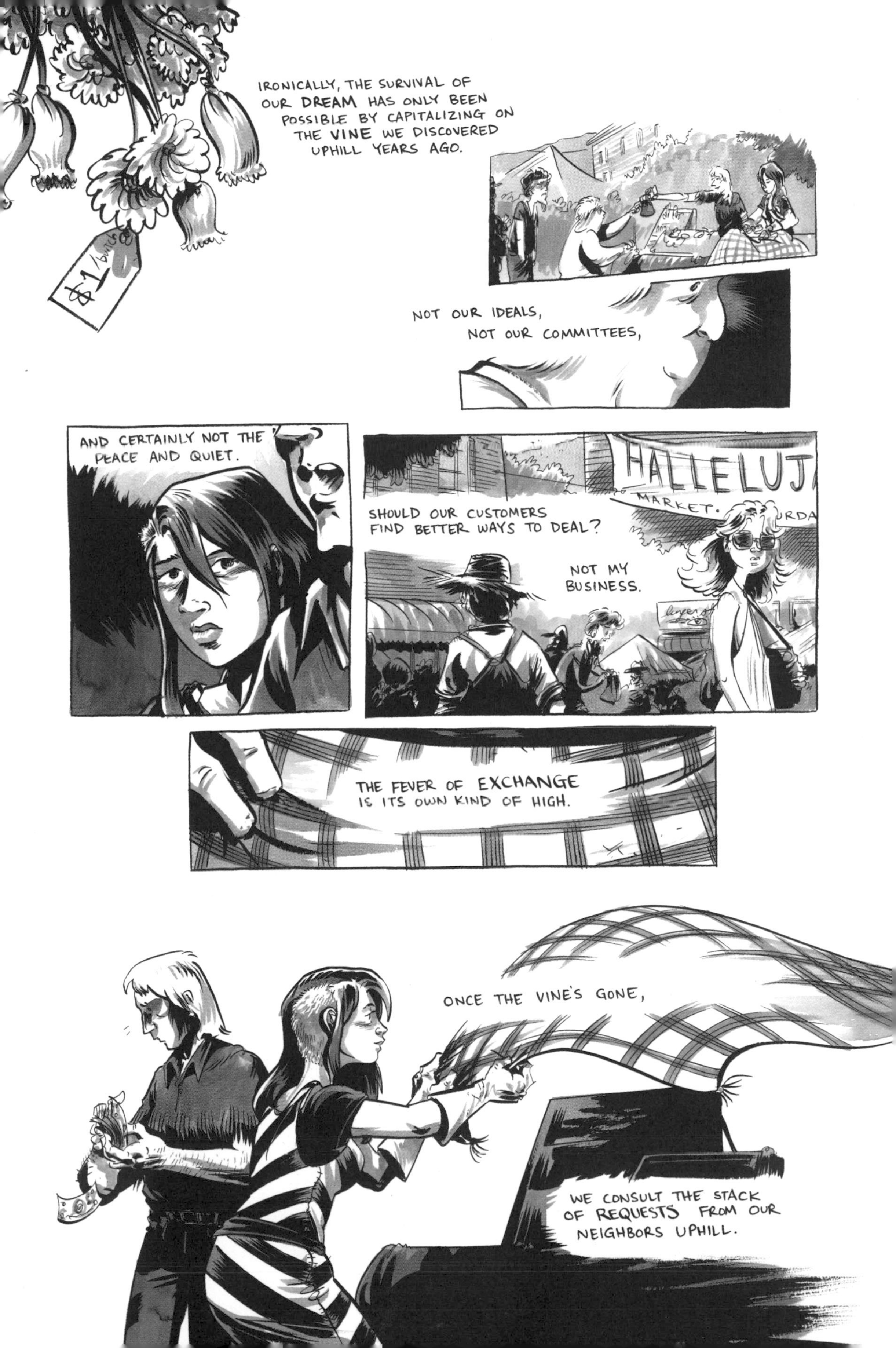
IRONICALLY, THE SURVIVAL OF OUR DREAM HAS ONLY BEEN POSSIBLE BY CAPITALIZING ON THE VINE WE DISCOVERED UPHILL YEARS AGO.
$1/bunch
NOT OUR IDEALS,
NOT OUR COMMITTEES,
AND CERTAINLY NOT THE PEACE AND QUIET.
MARKET
SHOULD OUR CUSTOMERS FIND BETTER WAYS TO DEAL?
NOT MY BUSINESS.
THE FEVER OF EXCHANGE IS ITS OWN KIND OF HIGH.
ONCE THE VINE'S GONE,
WE CONSULT THE STACK OF REQUESTS FROM OUR NEIGHBORS UPHILL.

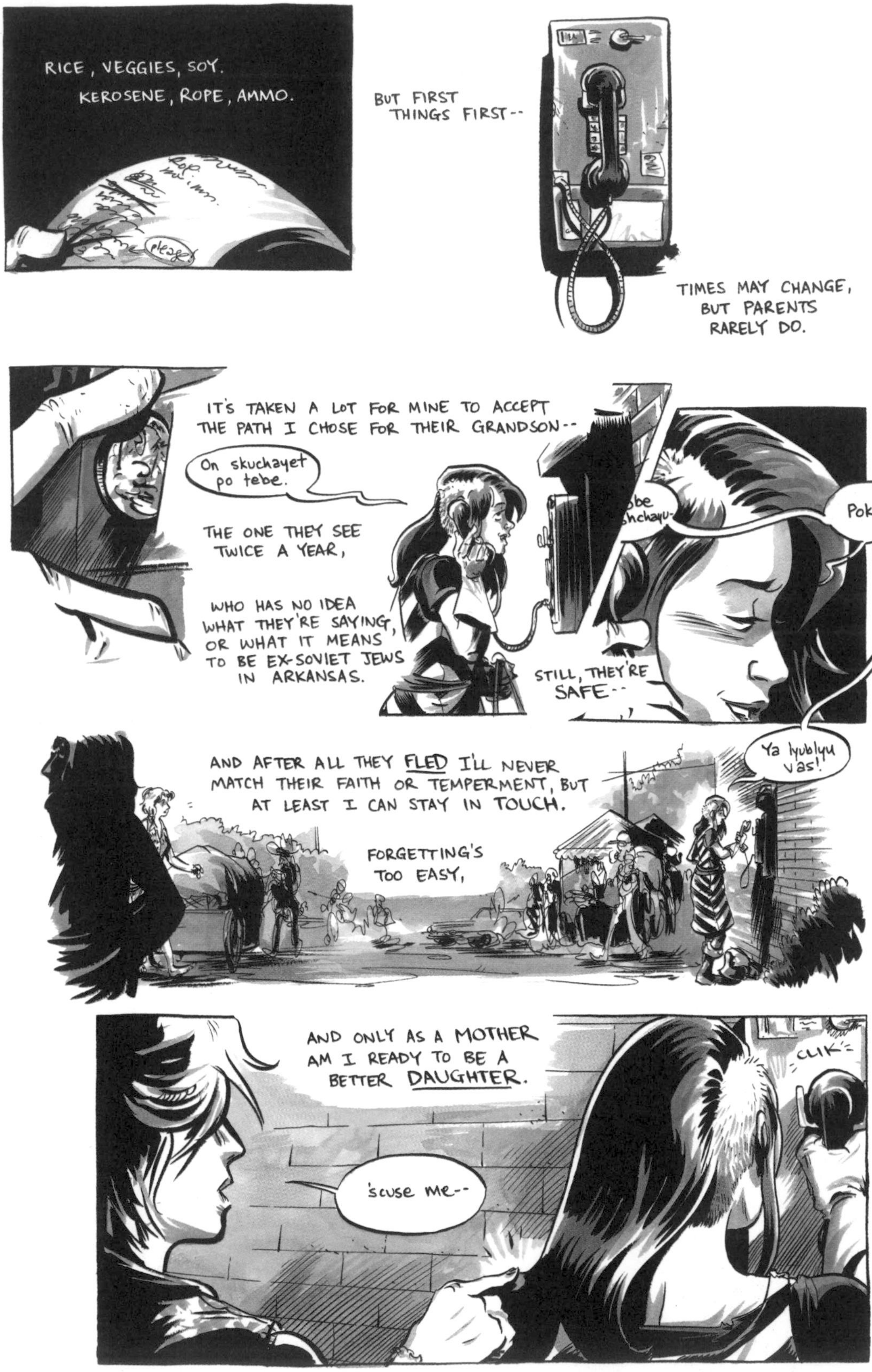

RICE, VEGGIES, SOY.
KEROSENE, ROPE, AMMO.
BUT FIRST THINGS FIRST--
TIMES MAY CHANGE, BUT PARENTS RARELY DO.
IT'S TAKEN A LOT FOR MINE TO ACCEPT THE PATH I CHOSE FOR THEIR GRANDSON--
On skuchayet po tebe.
THE ONE THEY SEE TWICE A YEAR,
WHO HAS NO IDEA WHAT THEY'RE SAYING, OR WHAT IT MEANS TO BE EX-SOVIET JEWS IN ARKANSAS.
Poka--
STILL, THEY'RE SAFE--
AND AFTER ALL THEY FLED I'LL NEVER MATCH THEIR FAITH OR TEMPERMENT, BUT AT LEAST I CAN STAY IN TOUCH.
Ya lyublyu vas!
FORGETTING'S TOO EASY,
AND ONLY AS A MOTHER AM I READY TO BE A BETTER DAUGHTER.
CLIK
'scuse me--

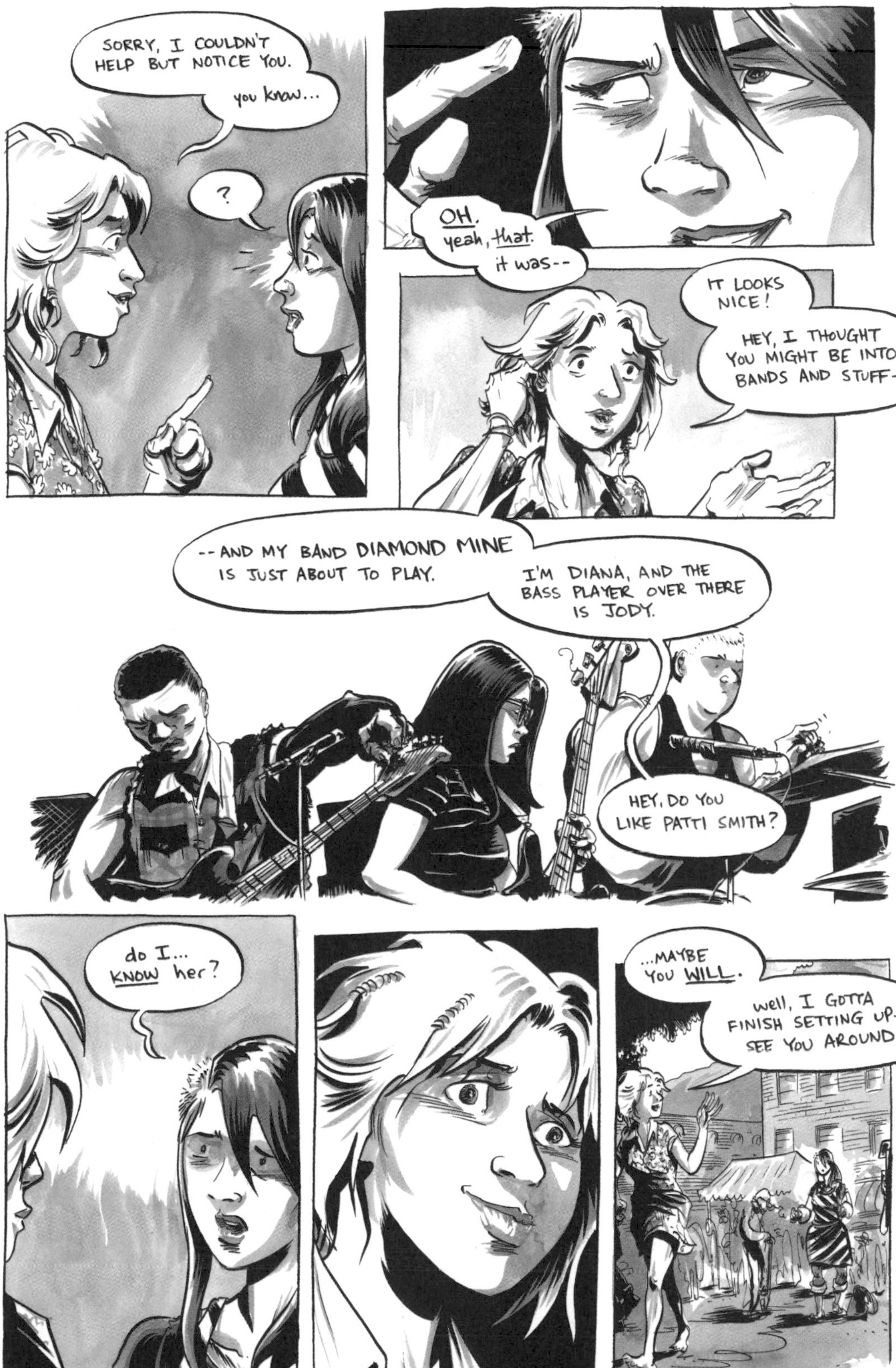
SORRY, I COULDN'T HELP BUT NOTICE YOU.
you know...
?
OH. yeah, that. it was--
IT LOOKS NICE!
HEY, I THOUGHT YOU MIGHT BE INTO BANDS AND STUFF--
--AND MY BAND DIAMOND MINE IS JUST ABOUT TO PLAY.
I'M DIANA, AND THE BASS PLAYER OVER THERE IS JODY.
HEY, DO YOU LIKE PATTI SMITH?
do I... KNOW her?
...MAYBE YOU WILL.
well, I GOTTA FINISH SETTING UP-- SEE YOU AROUND!

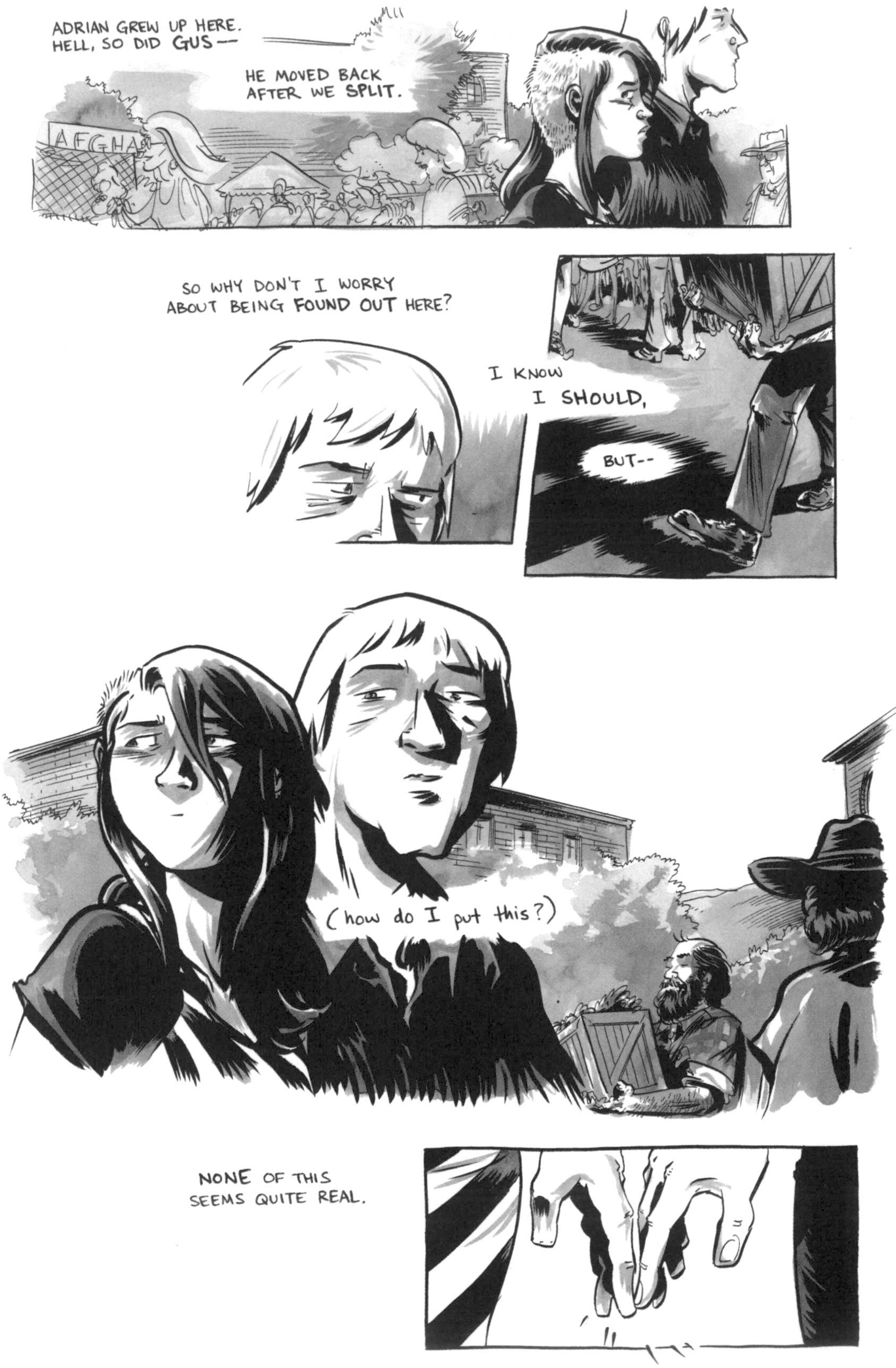
ADRIAN GREW UP HERE. HELL, SO DID GUS--
HE MOVED BACK AFTER WE SPLIT.
AFGHA
SO WHY DON'T I WORRY ABOUT BEING FOUND OUT HERE?
I KNOW I SHOULD,
BUT--
(how do I put this?)
NONE OF THIS SEEMS QUITE REAL.

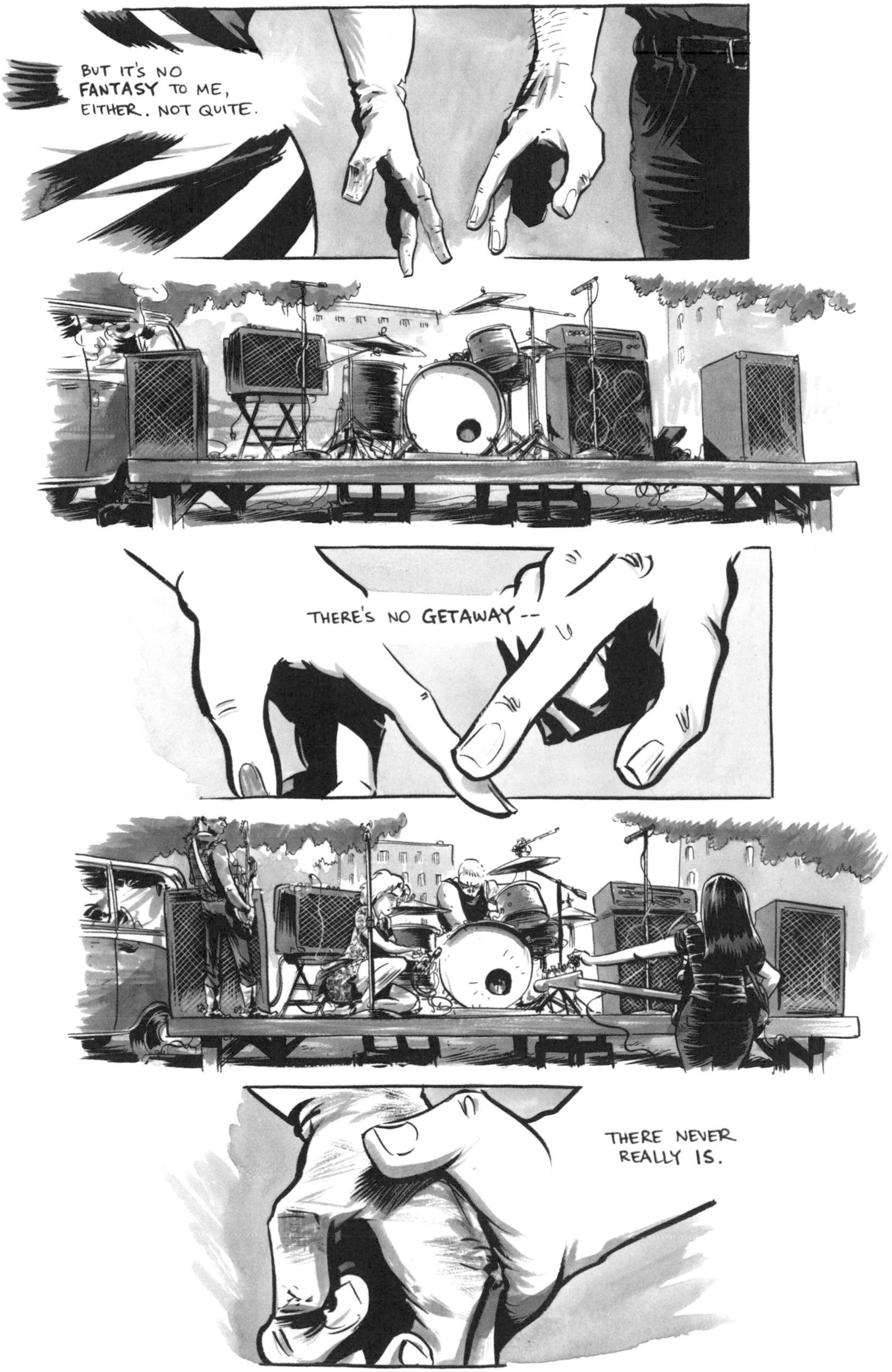
BUT IT'S NO FANTASY TO ME, EITHER. NOT QUITE.
THERE'S NO GETAWAY--
THERE NEVER REALLY IS.

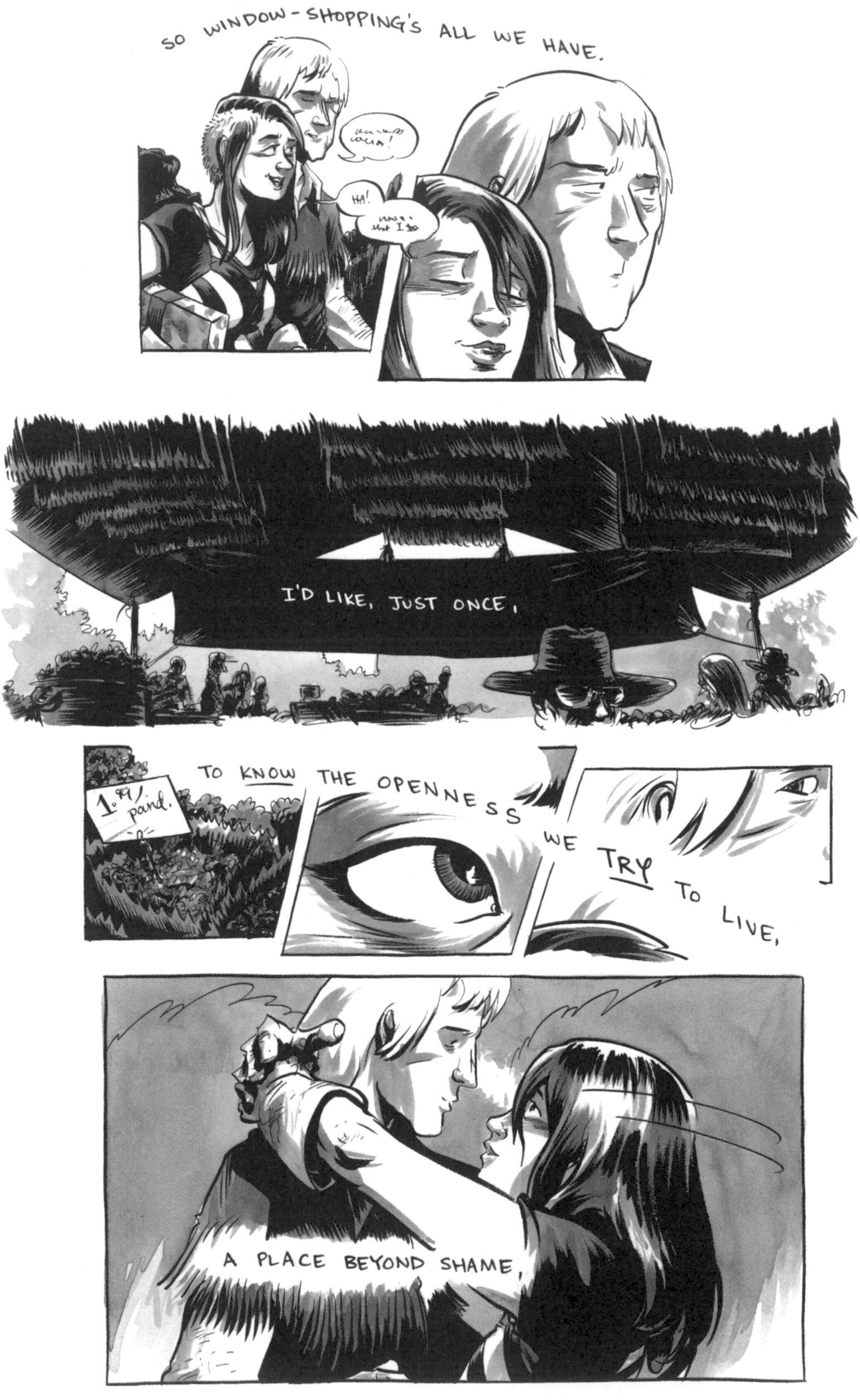
SO WINDOW-SHOPPING'S ALL WE HAVE.
HA!
I'D LIKE, JUST ONCE,
TO KNOW THE OPENNESS WE TRY TO LIVE,
A PLACE BEYOND SHAME,

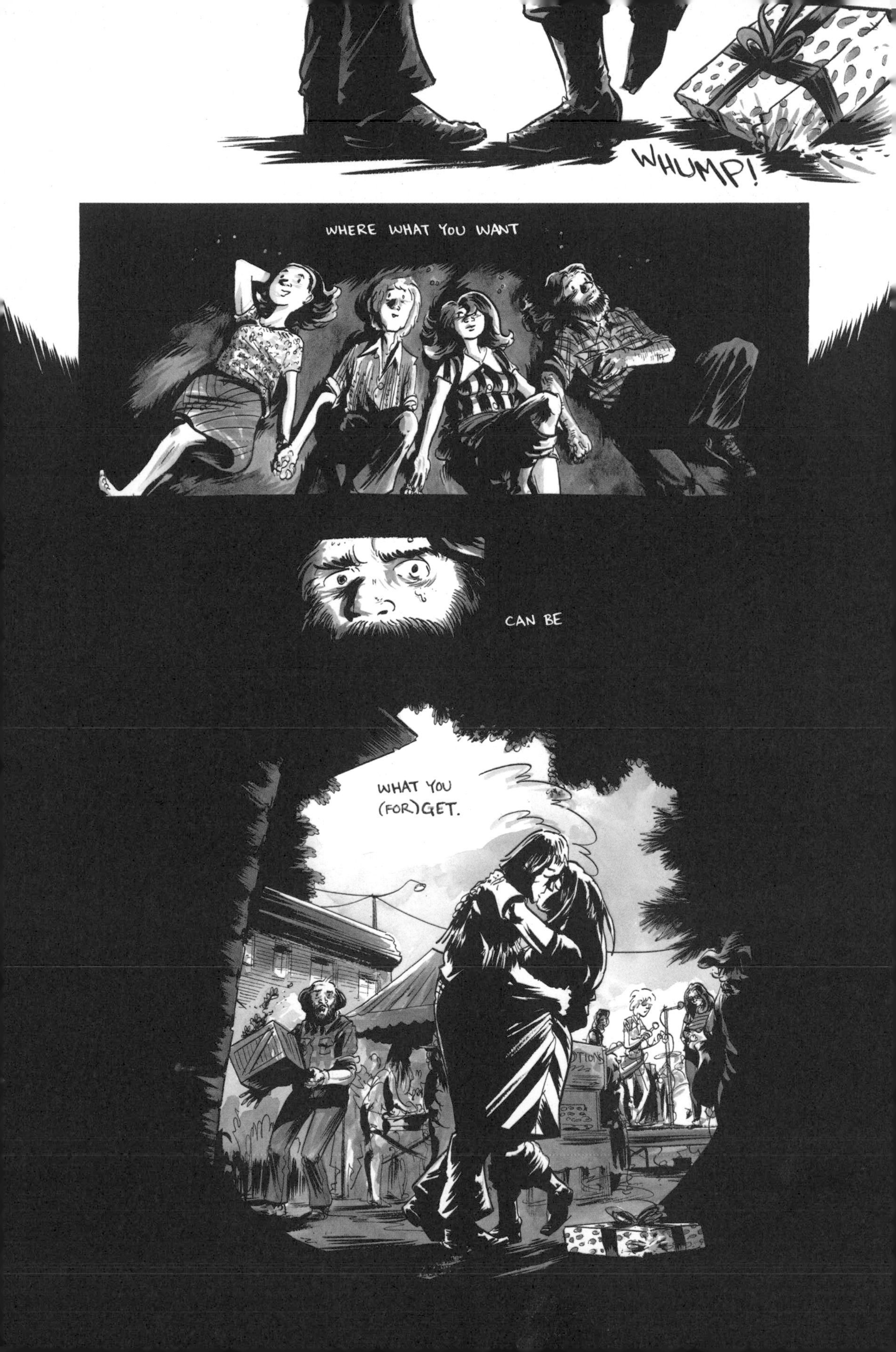
WHUMP!
WHERE WHAT YOU WANT
CAN BE
WHAT YOU
(FOR)GET.

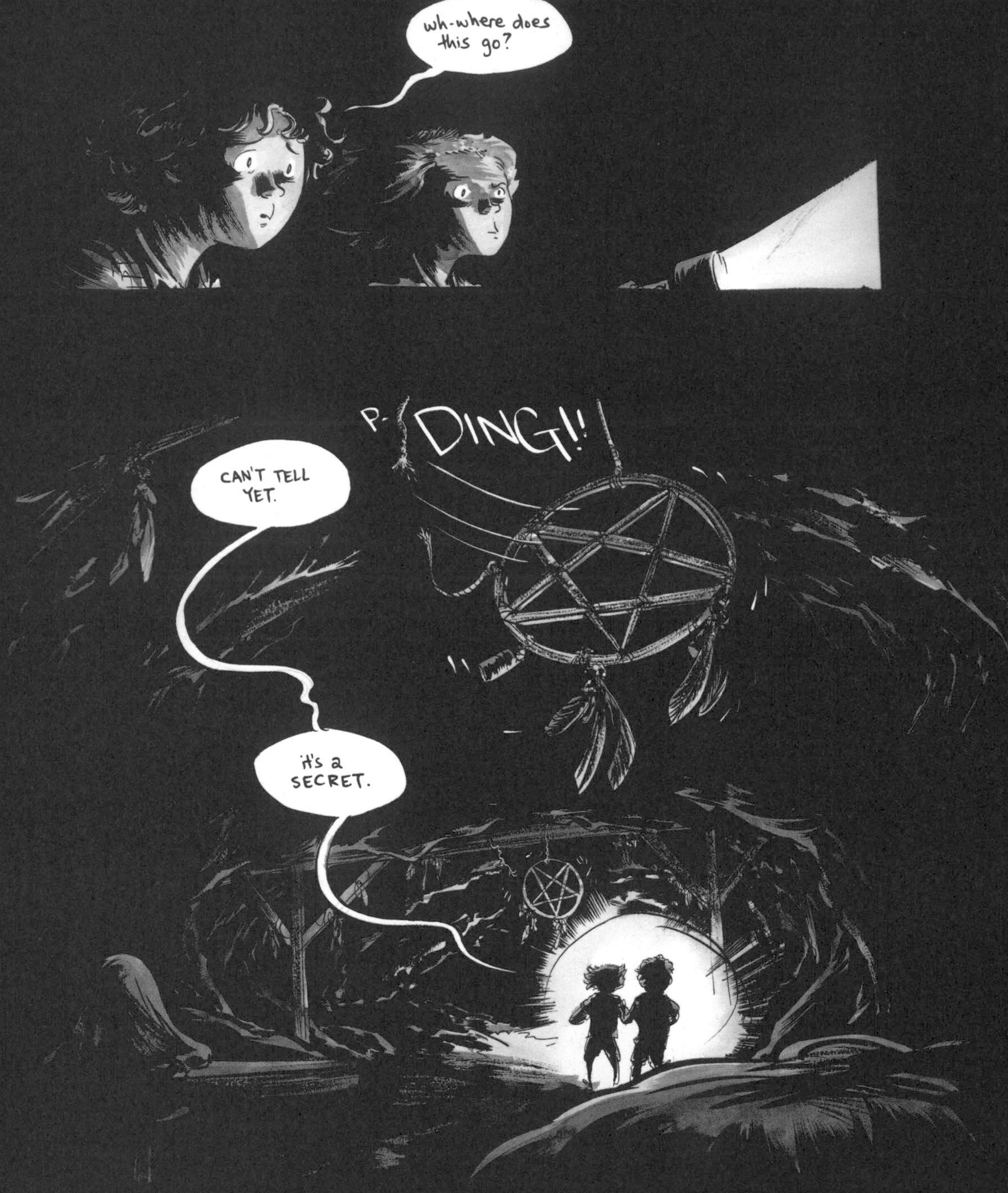
wh-where does this go?
P-DING!!
CAN'T TELL YET.
it's a SECRET.

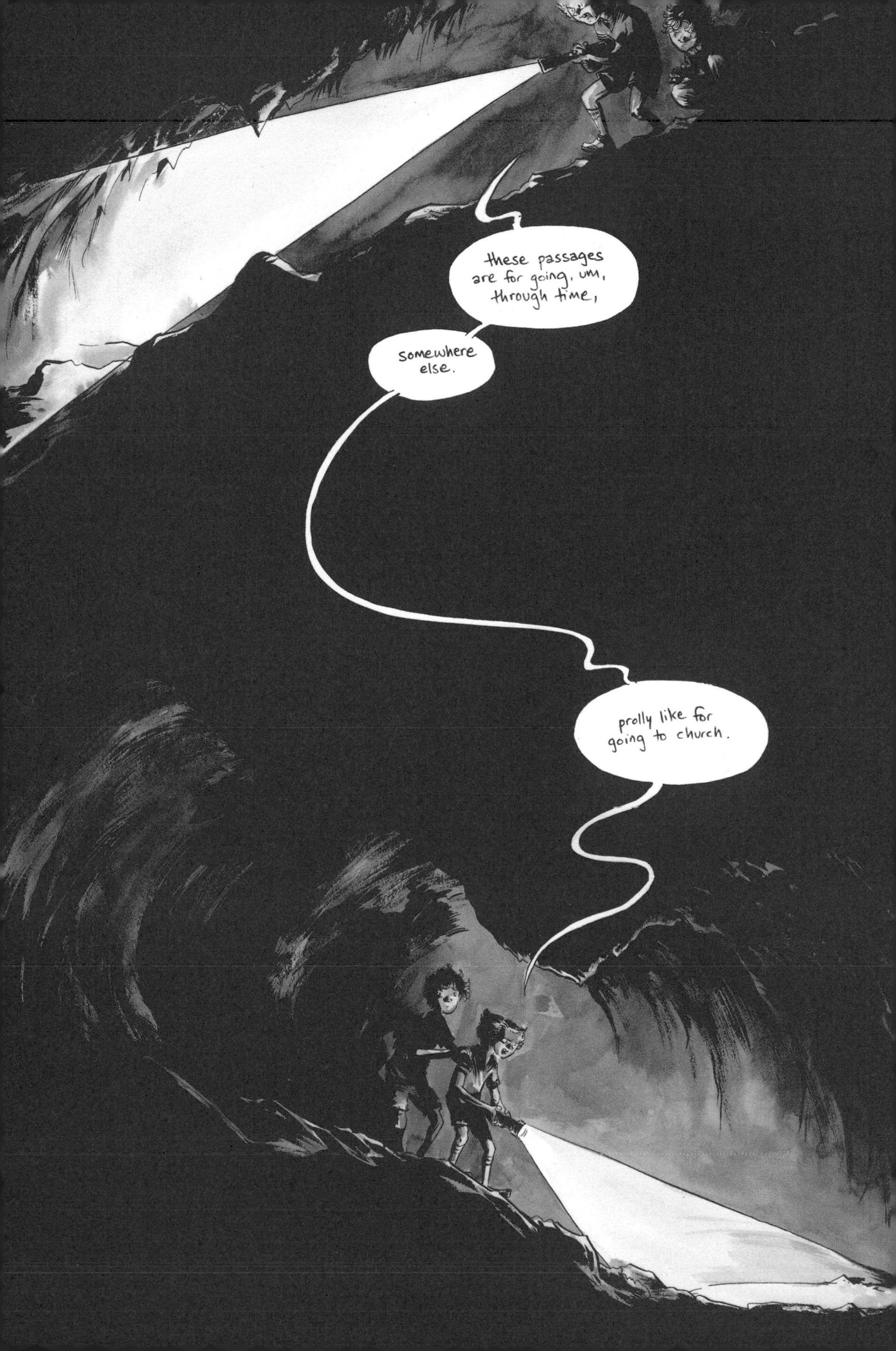
these passages are for going, um, through time,
somewhere else.
prolly like for going to church.

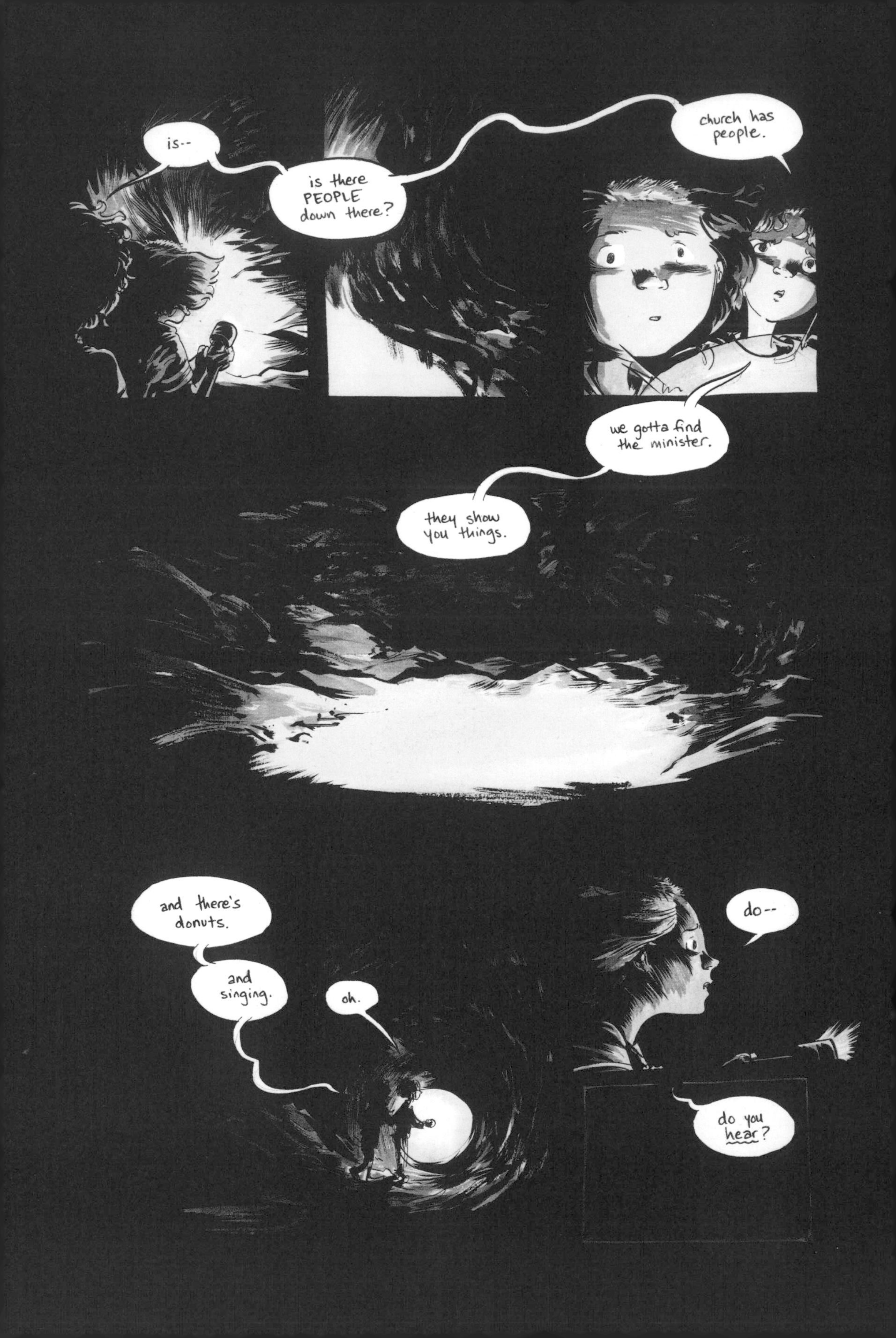
is--
is there PEOPLE down there?
church has people.
we gotta find the minister.
they show you things.
and there's donuts.
and singing.
oh.
do--
do you hear?

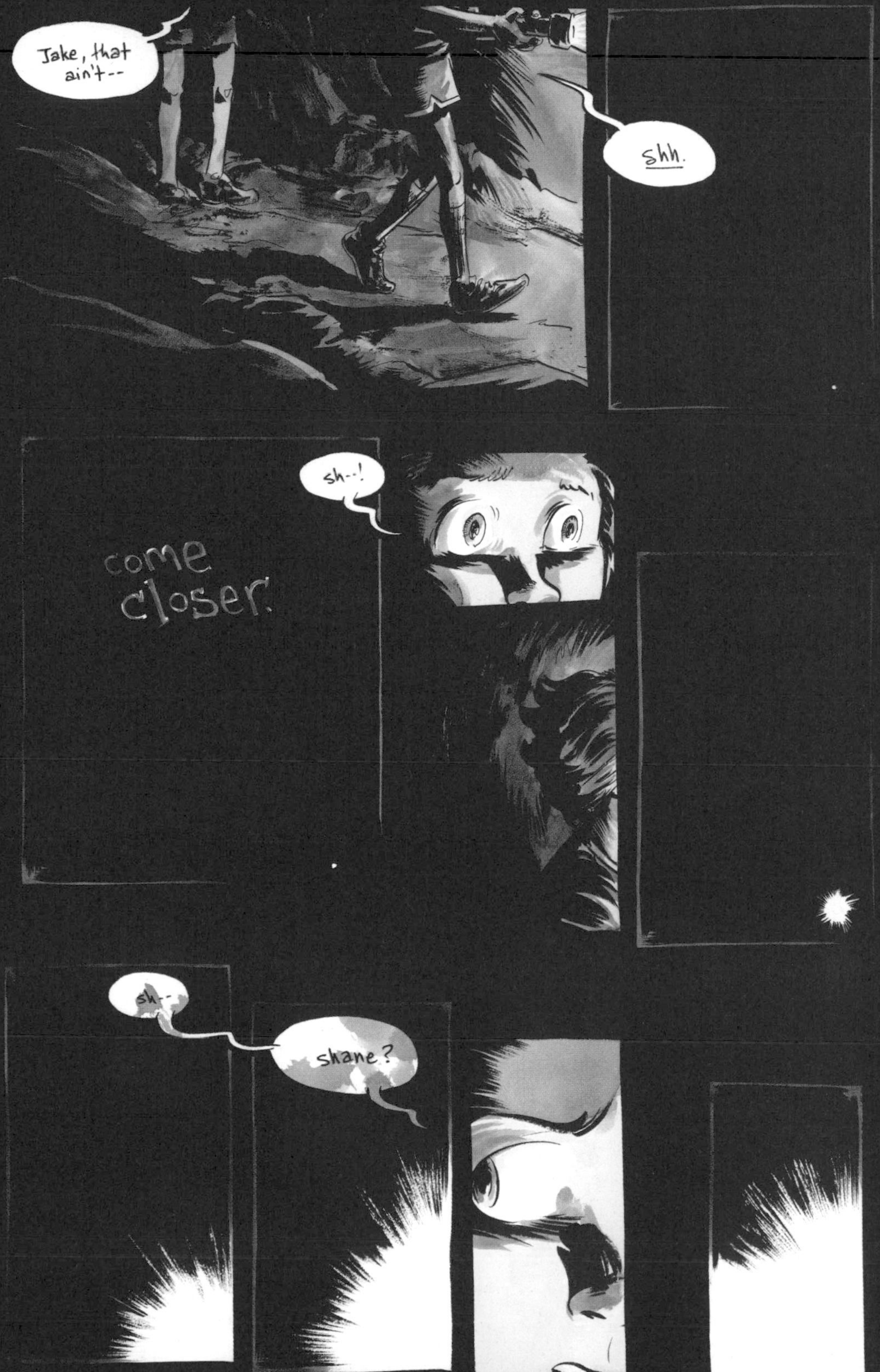
Jake, that ain't--
shh.
come closer.
sh--!
sh--
shane?

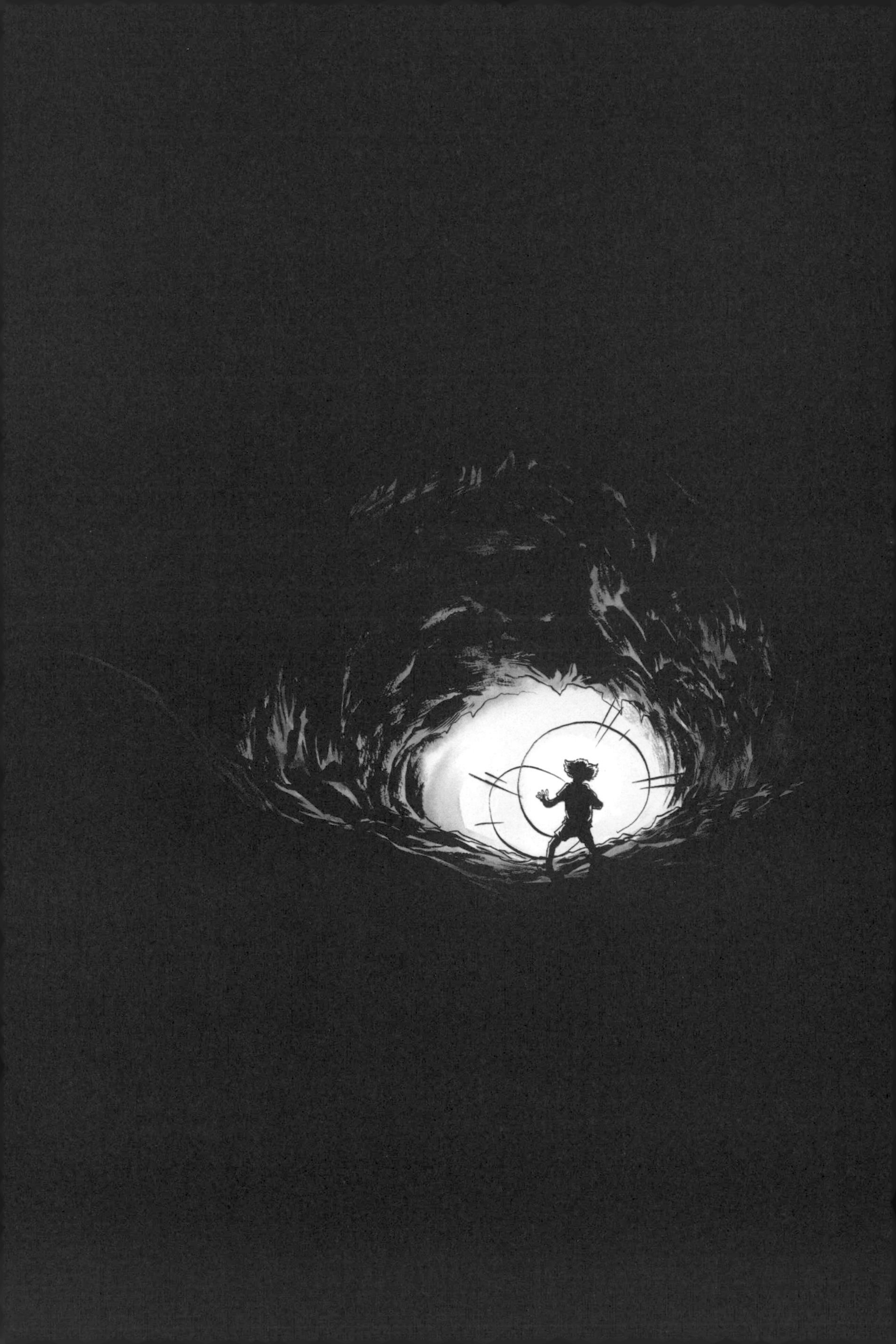

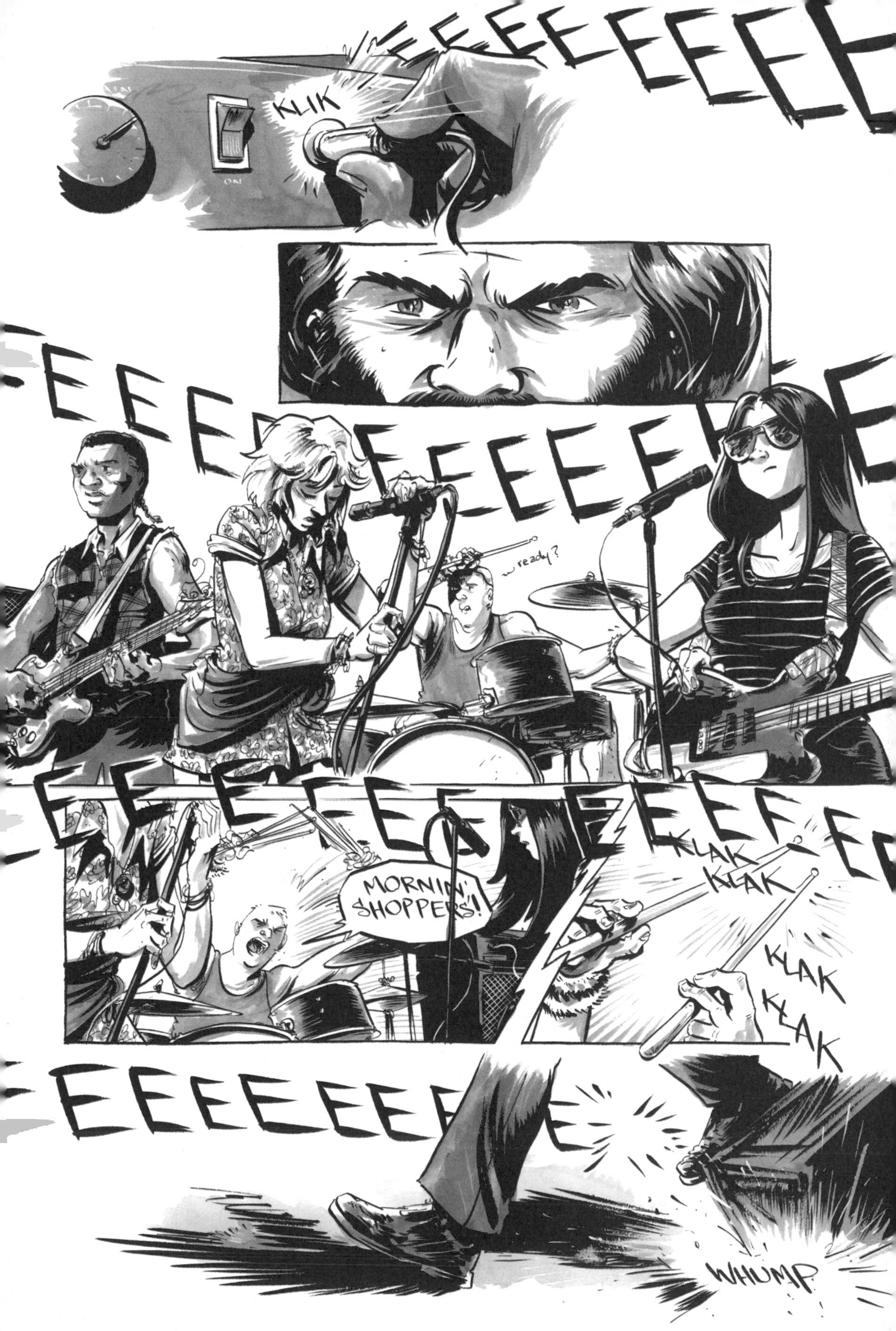
EEEEEEEEEEE
KLIK
ON
EEEEEEEEEEEEEE
ready?
EEEEEEEEEE
MORNIN' SHOPPERS!
KLAK
KLAK
KLAK
KLAK
EEEEEEEEE
WHUMP

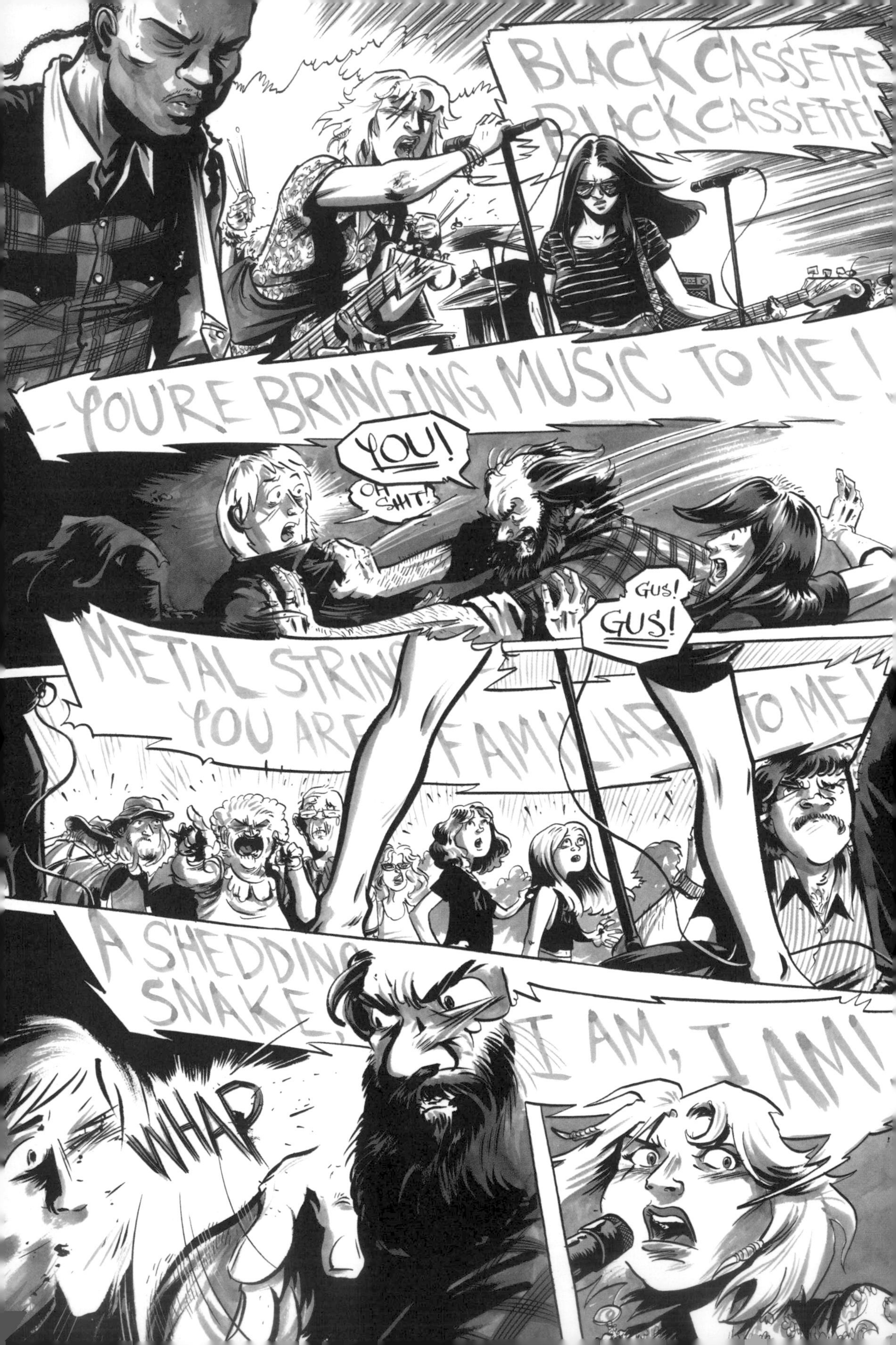
BLACK CASSETTE BLACK CASSETTE!
--YOU'RE BRINGING MUSIC TO ME!
YOU!
OH SHIT!
GUS!
GUS!
METAL STRING YOU ARE FAMILIAR TO ME!
A SHEDDING SNAKE,
I AM, I AM!
WHAP

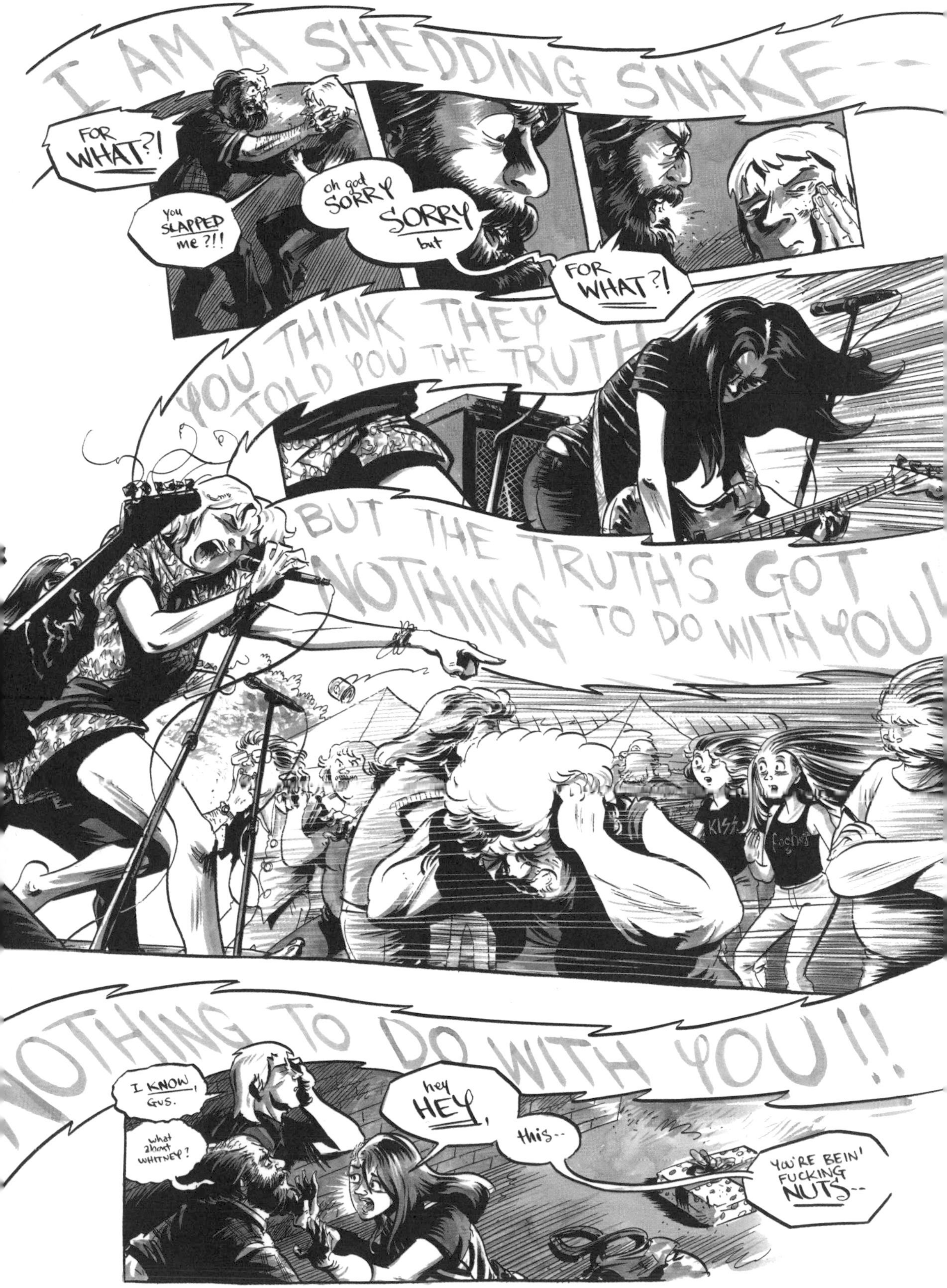

I AM A SHEDDING SNAKE--
FOR WHAT?!
YOU SLAPPED ME?!!
oh god SORRY SORRY but
FOR WHAT?!
YOU THINK THEY TOLD YOU THE TRUTH
BUT THE TRUTH'S GOT NOTHING TO DO WITH YOU
KISS
NOTHING TO DO WITH YOU!!
I KNOW, GUS.
what about WHITNEY?
hey HEY, this--
YOU'RE BEIN' FUCKING NUTS--

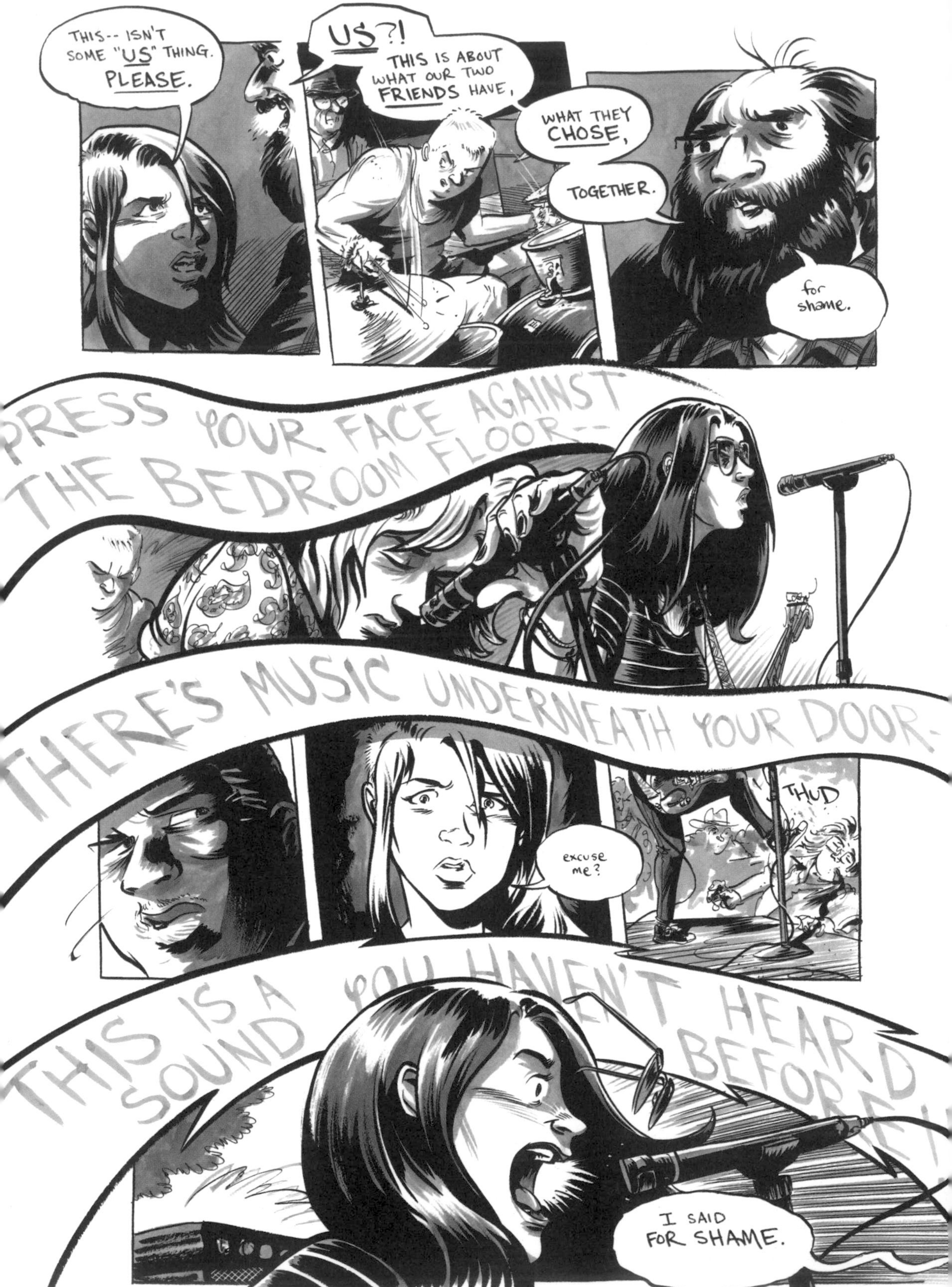

THIS-- ISN'T SOME "US" THING. PLEASE.
US?!
THIS IS ABOUT WHAT OUR TWO FRIENDS HAVE,
WHAT THEY CHOSE,
TOGETHER.
for shame.
PRESS YOUR FACE AGAINST THE BEDROOM FLOOR--
THERE'S MUSIC UNDERNEATH YOUR DOOR-
excuse me?
THUD
THIS IS A SOUND YOU HAVEN'T HEARD BEFORE
I SAID FOR SHAME.

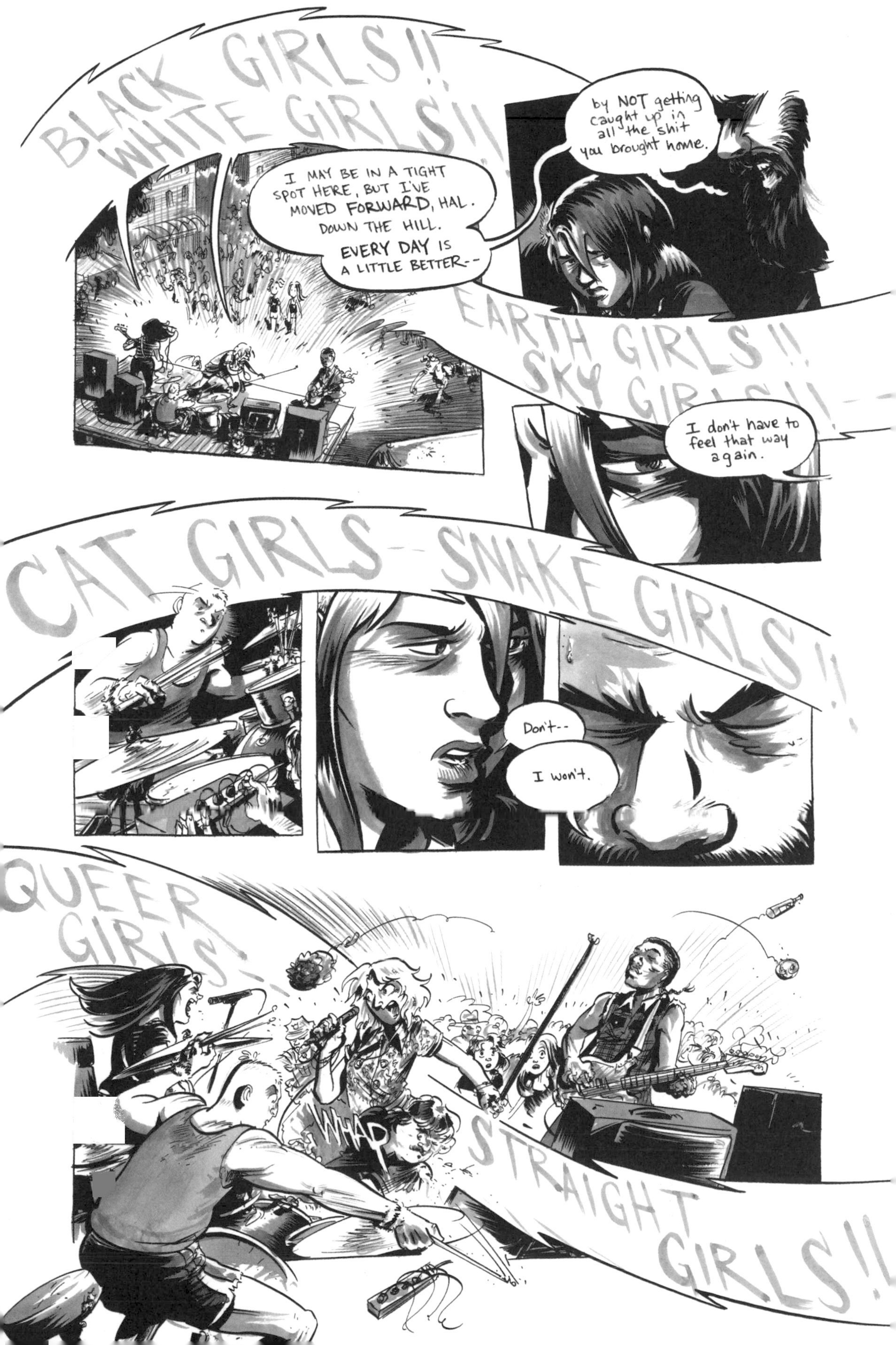
BLACK GIRLS!!
WHITE GIRLS!!
I MAY BE IN A TIGHT SPOT HERE, BUT I'VE MOVED FORWARD, HAL. DOWN THE HILL.
EVERY DAY IS A LITTLE BETTER--
by NOT getting caught up in all the shit you brought home.
EARTH GIRLS!!
SKY GIRLS!!--
I don't have to feel that way again.
CAT GIRLS--SNAKE GIRLS!!
Don't--
I won't.
QUEER GIRLS!!
WHAP
STRAIGHT GIRLS!!

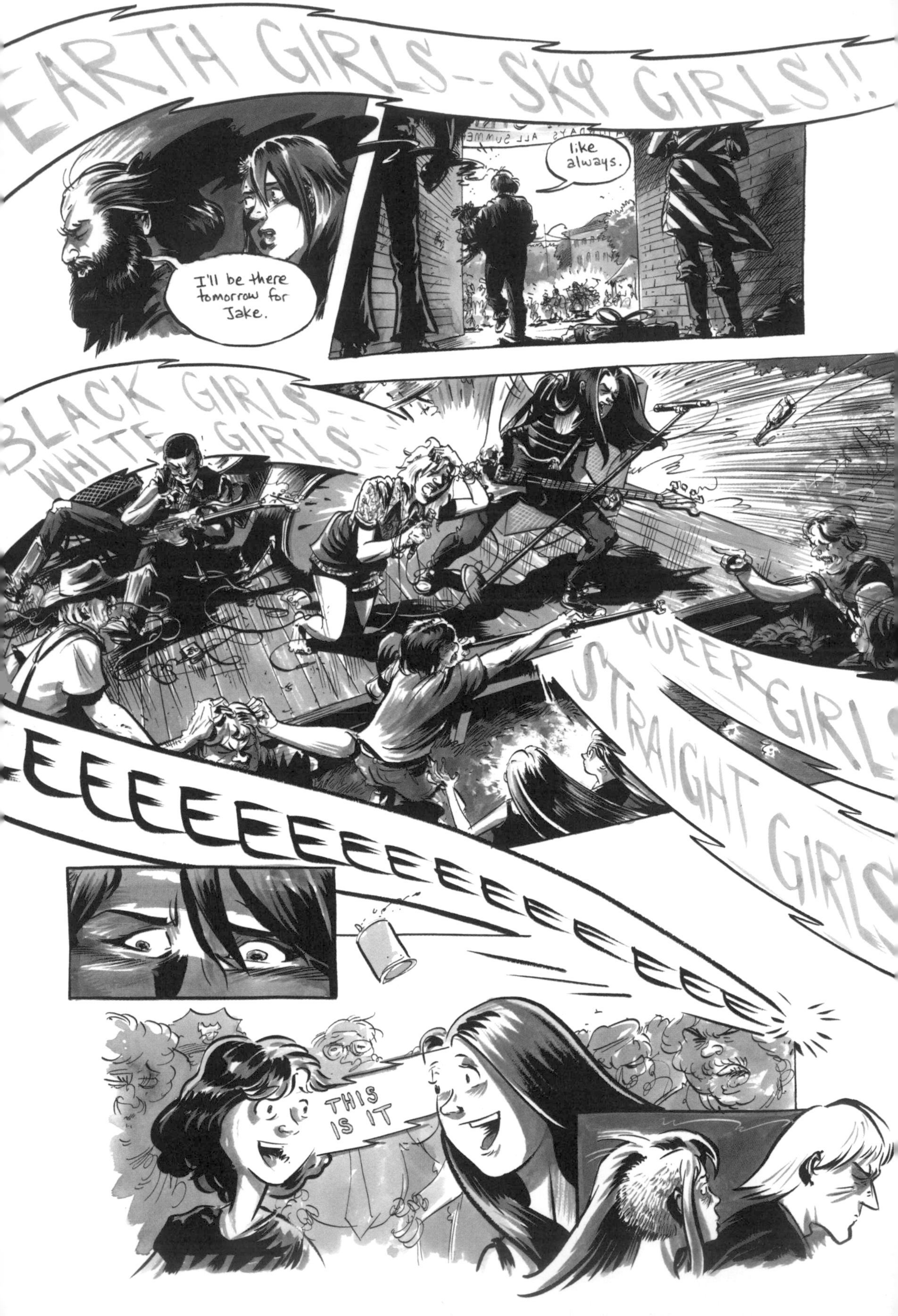
EARTH GIRLS-- SKY GIRLS!!
I'll be there tomorrow for Jake.
like always.
BLACK GIRLS WHITE GIRLS
QUEER GIRLS
STRAIGHT GIRLS
EEEEEEEEEEEEEEEEEEEEEE
THIS IS IT

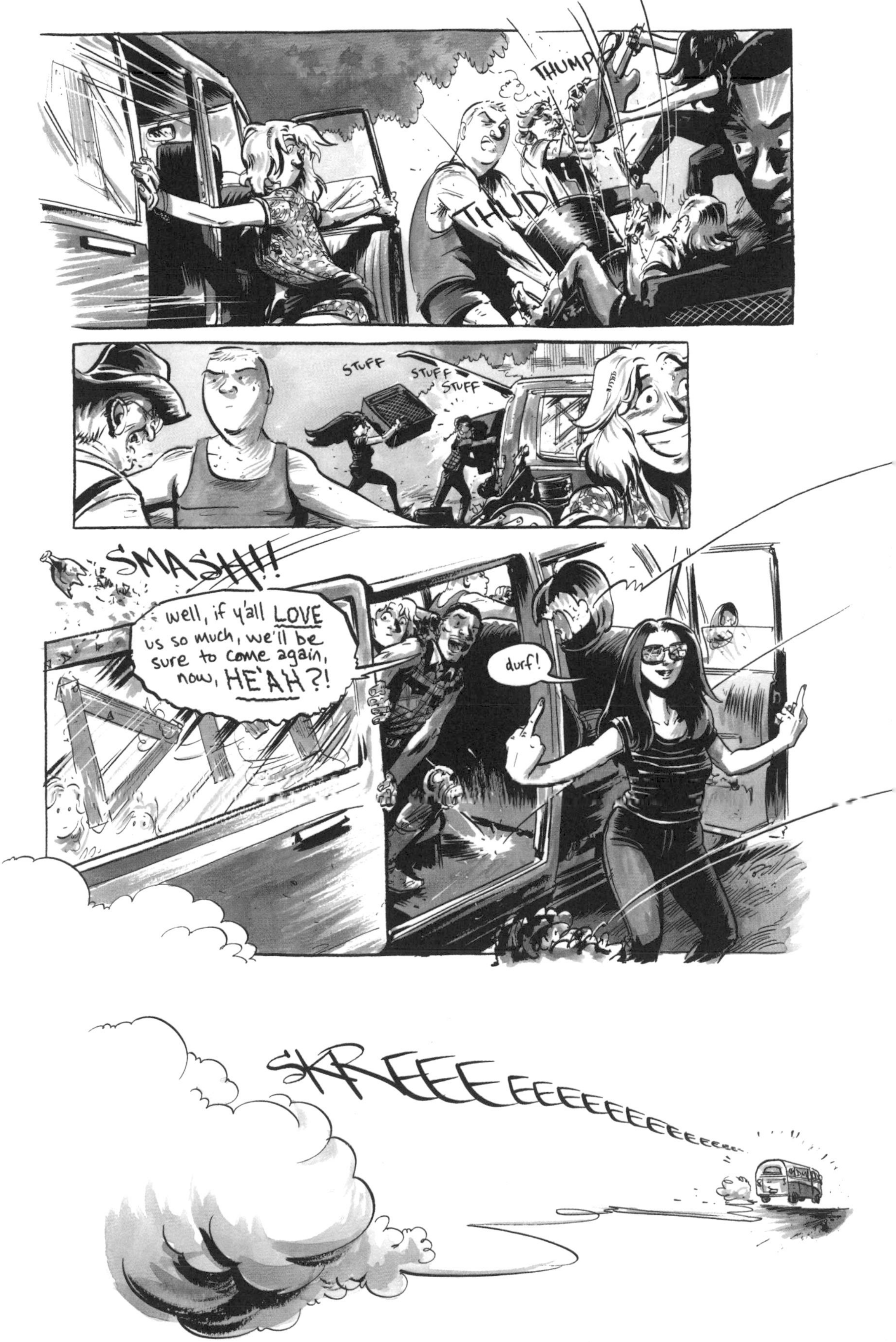
THUMP
THUD!
STUFF
STUFF
STUFF
SMASH!!
well, if y'all LOVE us so much, we'll be sure to come again, now, HE'AH?!
durf!
SKREEEEEEEEEEEEEEEEEEeee...

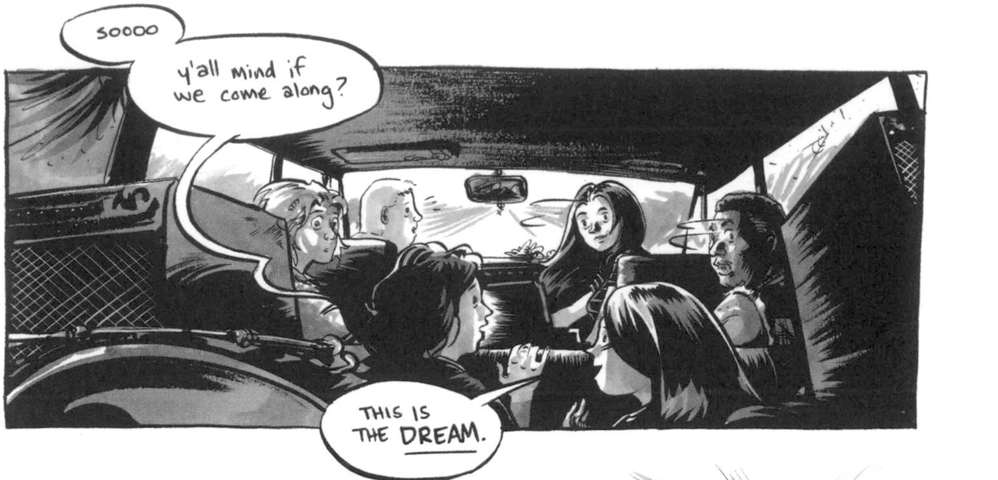
soooo
y'all mind if we come along?
THIS IS THE DREAM.

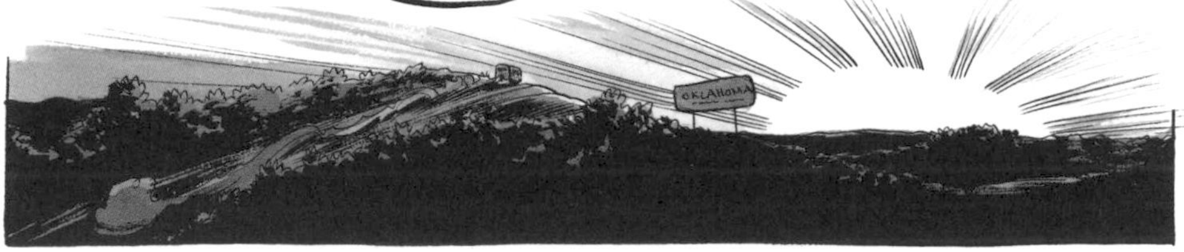
OKLAHOMA

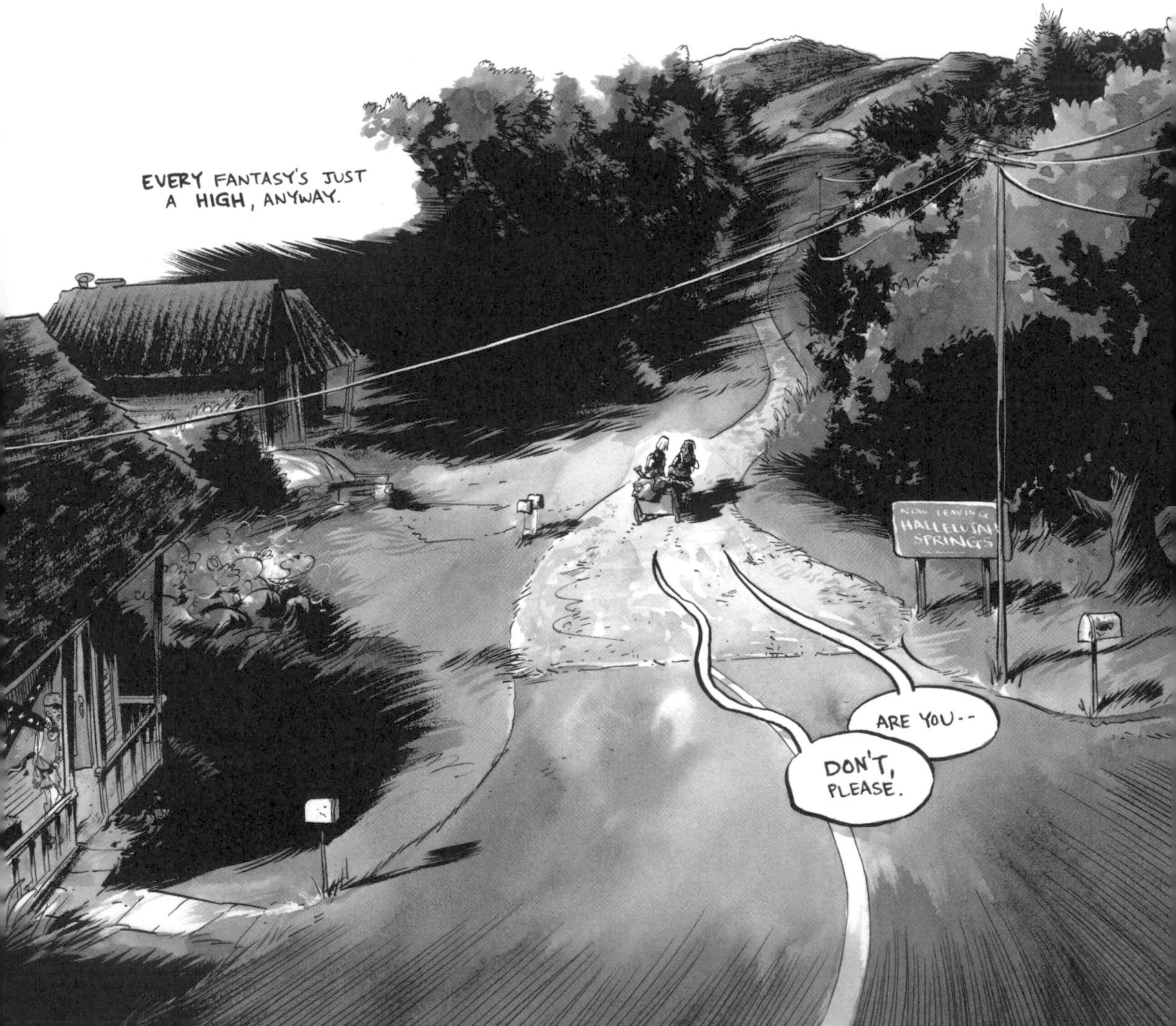
EVERY FANTASY'S JUST A HIGH, ANYWAY.
HALLELUJAH SPRINGS
ARE YOU--
DON'T, PLEASE.

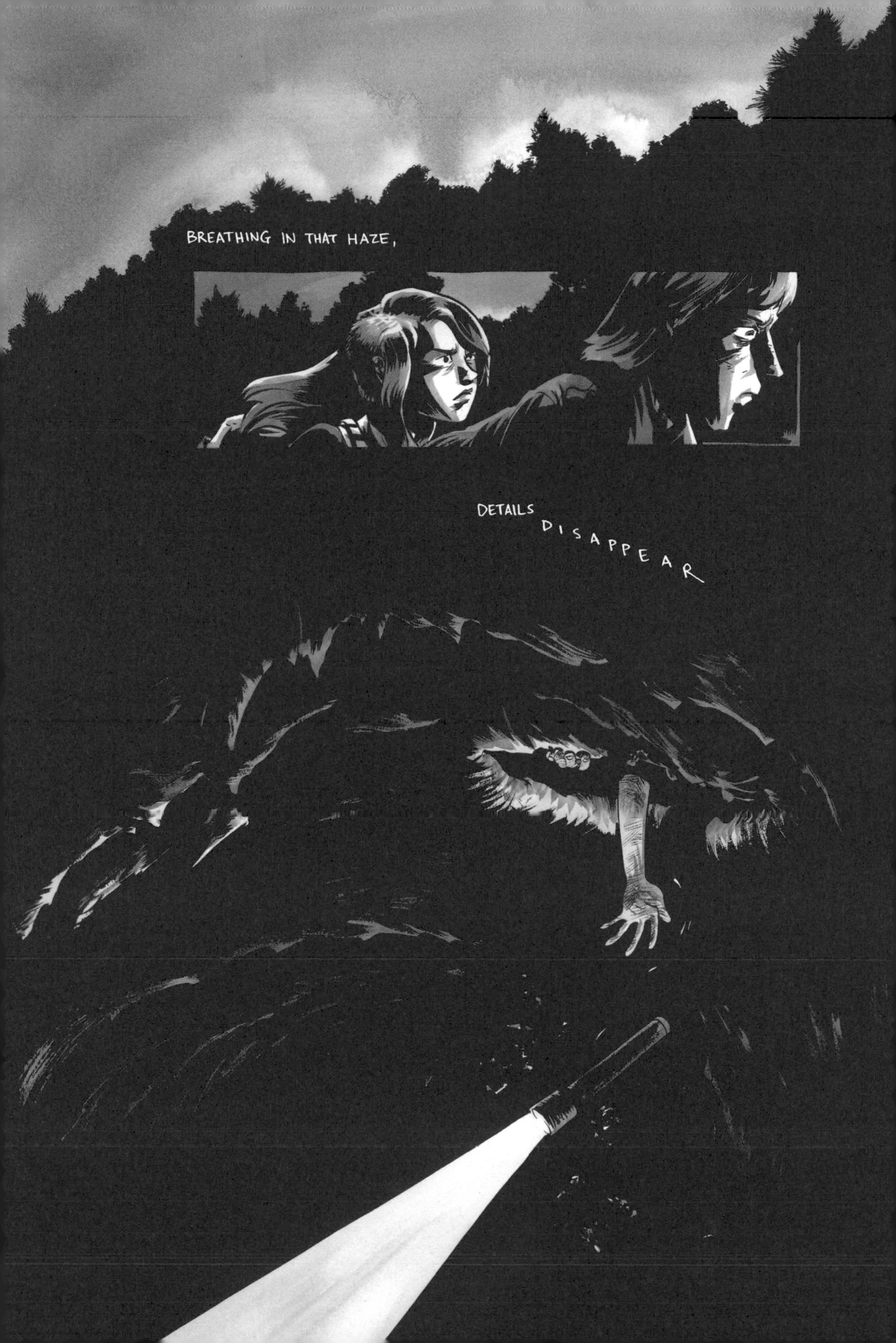
BREATHING IN THAT HAZE,
DETAILS DISAPPEAR

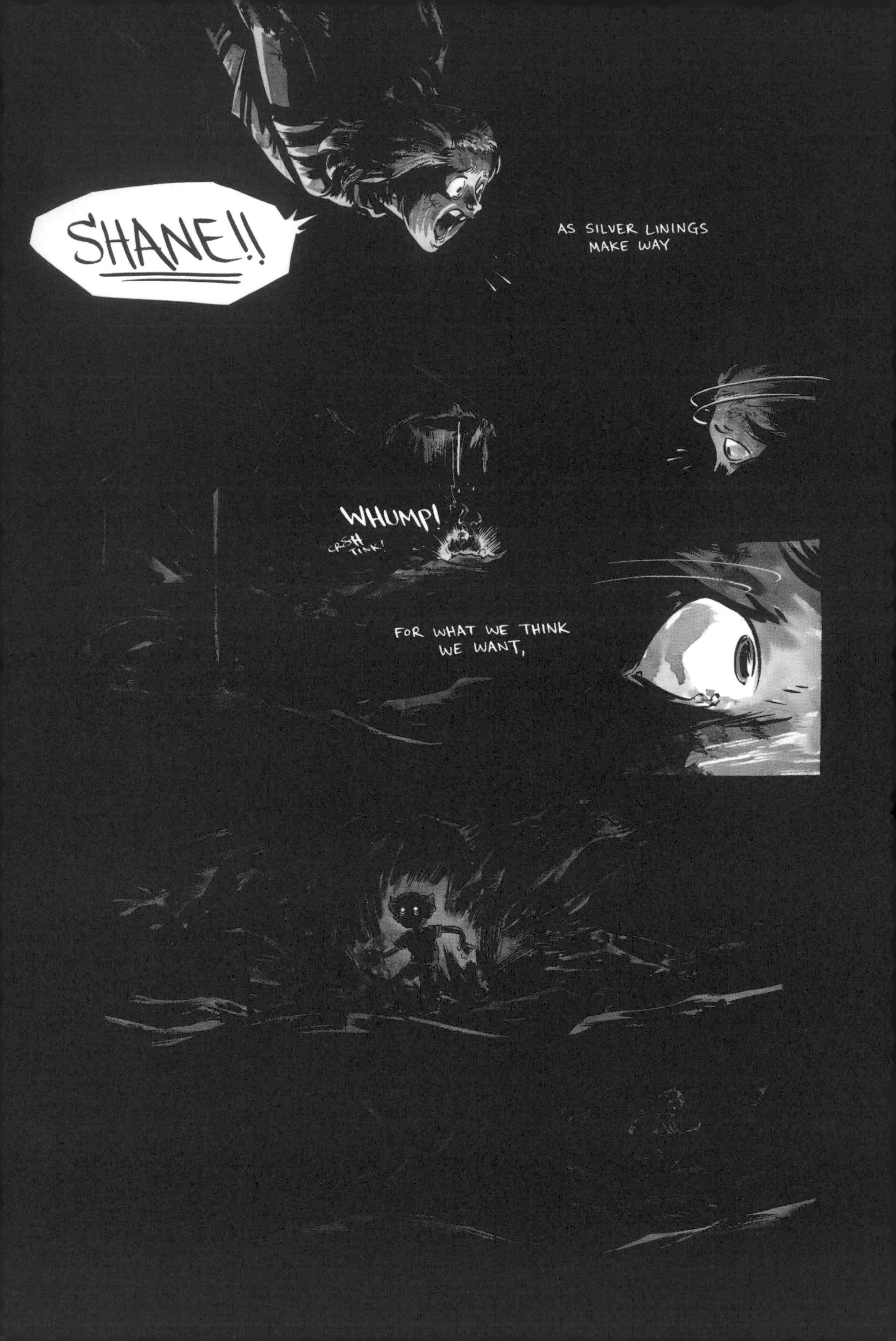
SHANE!!
AS SILVER LININGS MAKE WAY
WHUMP!
CRSH
TINK!
FOR WHAT WE THINK WE WANT,

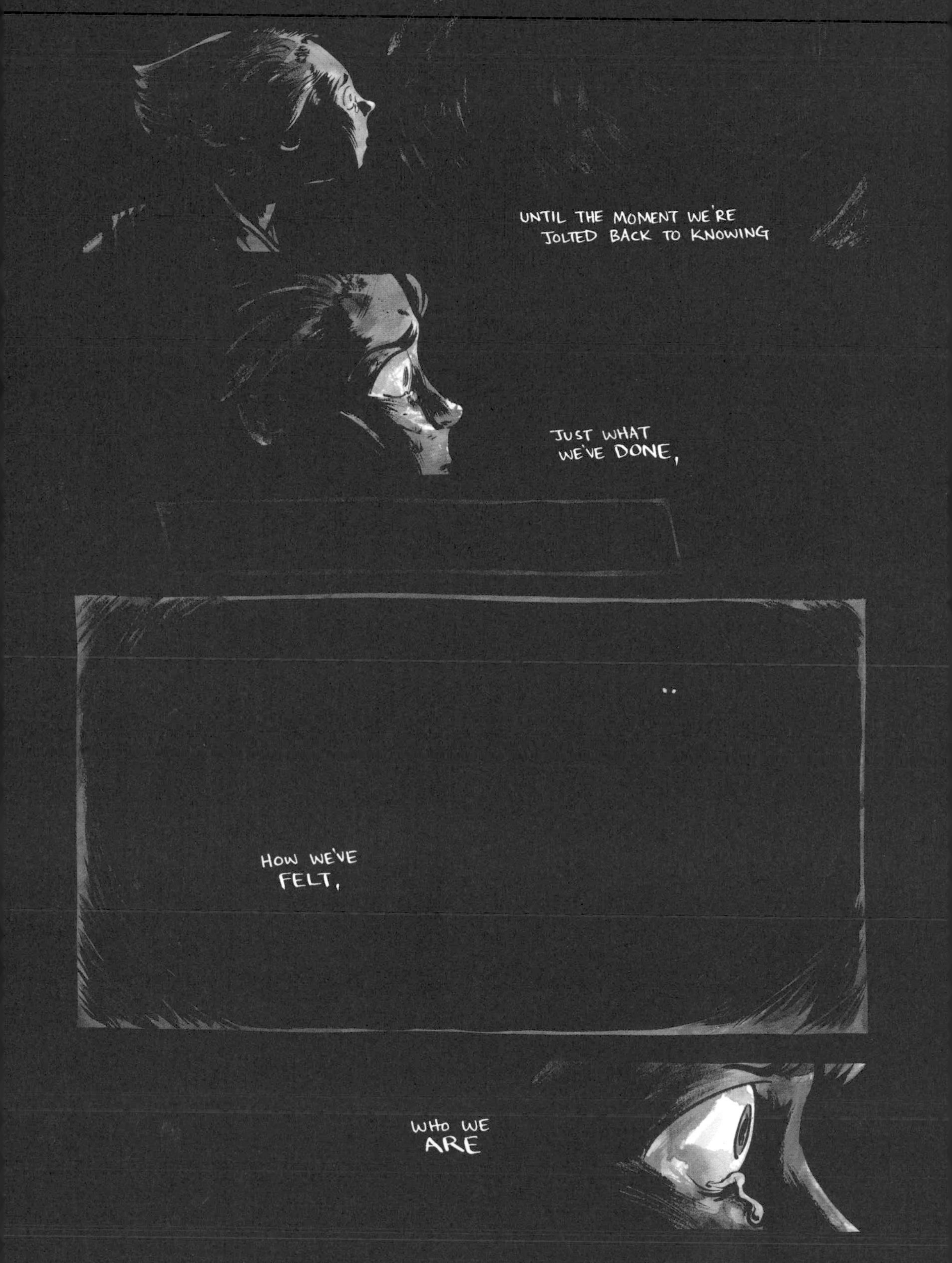
UNTIL THE MOMENT WE'RE JOLTED BACK TO KNOWING
JUST WHAT WE'VE DONE,
HOW WE'VE FELT,
WHO WE ARE

FANTASY IS

A BLIND WRAITH,

TRAILING

IN

FOG,

EASILY SCATTERED
BY THUNDER,

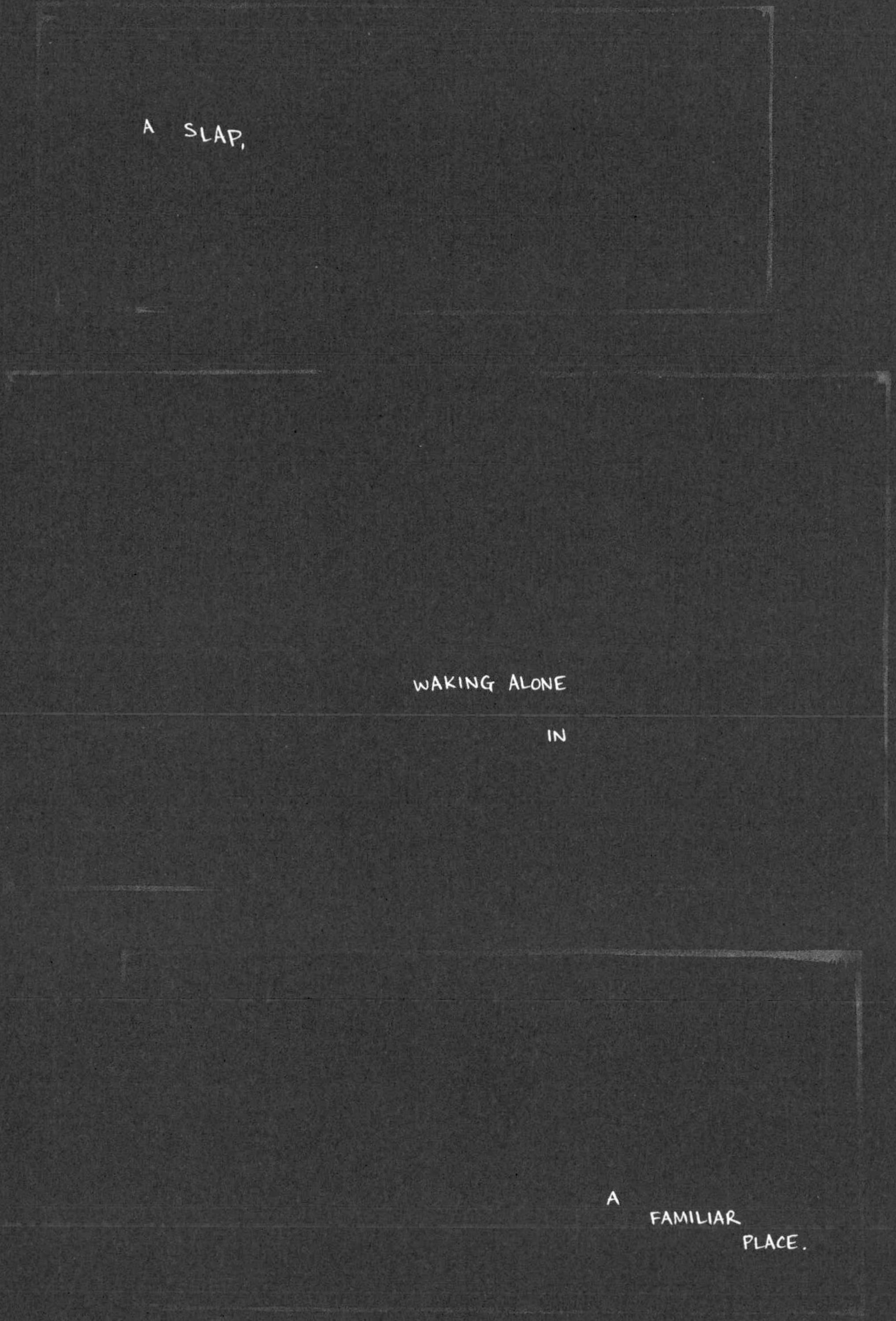
A SLAP.
WAKING ALONE
IN
A
FAMILIAR
PLACE.

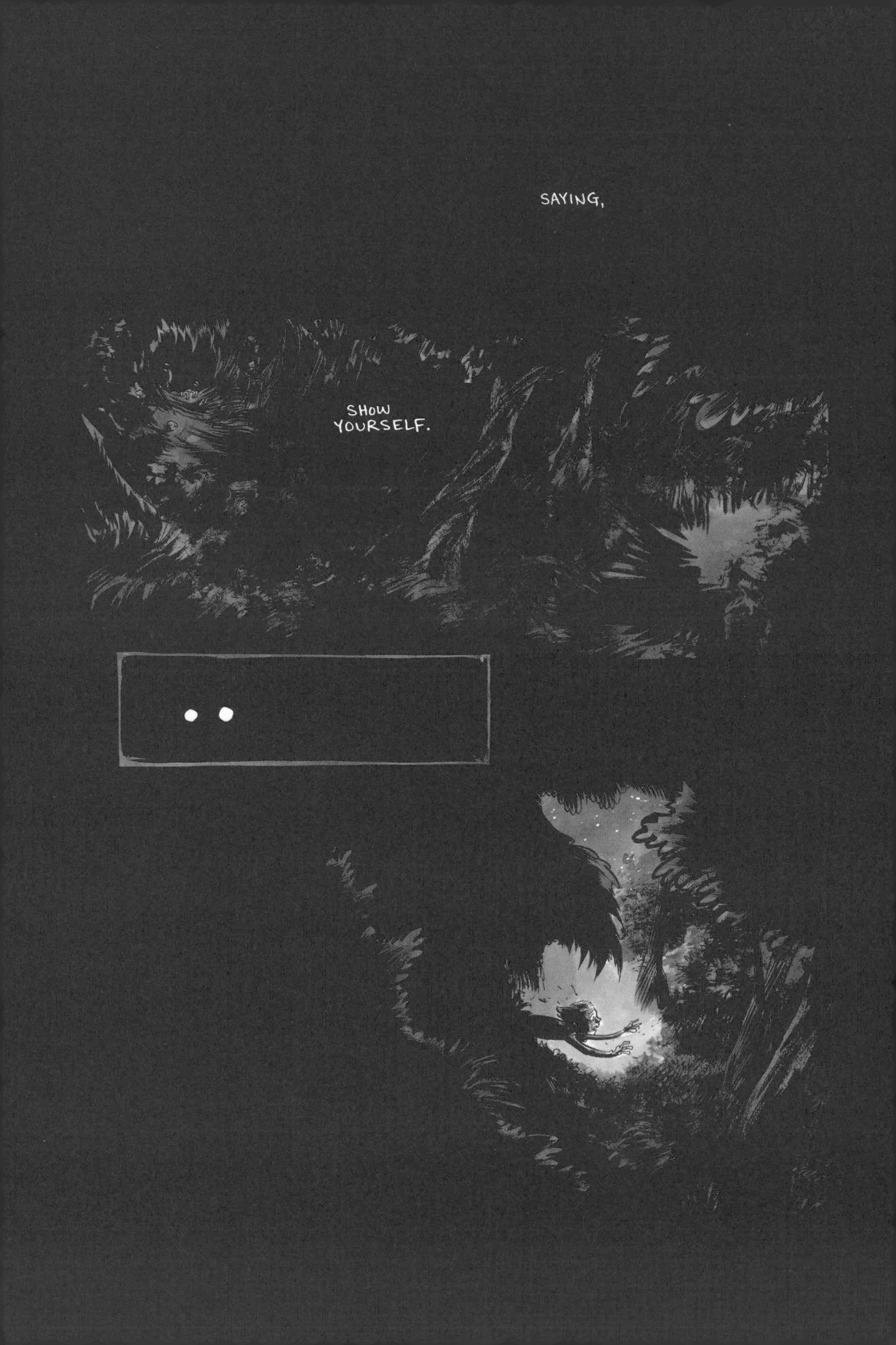
SAYING,
SHOW YOURSELF.

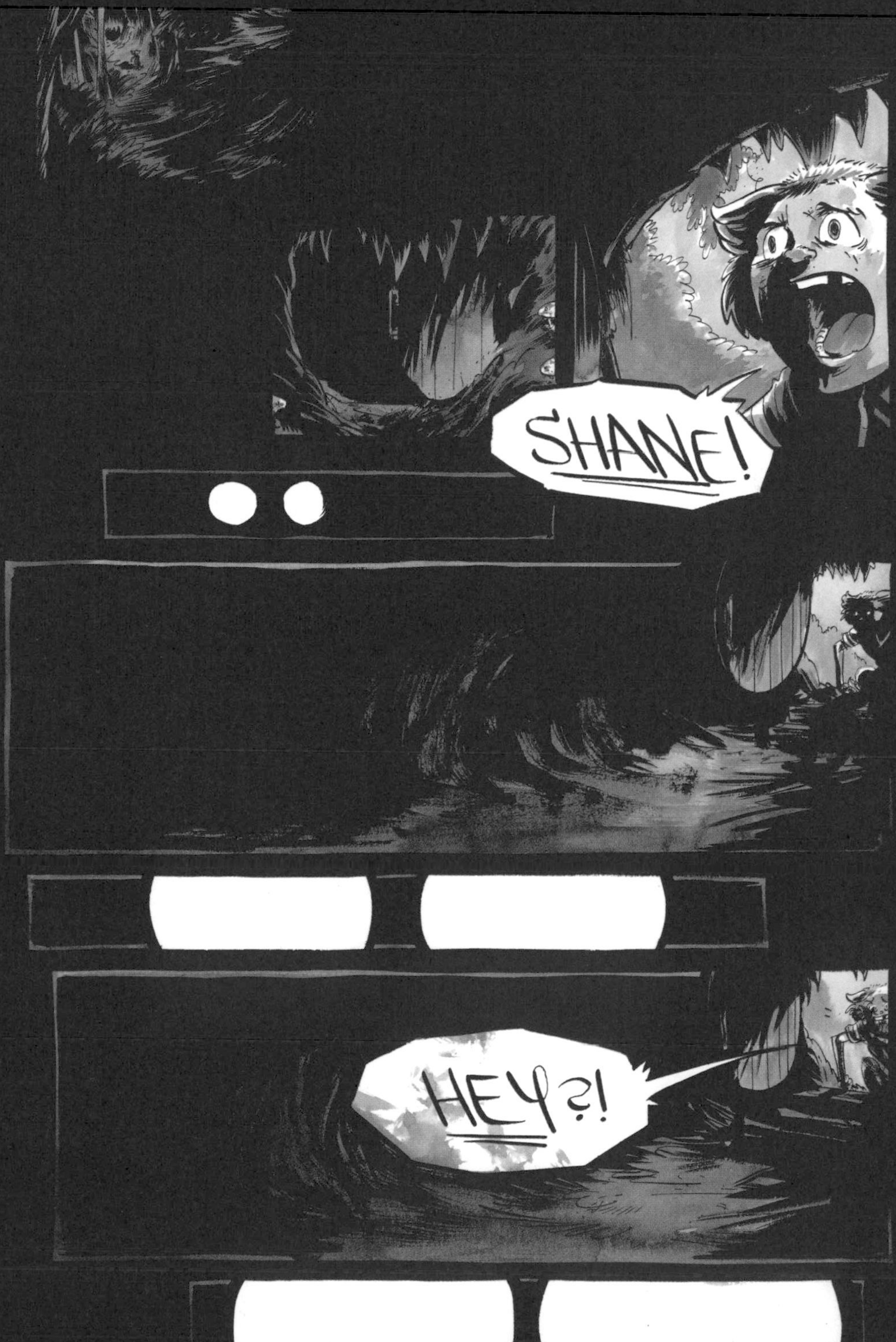
SHANE!
HEY?!

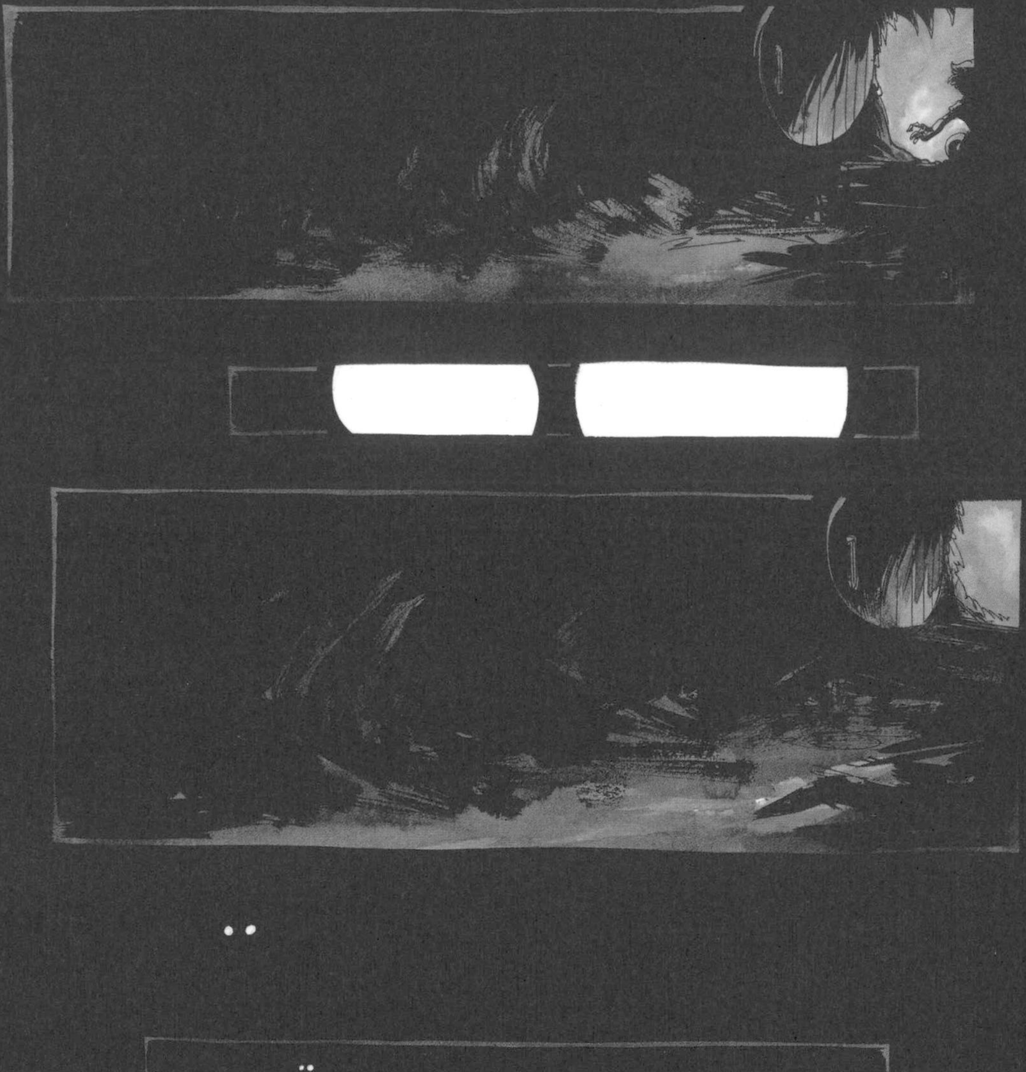

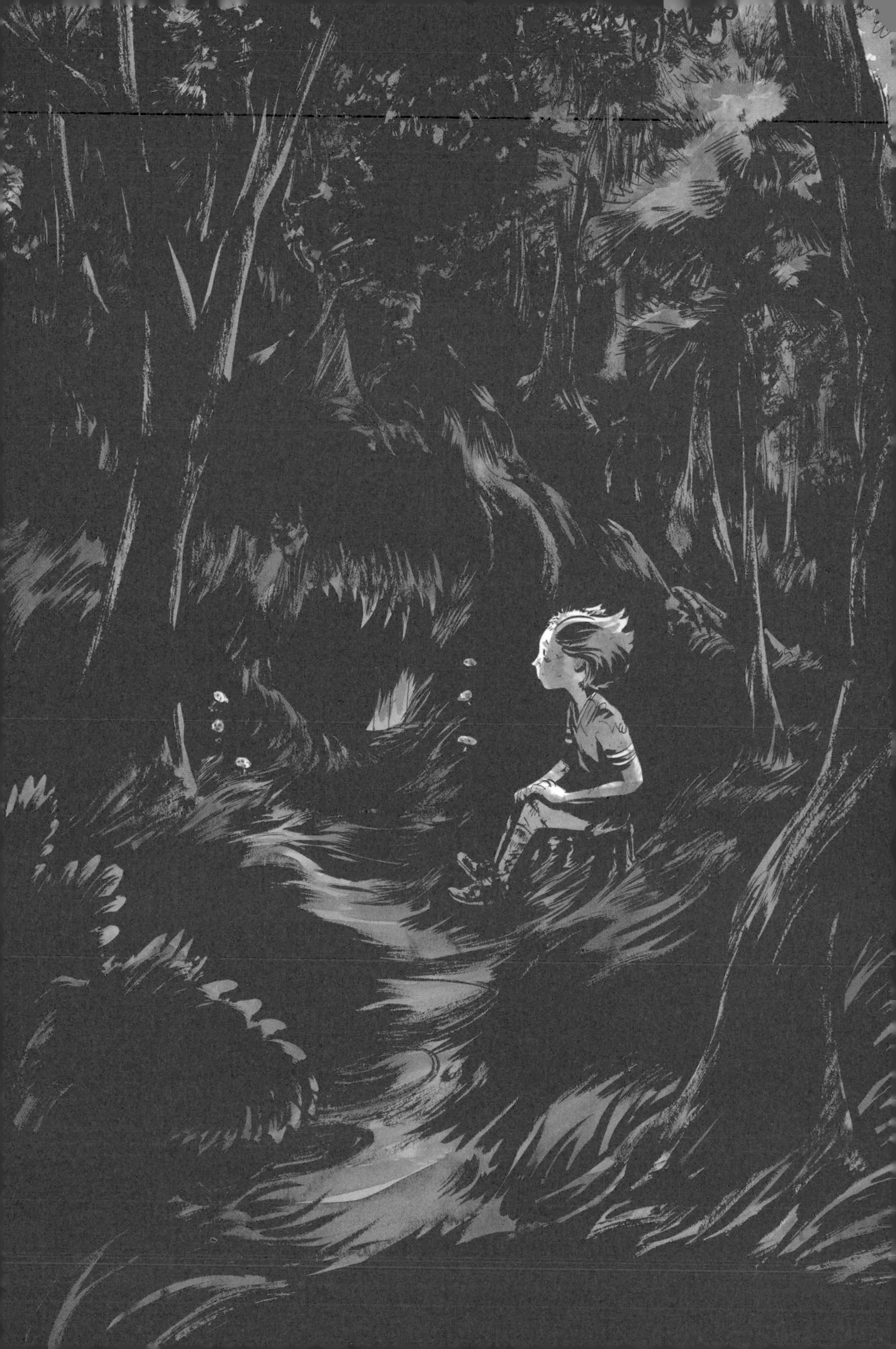

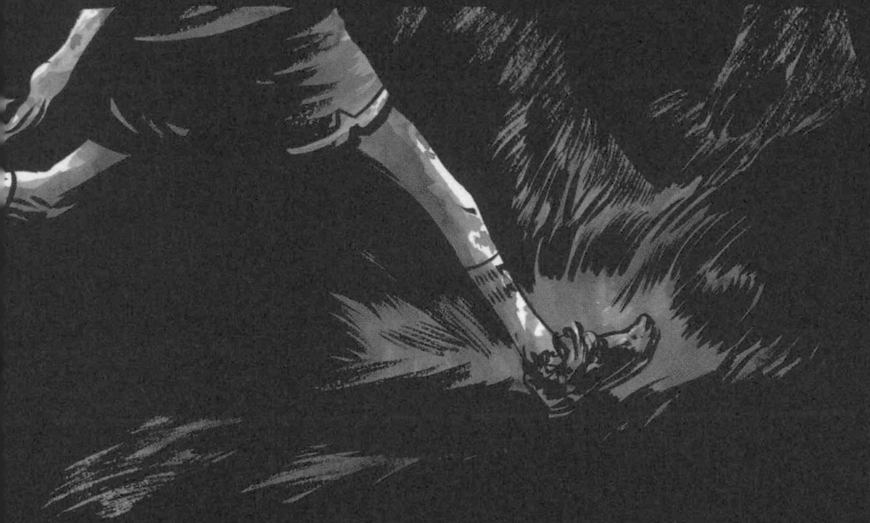

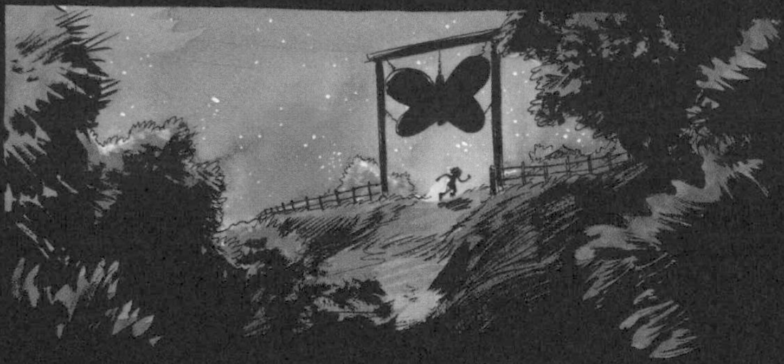

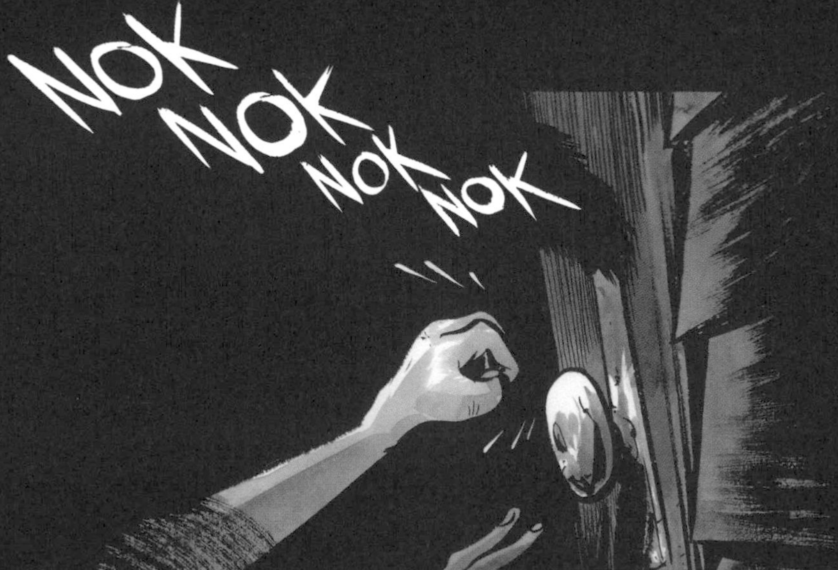
NOK
NOK
NOK
NOK

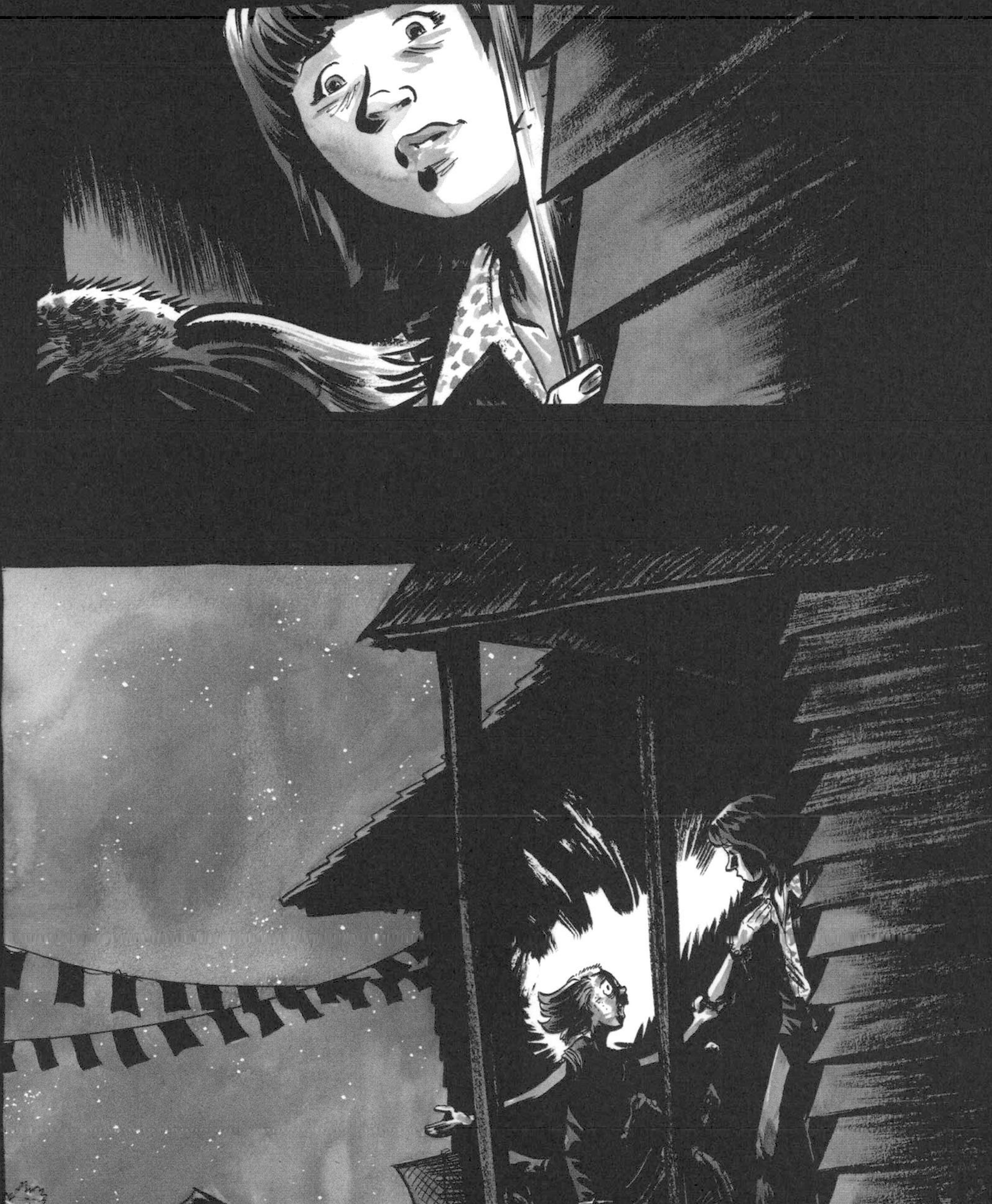

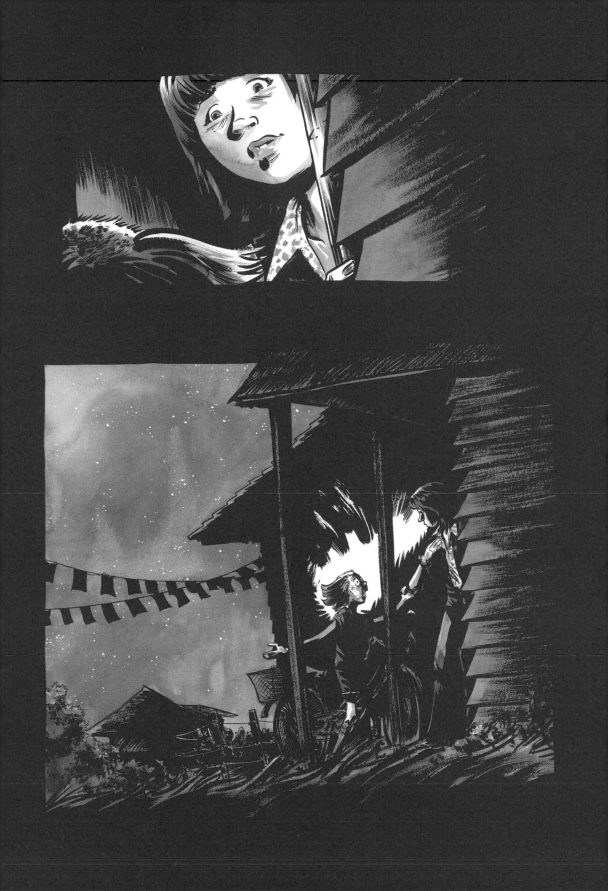

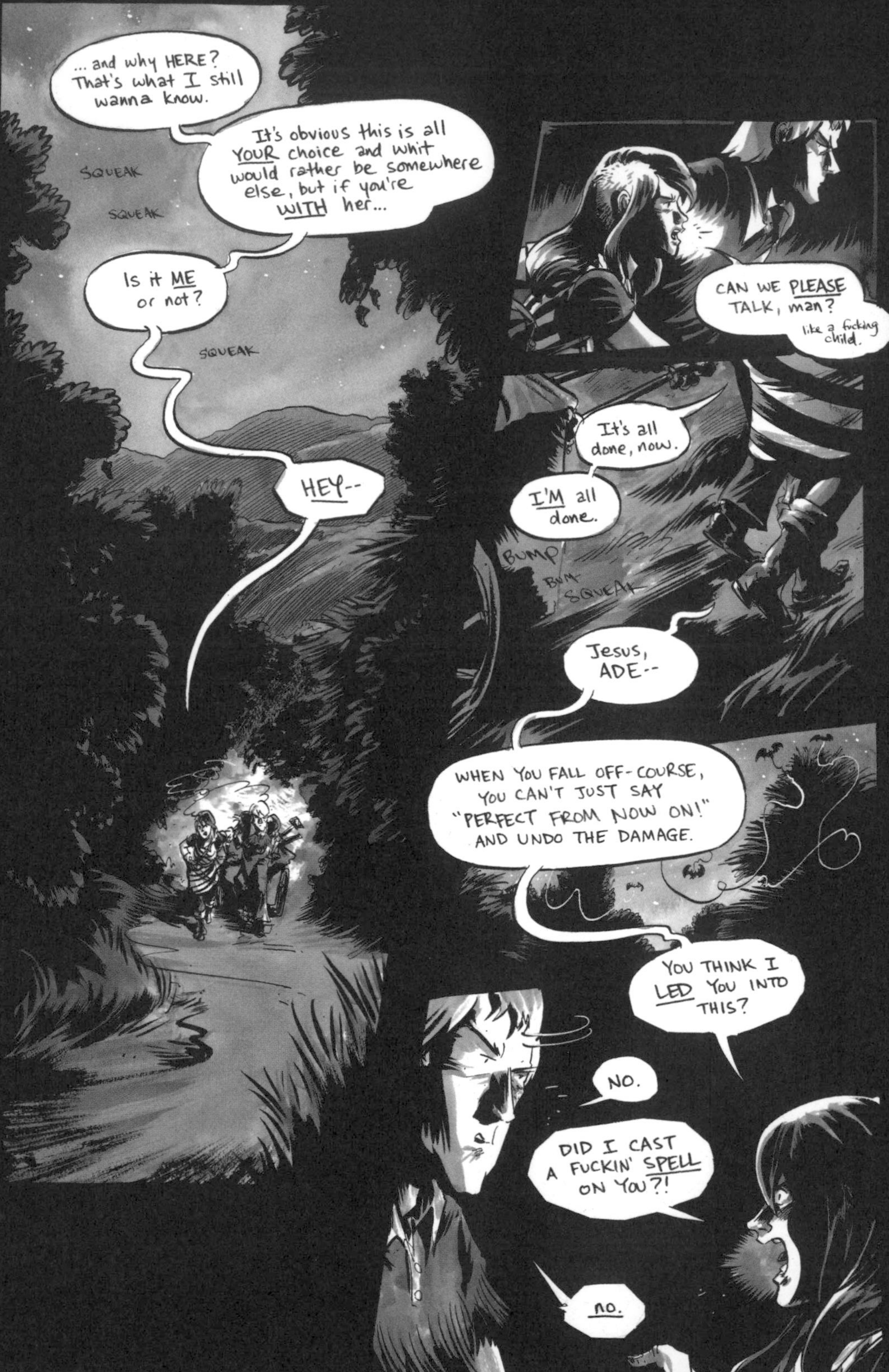

... and why HERE? That's what I still wanna know.
It's obvious this is all YOUR choice and whit would rather be somewhere else, but if you're WITH her...
SQUEAK
SQUEAK
Is it ME or not?
SQUEAK
HEY--
CAN WE PLEASE TALK, man?
like a fucking child.
It's all done, now.
I'M all done.
BUMP
BUM
SQUEAK
Jesus, ADE--
WHEN YOU FALL OFF-COURSE, YOU CAN'T JUST SAY "PERFECT FROM NOW ON!" AND UNDO THE DAMAGE.
YOU THINK I LED YOU INTO THIS?
NO.
DID I CAST A FUCKIN' SPELL ON YOU?!
no.

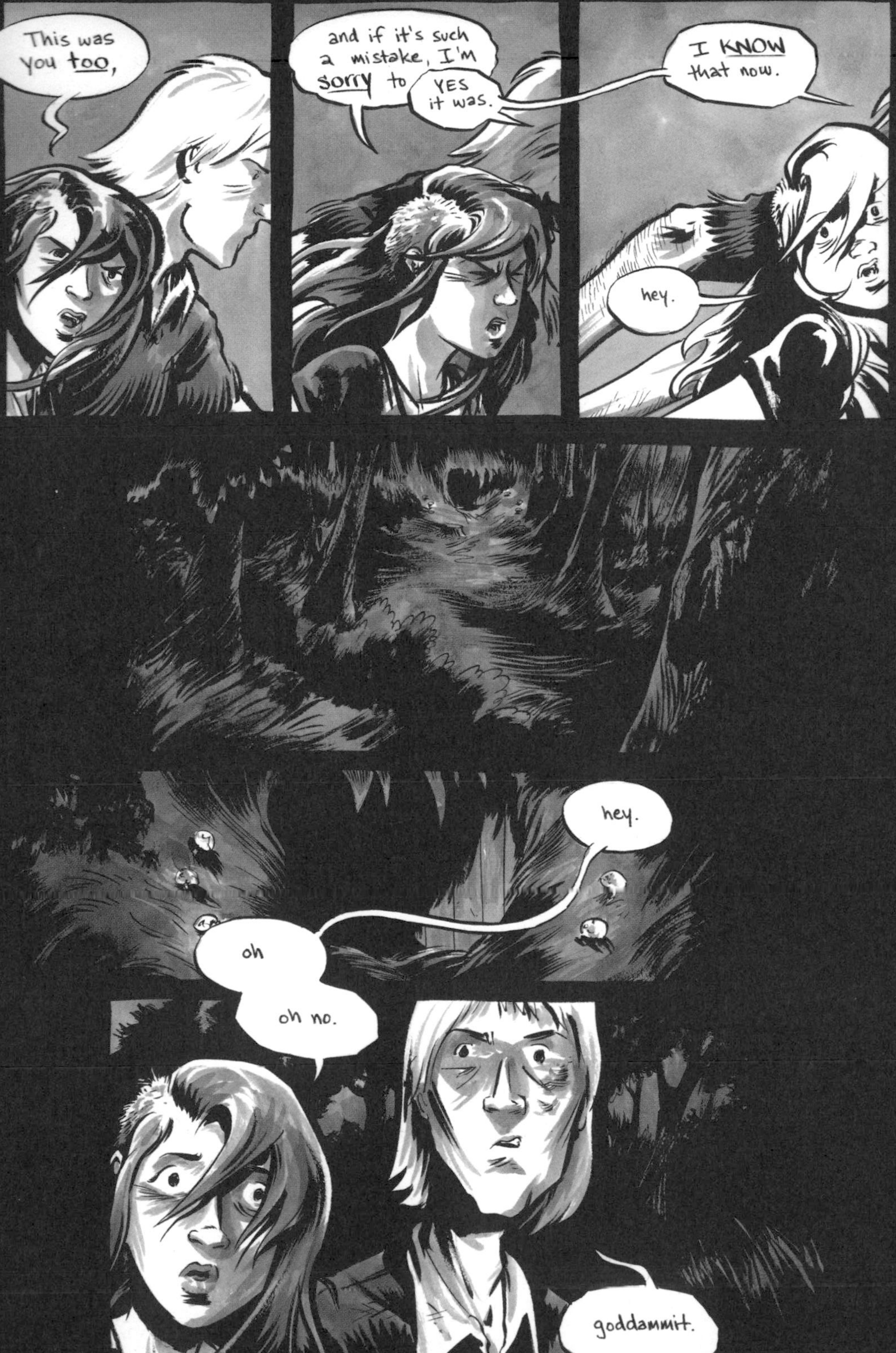
This was you too,
and if it's such a mistake, I'm sorry to
YES it was.
I KNOW that now.
hey.
hey.
oh
oh no.
goddammit.

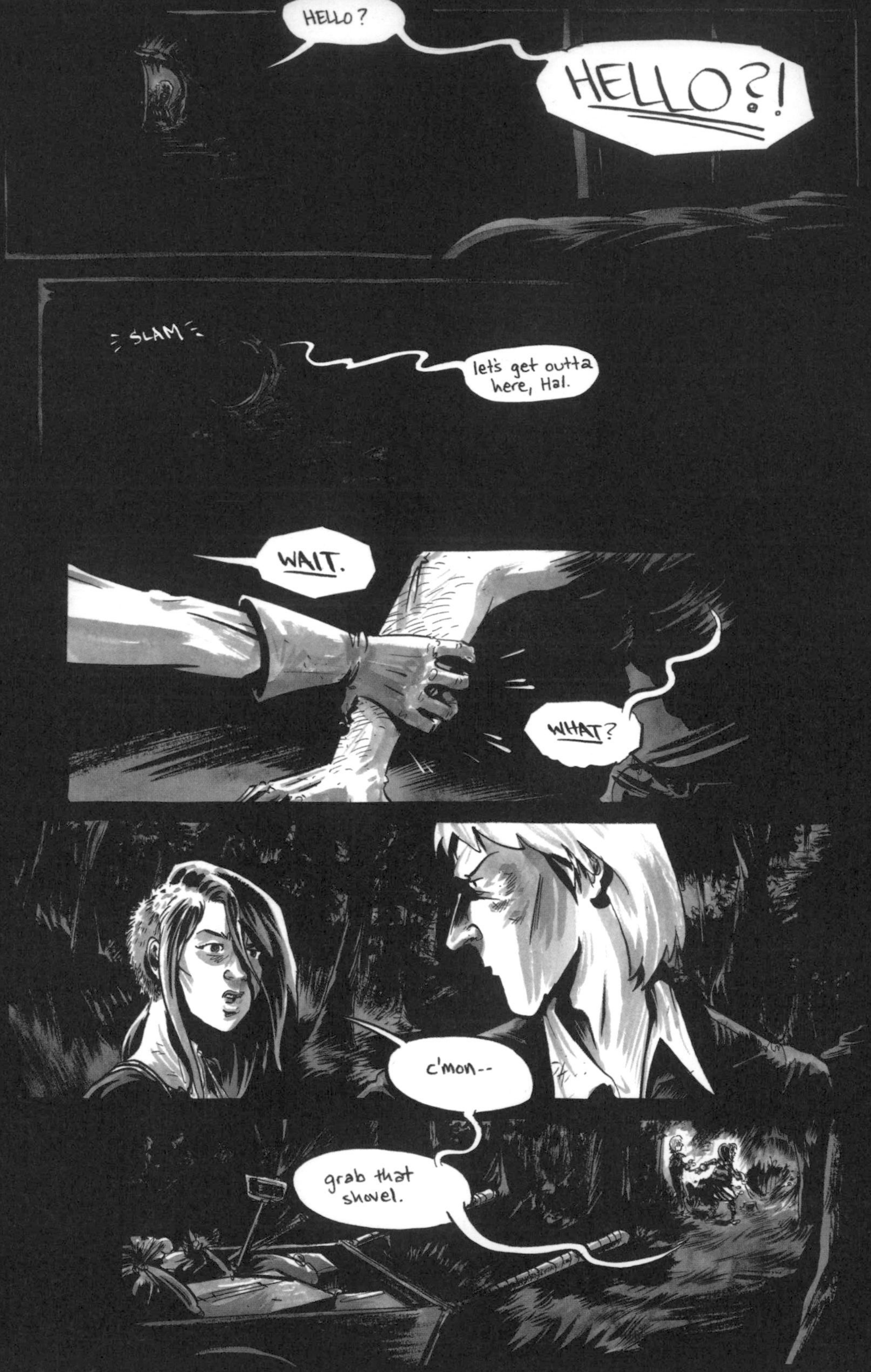
HELLO?
HELLO?!
SLAM
let's get outta here, Hal.
WAIT.
WHAT?
c'mon--
grab that shovel.

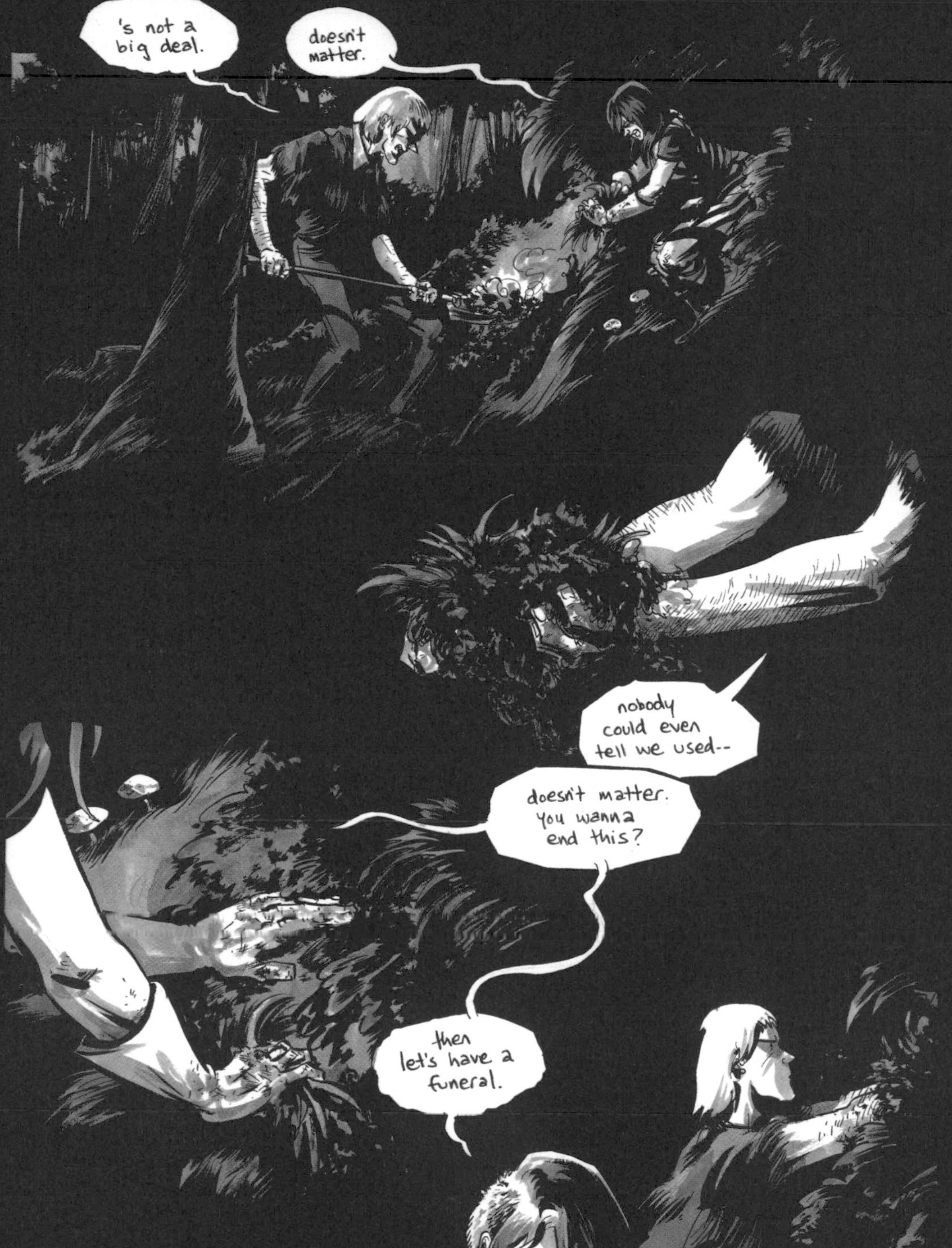

's not a big deal.
doesn't matter.
nobody could even tell we used--
doesn't matter. you wanna end this?
then let's have a funeral.

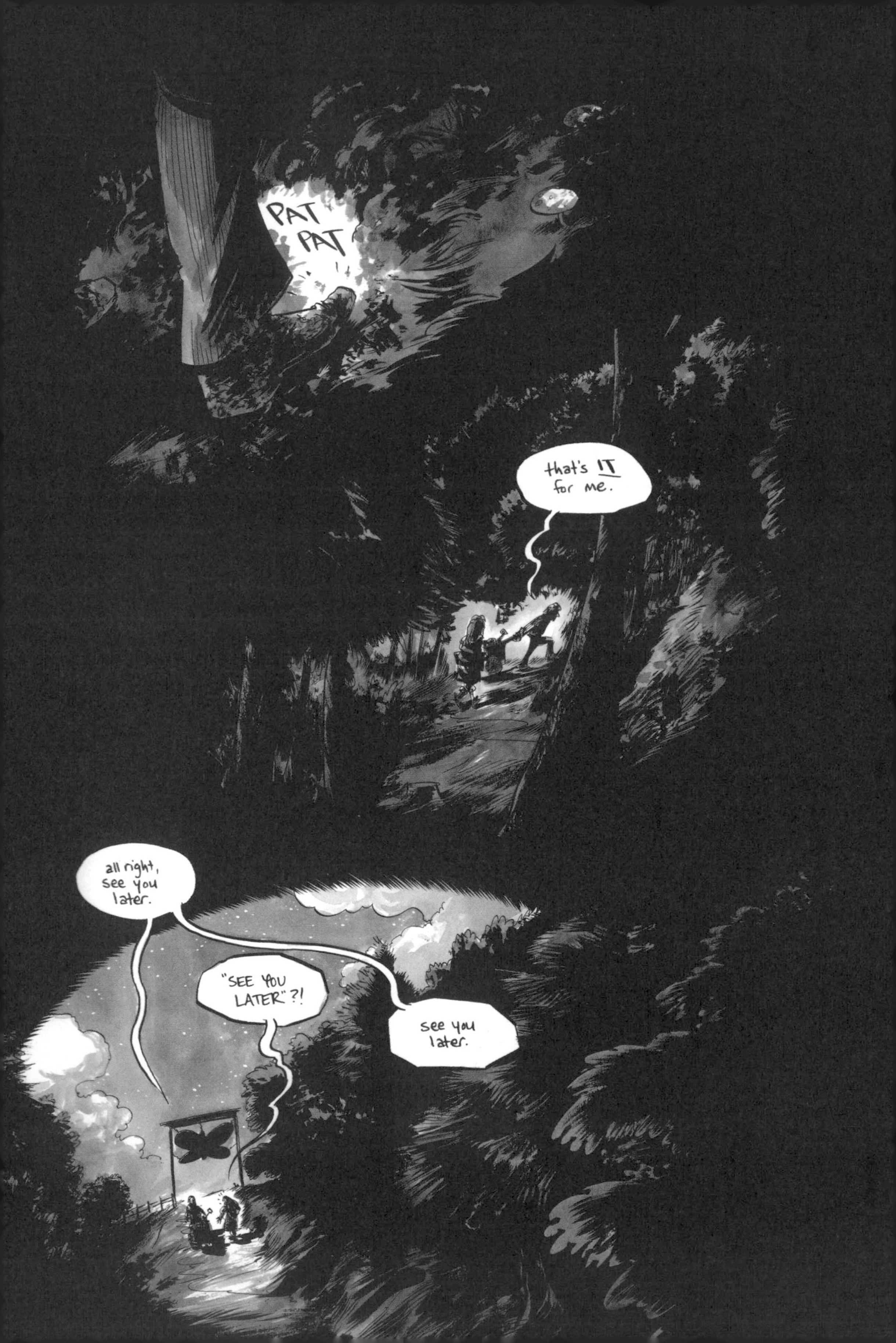
PAT PAT
that's IT for me.
all right, see you later.
see you later.
"SEE YOU LATER"?!

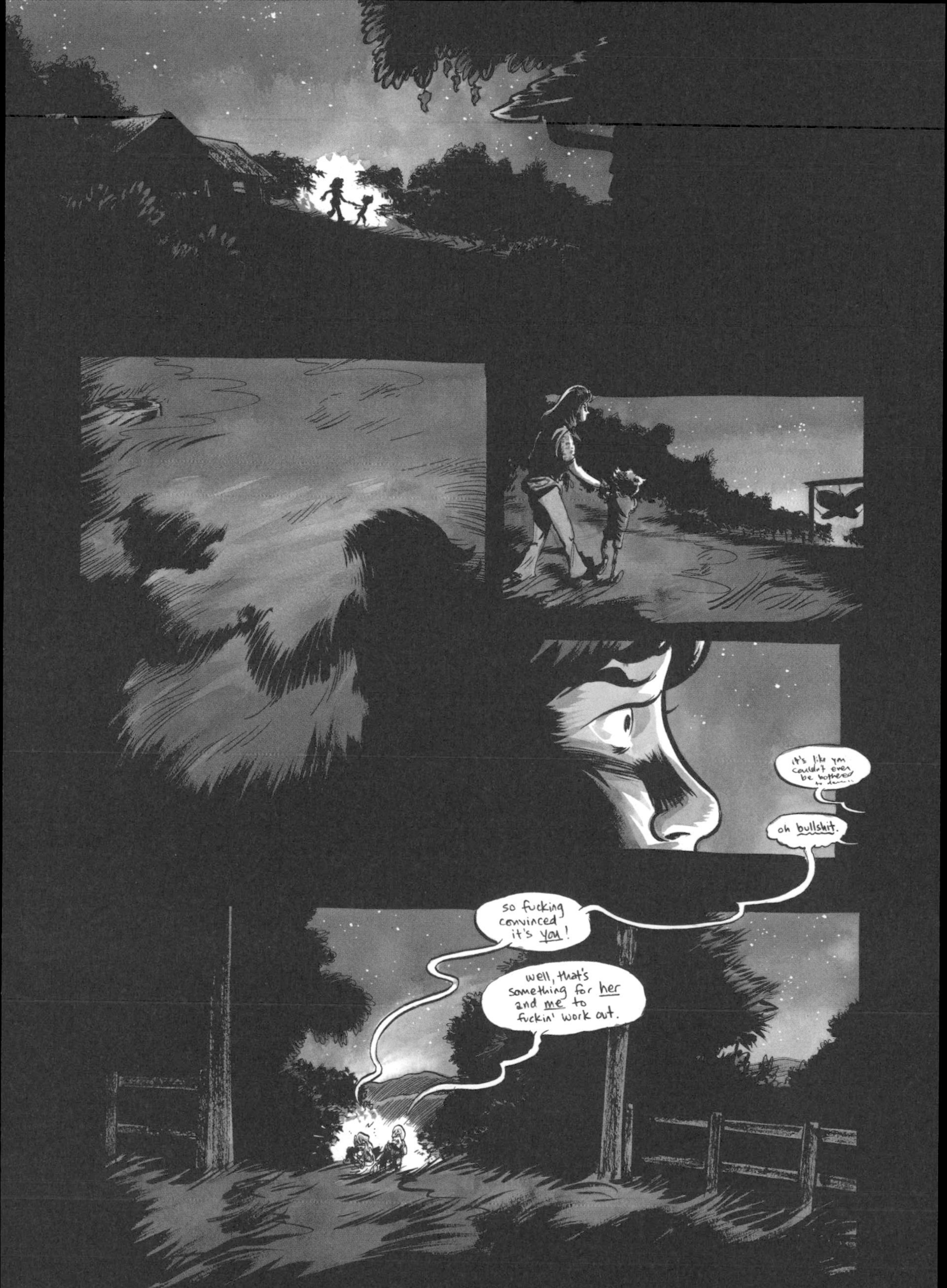
it's like you couldn't even be bothered
oh bullshit.
so fucking convinced it's you!
well, that's something for her and me to fuckin' work out.

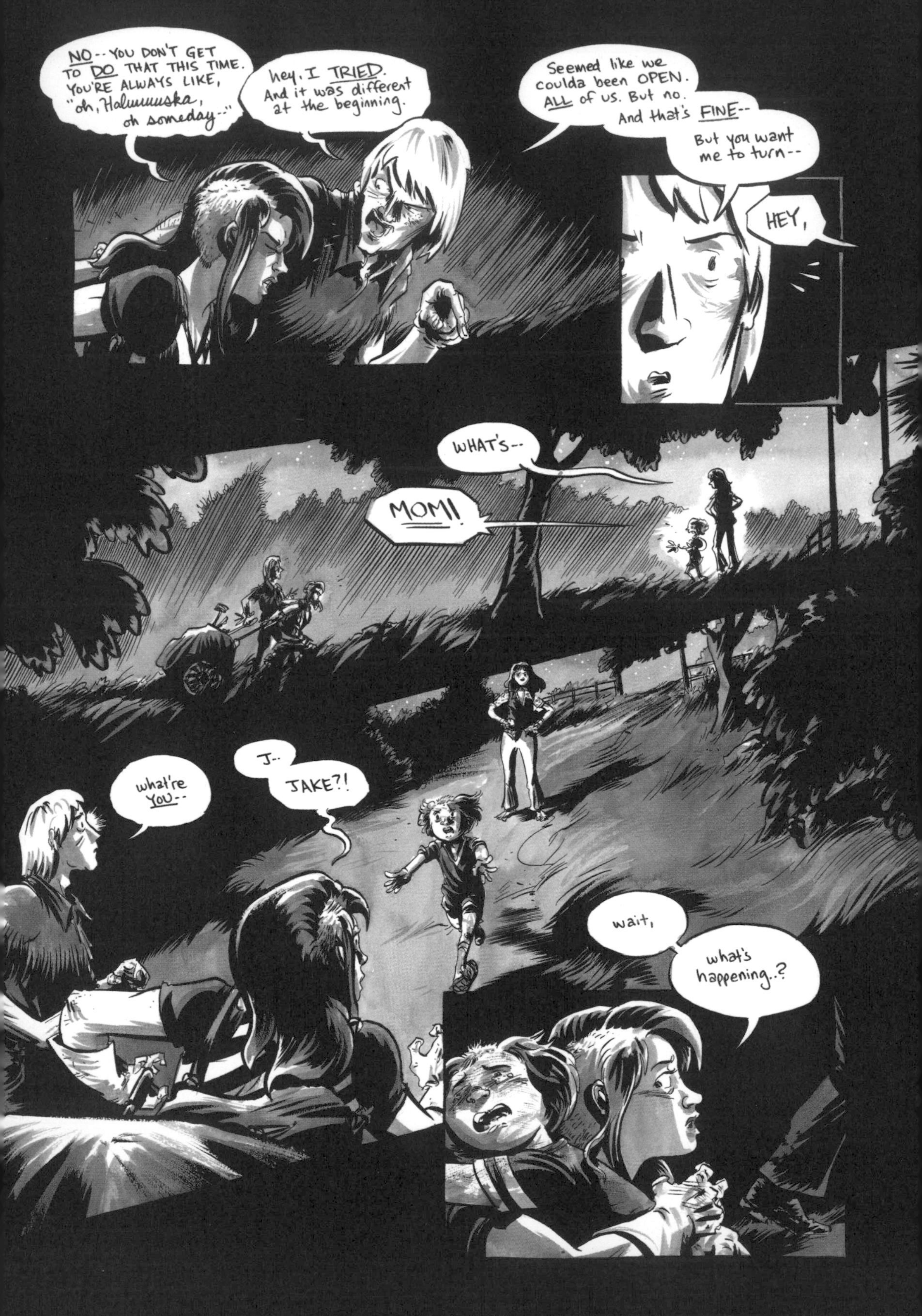
NO-- YOU DON'T GET TO DO THAT THIS TIME. YOU'RE ALWAYS LIKE, "oh, Halmmuska, oh someday--"
hey, I TRIED. And it was different at the beginning.
Seemed like we coulda been OPEN. ALL of us. But no.
And that's FINE--
But you want me to turn--
HEY,
WHAT'S--
MOM!
what're YOU--
J--
JAKE?!
wait,
what's happening..?

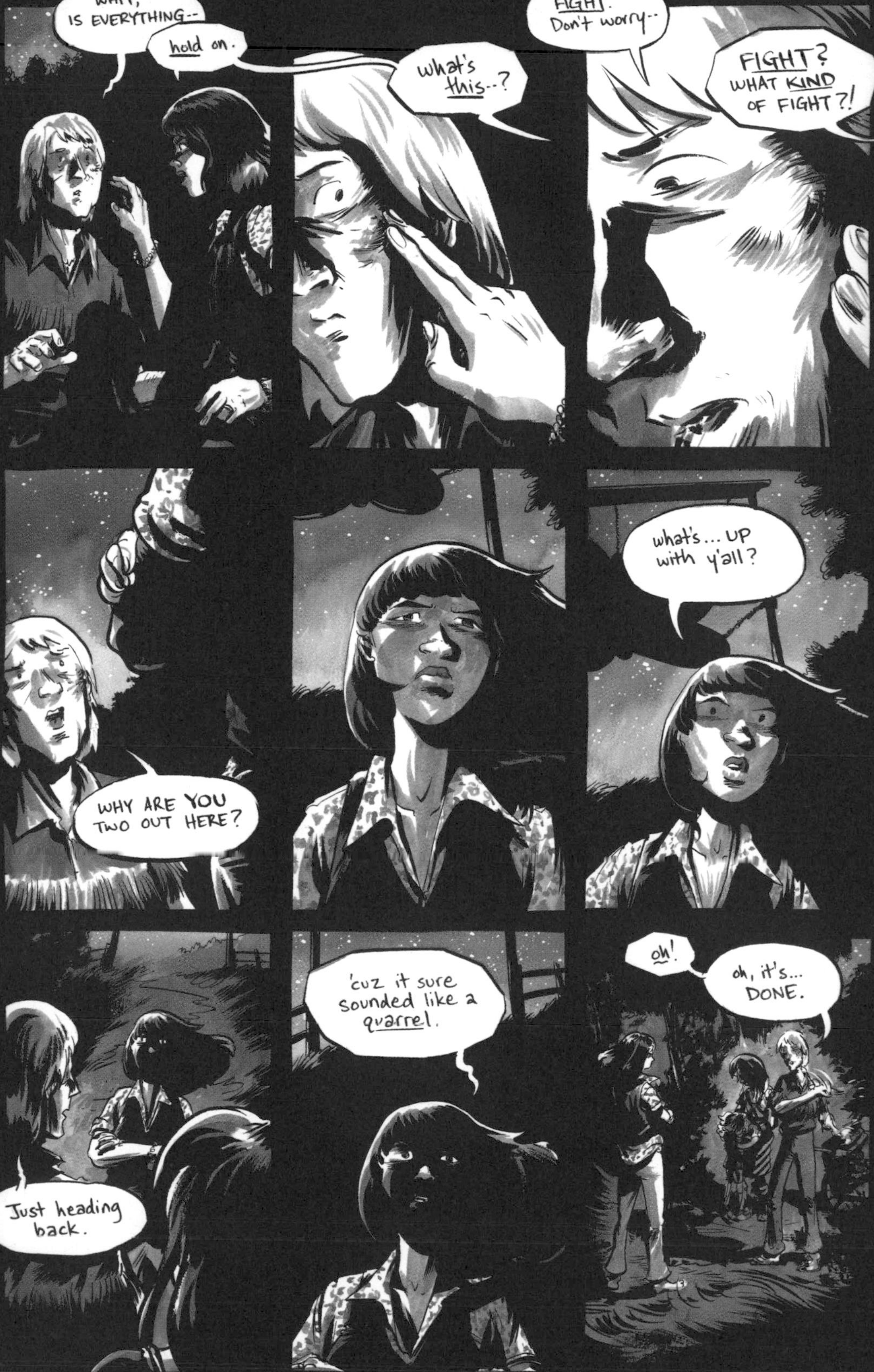
WHIT, IS EVERYTHING--
hold on.
what's this--?
FIGHT. Don't worry--
FIGHT? WHAT KIND OF FIGHT?!
WHY ARE YOU TWO OUT HERE?
what's... UP with y'all?
Just heading back.
'cuz it sure sounded like a quarrel.
oh!
oh, it's... DONE.

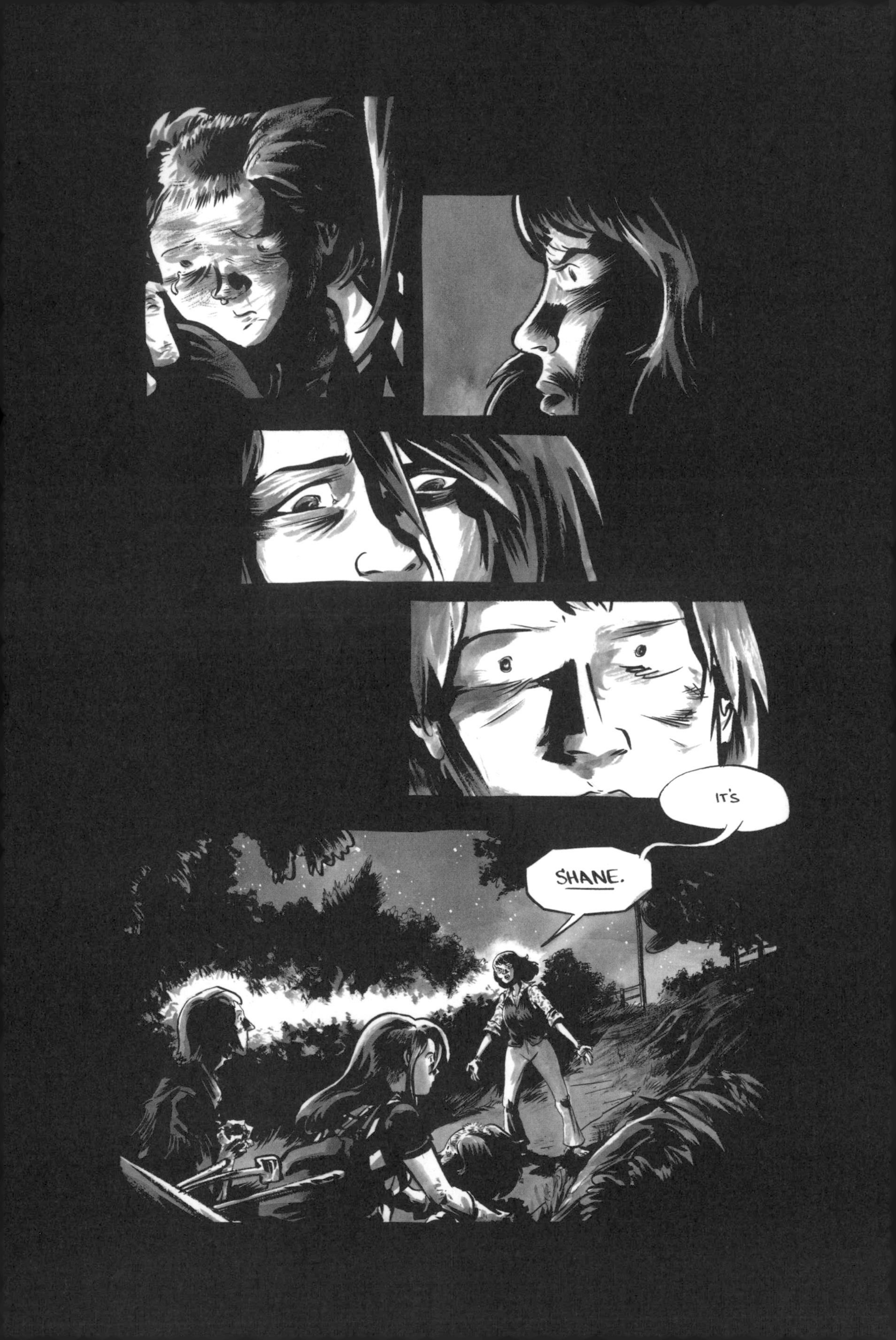
IT'S
SHANE.

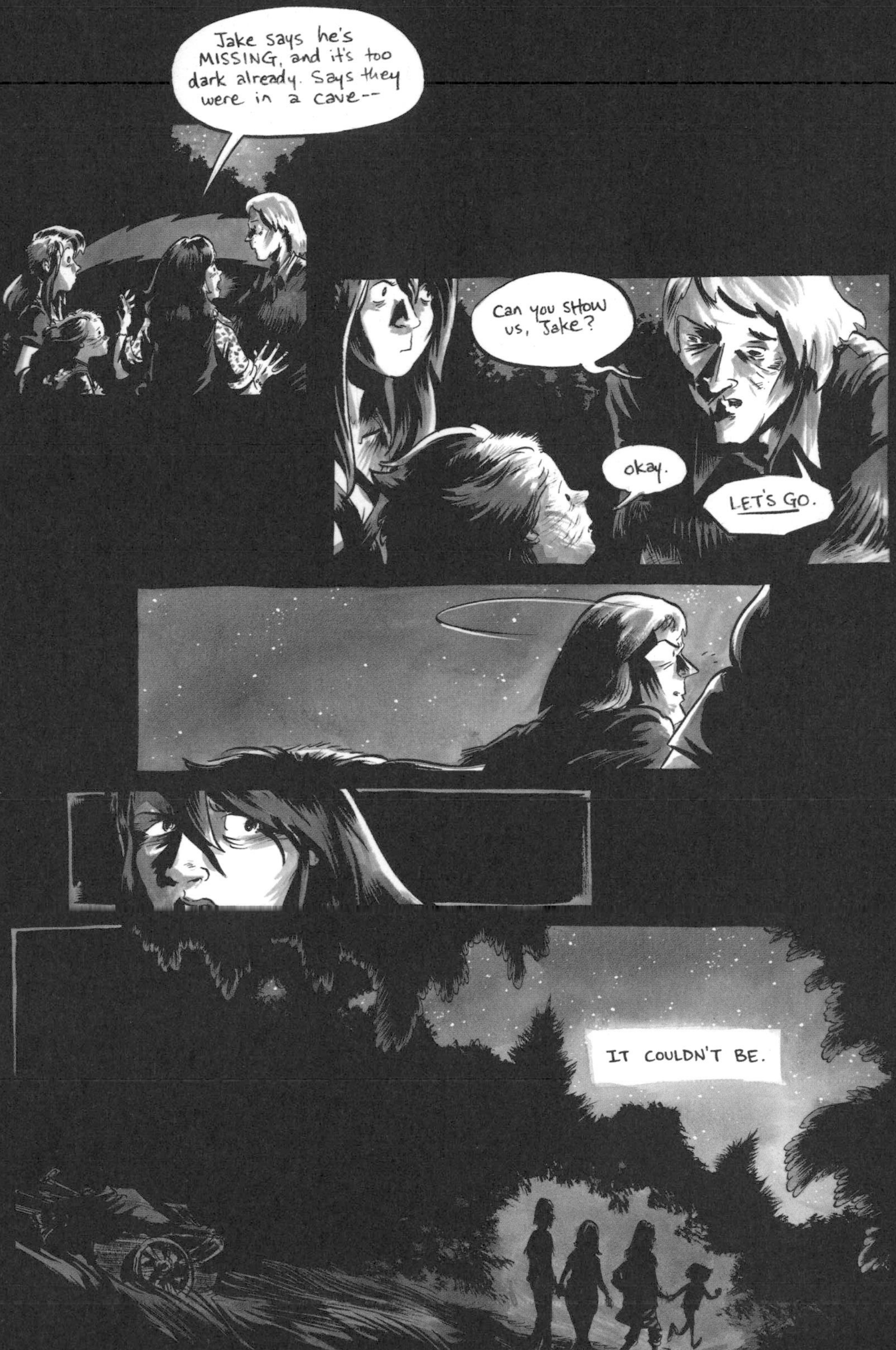
Jake says he's MISSING, and it's too dark already. Says they were in a cave--
Can you SHOW us, Jake?
okay.
LET'S GO.
IT COULDN'T BE.

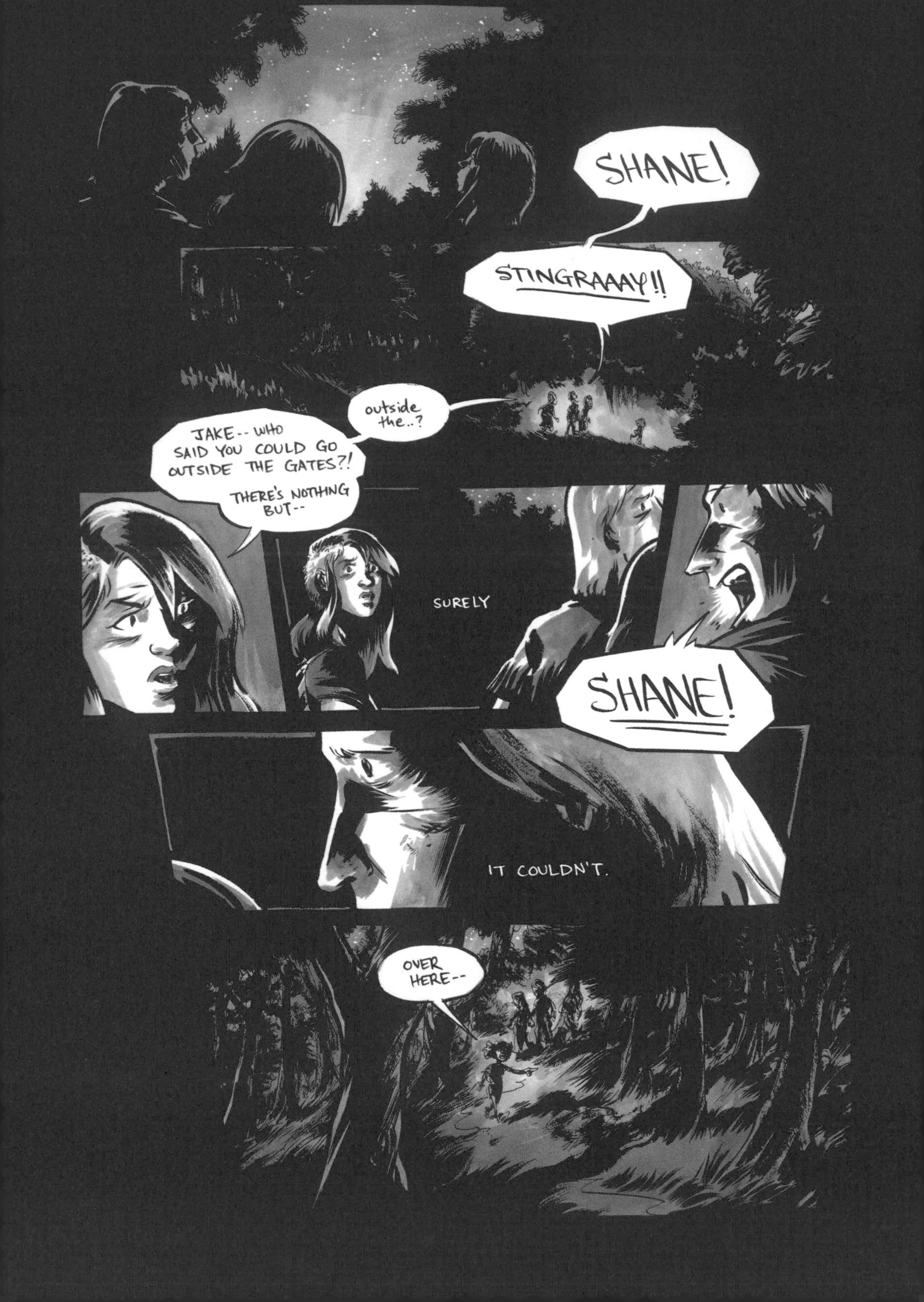
SHANE!
STINGRAAAY!!
outside the..?
JAKE-- WHO SAID YOU COULD GO OUTSIDE THE GATES?!
THERE'S NOTHING BUT--
SURELY
SHANE!
IT COULDN'T.
OVER HERE--

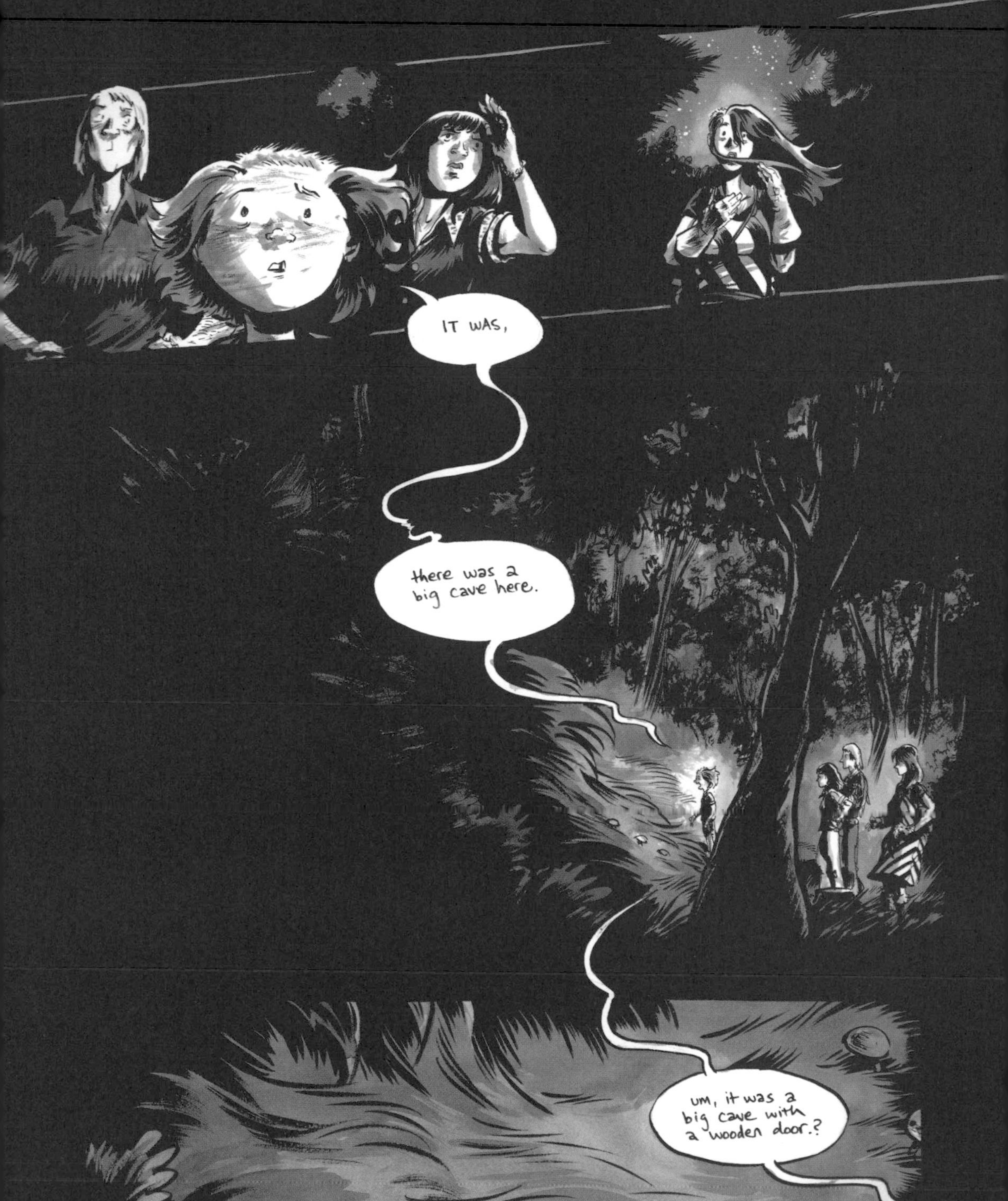

IT WAS,
there was a big cave here.
um, it was a big cave with a wooden door.?

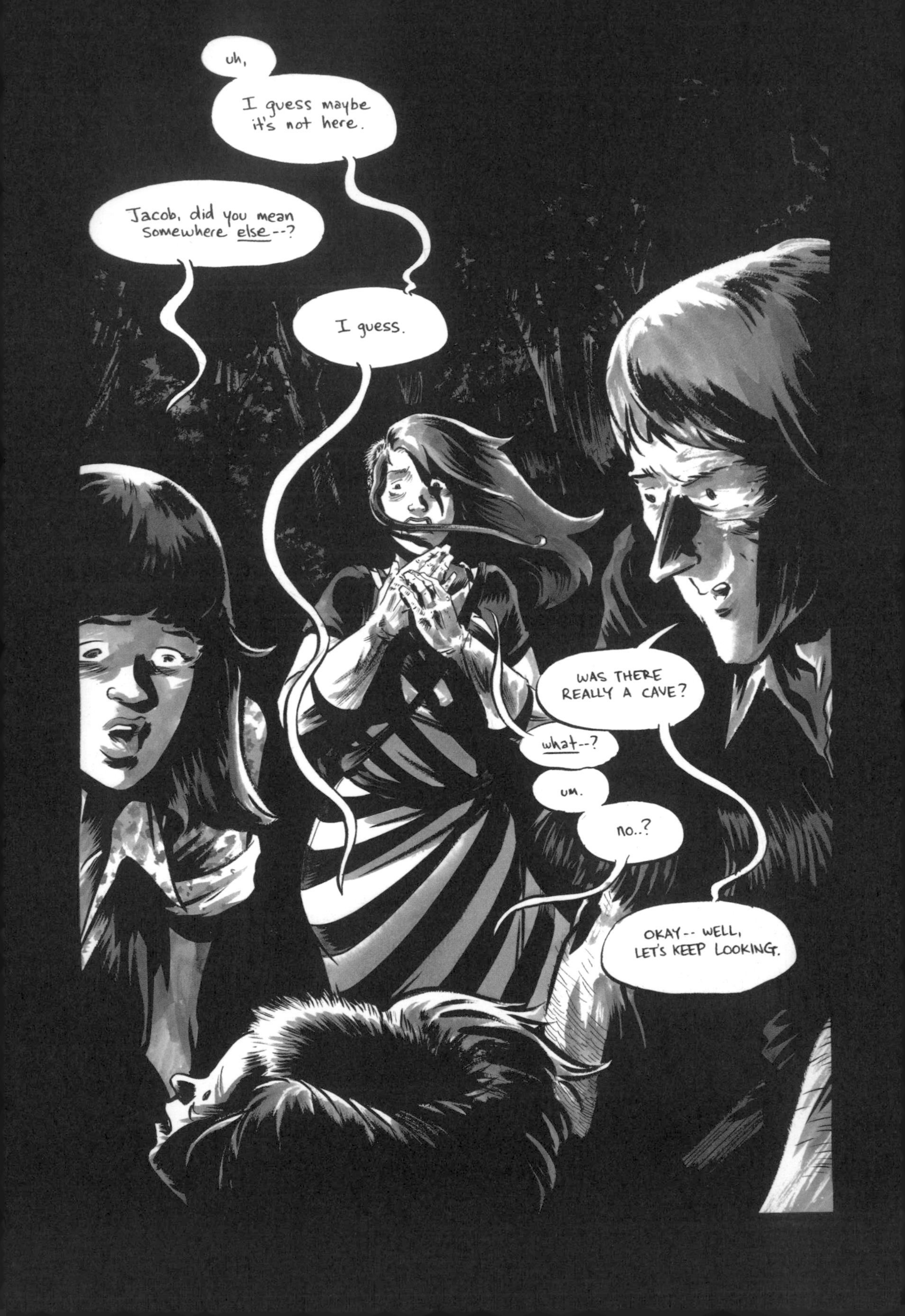
uh,
I guess maybe it's not here.
Jacob, did you mean somewhere else--?
I guess.
WAS THERE REALLY A CAVE?
what--?
um.
no..?
OKAY-- WELL, LET'S KEEP LOOKING.

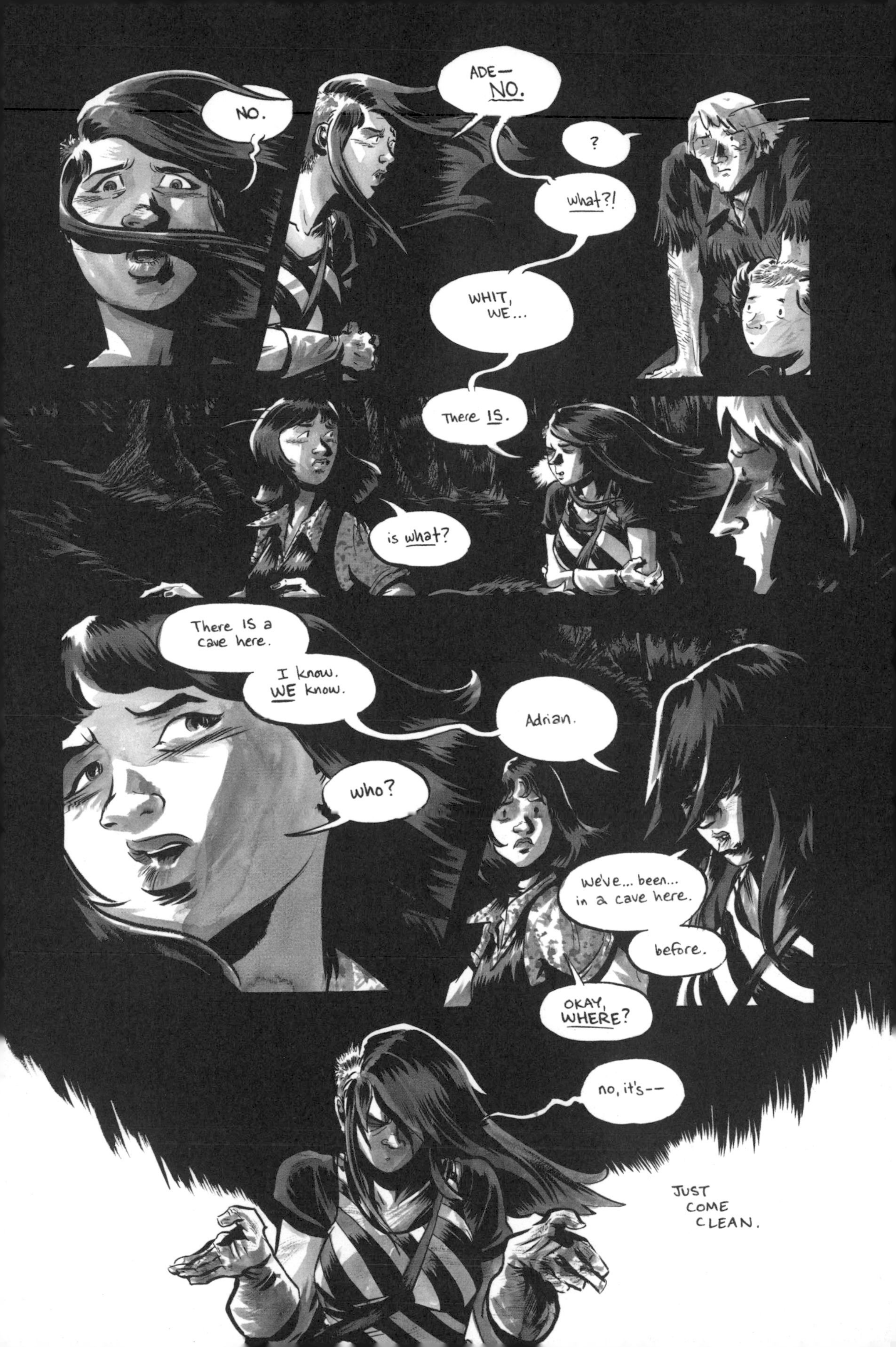
NO.
ADE—
NO.
?
what?!
WHIT,
WE...
There IS.
is what?
There IS a cave here.
I know. WE know.
Adrian.
who?
we've... been... in a cave here.
before.
OKAY, WHERE?
no, it's--
JUST COME CLEAN.

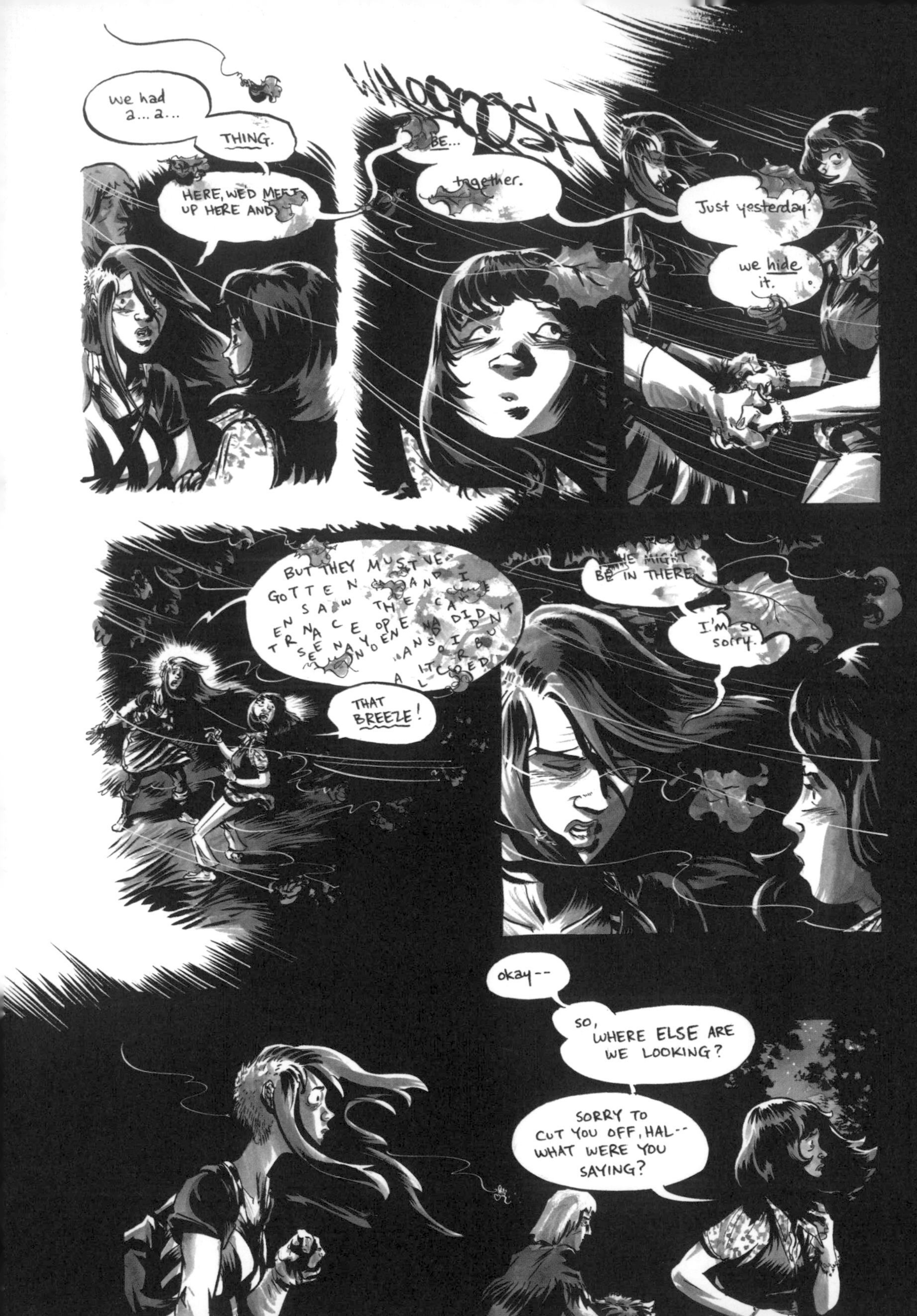

we had a... a...
THING.
HERE, WE'D MEET UP HERE AND
WHOOOOSH
BE...
together.
Just yesterday.
we hide it.
BUT THEY MUST'VE
THAT BREEZE!
BE IN THERE
I'M SO sorry.
okay--
SO, WHERE ELSE ARE WE LOOKING?
SORRY TO CUT YOU OFF, HAL-- WHAT WERE YOU SAYING?

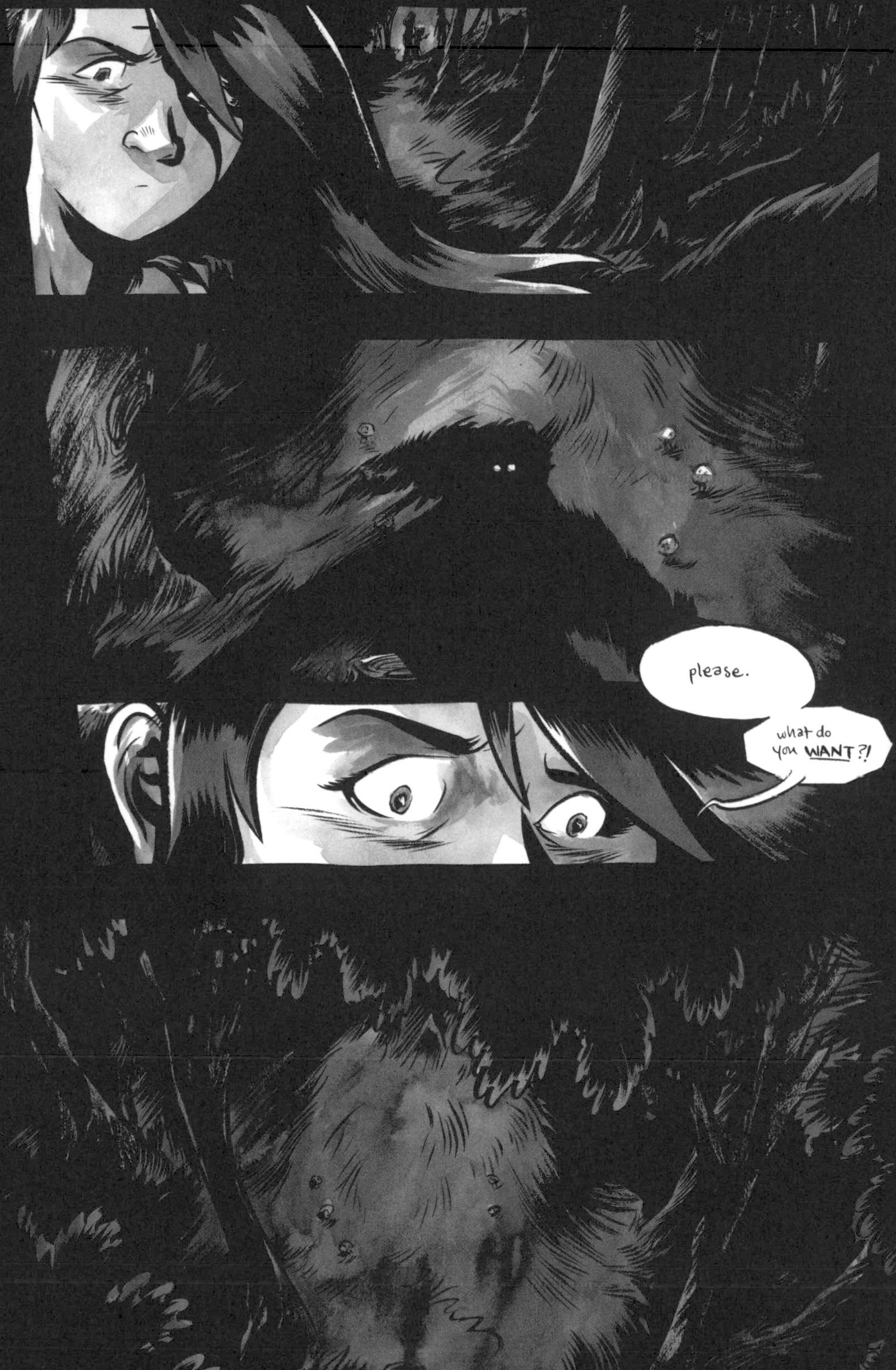
please.
what do you WANT?!

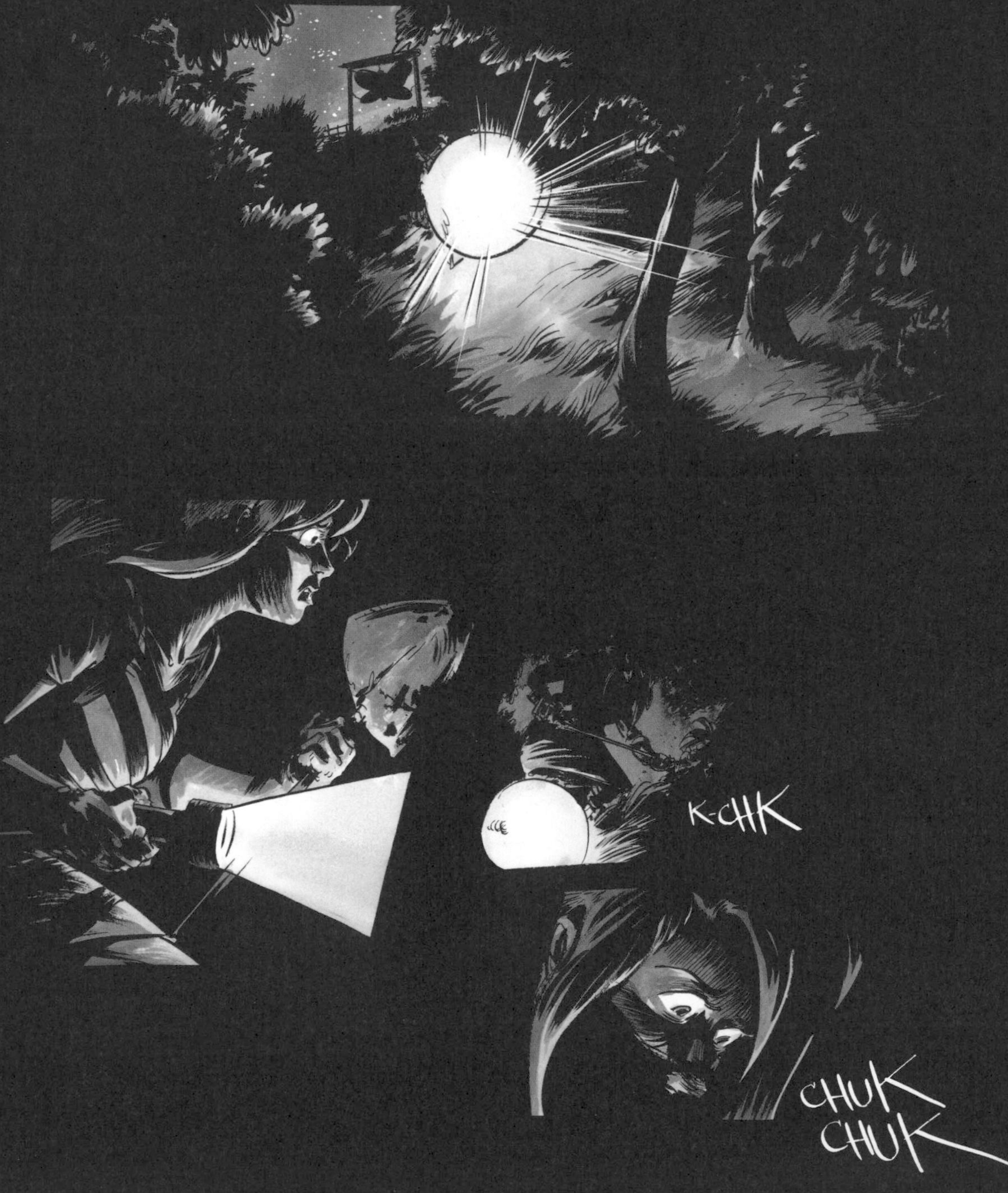
K-CHK
CHUK
CHUK

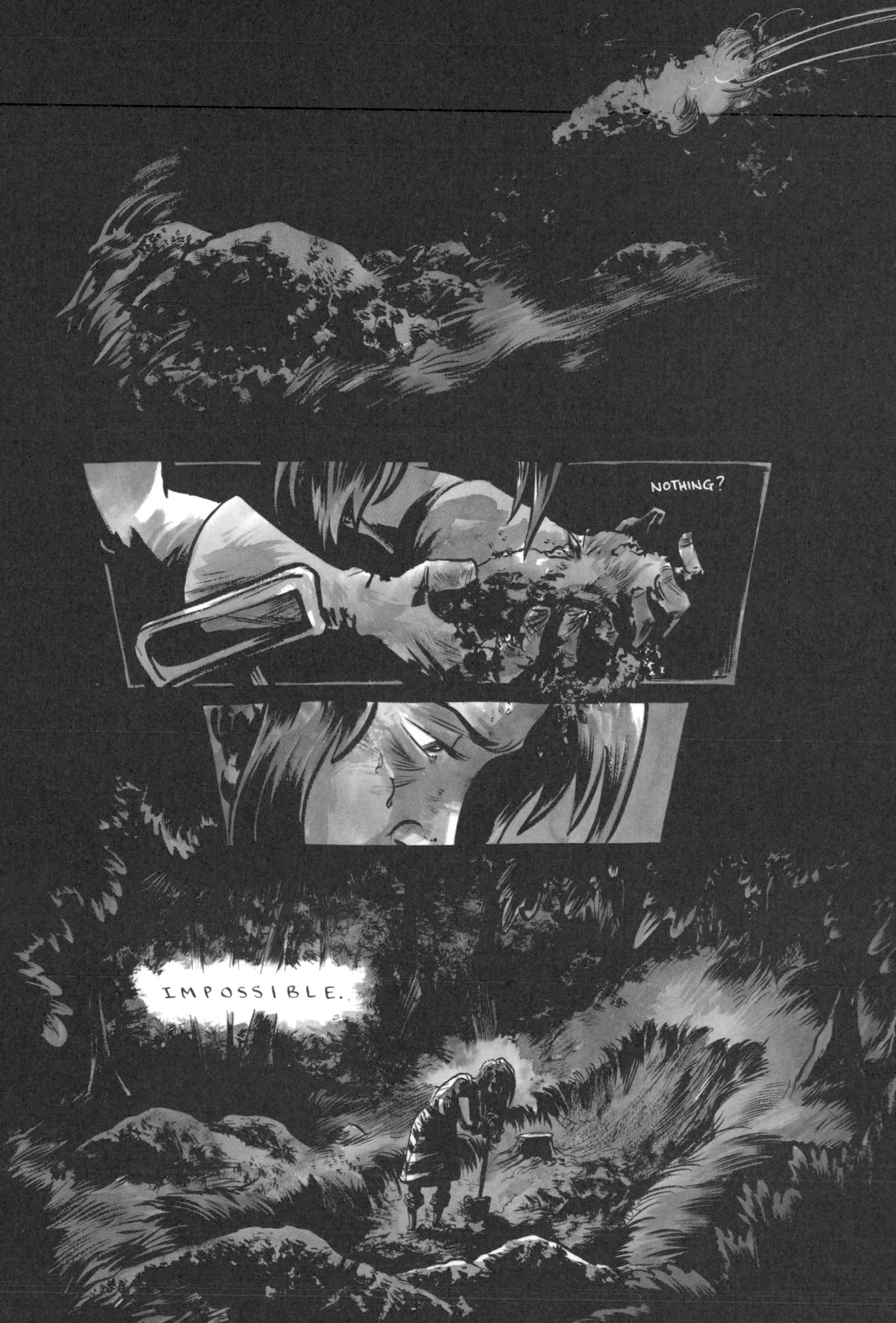
NOTHING?
IMPOSSIBLE.

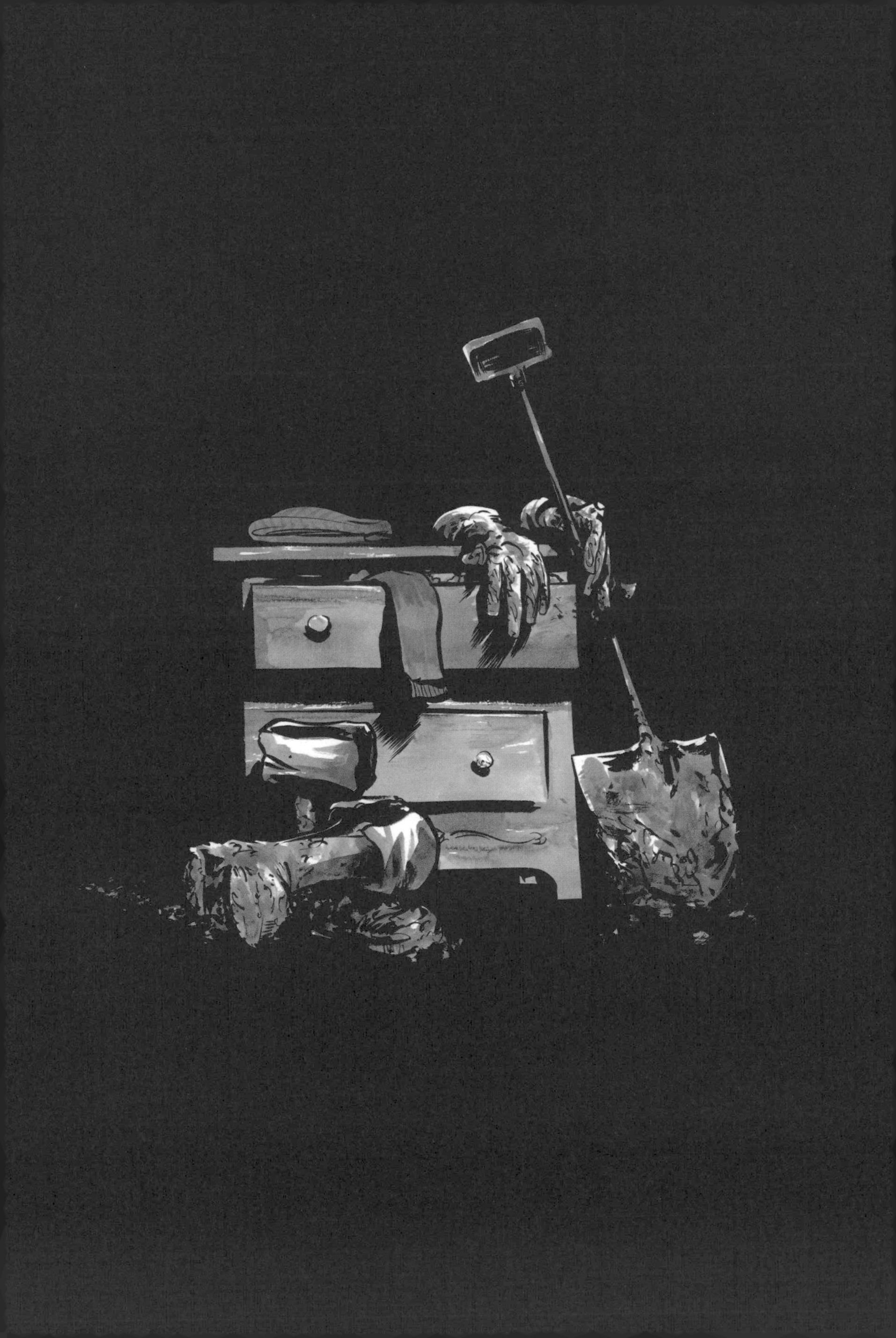

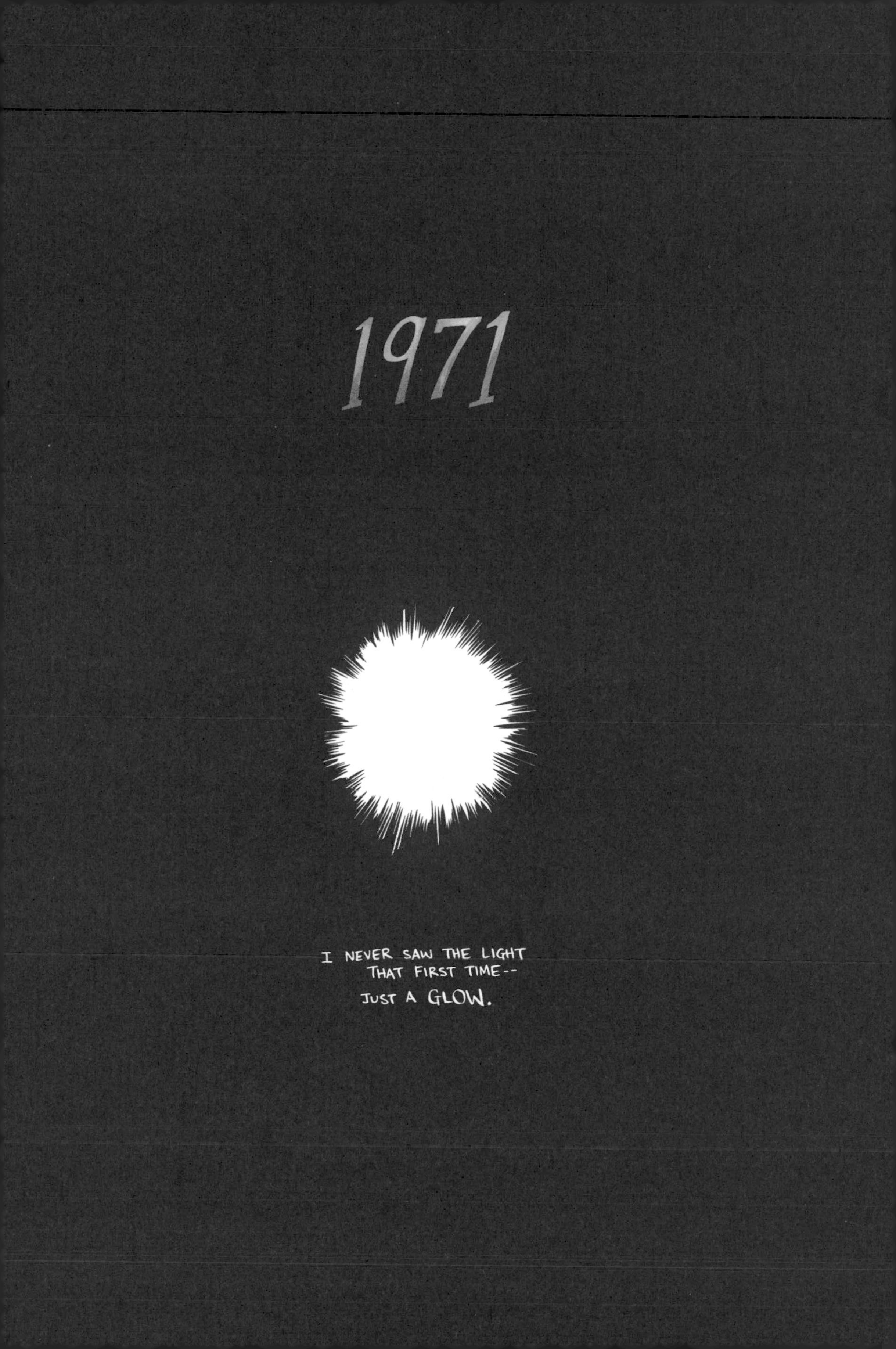
1971
I NEVER SAW THE LIGHT
THAT FIRST TIME--
JUST A GLOW.

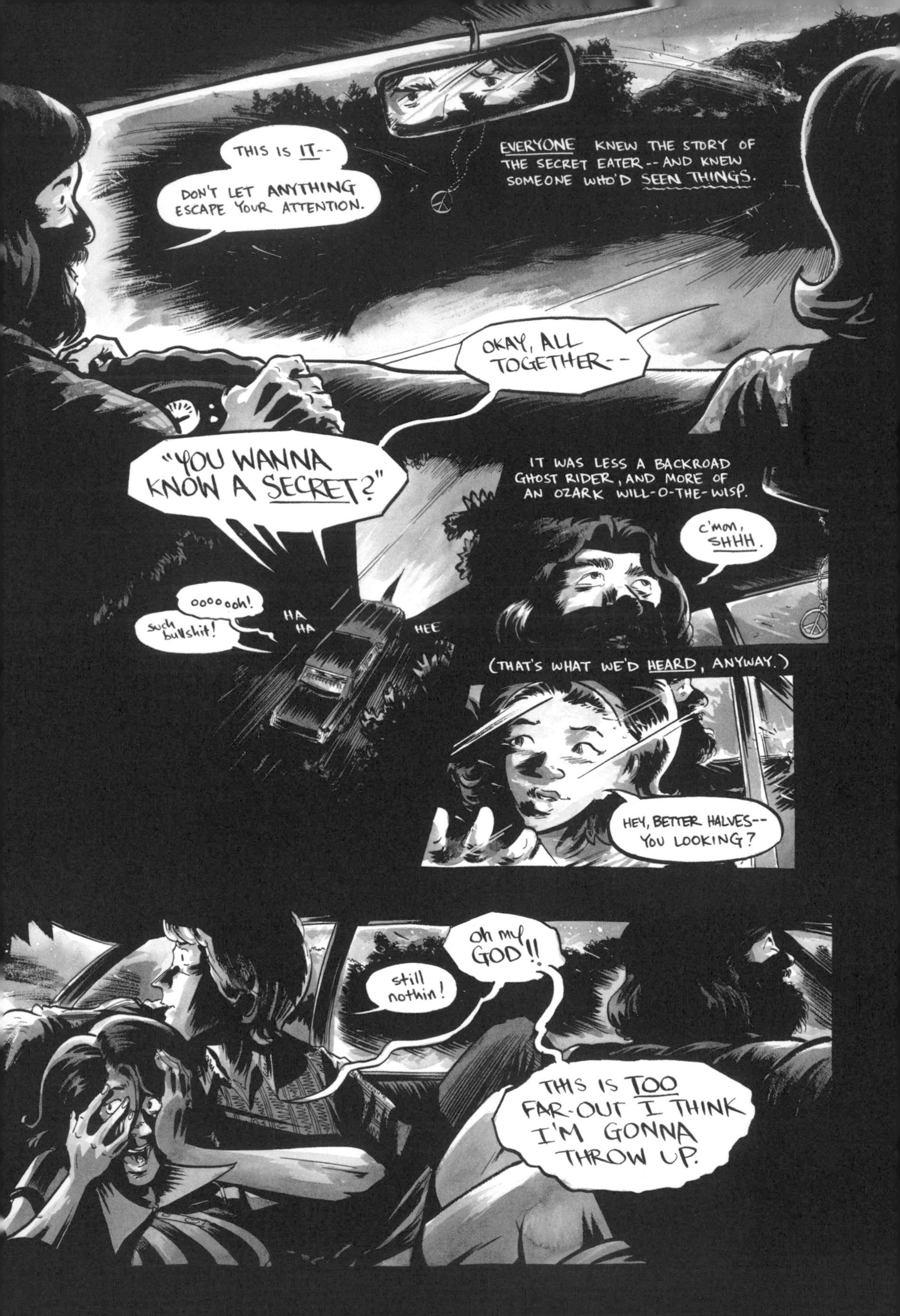
THIS IS IT--
DON'T LET ANYTHING ESCAPE YOUR ATTENTION.
EVERYONE KNEW THE STORY OF THE SECRET EATER--AND KNEW SOMEONE WHO'D SEEN THINGS.
OKAY, ALL TOGETHER--
"YOU WANNA KNOW A SECRET?"
IT WAS LESS A BACKROAD GHOST RIDER, AND MORE OF AN OZARK WILL-O-THE-WISP.
c'mon, SHHH.
ooooooh!
such bullshit!
HA HA
HEE
(THAT'S WHAT WE'D HEARD, ANYWAY.)
HEY, BETTER HALVES--YOU LOOKING?
oh my GOD!!
still nothin!
THIS IS TOO FAR-OUT I THINK I'M GONNA THROW UP.

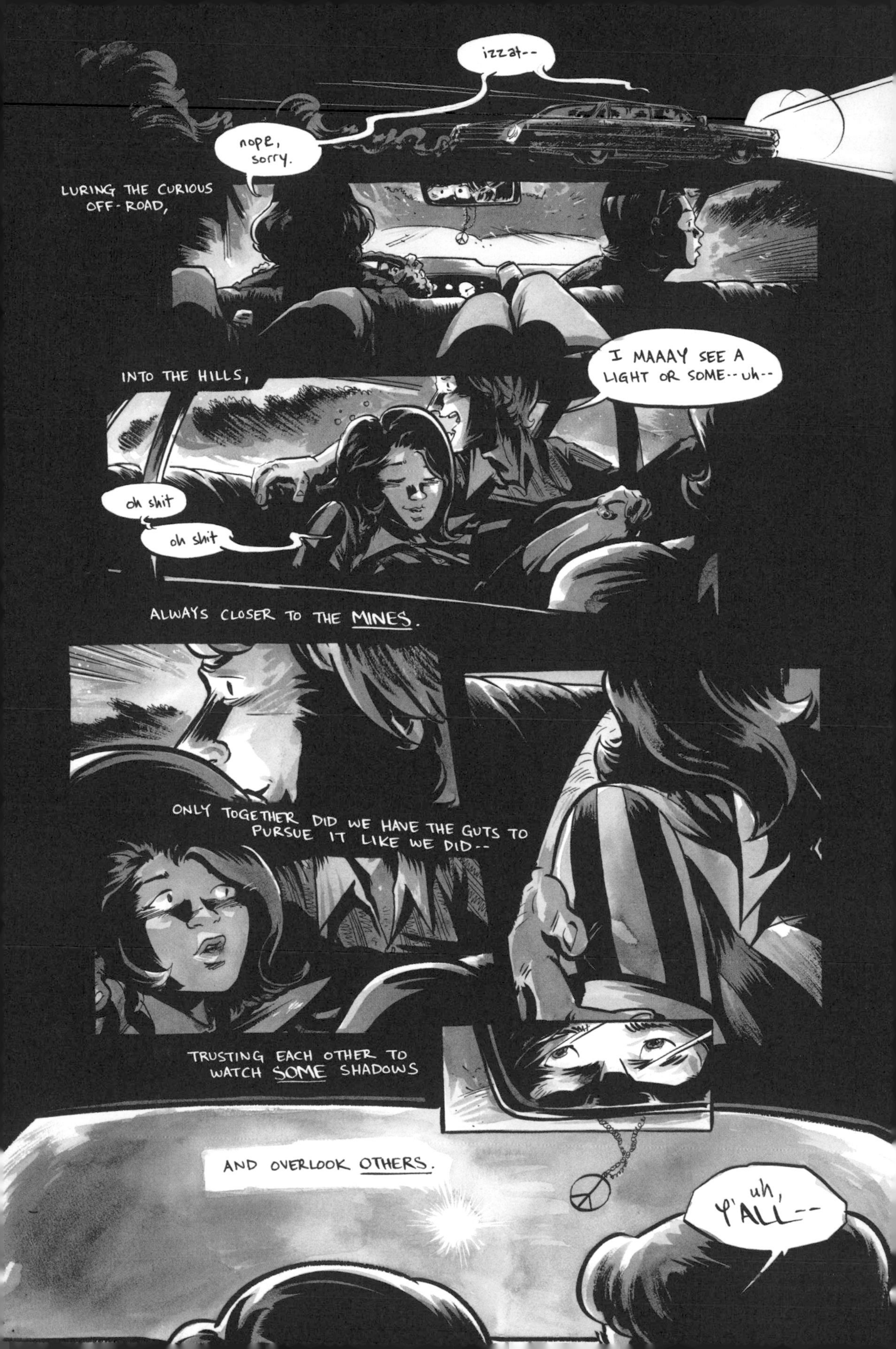

izzat--
nope, sorry.
LURING THE CURIOUS OFF-ROAD,
INTO THE HILLS,
I MAAAY SEE A LIGHT OR SOME--uh--
oh shit
oh shit
ALWAYS CLOSER TO THE MINES.
ONLY TOGETHER DID WE HAVE THE GUTS TO PURSUE IT LIKE WE DID--
TRUSTING EACH OTHER TO WATCH SOME SHADOWS
AND OVERLOOK OTHERS.
uh, Y'ALL--

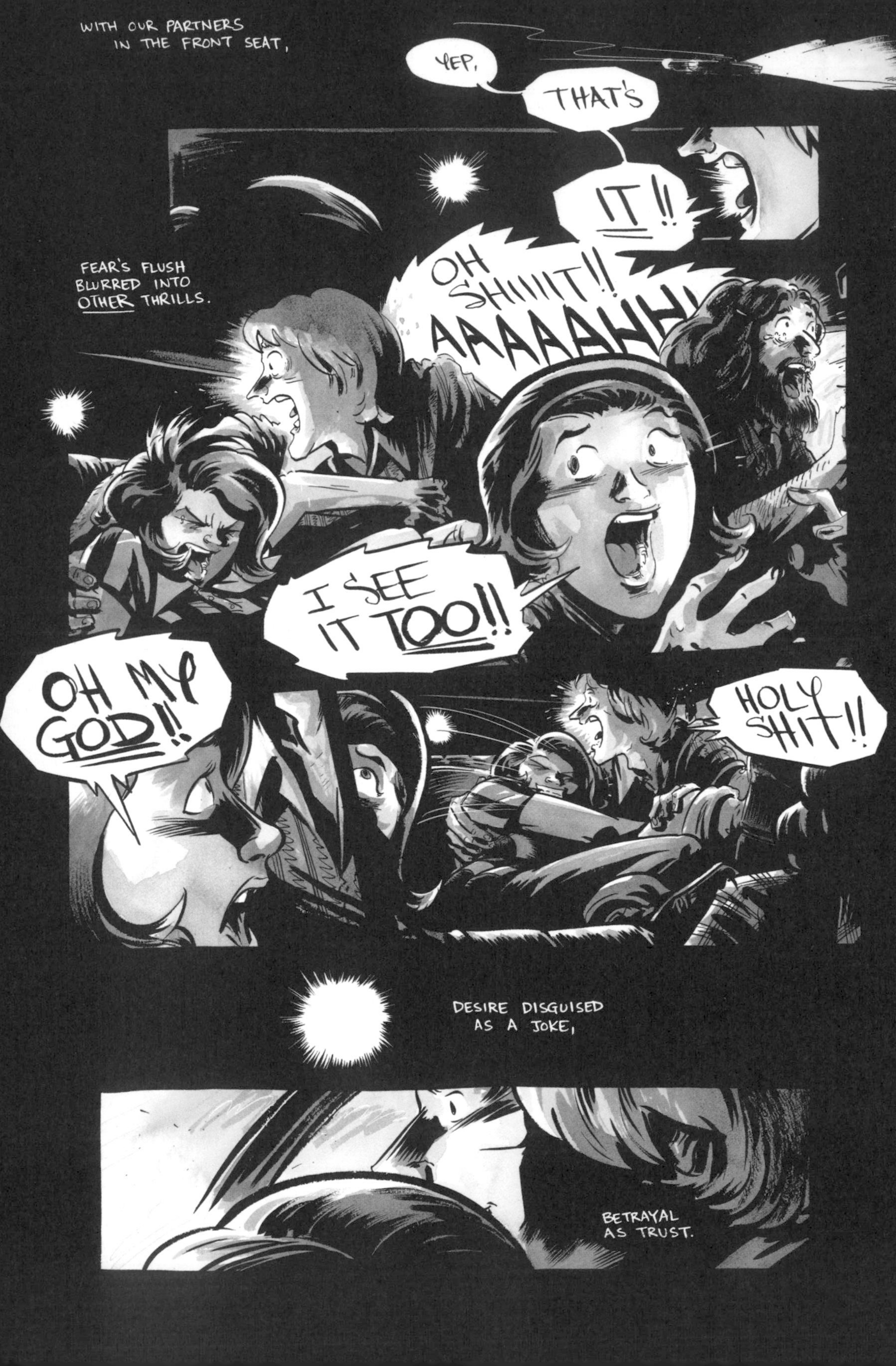
WITH OUR PARTNERS IN THE FRONT SEAT,
YEP,
THAT'S
IT!!
FEAR'S FLUSH BLURRED INTO OTHER THRILLS.
OH SHIIIIT!!
AAAAAHH
I SEE IT TOO!!
OH MY GOD!!
HOLY SHIT!!
DESIRE DISGUISED AS A JOKE,
BETRAYAL AS TRUST.

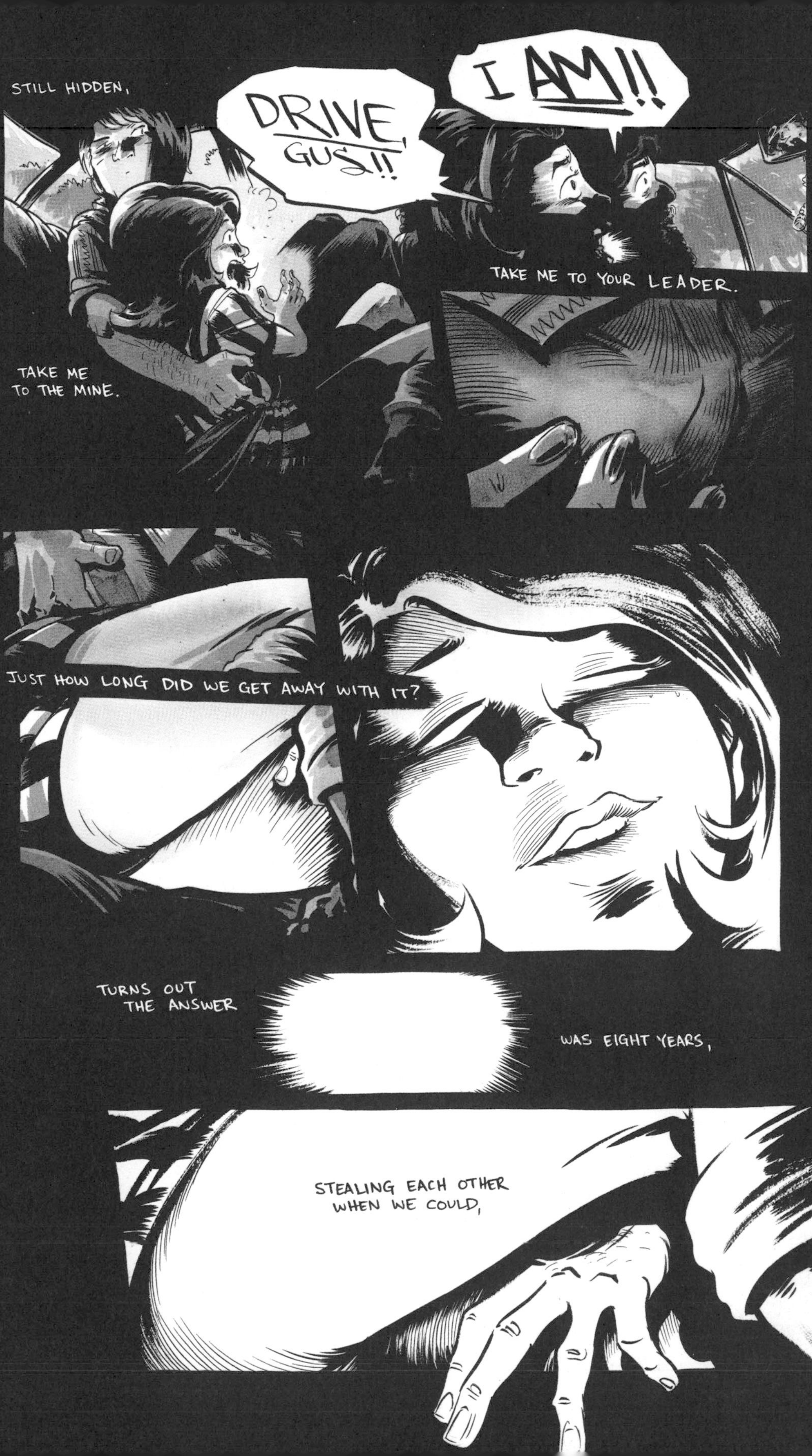
STILL HIDDEN,
DRIVE, GUS!!
I AM!!
TAKE ME TO YOUR LEADER.
TAKE ME TO THE MINE.
JUST HOW LONG DID WE GET AWAY WITH IT?
TURNS OUT THE ANSWER
WAS EIGHT YEARS,
STEALING EACH OTHER WHEN WE COULD,

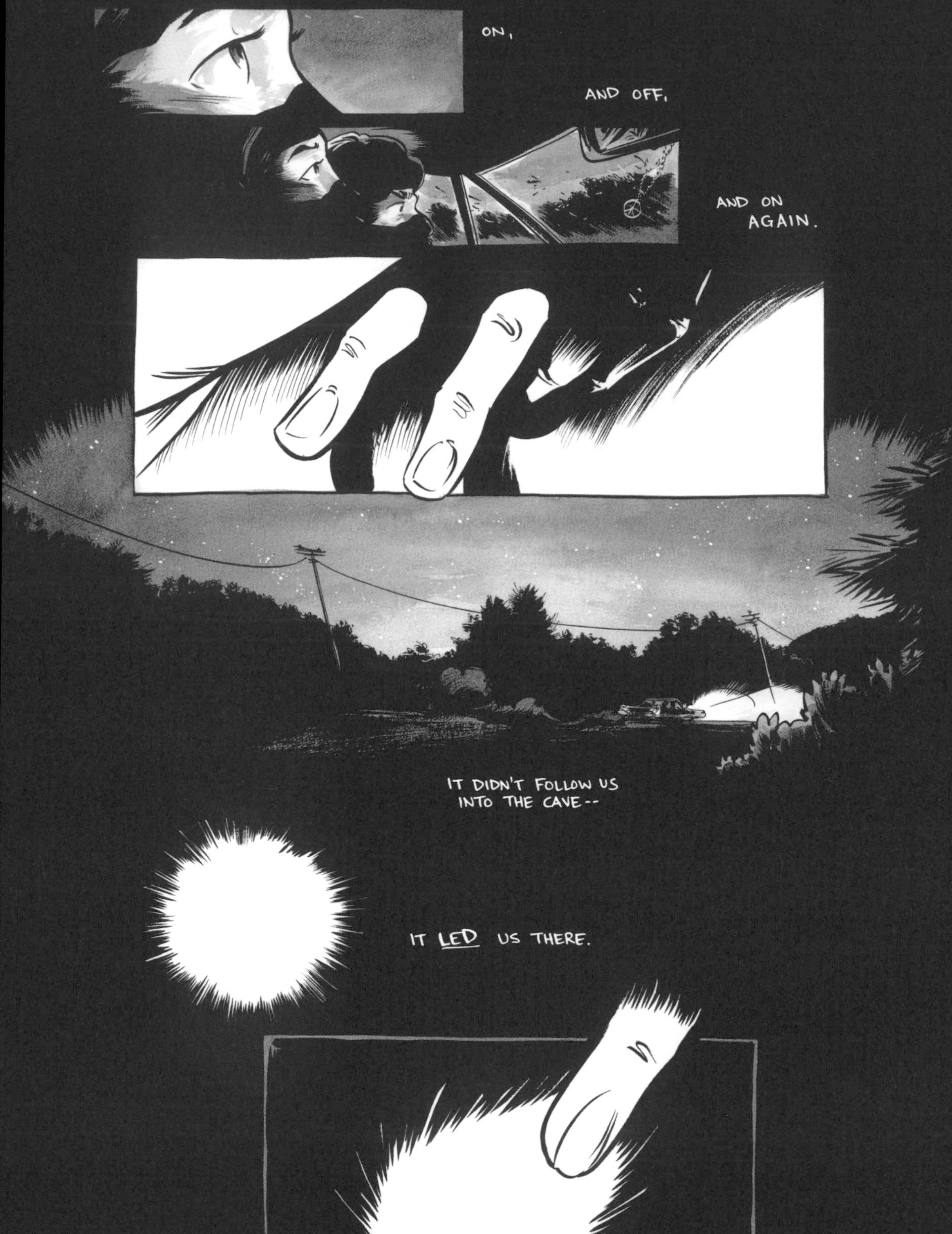
ON,
AND OFF,
AND ON AGAIN.
IT DIDN'T FOLLOW US INTO THE CAVE--
IT LED US THERE.

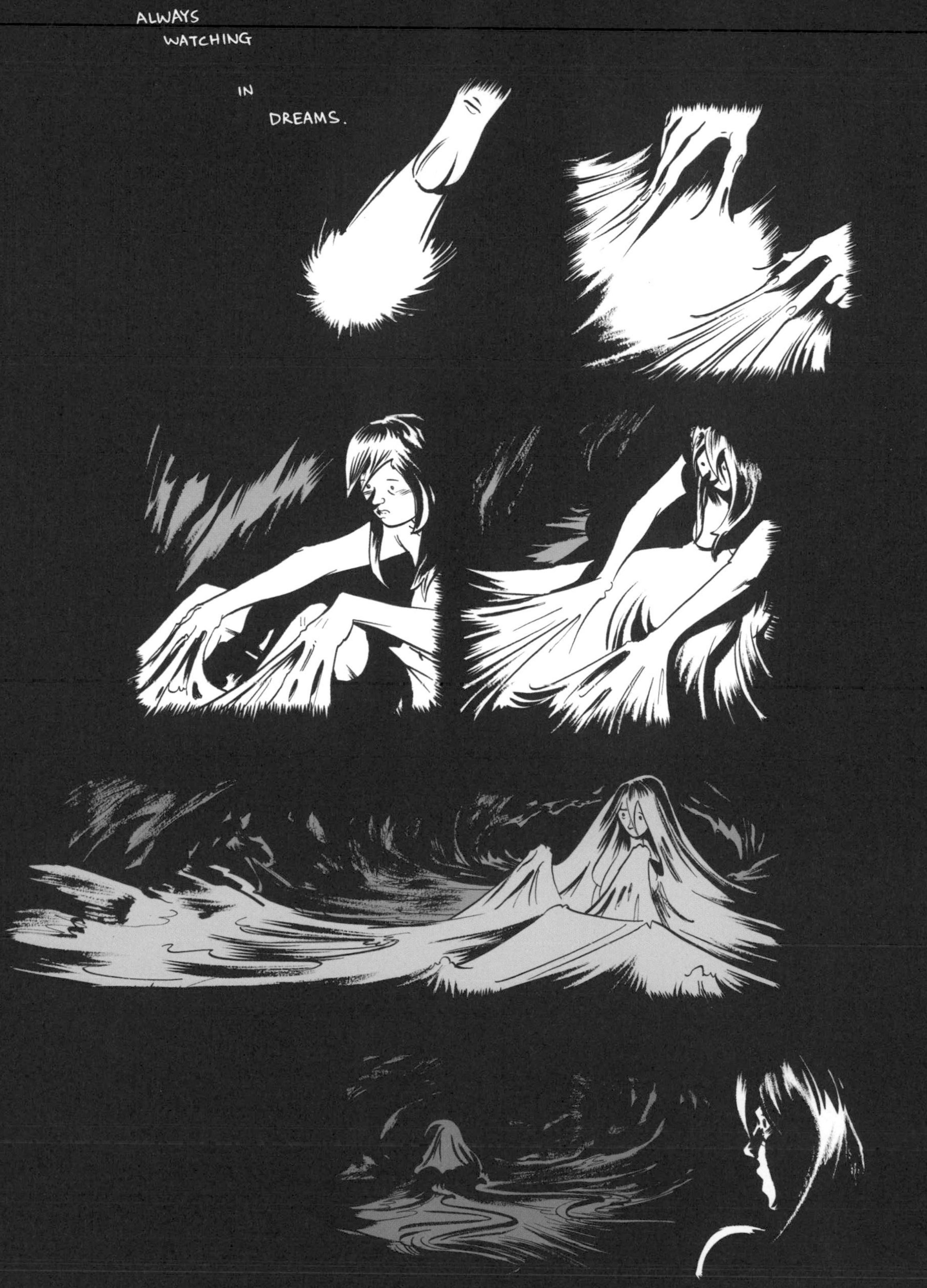
ALWAYS
WATCHING
IN
DREAMS.

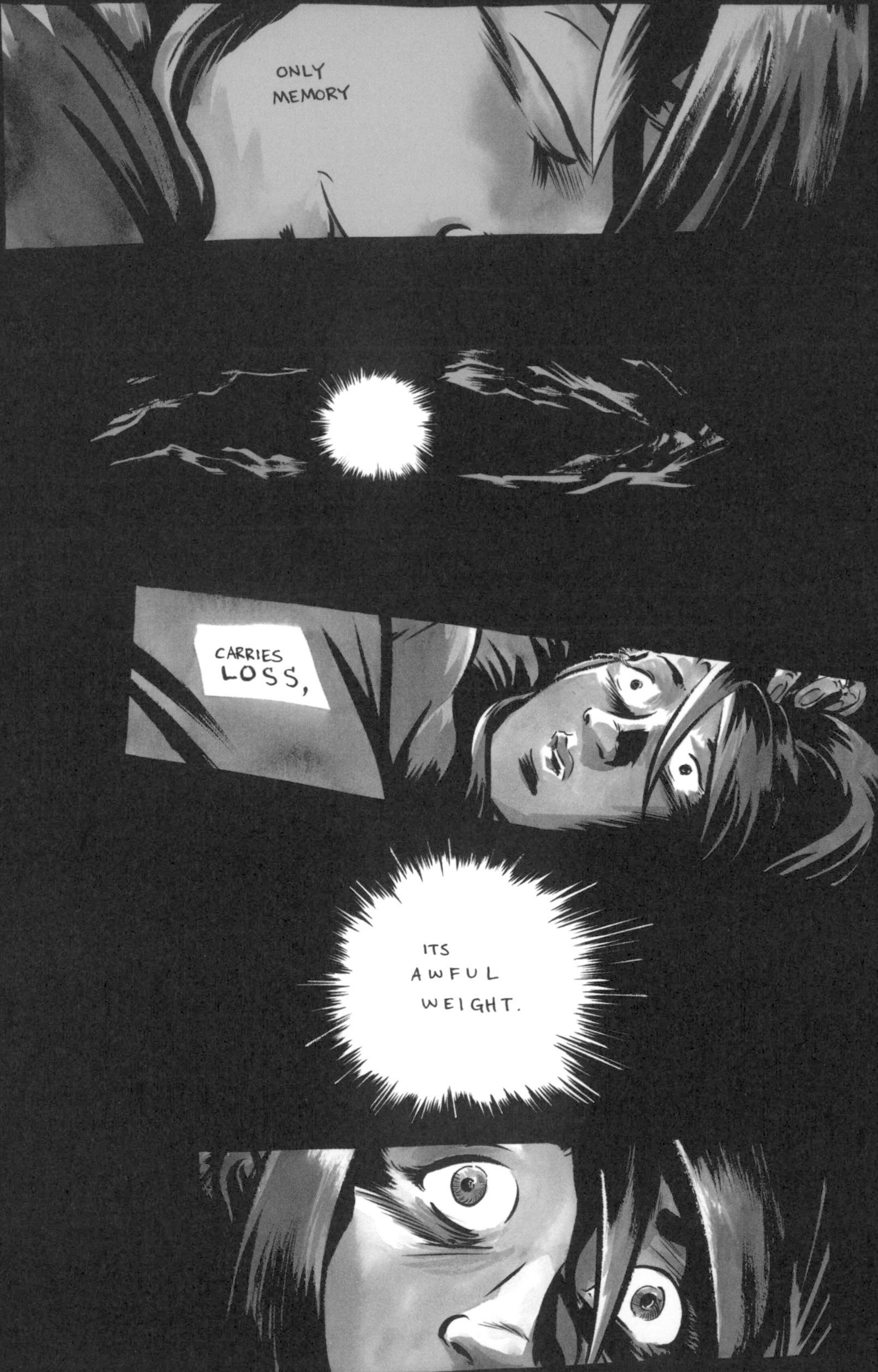
ONLY MEMORY
CARRIES LOSS,
ITS AWFUL WEIGHT.

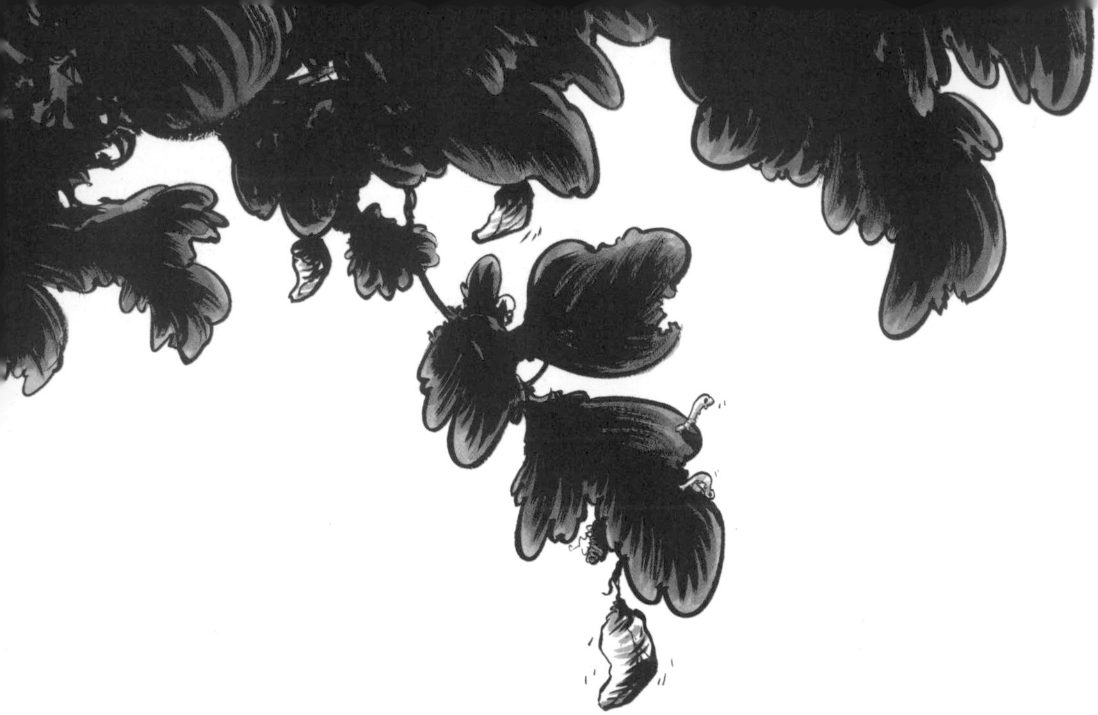

THEN CAME THE
FORGETTING.

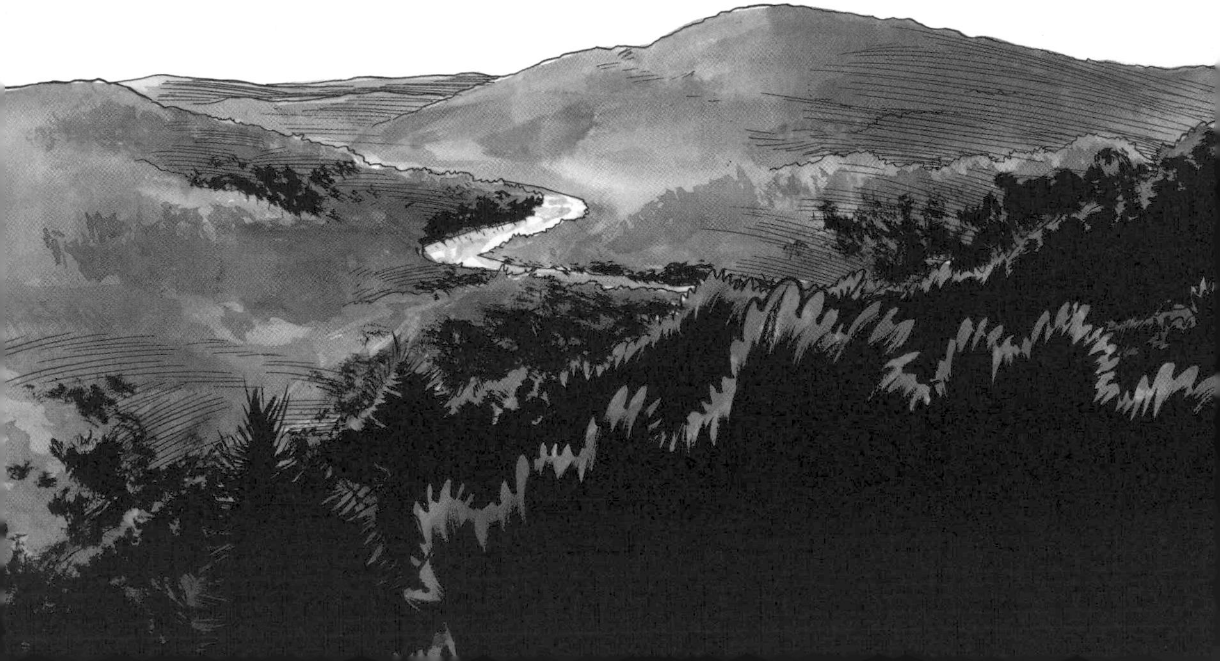

SUNDAY

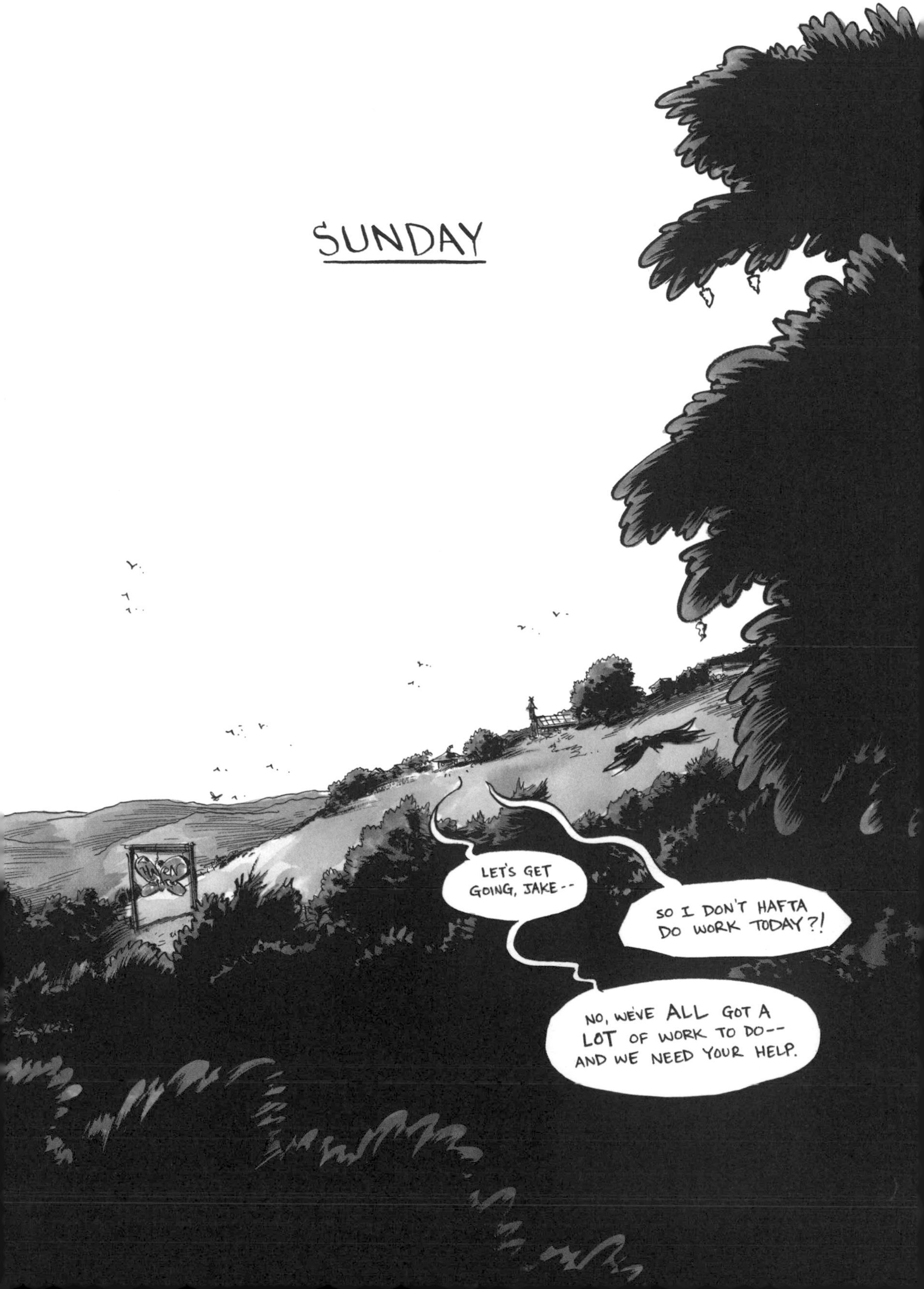
LET'S GET GOING, JAKE--
SO I DON'T HAFTA DO WORK TODAY?!
NO, WE'VE ALL GOT A LOT OF WORK TO DO-- AND WE NEED YOUR HELP.

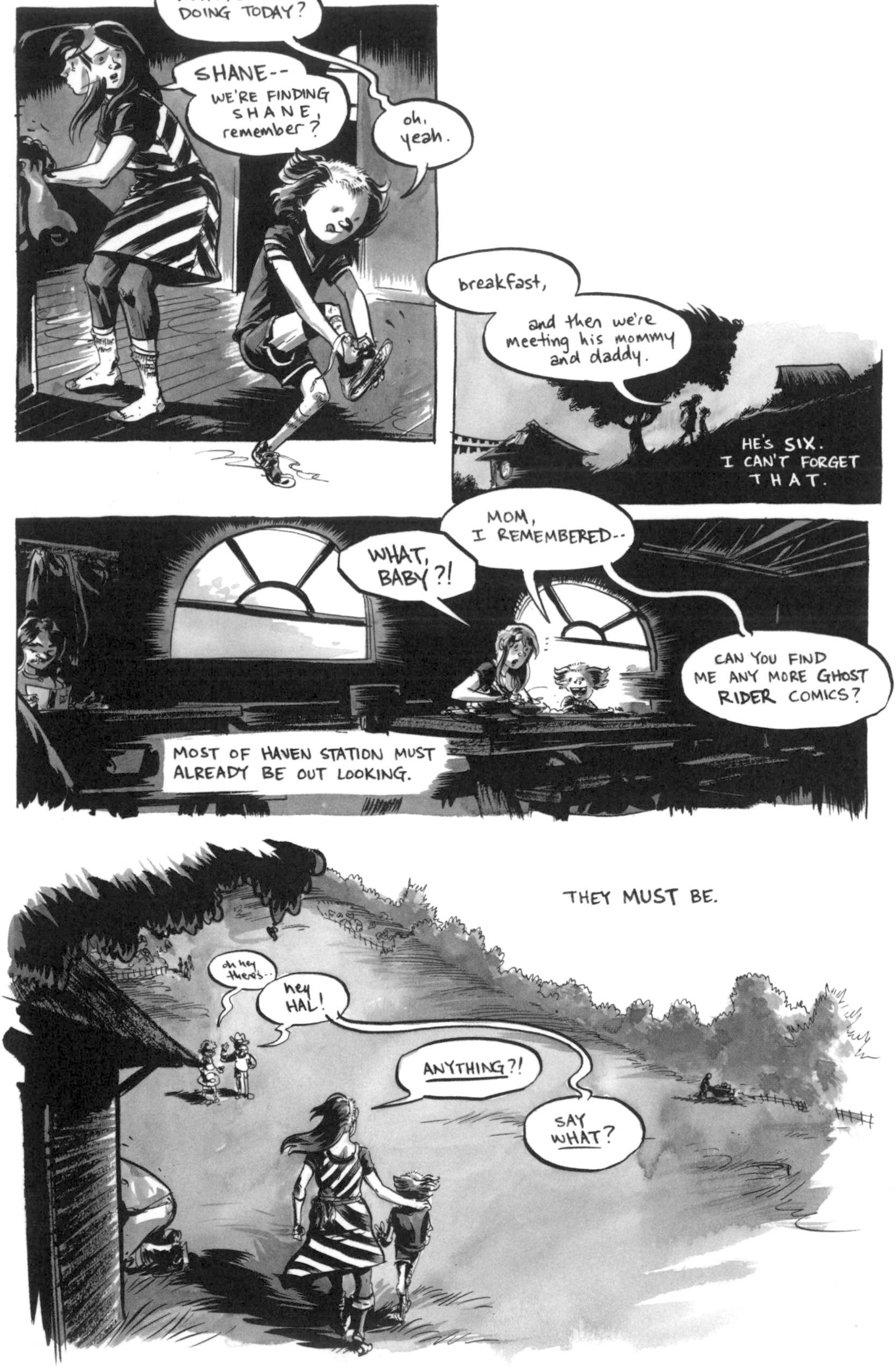
WHAT'RE WE DOING TODAY?
SHANE-- WE'RE FINDING SHANE, remember?
oh, yeah.
breakfast,
and then we're meeting his mommy and daddy.
HE'S SIX. I CAN'T FORGET THAT.
WHAT, BABY?!
MOM, I REMEMBERED--
CAN YOU FIND ME ANY MORE GHOST RIDER COMICS?
MOST OF HAVEN STATION MUST ALREADY BE OUT LOOKING.
THEY MUST BE.
oh hey there's--
hey HAL!
ANYTHING?!
SAY WHAT?

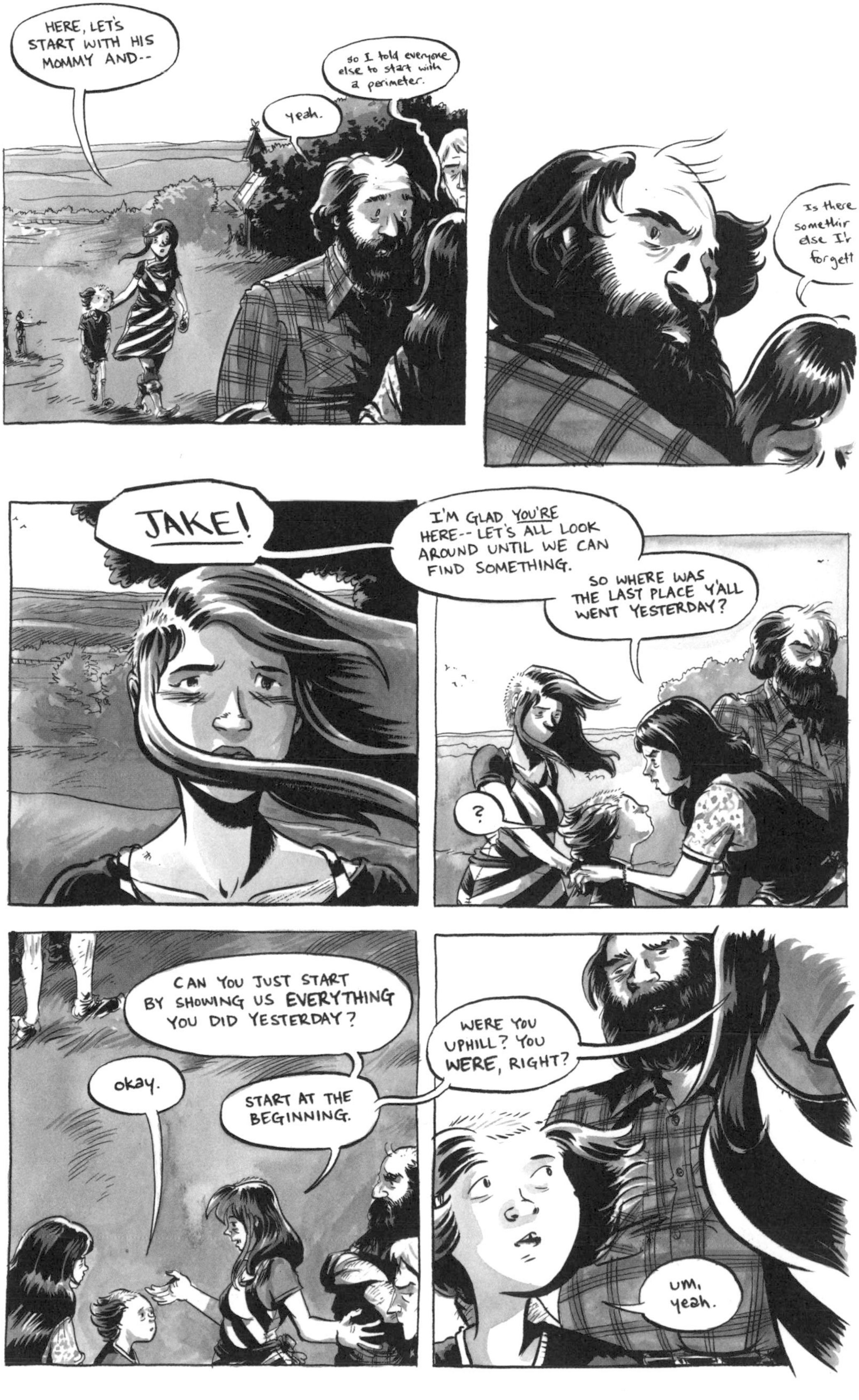
HERE, LET'S START WITH HIS MOMMY AND--
so I told everyone else to start with a perimeter.
yeah.
Is there somethir else I'r forgett
JAKE!
I'M GLAD YOU'RE HERE-- LET'S ALL LOOK AROUND UNTIL WE CAN FIND SOMETHING.
SO WHERE WAS THE LAST PLACE Y'ALL WENT YESTERDAY?
?
CAN YOU JUST START BY SHOWING US EVERYTHING YOU DID YESTERDAY?
okay.
START AT THE BEGINNING.
WERE YOU UPHILL? YOU WERE, RIGHT?
um, yeah.

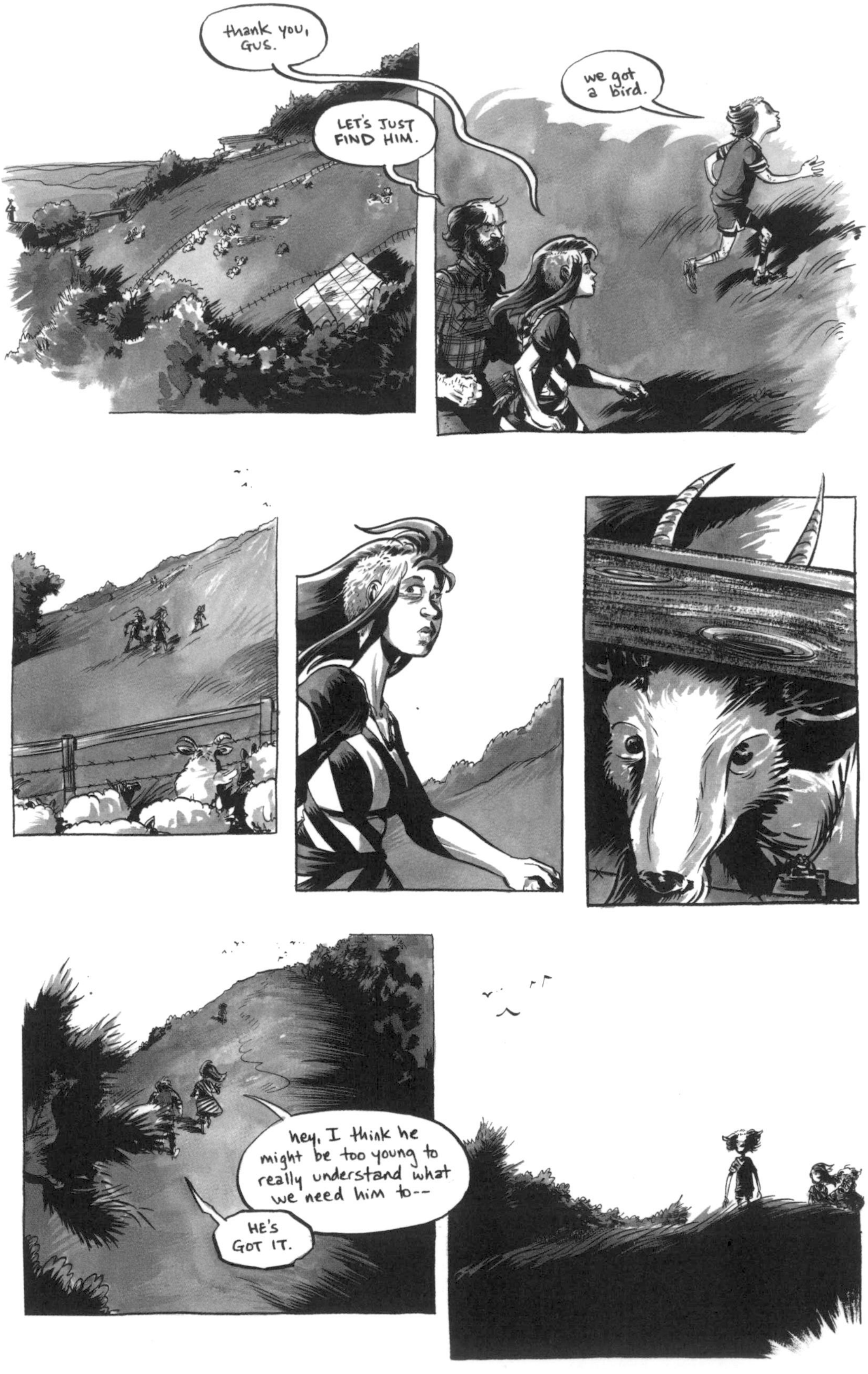
thank you, GUS.
LET'S JUST FIND HIM.
we got a bird.
hey, I think he might be too young to really understand what we need him to--
HE'S GOT IT.

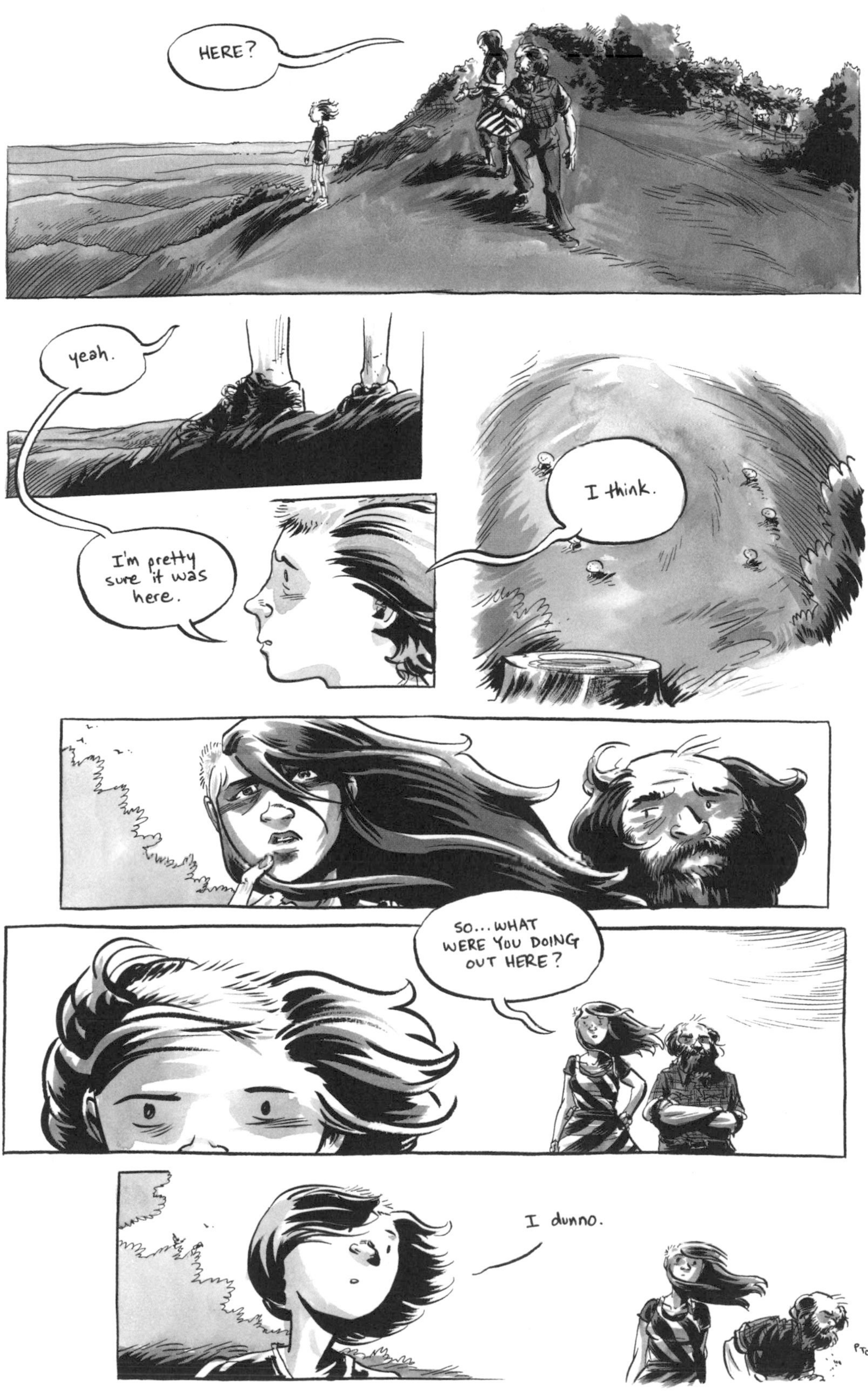
HERE?
yeah.
I'm pretty sure it was here.
I think.
SO... WHAT WERE YOU DOING OUT HERE?
I dunno.
PTOO

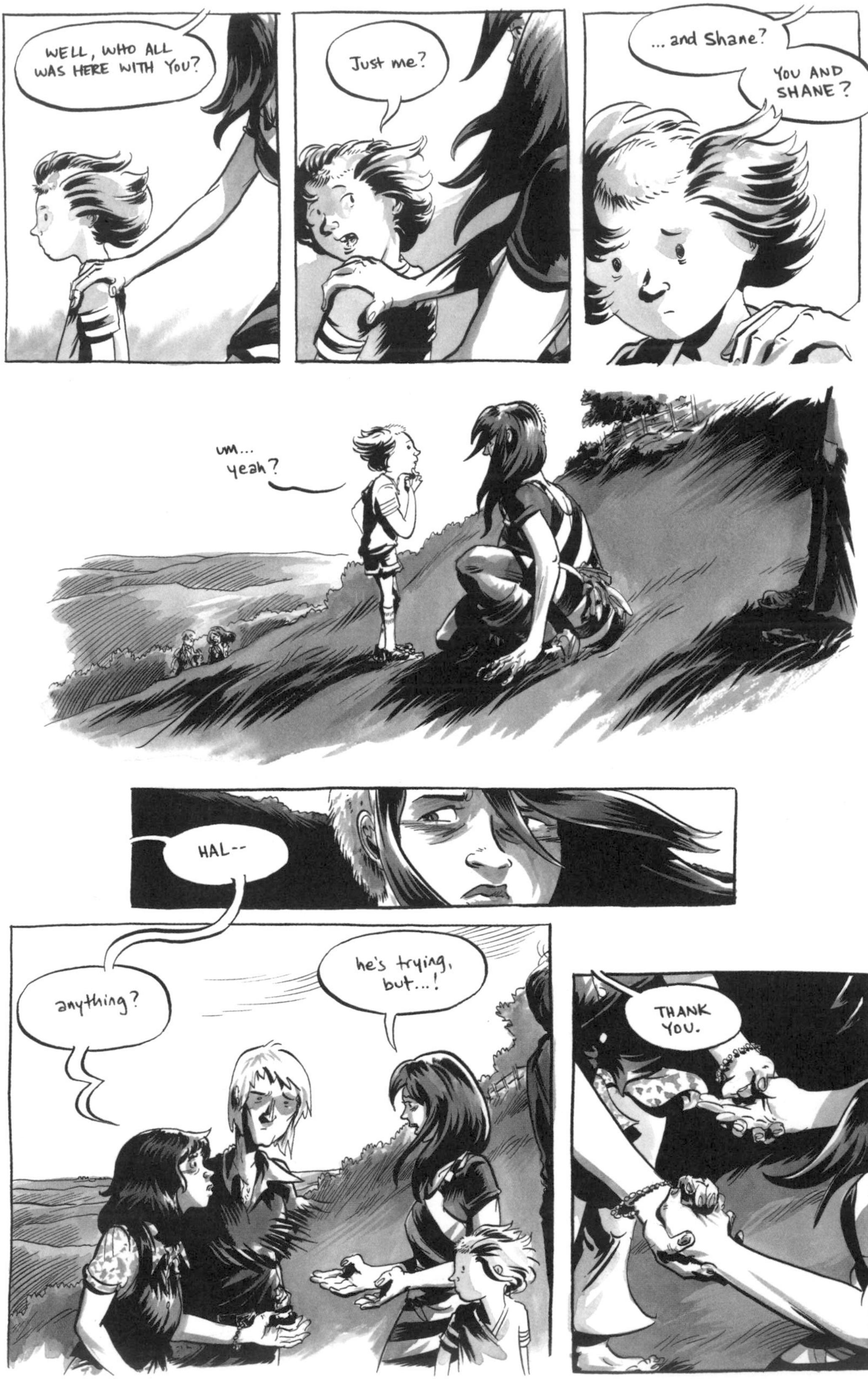
WELL, WHO ALL WAS HERE WITH YOU?
Just me?
... and Shane?
YOU AND SHANE?
um... yeah?
HAL--
anything?
he's trying, but...!
THANK YOU.

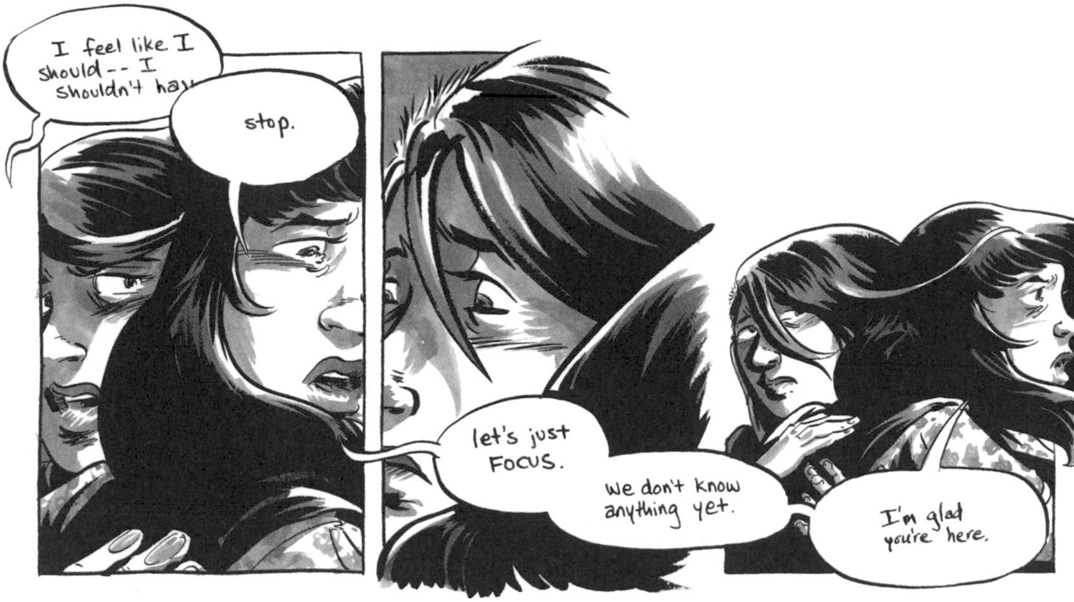
I feel like I should-- I shouldn't hav
stop.
let's just FOCUS.
We don't know anything yet.
I'm glad you're here.

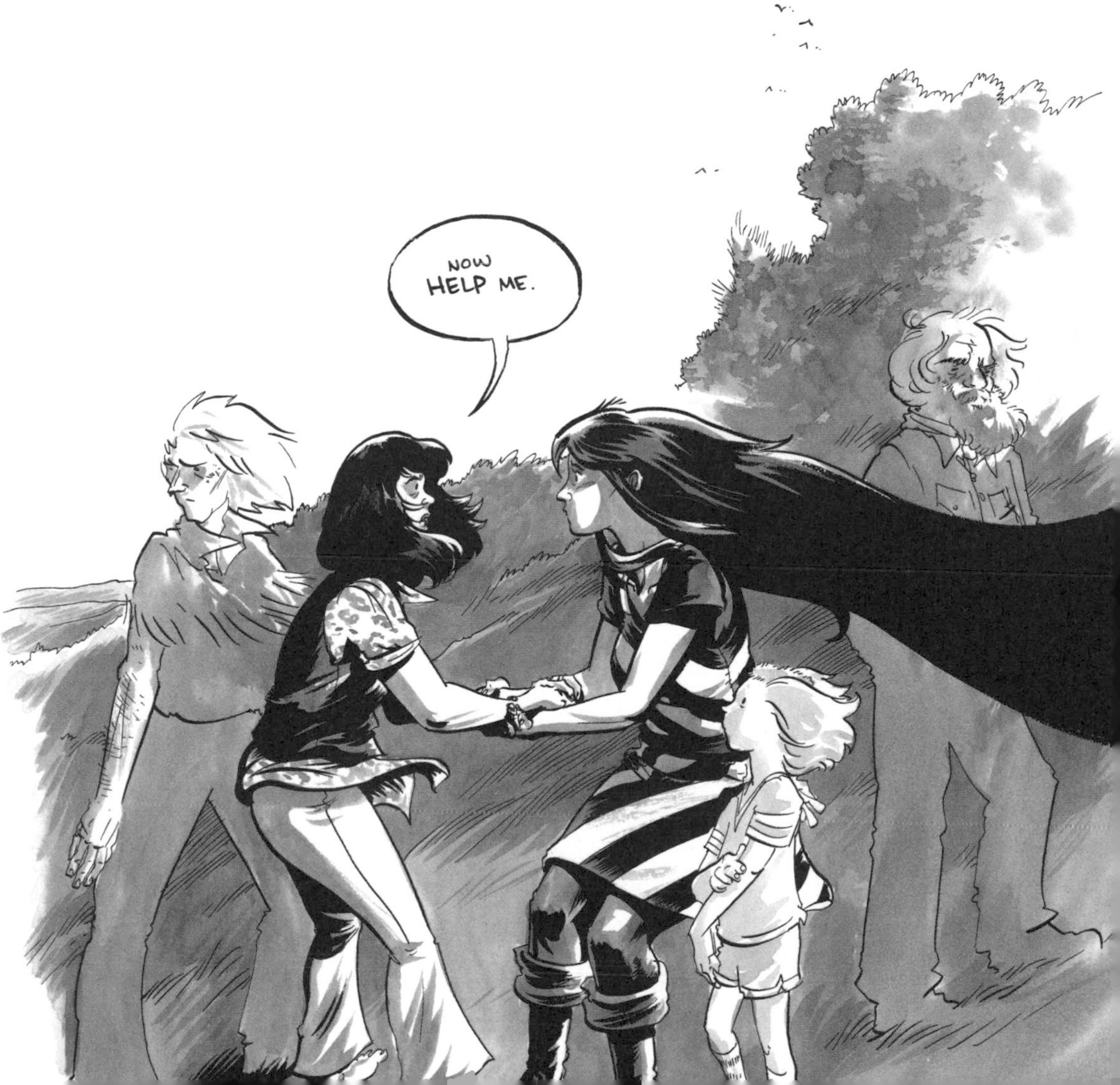
NOW HELP ME.

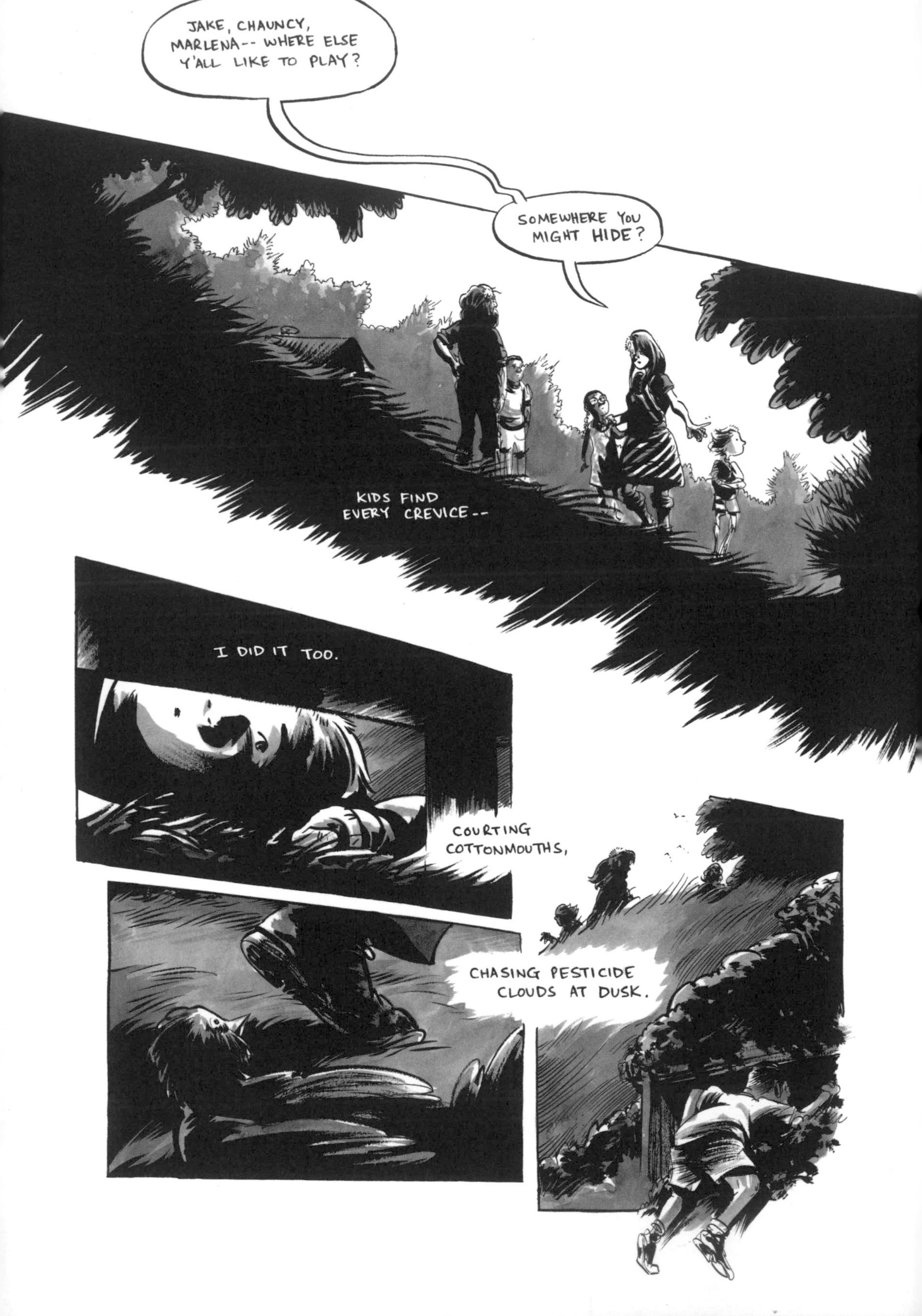

JAKE, CHAUNCY, MARLENA-- WHERE ELSE Y'ALL LIKE TO PLAY?
SOMEWHERE YOU MIGHT HIDE?
KIDS FIND EVERY CREVICE--
I DID IT TOO.
COURTING COTTONMOUTHS,
CHASING PESTICIDE CLOUDS AT DUSK.

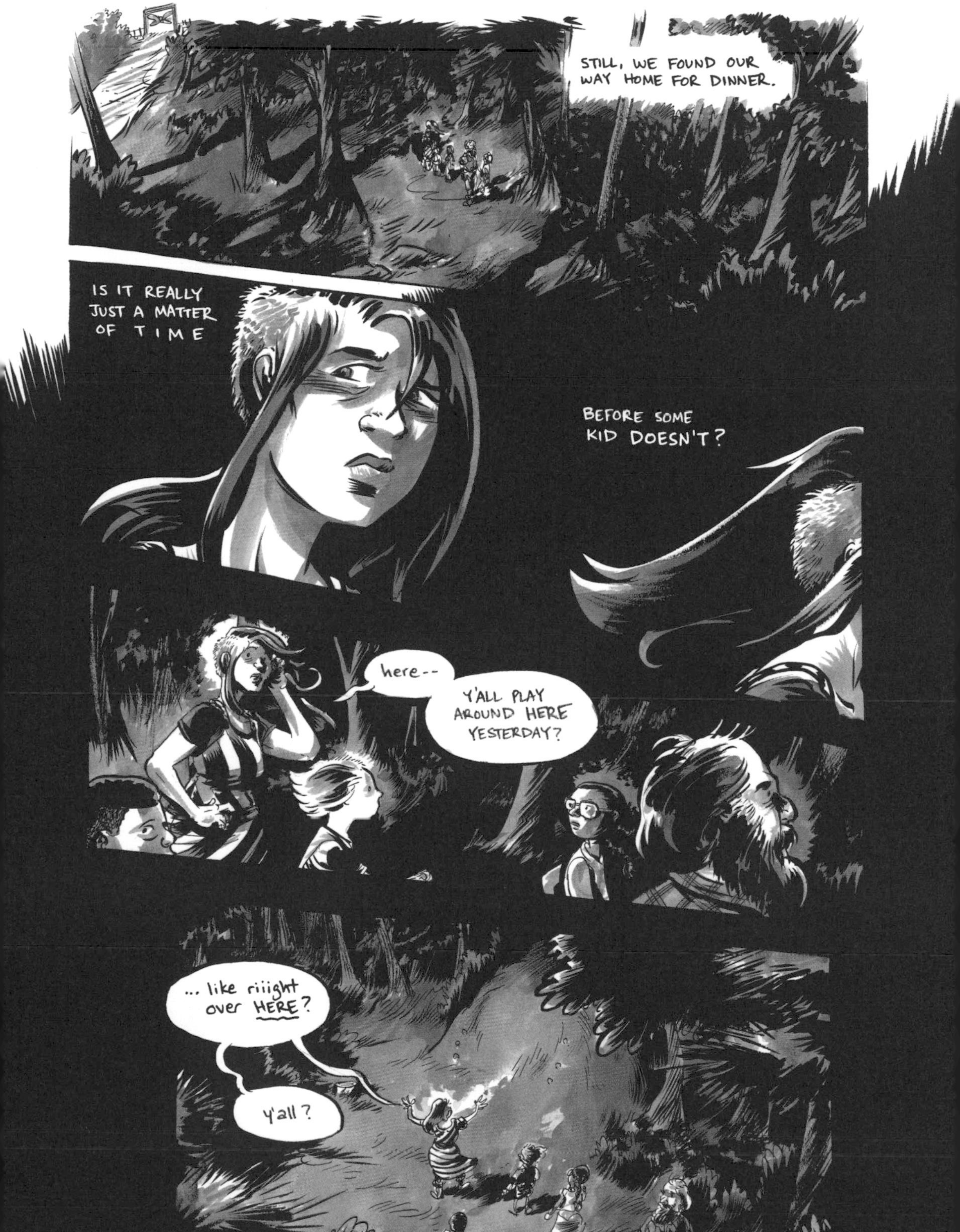
STILL, WE FOUND OUR WAY HOME FOR DINNER.
IS IT REALLY JUST A MATTER OF TIME
BEFORE SOME KID DOESN'T?
here--
Y'ALL PLAY AROUND HERE YESTERDAY?
... like riiight over HERE?
y'all?

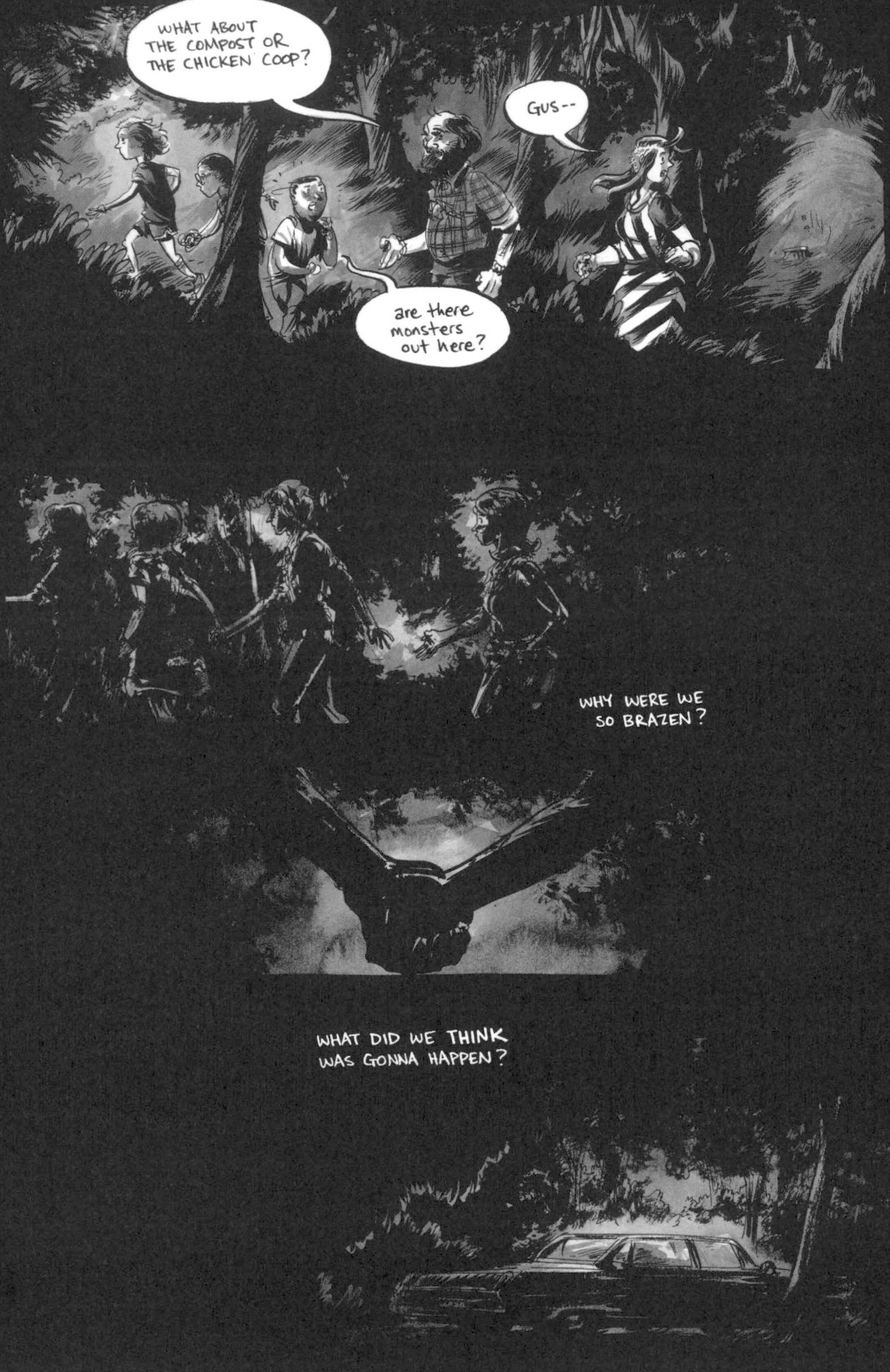
WHAT ABOUT THE COMPOST OR THE CHICKEN COOP?
GUS--
are there monsters out here?
WHY WERE WE SO BRAZEN?
WHAT DID WE THINK WAS GONNA HAPPEN?

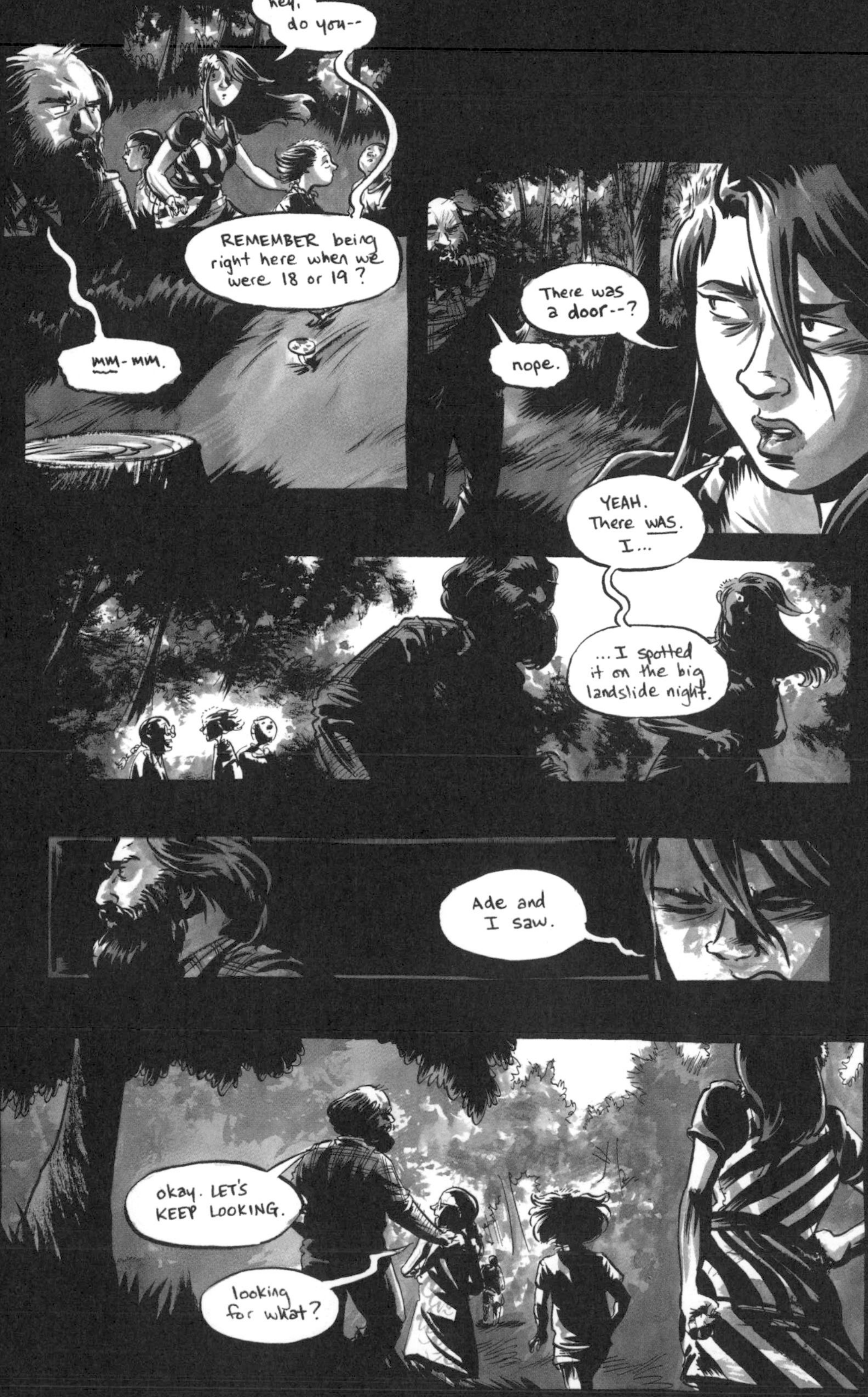
hey, do you--
REMEMBER being right here when we were 18 or 19 ?
mm-mm.
There was a door--?
nope.
YEAH. There WAS. I...
...I spotted it on the big landslide night.
Ade and I saw.
okay. LET'S KEEP LOOKING.
looking for what?

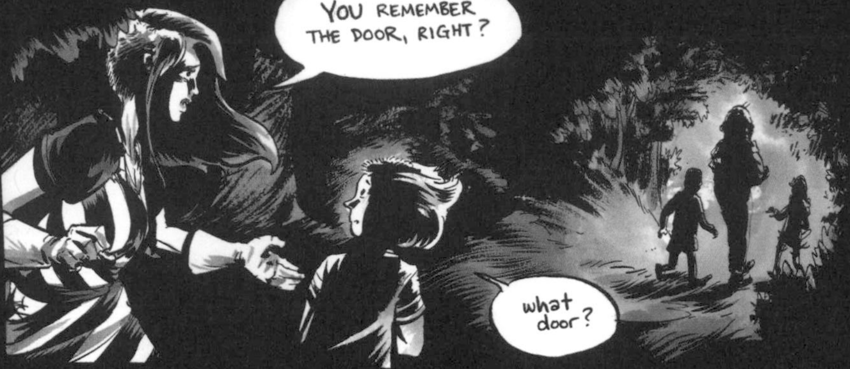
YOU REMEMBER THE DOOR, RIGHT?
what door?

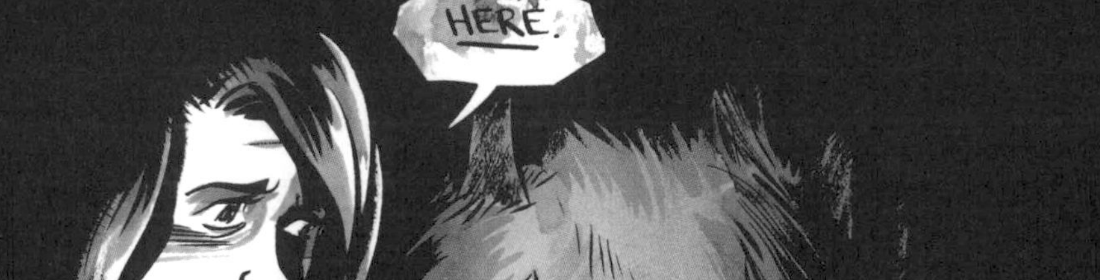
HERE.
where?

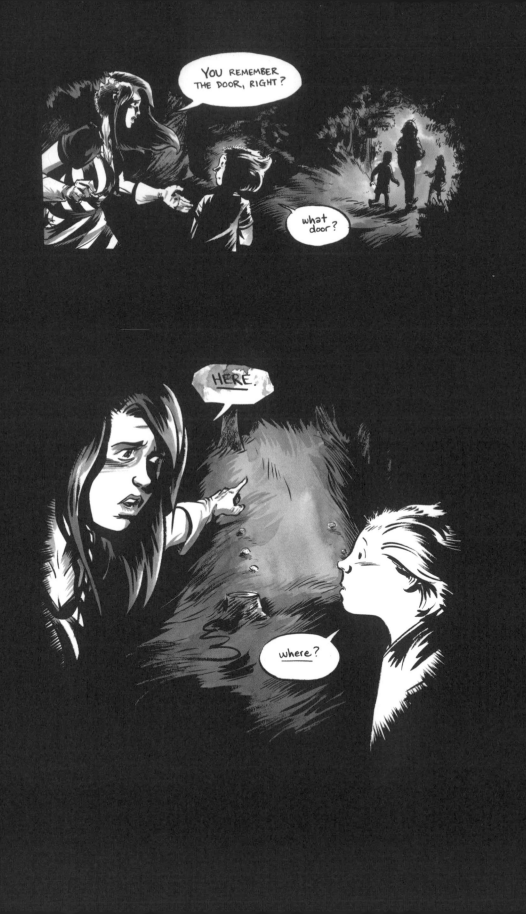

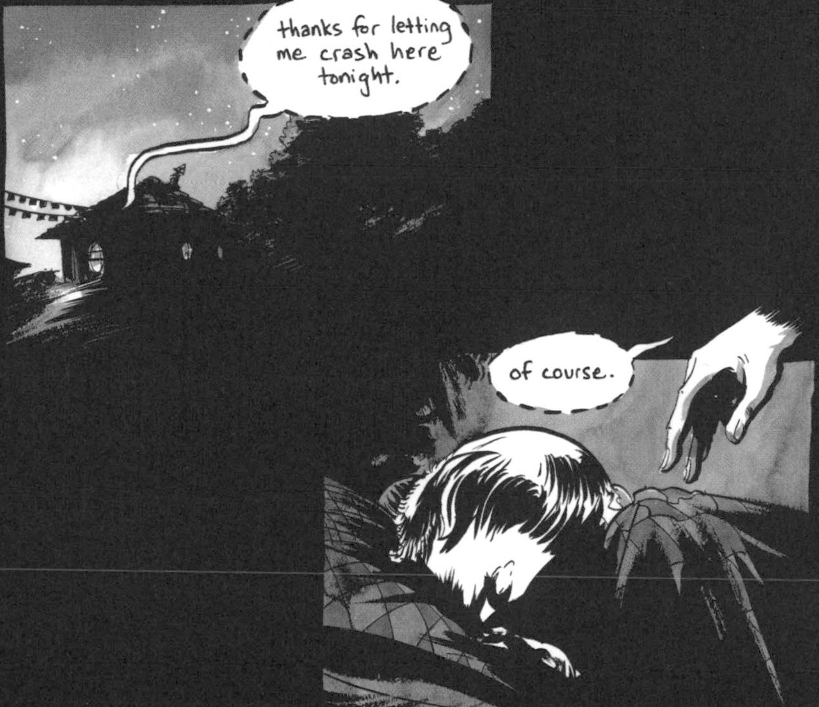
thanks for letting me crash here tonight.
of course.

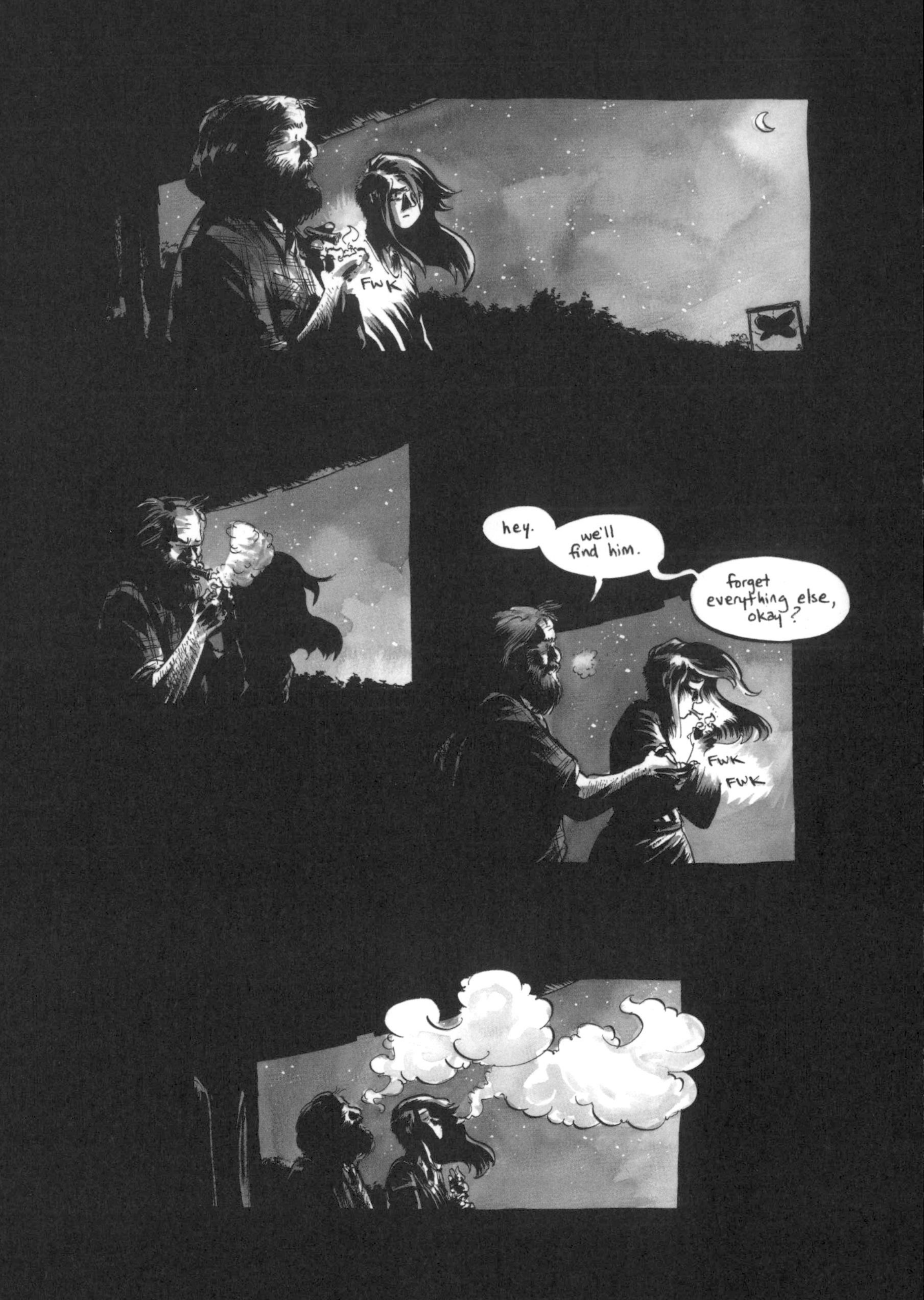
FWK
hey.
we'll find him.
forget everything else, okay?
FWK
FWK

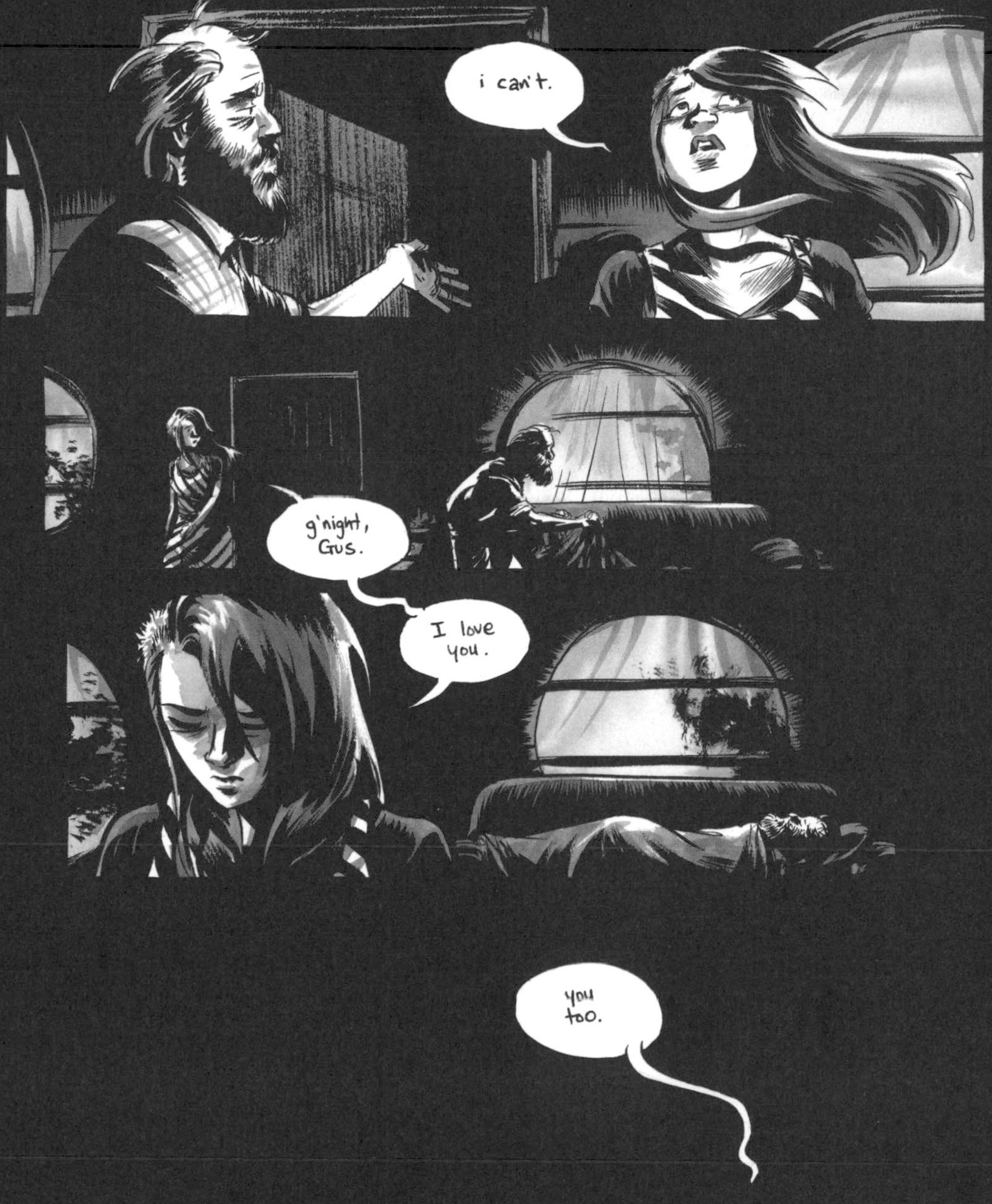
i can't.
g'night, Gus.
I love you.
you too.

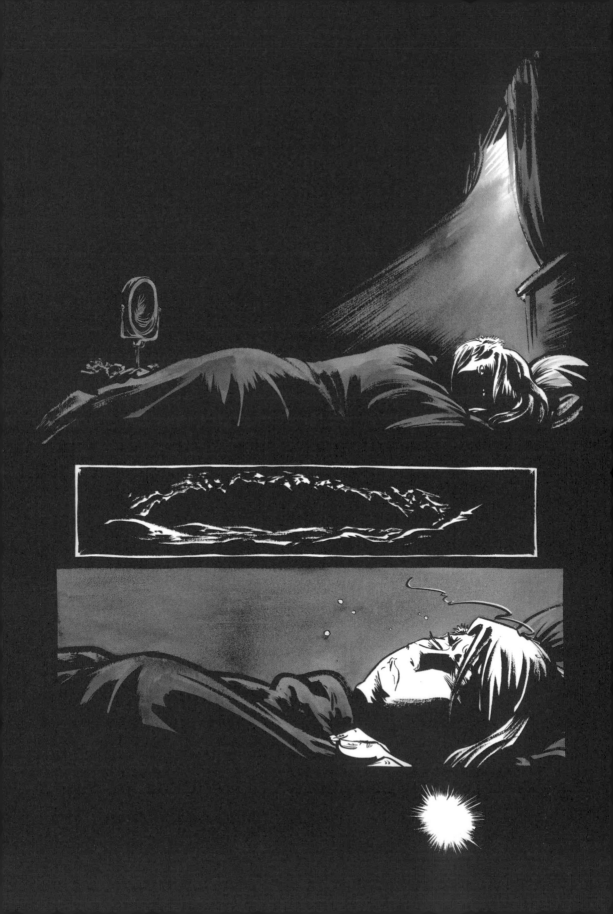

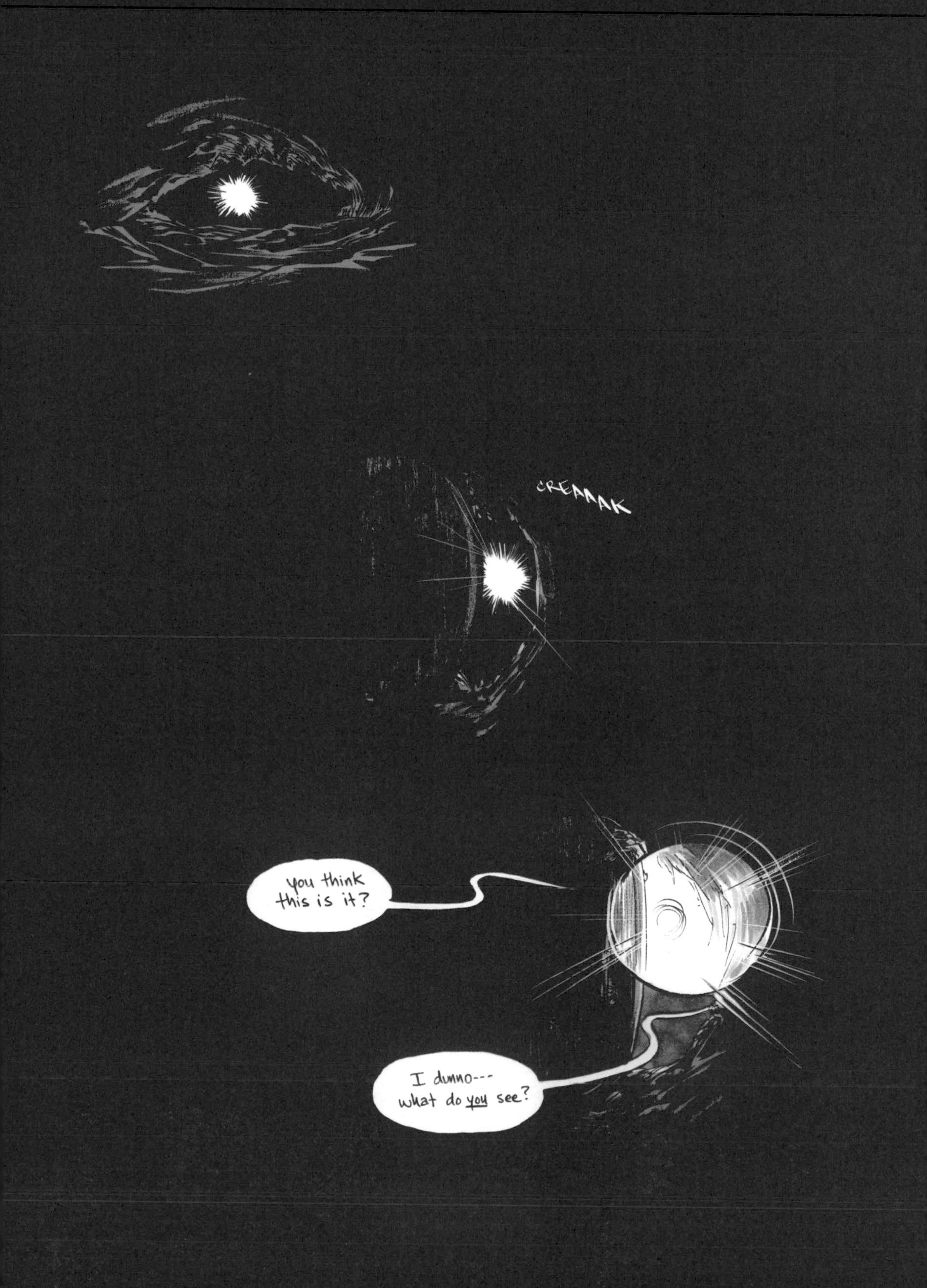
CREAAAK
you think this is it?
I dunno--- what do you see?

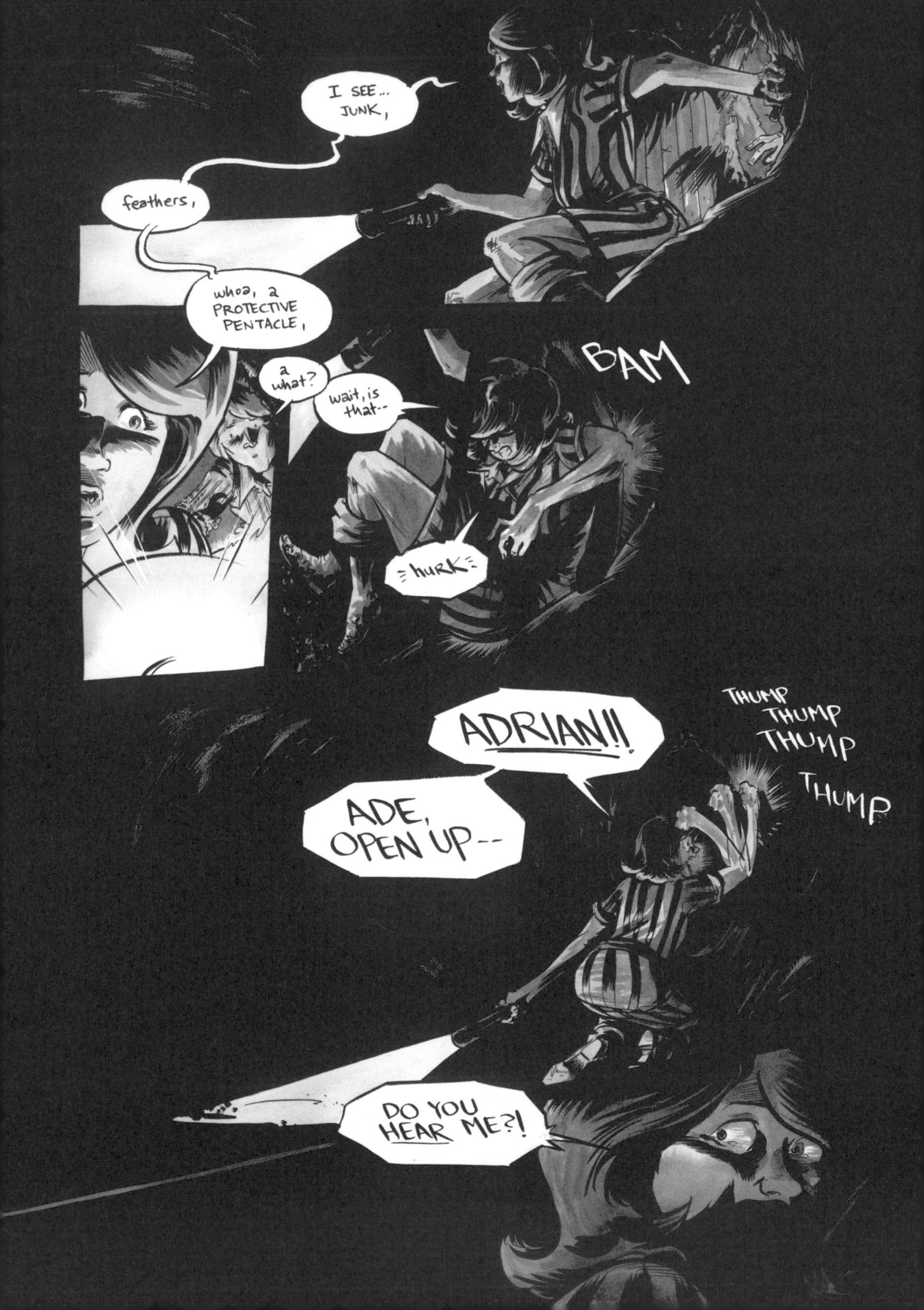

I SEE... JUNK,
feathers,
whoa, a PROTECTIVE PENTACLE,
a what?
wait, is that--
BAM
hurk
ADRIAN!!
ADE, OPEN UP--
THUMP THUMP THUMP
THUMP
DO YOU HEAR ME?!

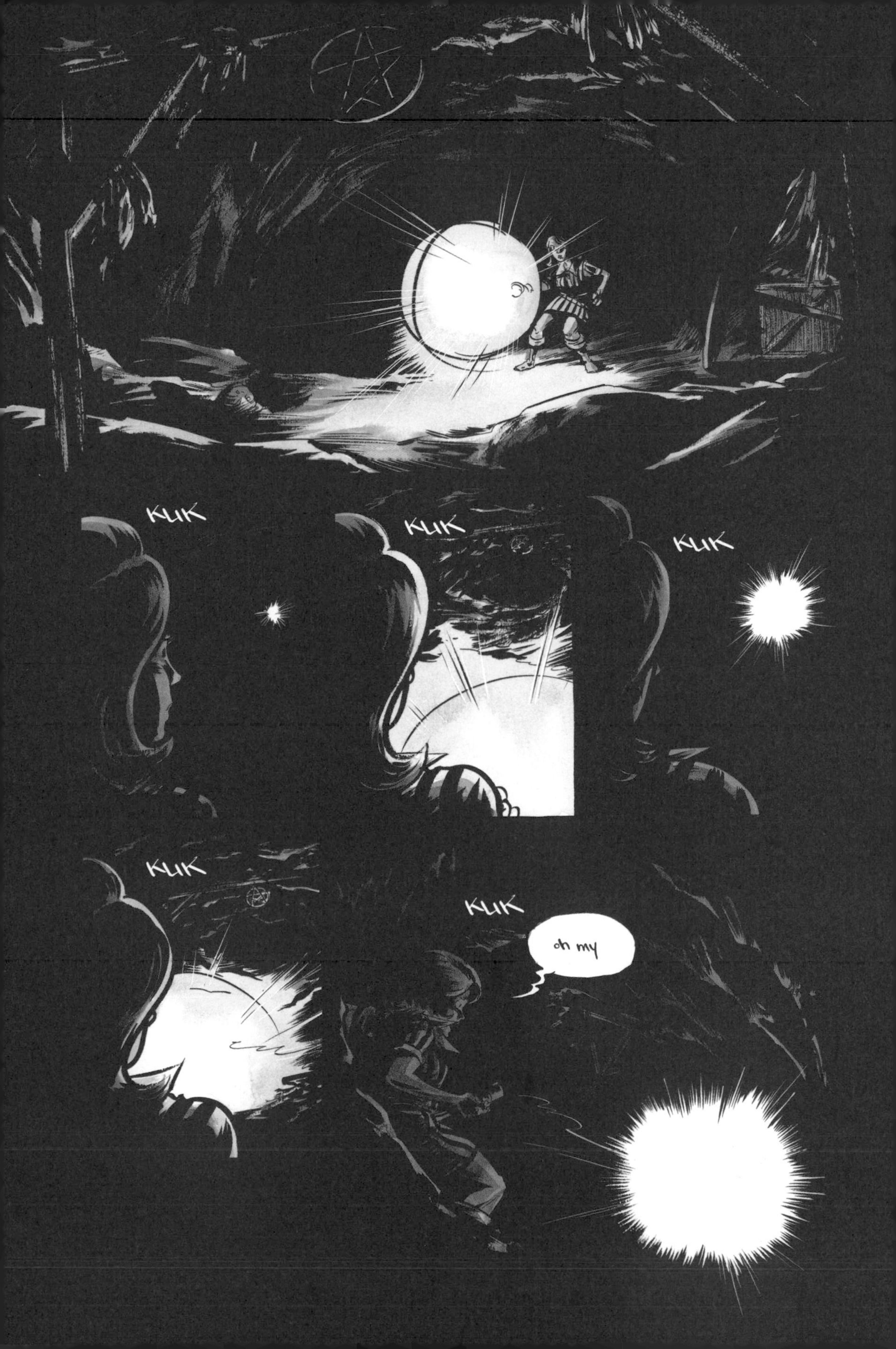
KUK
KUK
KUK
KUK
KUK
oh my

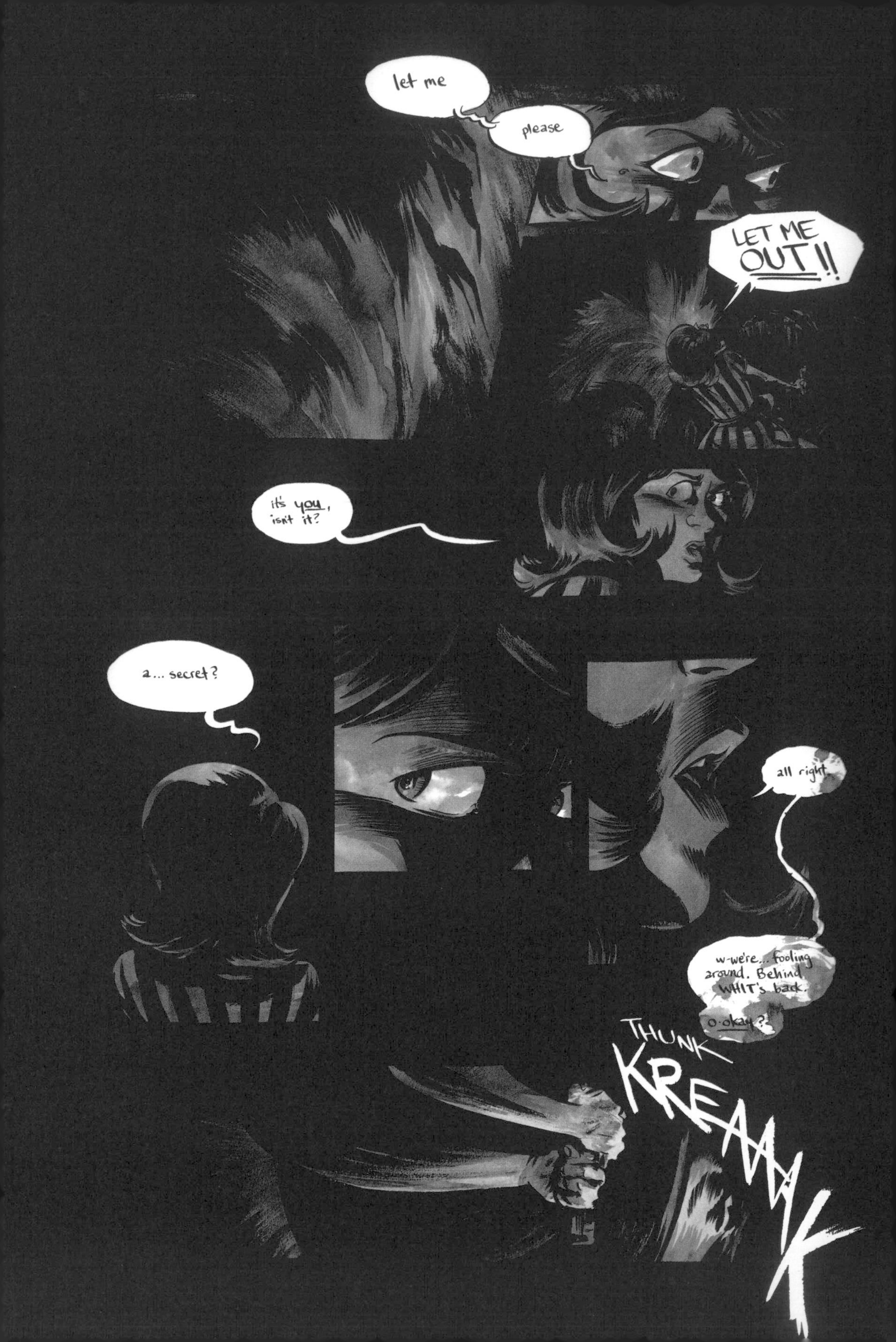
let me
please
LET ME OUT!!
it's you, isn't it?
a... secret?
all right.
w-we're... fooling around. Behind WHIT's back.
o-okay?
THUNK
KREAAAK

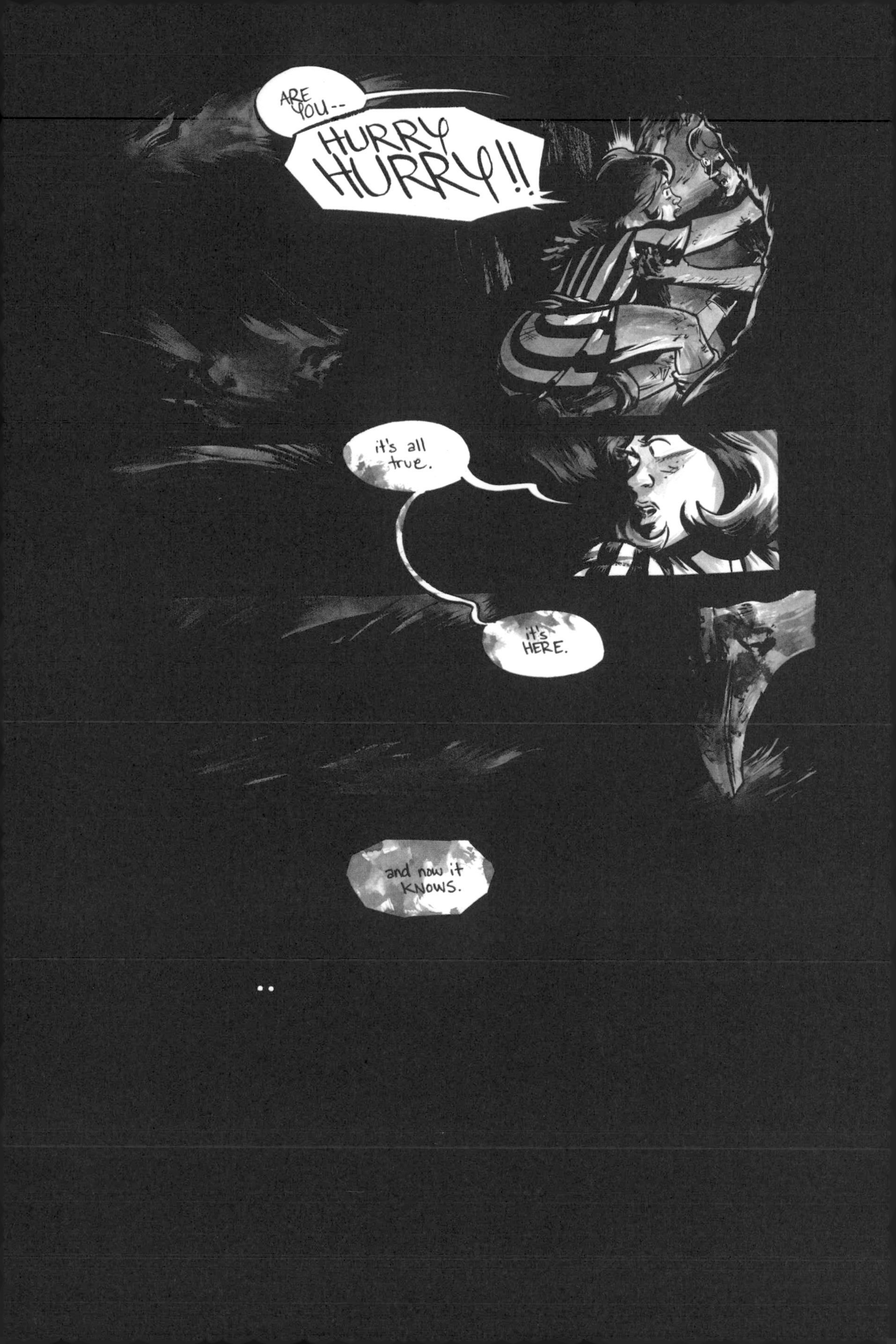
ARE YOU--
HURRY HURRY!!
it's all true.
it's HERE.
and now it KNOWS.

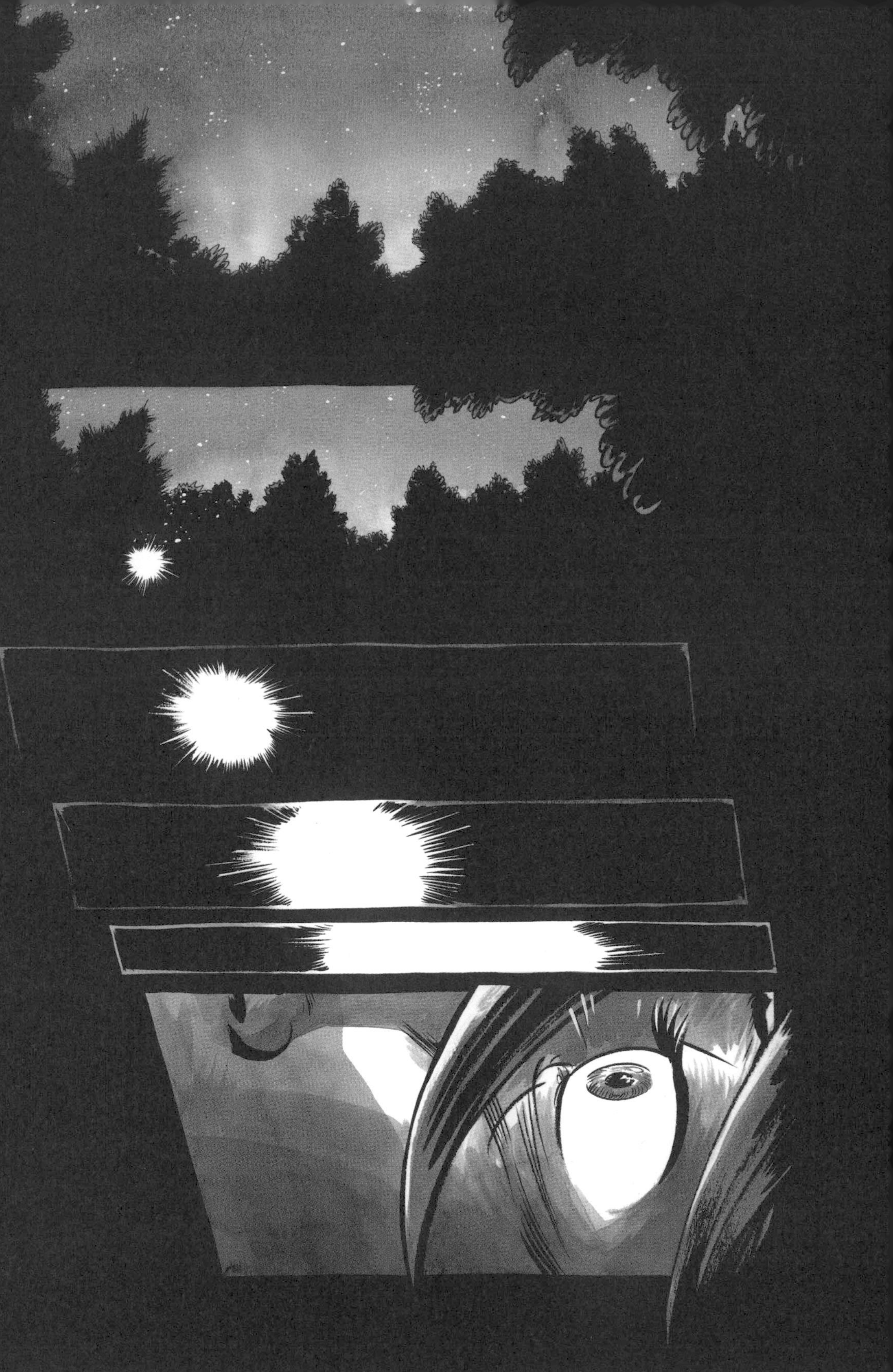

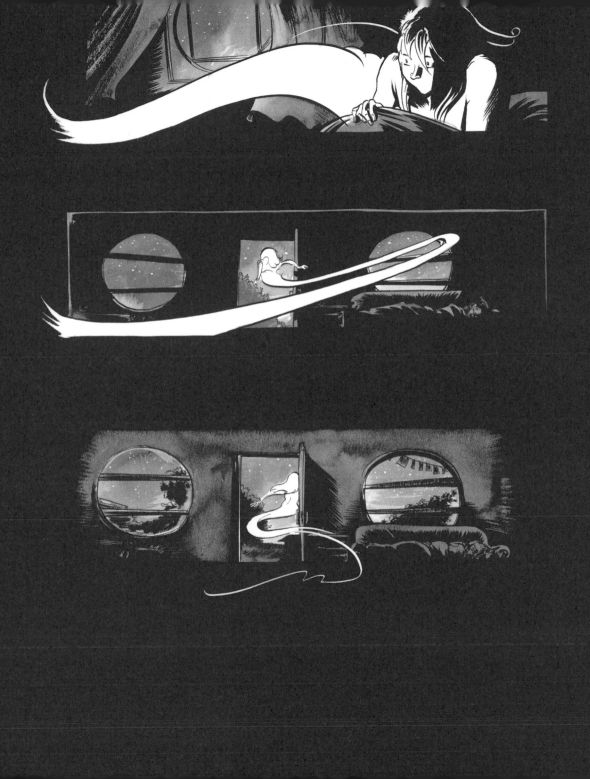

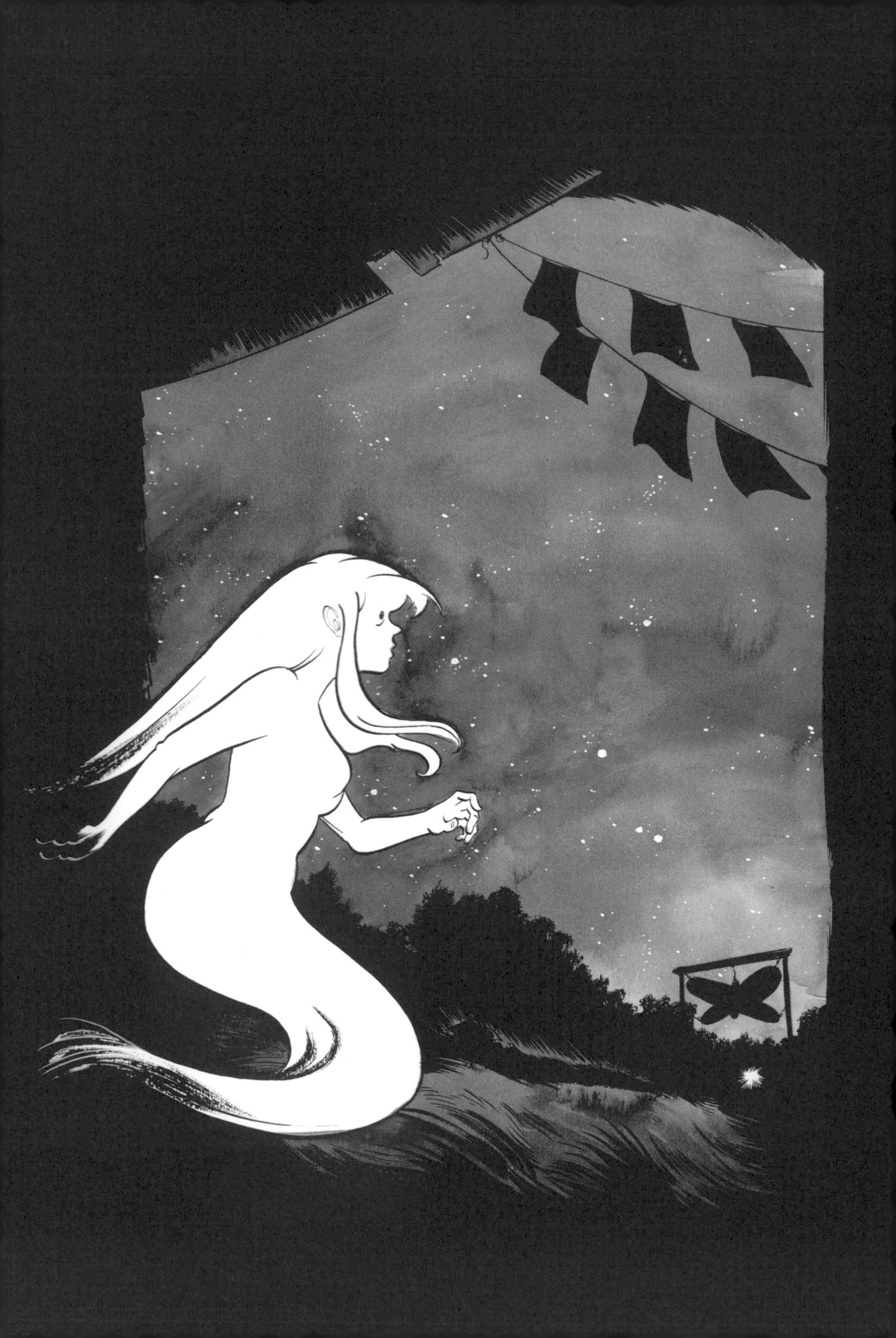

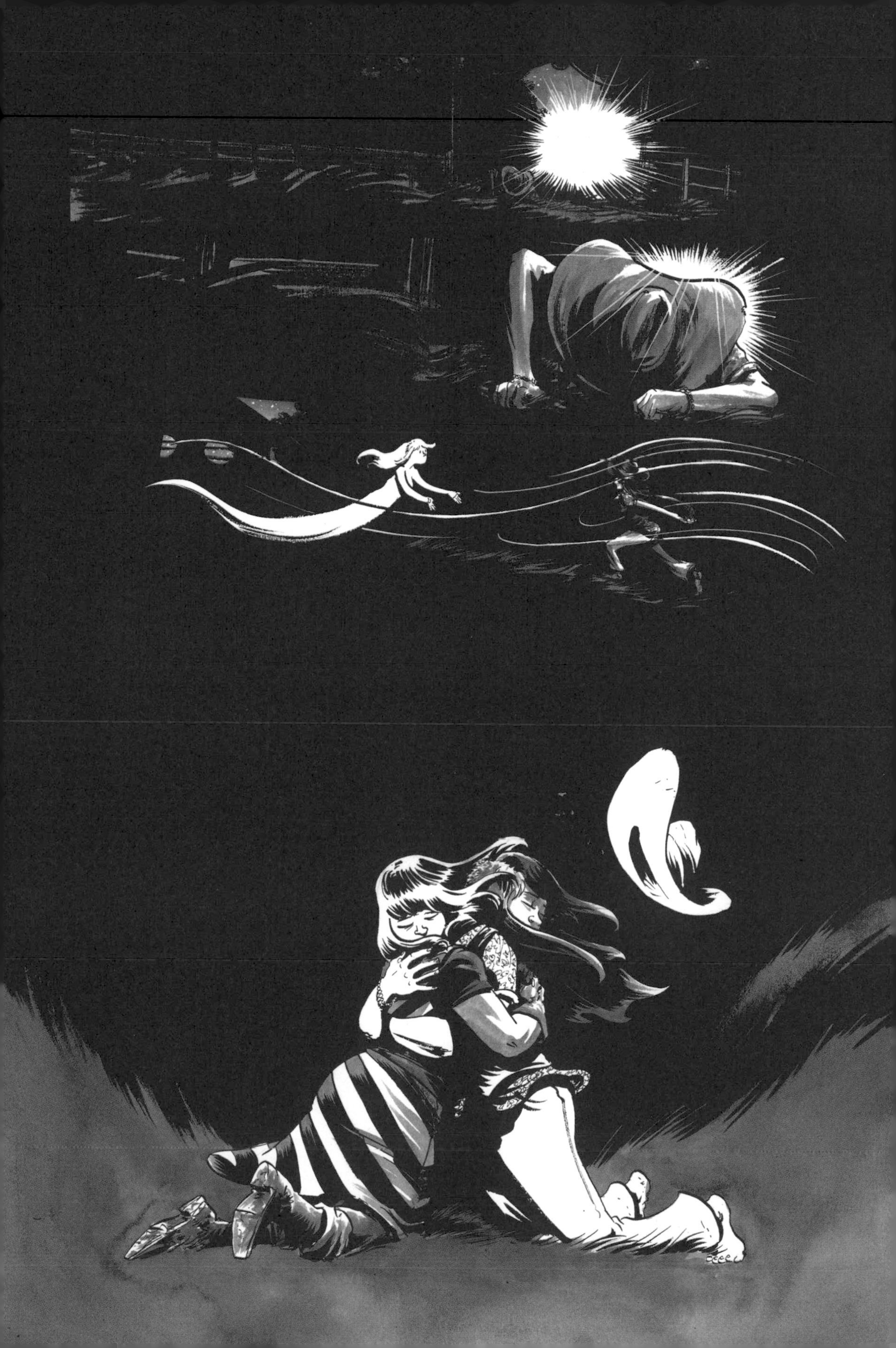

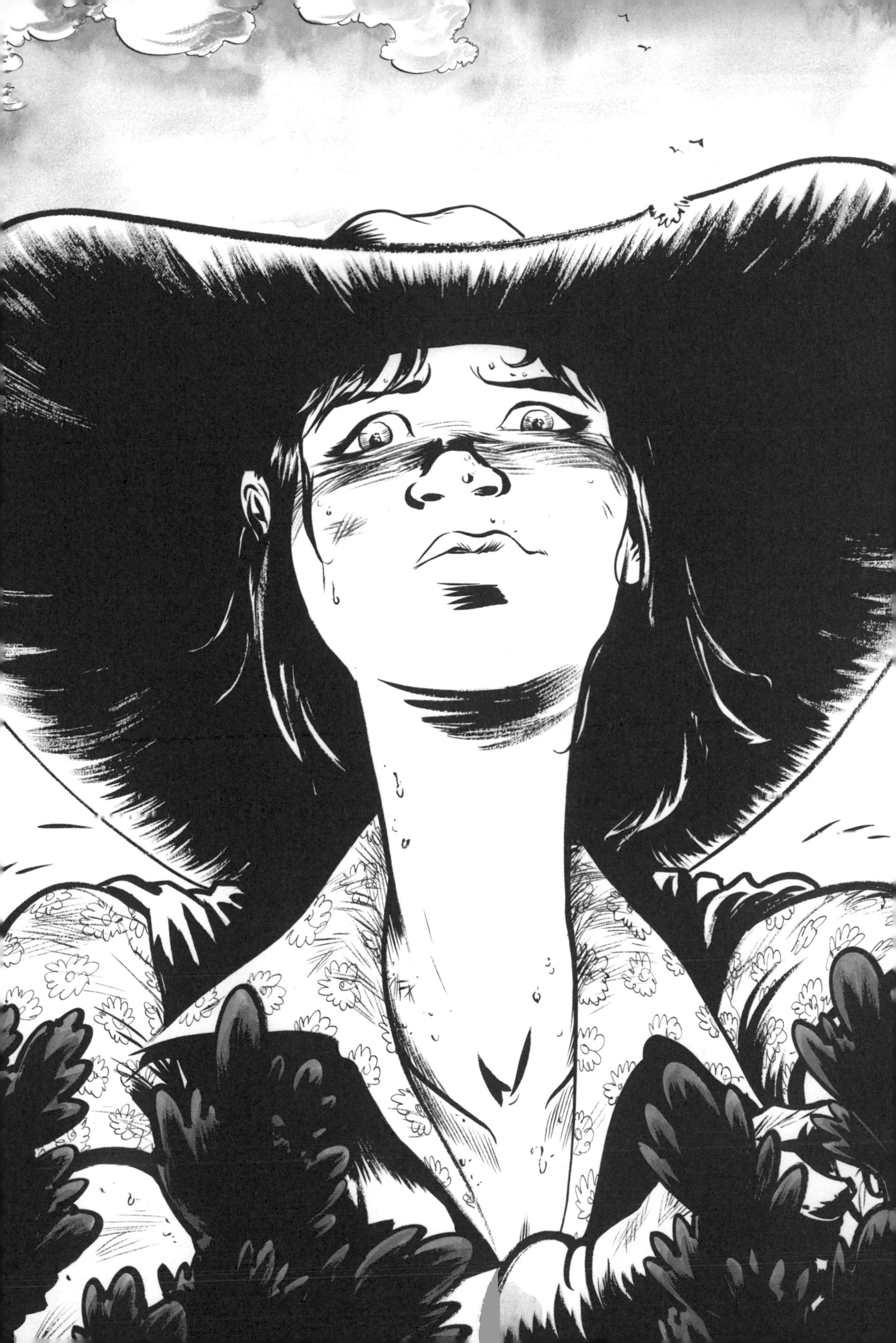

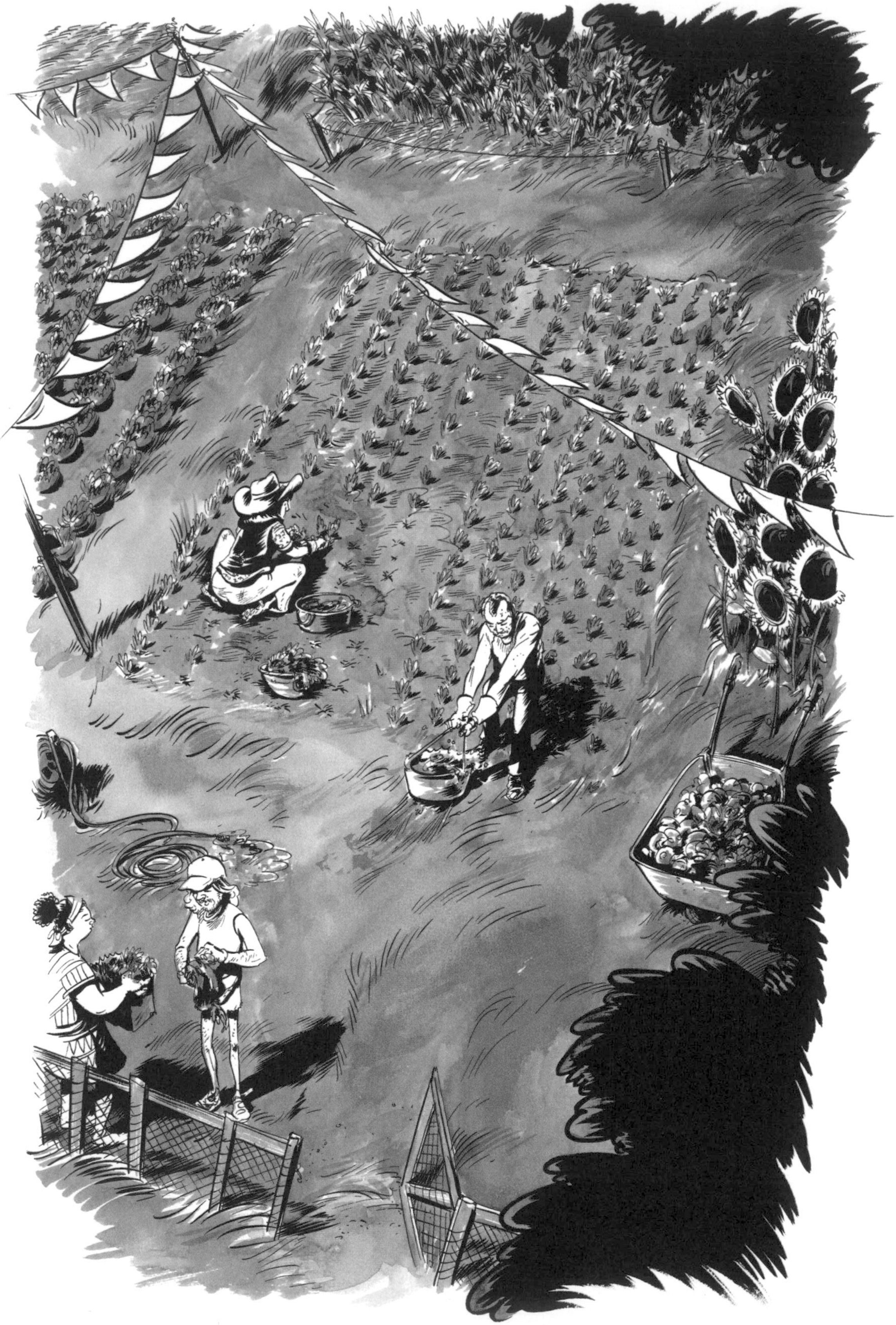

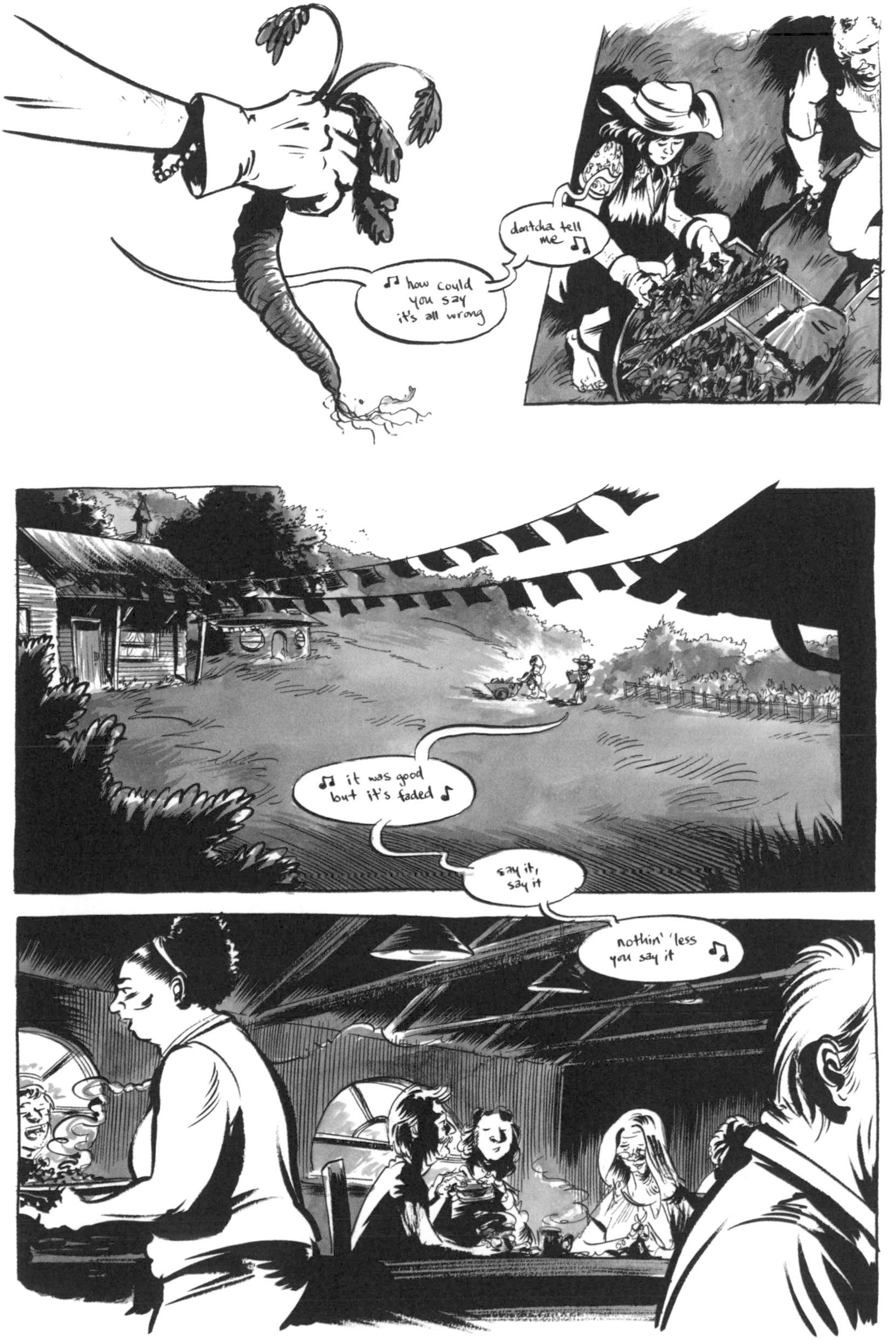
how could you say it's all wrong
dontcha tell me
it was good but it's faded
say it, say it
nothin' 'less you say it

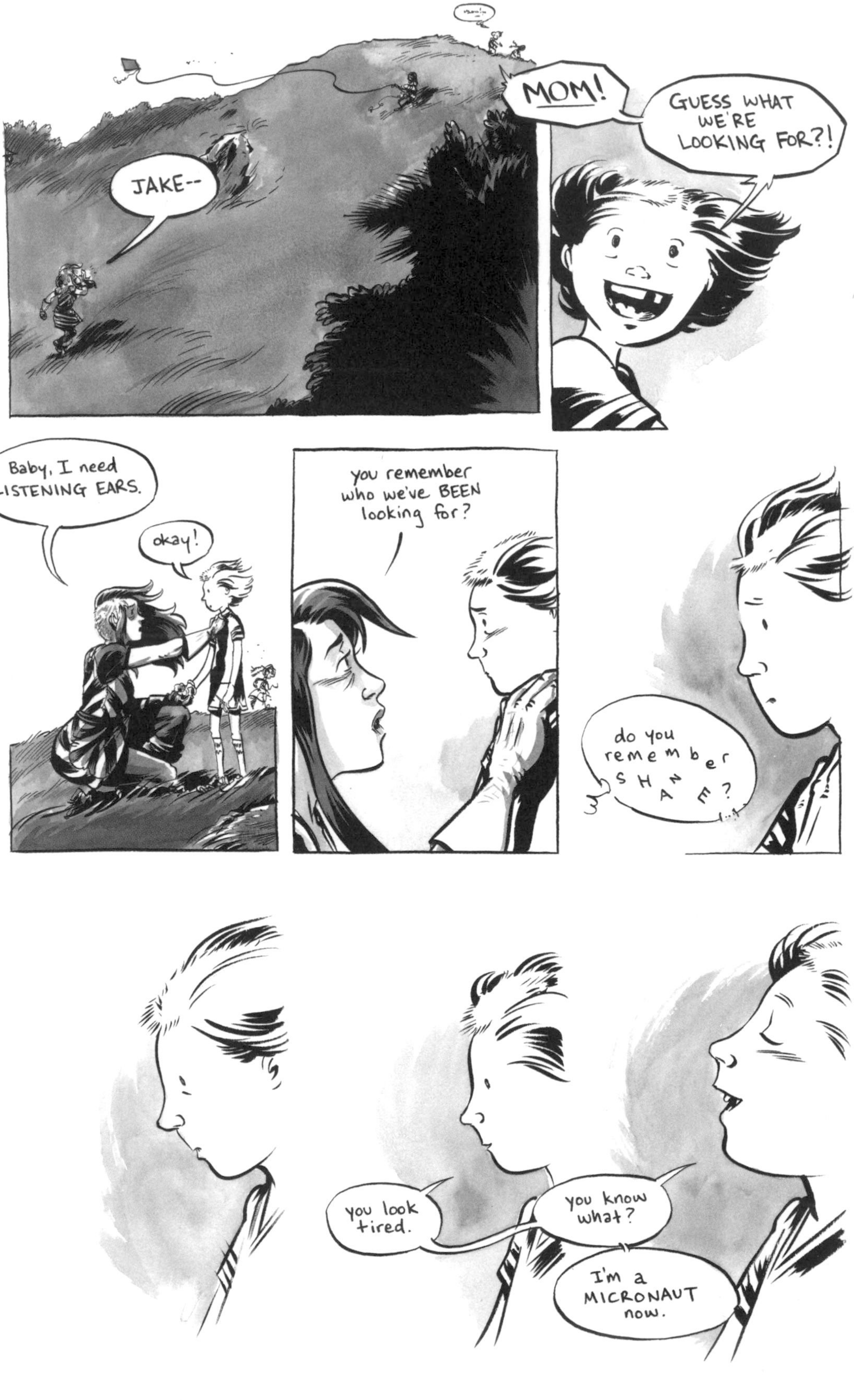
JAKE--
MOM!
GUESS WHAT WE'RE LOOKING FOR?!
Baby, I need LISTENING EARS.
okay!
you remember who we've BEEN looking for?
do you remember SHANE?
you look tired.
you know what?
I'm a MICRONAUT now.

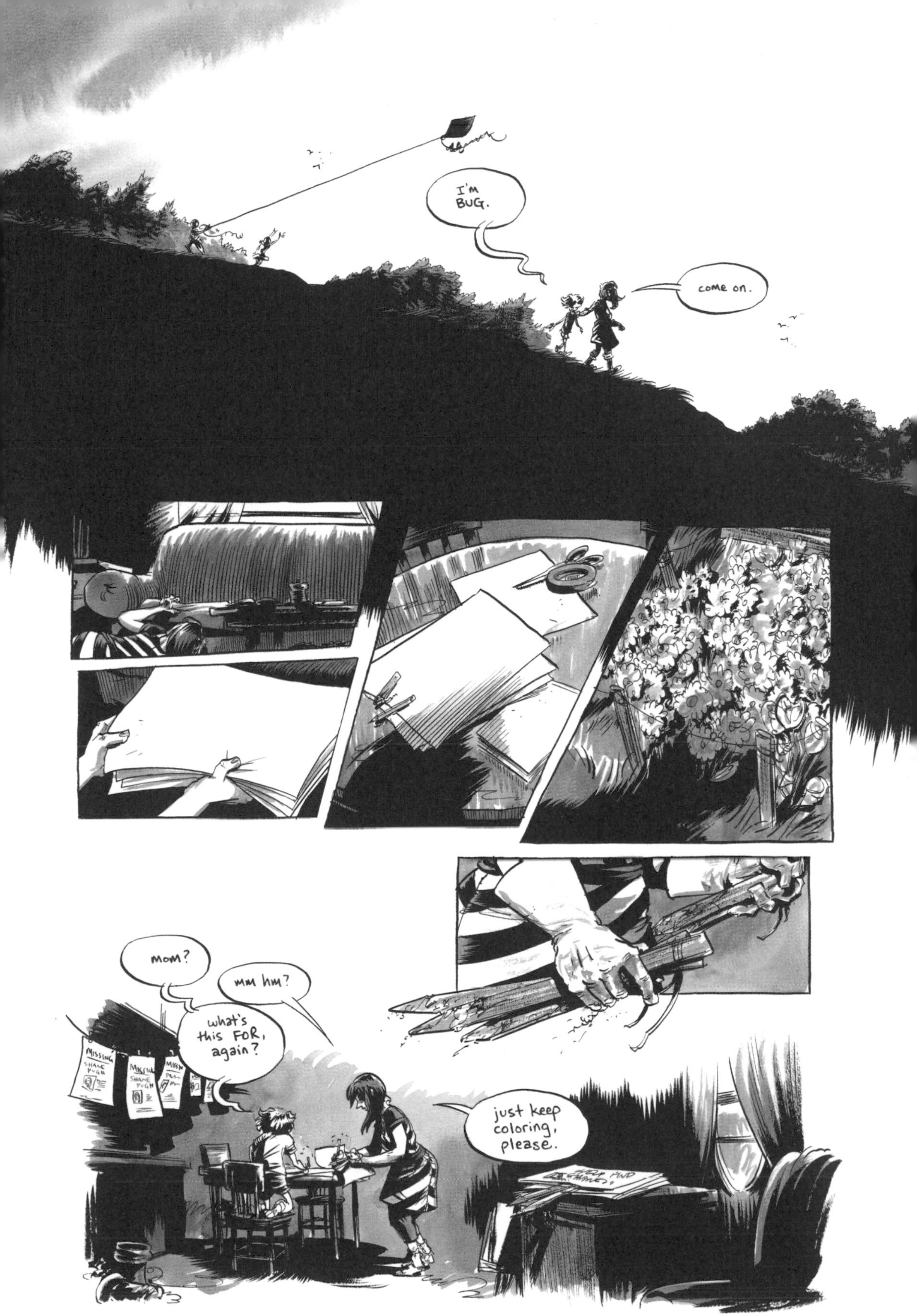

I'm BUG.
come on.
mom?
mm hm?
what's this FOR, again?
MISSING
SHANE PUGH
just keep coloring, please.

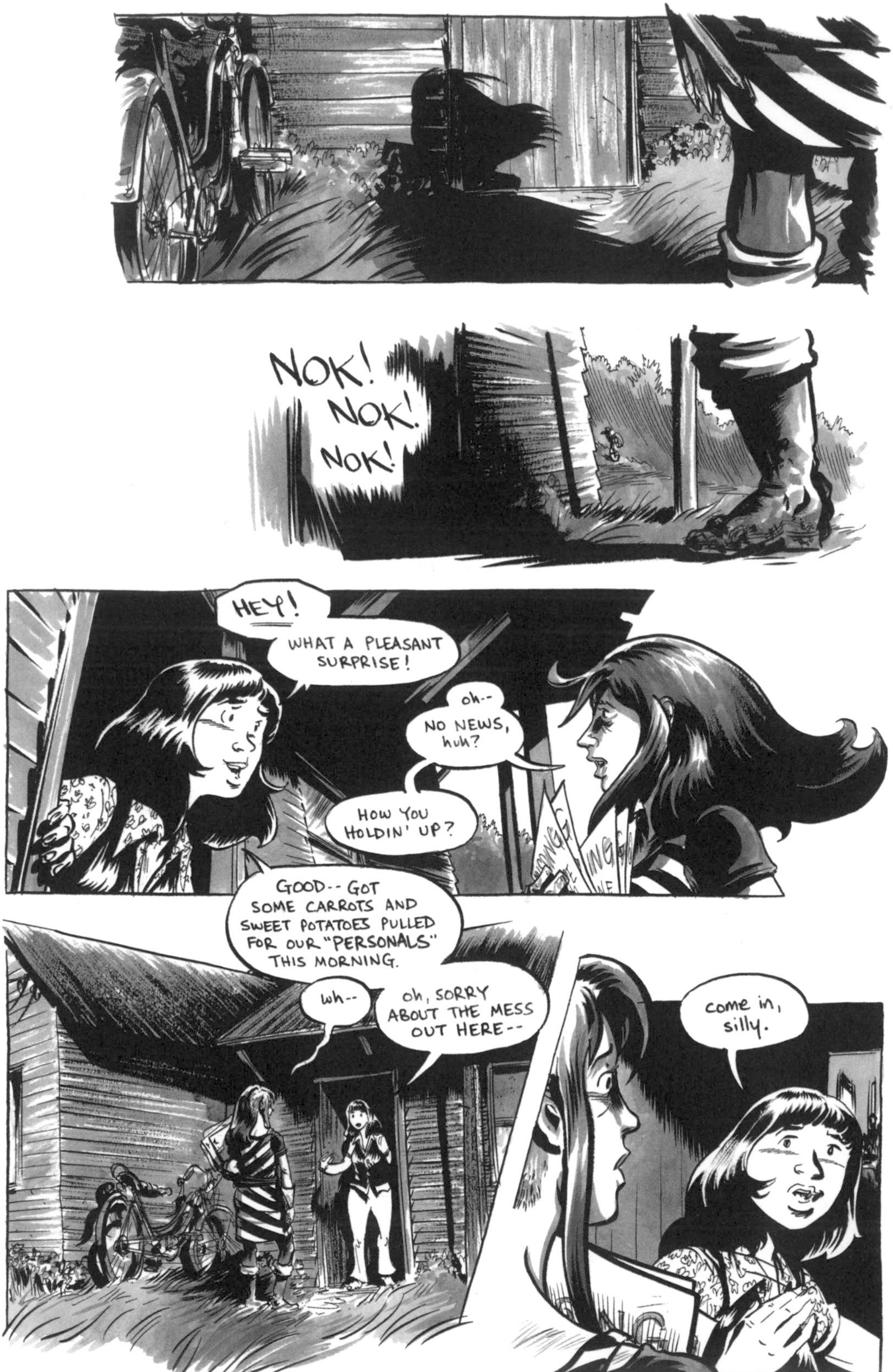
NOK!
NOK!
NOK!
HEY!
WHAT A PLEASANT SURPRISE!
oh--
NO NEWS, huh?
HOW YOU HOLDIN' UP?
GOOD-- GOT SOME CARROTS AND SWEET POTATOES PULLED FOR OUR "PERSONALS" THIS MORNING.
wh--
oh, SORRY ABOUT THE MESS OUT HERE--
come in, silly.

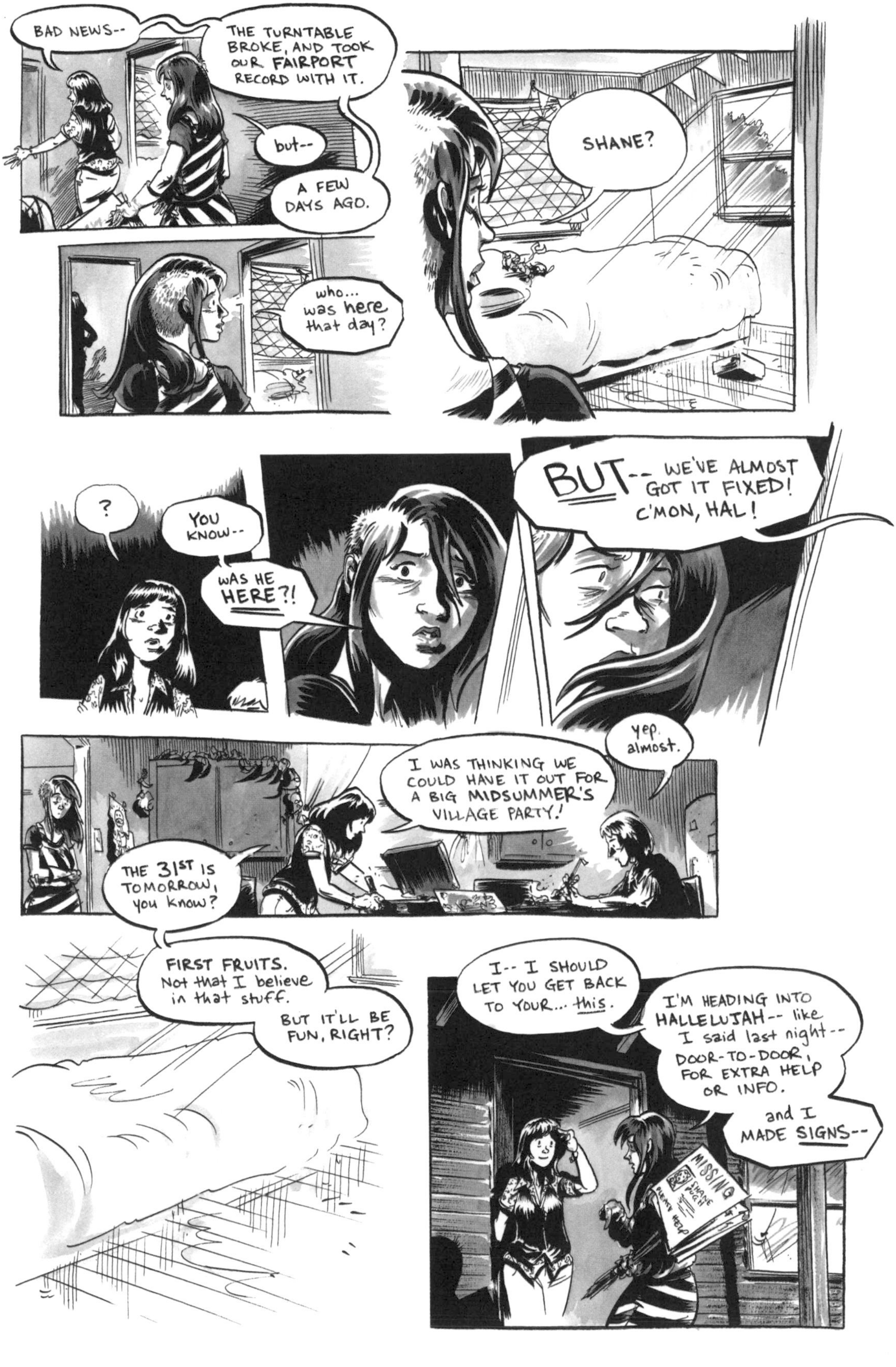
BAD NEWS--
THE TURNTABLE BROKE, AND TOOK OUR FAIRPORT RECORD WITH IT.
but--
A FEW DAYS AGO.
SHANE?
who... was here that day?
?
YOU KNOW--
WAS HE HERE?!
BUT-- WE'VE ALMOST GOT IT FIXED! C'MON, HAL!
I WAS THINKING WE COULD HAVE IT OUT FOR A BIG MIDSUMMER'S VILLAGE PARTY!
yep. almost.
THE 31ST IS TOMORROW, you know?
FIRST FRUITS. Not that I believe in that stuff.
BUT IT'LL BE FUN, RIGHT?
I-- I SHOULD LET YOU GET BACK TO YOUR... this.
I'M HEADING INTO HALLELUJAH-- like I said last night-- DOOR-TO-DOOR, FOR EXTRA HELP OR INFO.
and I MADE SIGNS--
MISSING

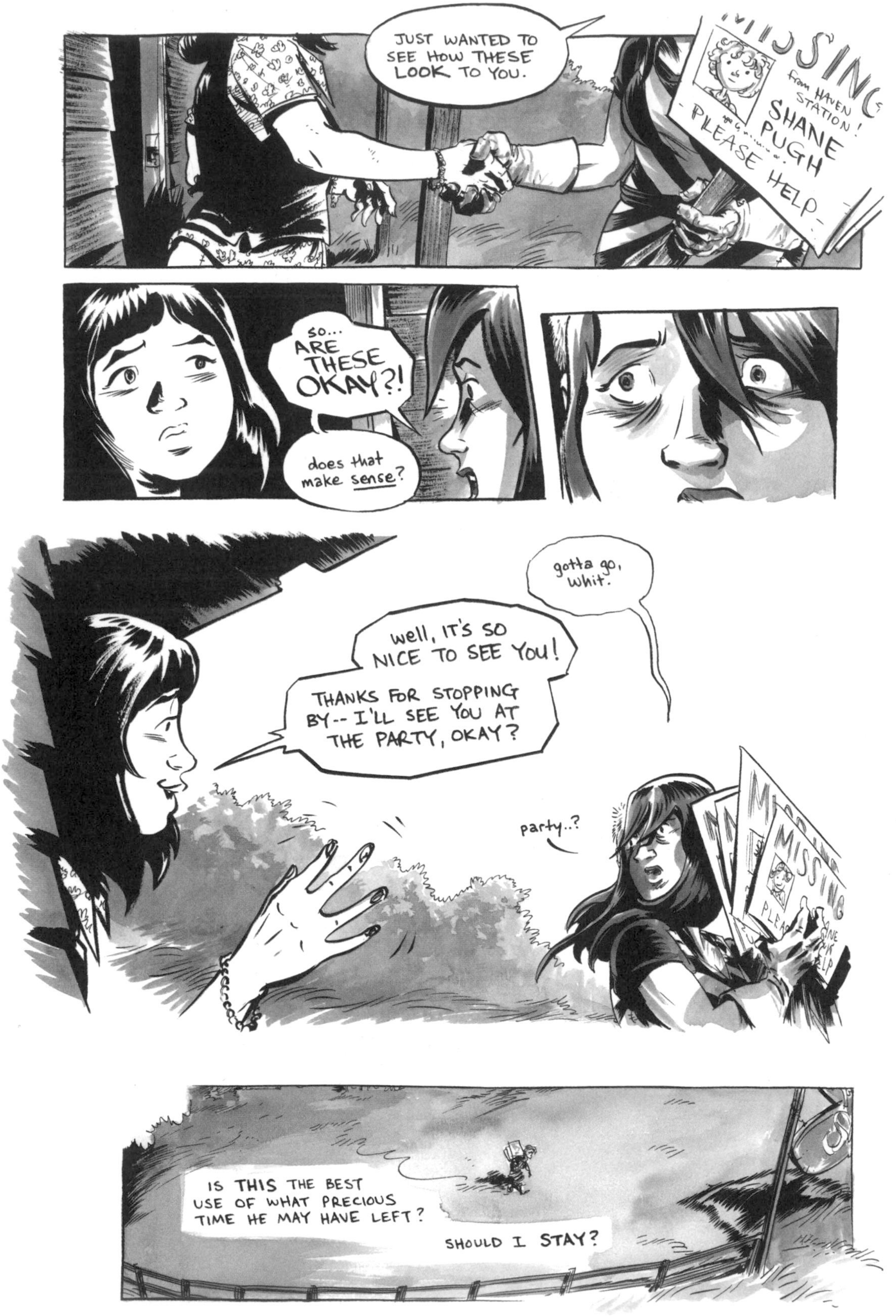

JUST WANTED TO SEE HOW THESE LOOK TO YOU.
MISSING from HAVEN STATION! SHANE PUGH -PLEASE HELP-
so... ARE THESE OKAY?!
does that make sense?
gotta go, whit.
well, IT'S SO NICE TO SEE YOU!
THANKS FOR STOPPING BY-- I'LL SEE YOU AT THE PARTY, OKAY?
party..?
IS THIS THE BEST USE OF WHAT PRECIOUS TIME HE MAY HAVE LEFT?
SHOULD I STAY?

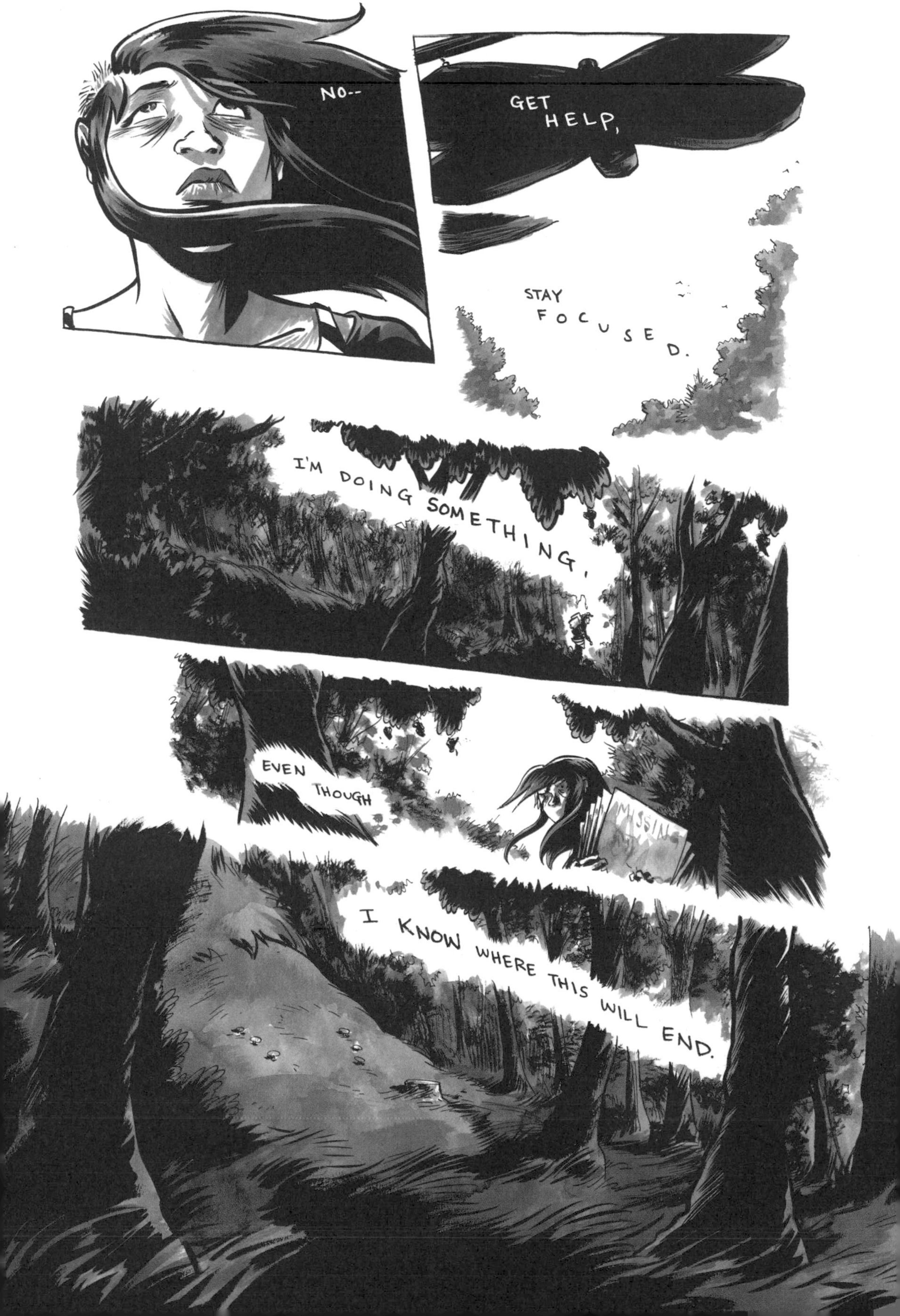
NO--
GET HELP,
STAY FOCUSED.
I'M DOING SOMETHING,
EVEN THOUGH
MISSING
I KNOW WHERE THIS WILL END.

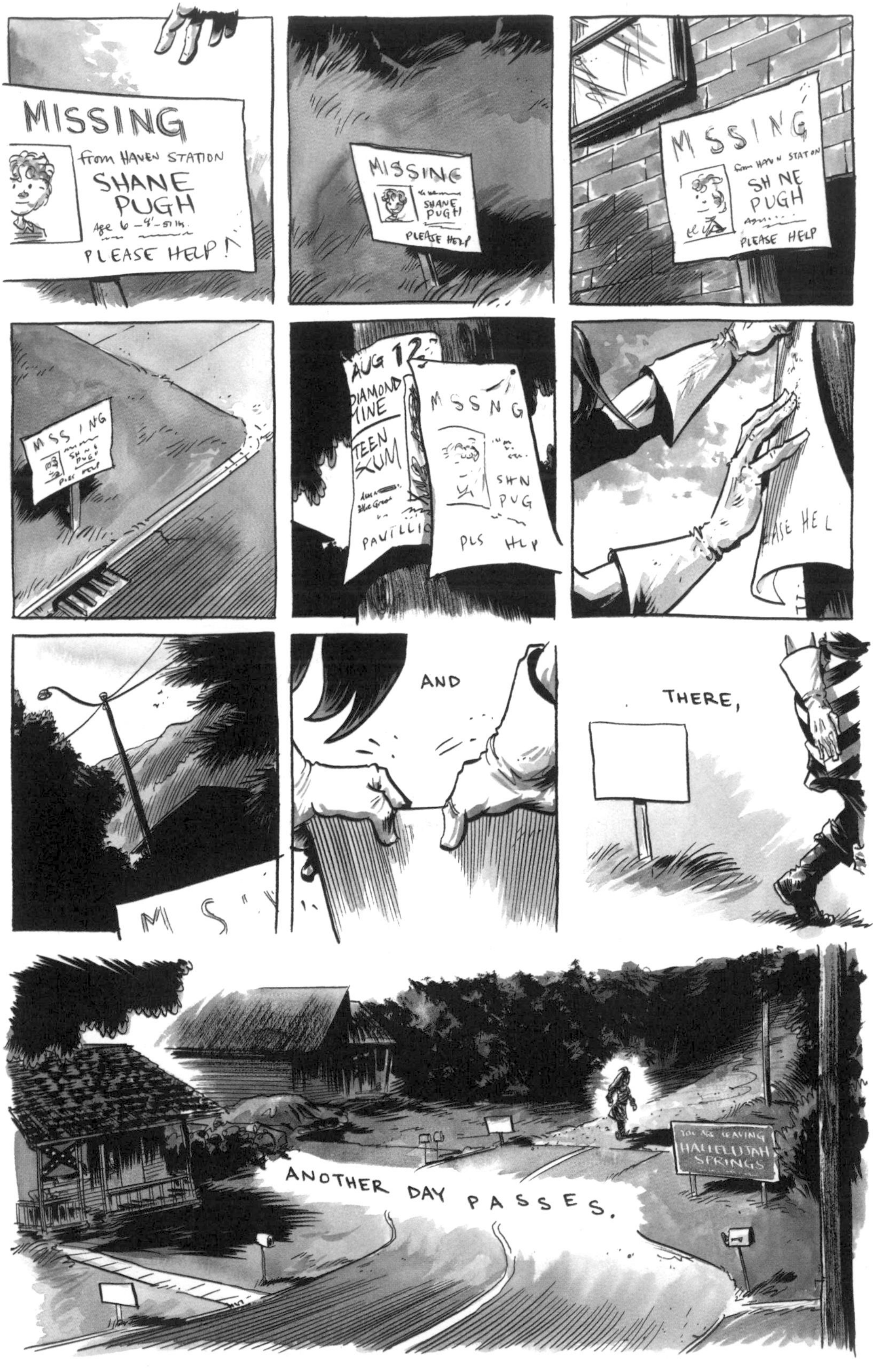

MISSING
from HAVEN STATION
SHANE PUGH
PLEASE HELP!
MISSING
SHANE PUGH
PLEASE HELP
MISSING
SHNE PUGH
PLEASE HELP
AUG 12
DIAMOND MINE
TEEN SKUM
PAVILLIO
MSSNG
SHN PUG
PLS HELP
ASE HEL
AND
THERE,
YOU ARE LEAVING
HALLELUJAH SPRINGS
ANOTHER DAY PASSES.

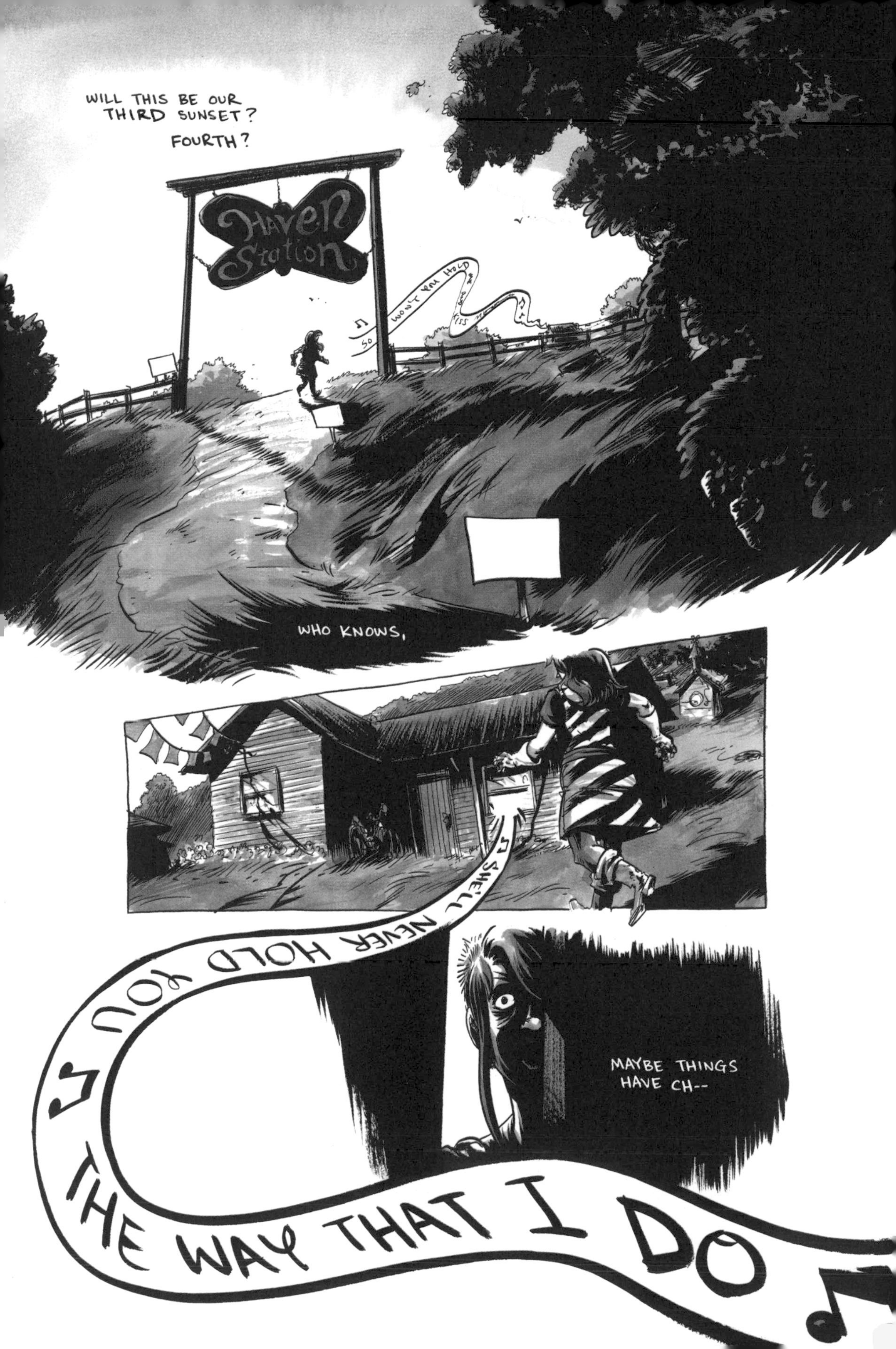
WILL THIS BE OUR THIRD SUNSET?
FOURTH?
Haven Station
SO WON'T YOU HOLD ME AND KISS ME
WHO KNOWS,
SHE'LL NEVER HOLD YOU
MAYBE THINGS HAVE CH--
THE WAY THAT I DO

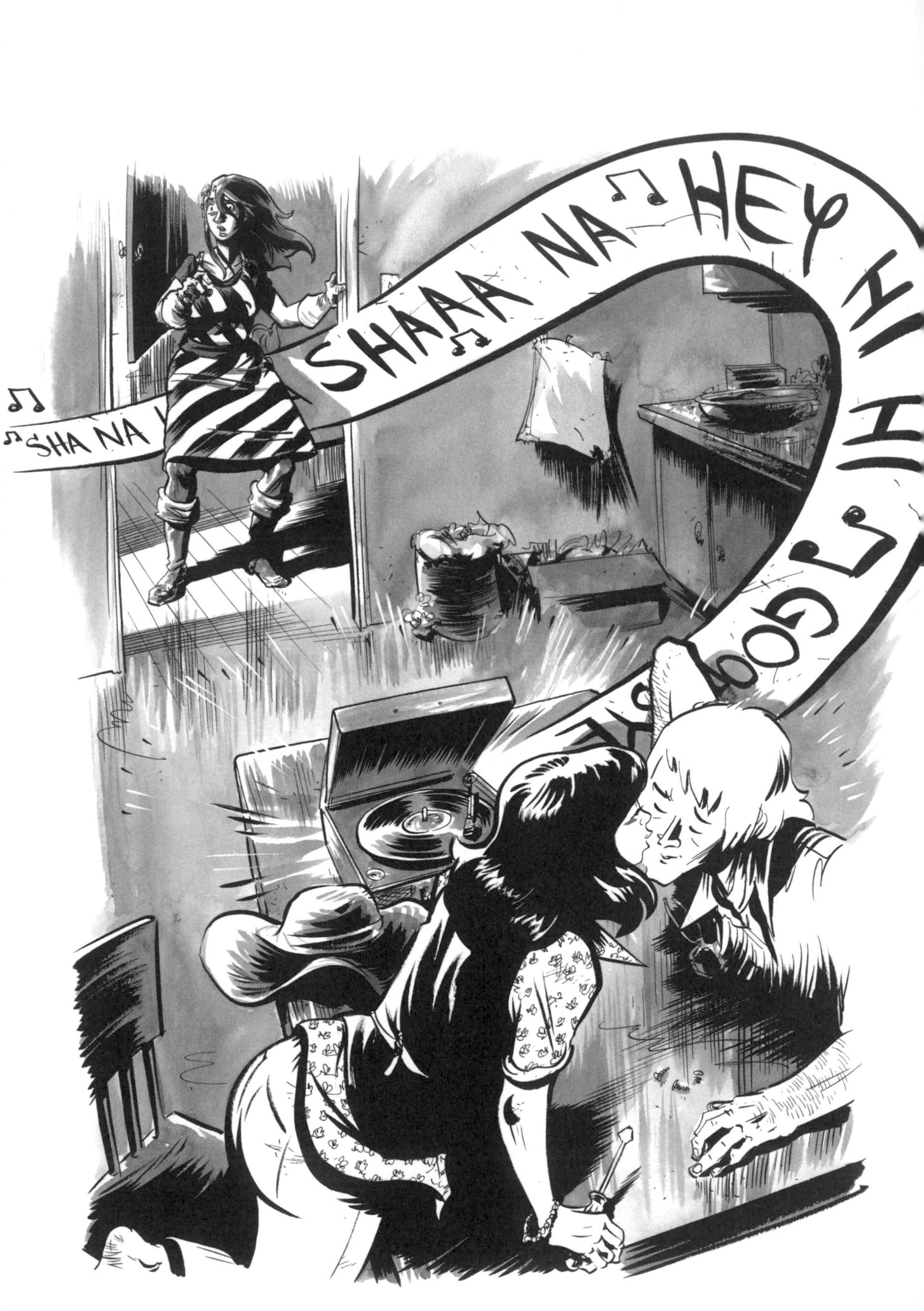
SHA NA
SHAAA NA
HEY HI HI GOO

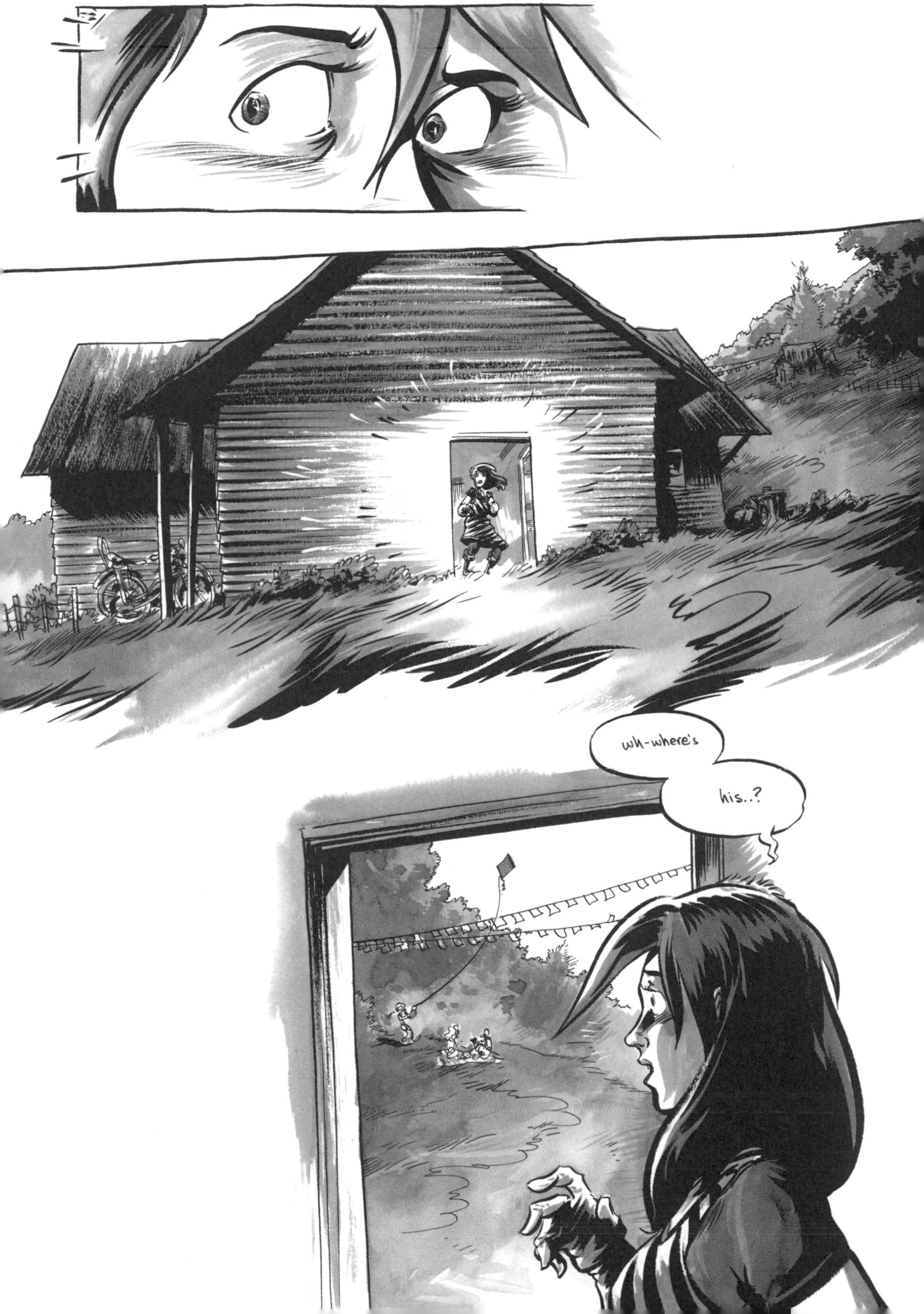
wh-where's
his..?

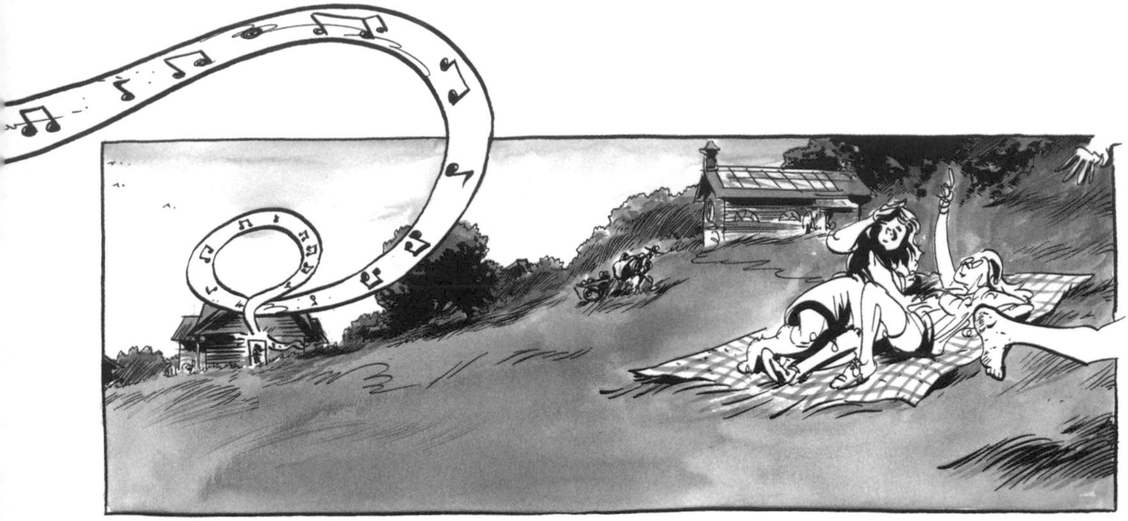

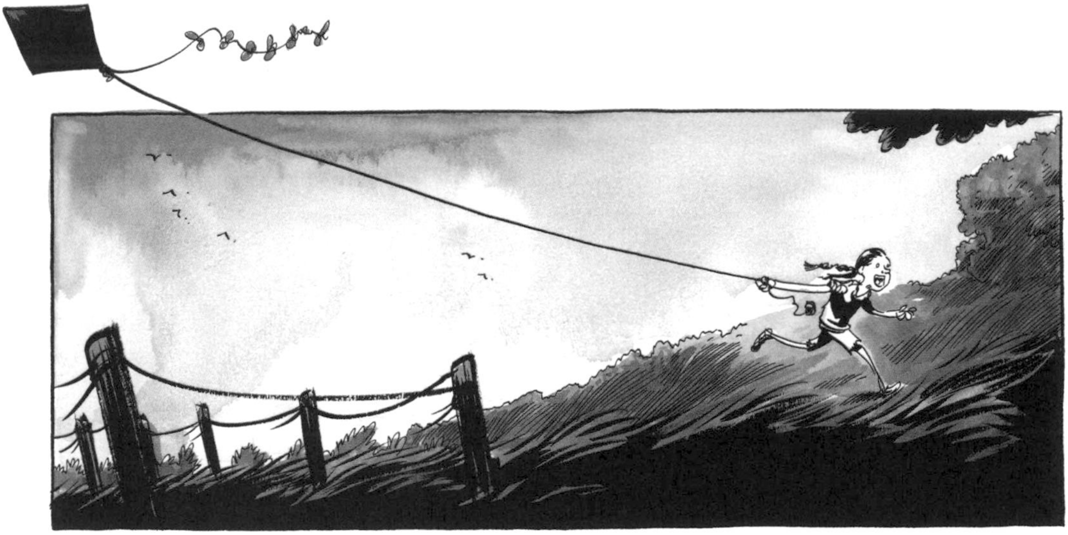

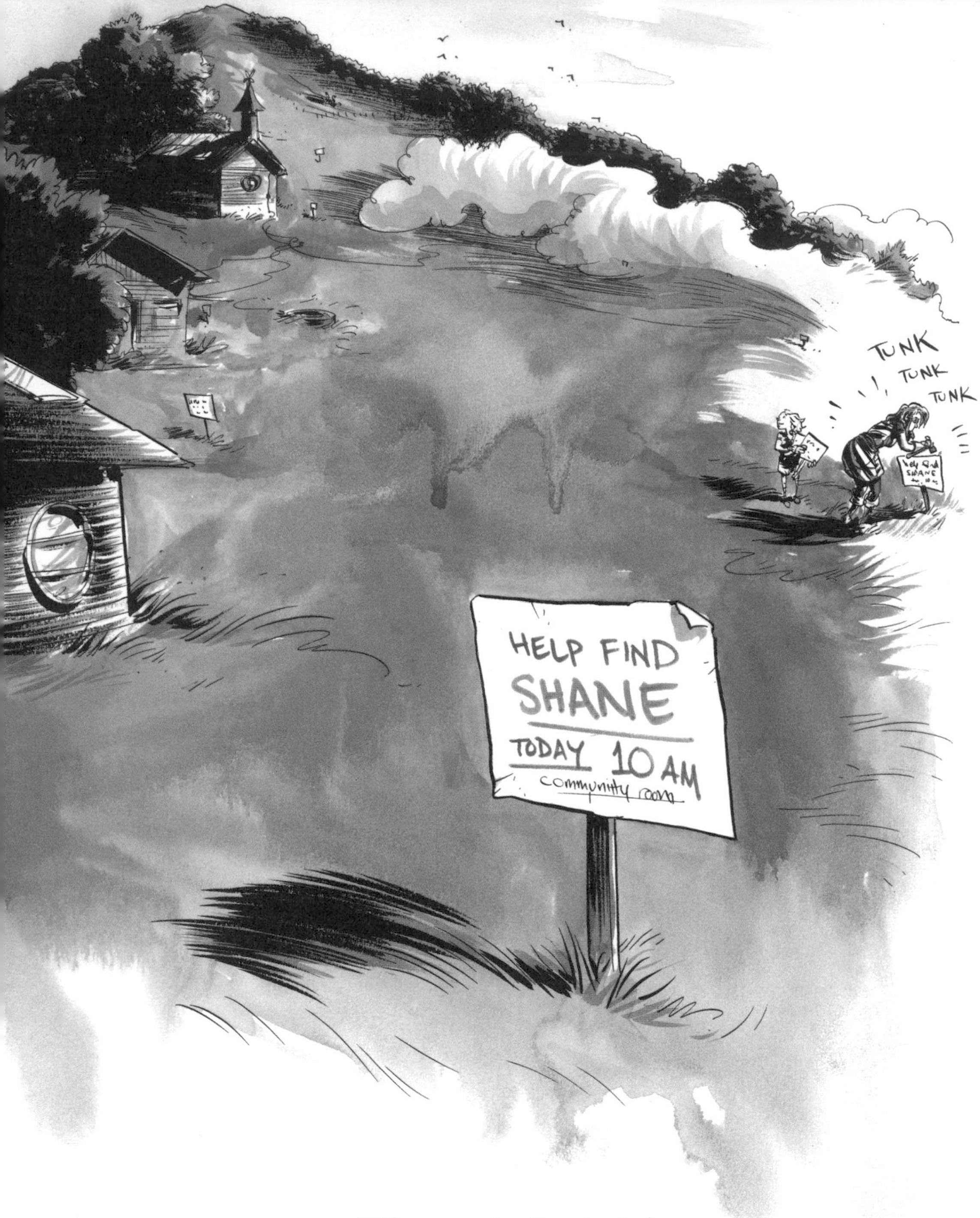
TUNK
TUNK
TUNK
HELP FIND
SHANE
TODAY 10 AM
community room

TUESDAY

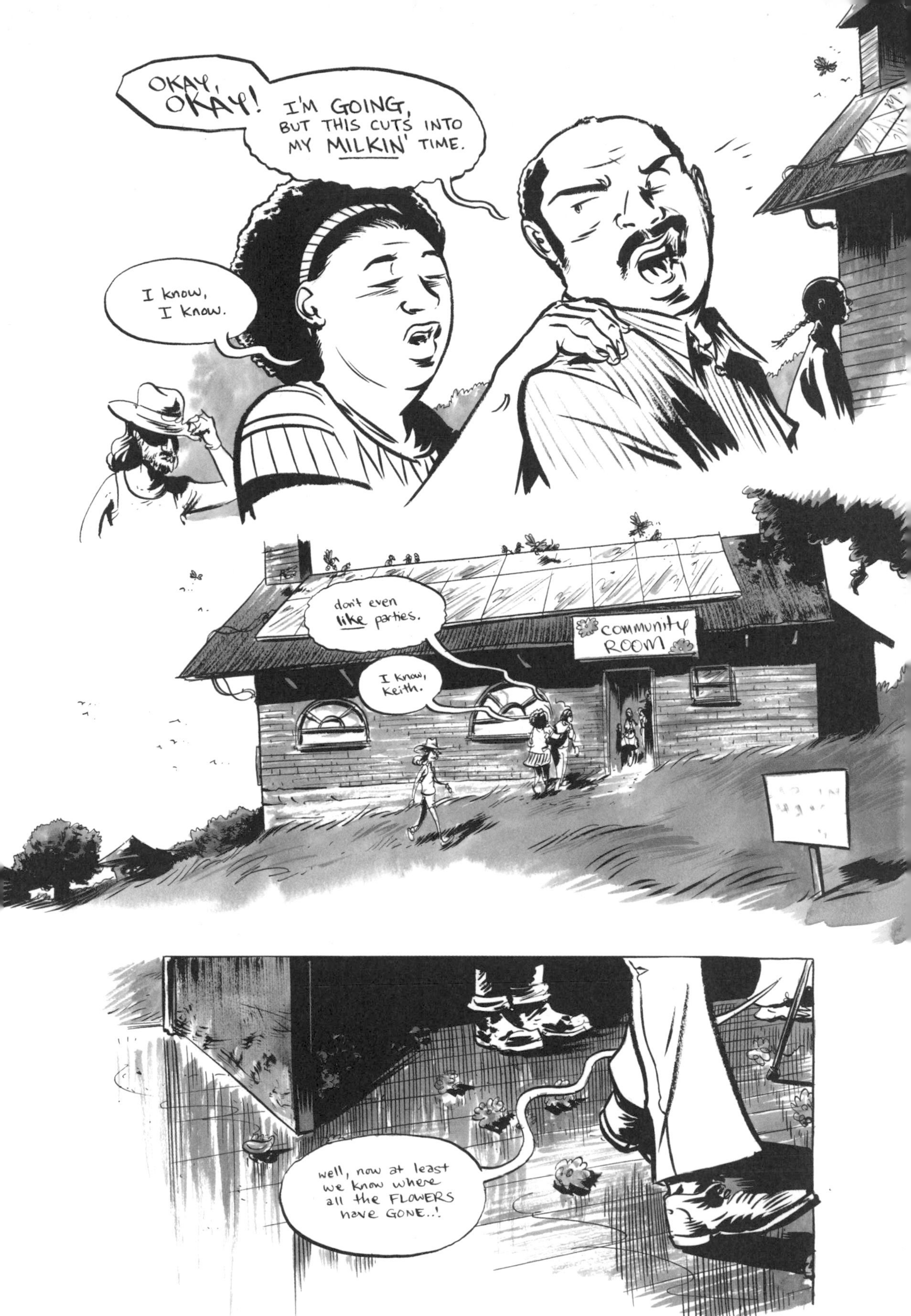
OKAY, OKAY! I'M GOING, BUT THIS CUTS INTO MY MILKIN' TIME.
I know, I know.
don't even like parties.
I know, Keith.
COMMUNITY ROOM
well, now at least we know where all the FLOWERS have GONE..!

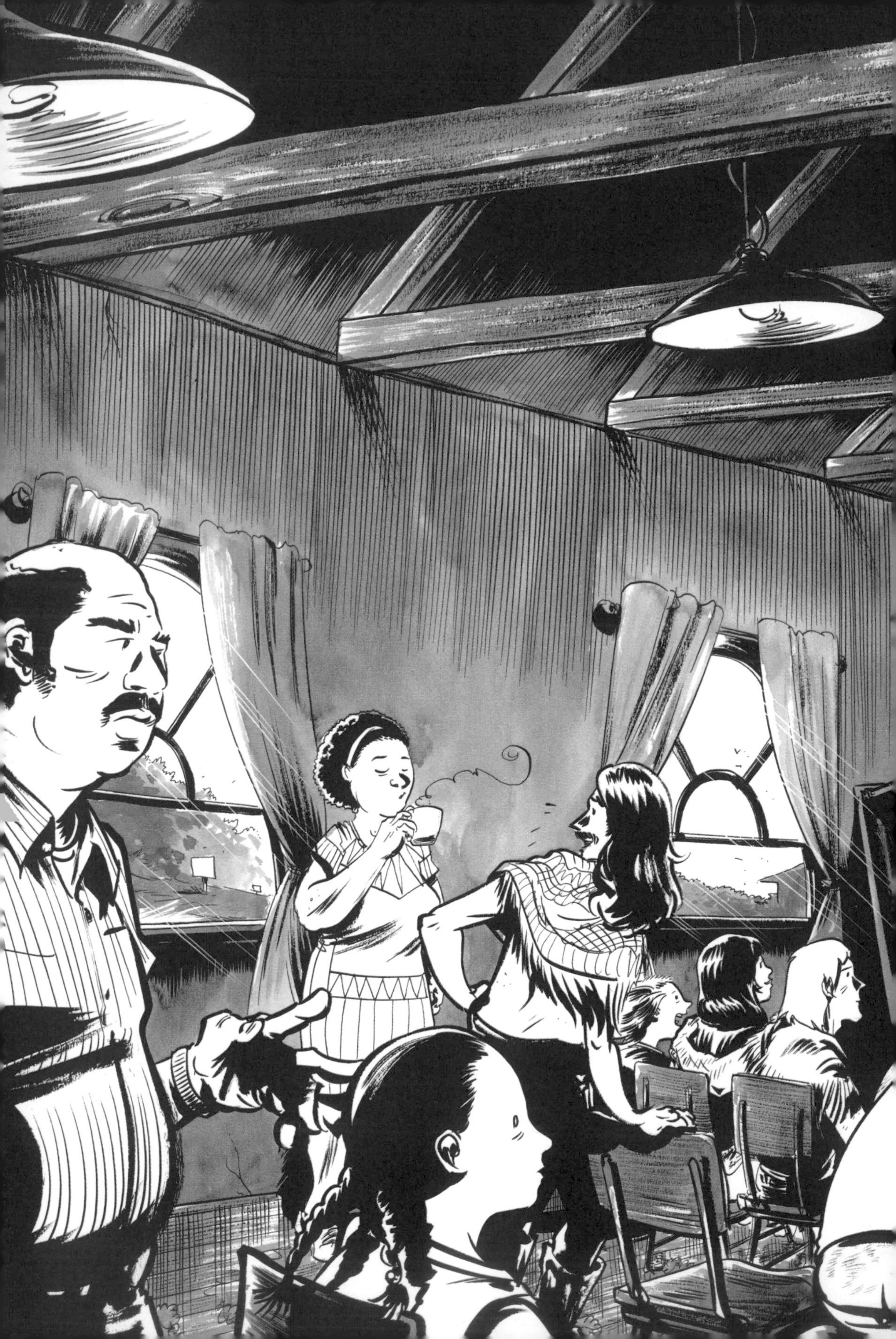

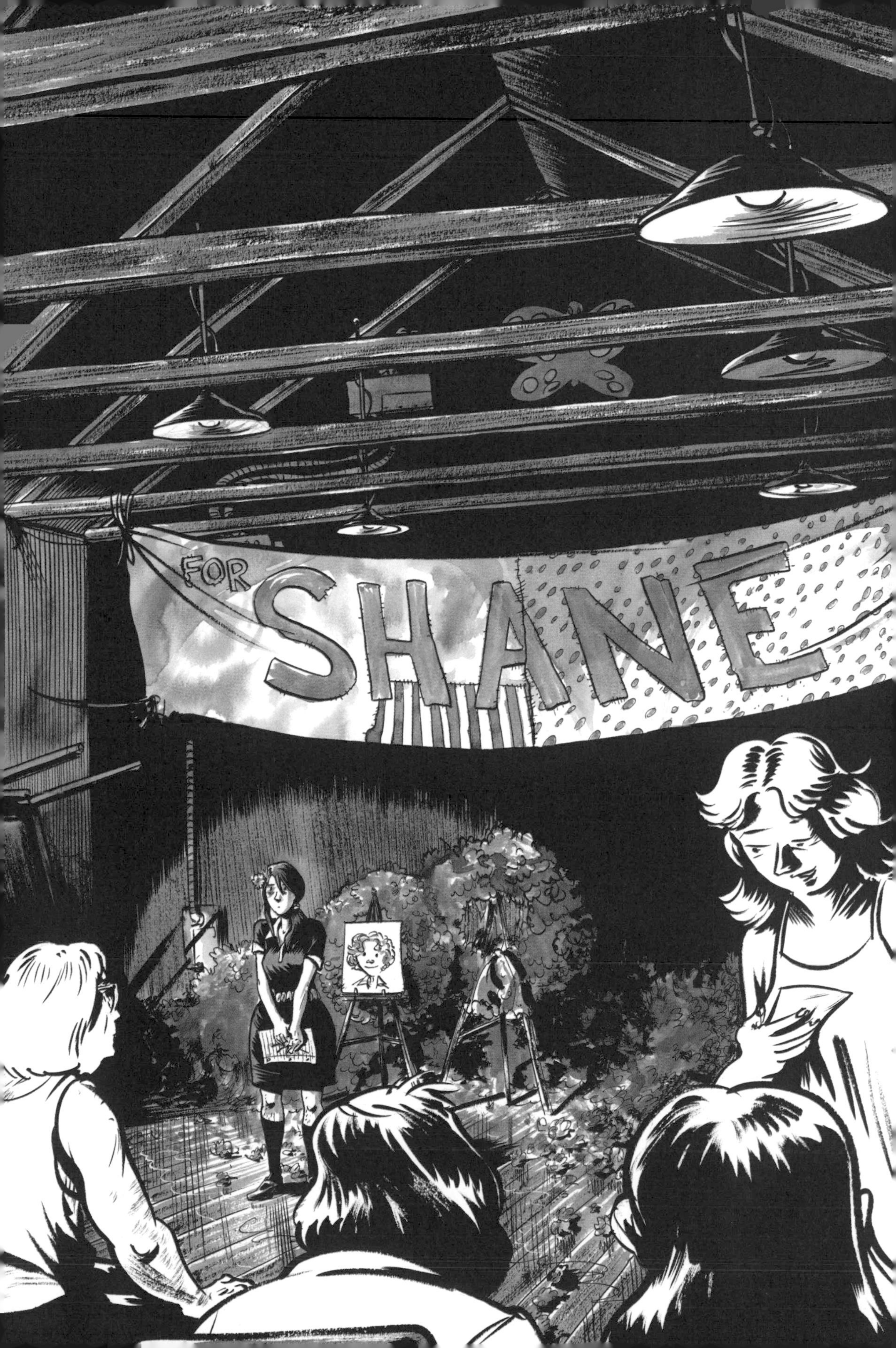

FOR SHANE

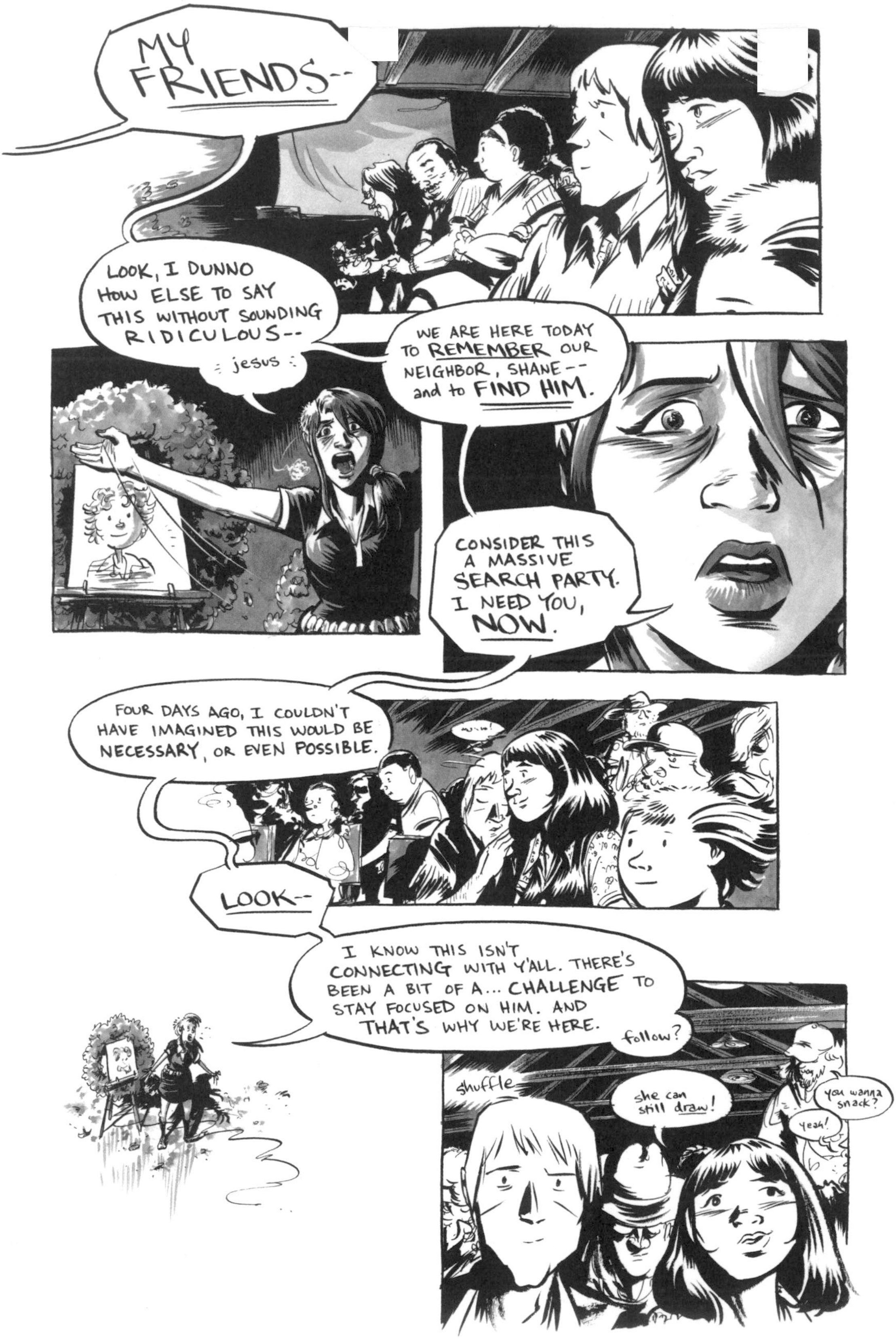
MY FRIENDS--
LOOK, I DUNNO HOW ELSE TO SAY THIS WITHOUT SOUNDING RIDICULOUS--
jesus
WE ARE HERE TODAY TO REMEMBER OUR NEIGHBOR, SHANE-- and to FIND HIM.
CONSIDER THIS A MASSIVE SEARCH PARTY. I NEED YOU, NOW.
FOUR DAYS AGO, I COULDN'T HAVE IMAGINED THIS WOULD BE NECESSARY, OR EVEN POSSIBLE.
LOOK--
I KNOW THIS ISN'T CONNECTING WITH Y'ALL. THERE'S BEEN A BIT OF A... CHALLENGE TO STAY FOCUSED ON HIM. AND THAT'S WHY WE'RE HERE.
follow?
shuffle
she can still draw!
you wanna snack?
yeah!

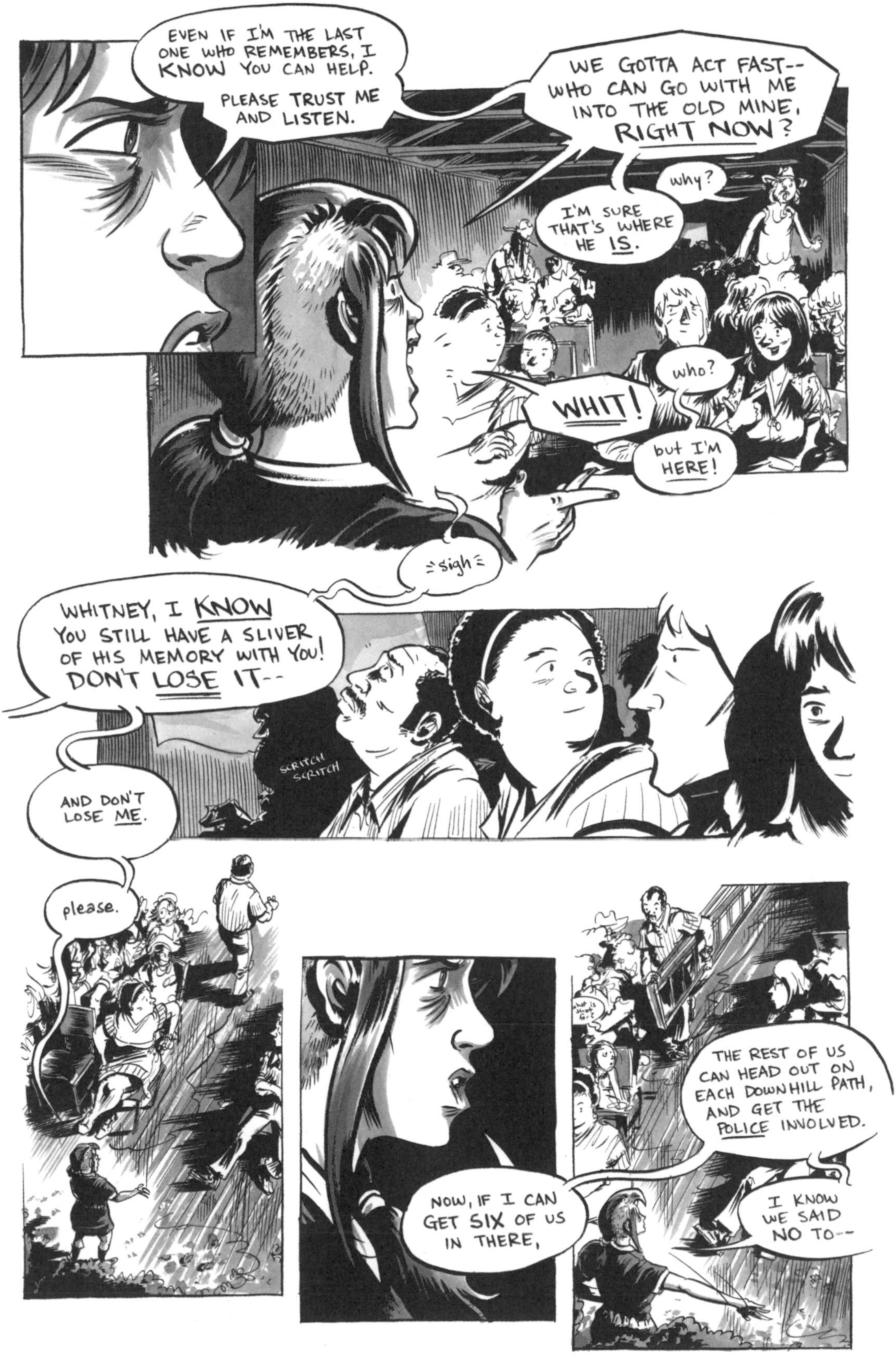
EVEN IF I'M THE LAST ONE WHO REMEMBERS, I KNOW YOU CAN HELP.
PLEASE TRUST ME AND LISTEN.
WE GOTTA ACT FAST-- WHO CAN GO WITH ME INTO THE OLD MINE, RIGHT NOW?
why?
I'M SURE THAT'S WHERE HE IS.
who?
WHIT!
but I'M HERE!
sigh
WHITNEY, I KNOW YOU STILL HAVE A SLIVER OF HIS MEMORY WITH YOU! DON'T LOSE IT--
SCRITCH SCRITCH
AND DON'T LOSE ME.
please.
NOW, IF I CAN GET SIX OF US IN THERE,
THE REST OF US CAN HEAD OUT ON EACH DOWNHILL PATH, AND GET THE POLICE INVOLVED.
I KNOW WE SAID NO TO--

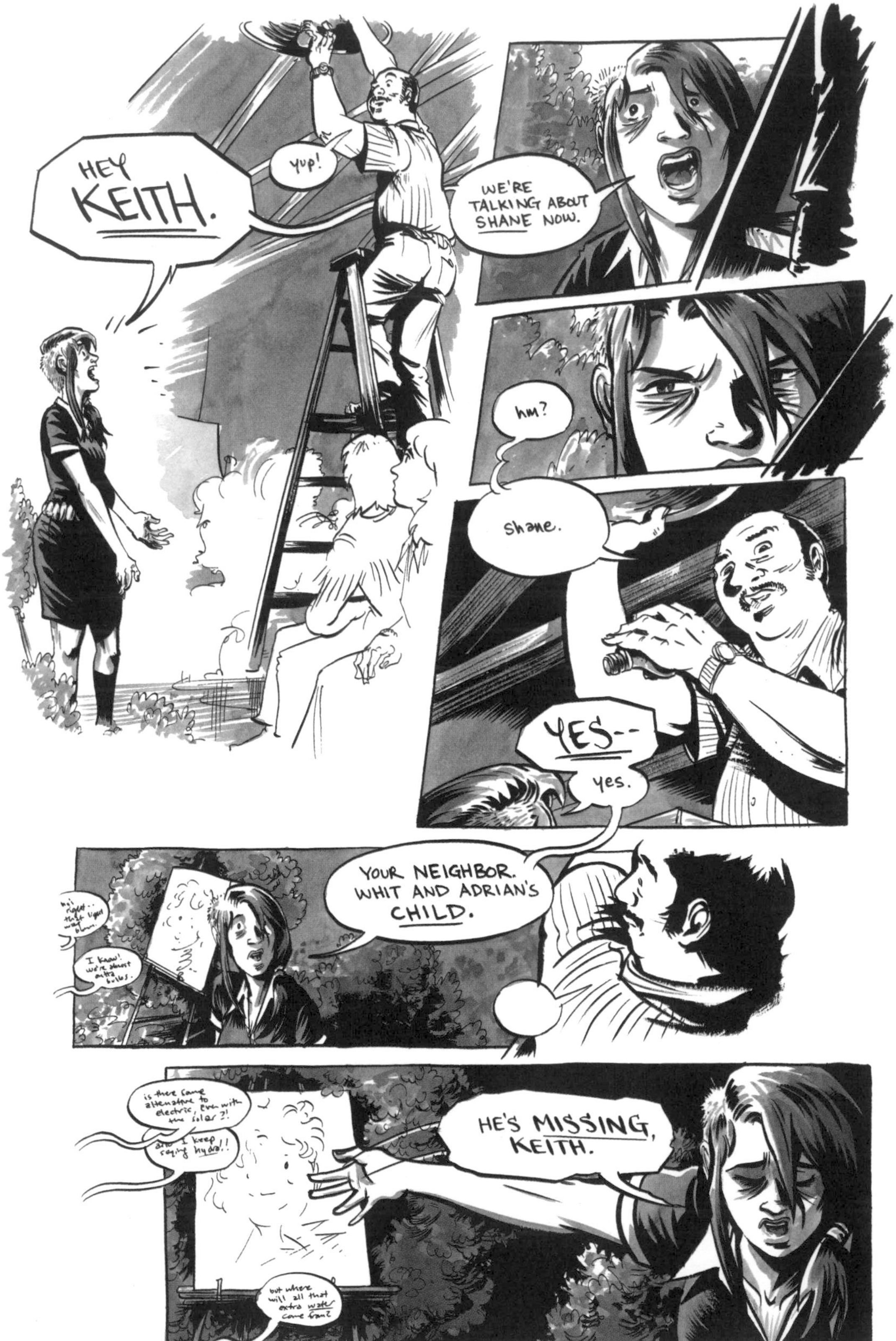
HEY KEITH.
yup!
WE'RE TALKING ABOUT SHANE NOW.
hm?
shane.
YES--
yes.
YOUR NEIGHBOR. WHIT AND ADRIAN'S CHILD.
I know! we're almost outta bulbs.
is there some alternative to electric, even with the solar?!
and I keep saying hydro!!
HE'S MISSING, KEITH.
but where will all that extra water come from?

okay.

CLEARLY something is happening.

ha!

maybe only I did!

A dark magic is at work. Or SOMETHING.

I know that sounds absurd,

but so do YOU.

It re

well, that's the last I heard, anyway. It was about his sister.

so what do you think was the best

oh yeah, me too.

there an em

I--

hey, you want some help with that?

Sure, if you don't mind!

I have something to tell you.

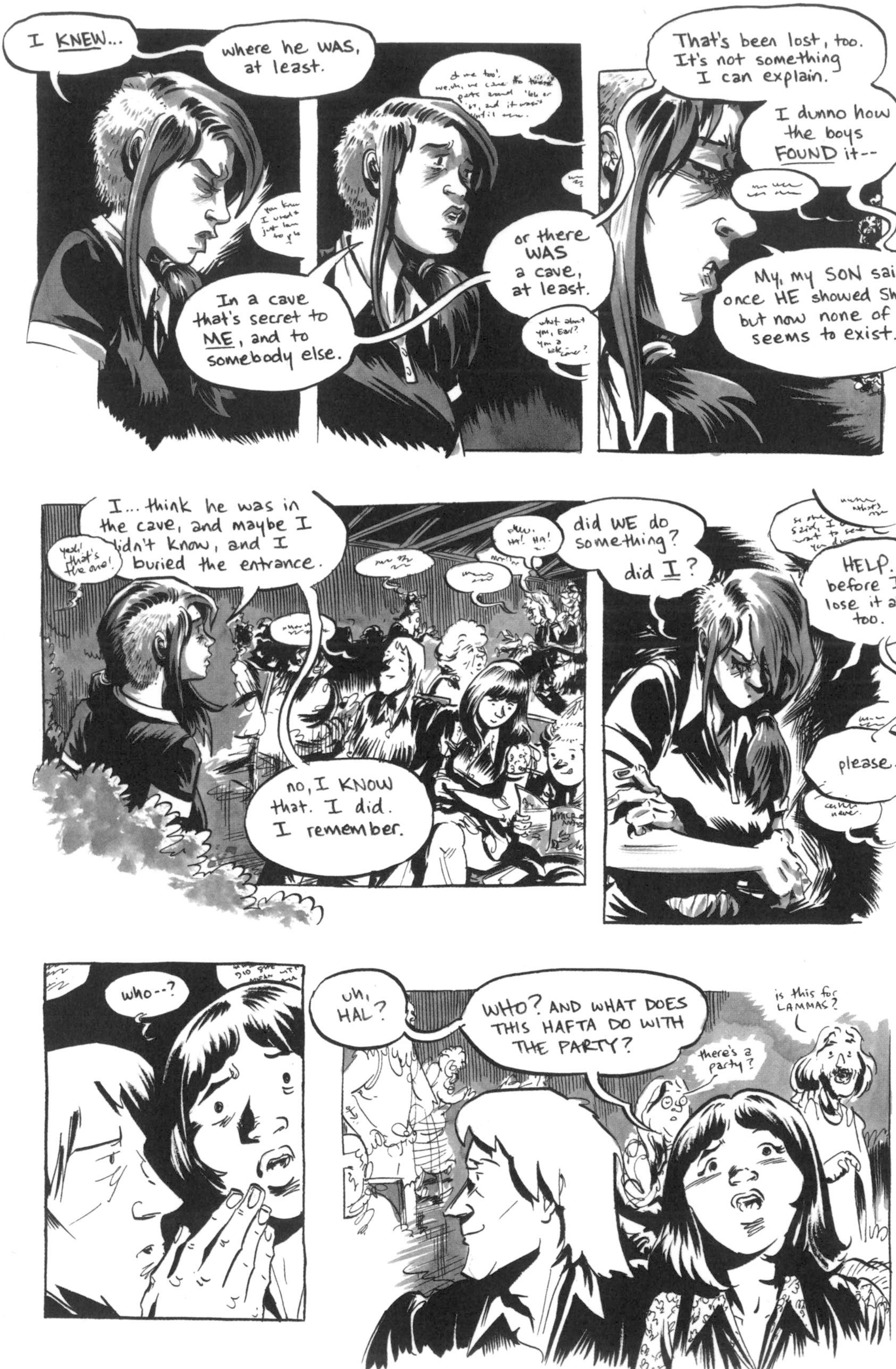
I KNEW...
where he WAS, at least.
In a cave that's secret to ME, and to somebody else.
or there WAS a cave, at least.
That's been lost, too. It's not something I can explain.
I dunno how the boys FOUND it--
My, my SON said once HE showed Shane, but now none of it seems to exist.
I... think he was in the cave, and maybe I didn't know, and I buried the entrance.
yeah! that's the one!
no, I KNOW that. I did. I remember.
did WE do something?
did I?
HELP. before I lose it all, too.
please.
who--?
uh, HAL?
WHO? AND WHAT DOES THIS HAFTA DO WITH THE PARTY?
there's a party?
is this for LAMMAS?

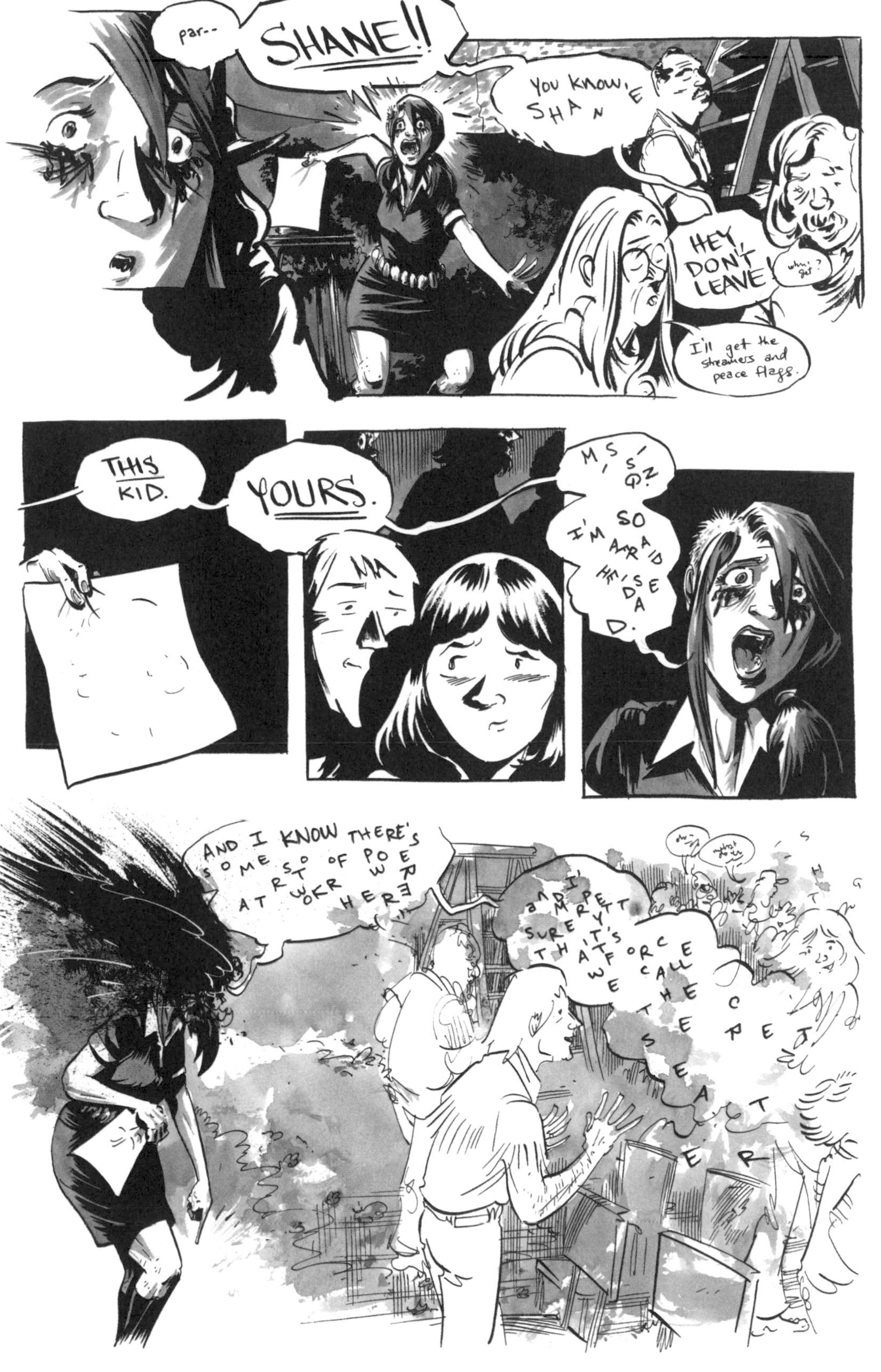
par--
SHANE!!
You know, SHANE
HEY, DON'T LEAVE!
I'll get the streamers and peace flags.
THIS KID.
YOURS.
M S I S Q Z
I'M SO AARAID HE IS DEAD.
AND I KNOW THERE'S SOME ST OF POER AT RWOKR WER HERE

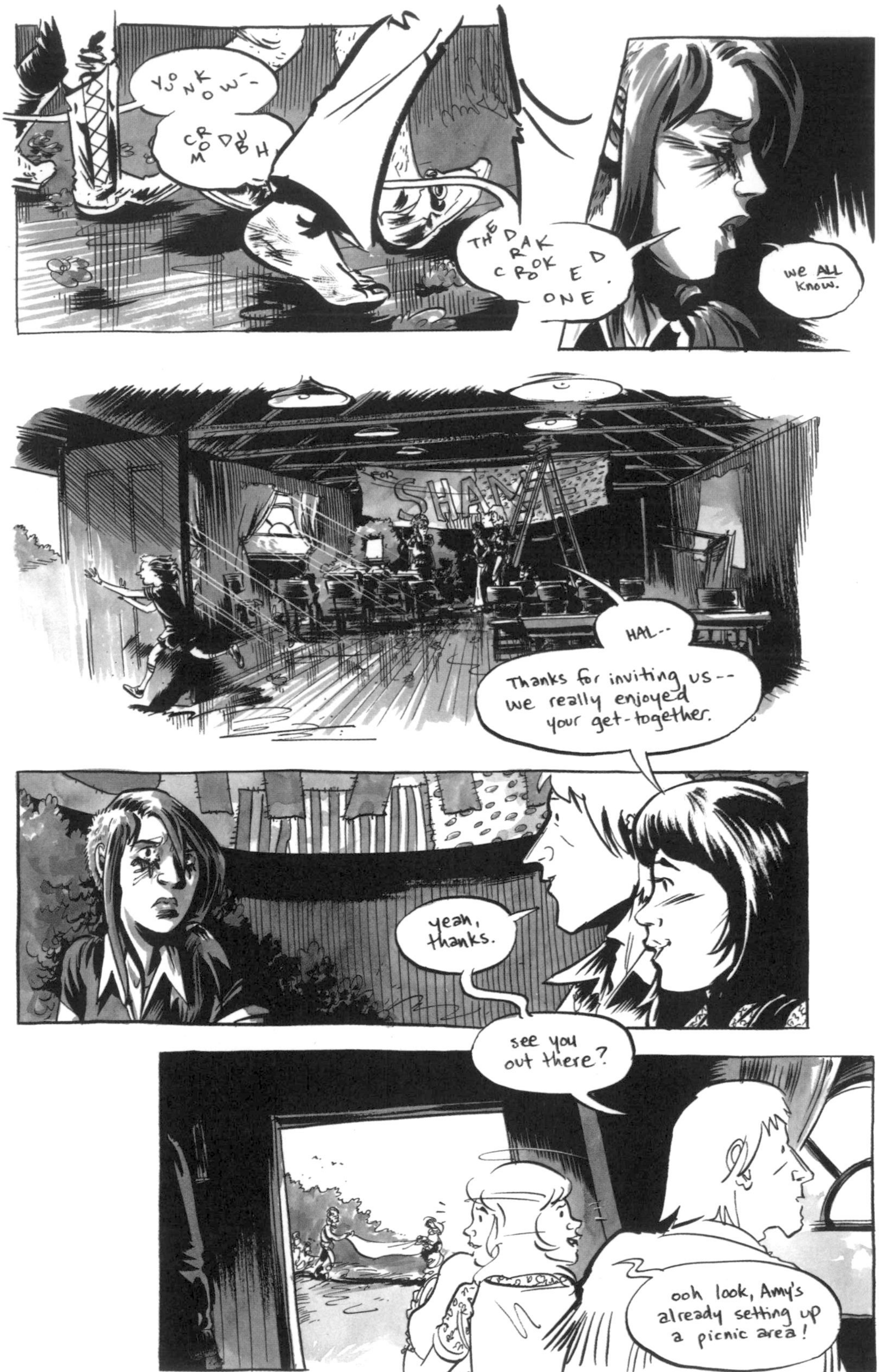
YOU KNOW--
CRMODUBH
THE DARK CROOKED ONE.
we ALL know.
HAL--
Thanks for inviting us-- we really enjoyed your get-together.
yeah, thanks.
see you out there?
ooh look, Amy's already setting up a picnic area!

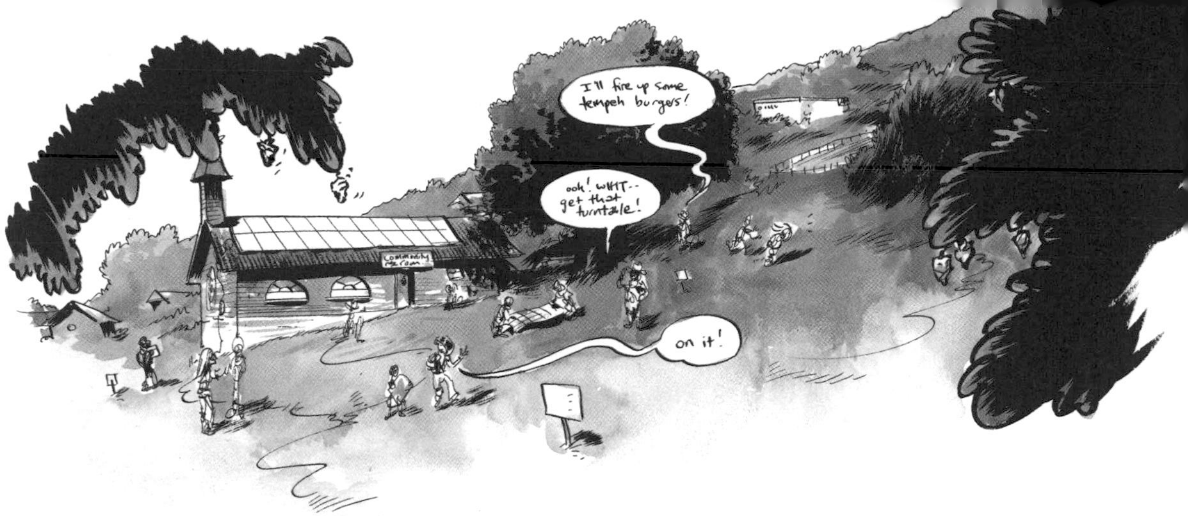
I'll fire up some tempeh burgers!
ook! WHT-- get that turntable!
on it!

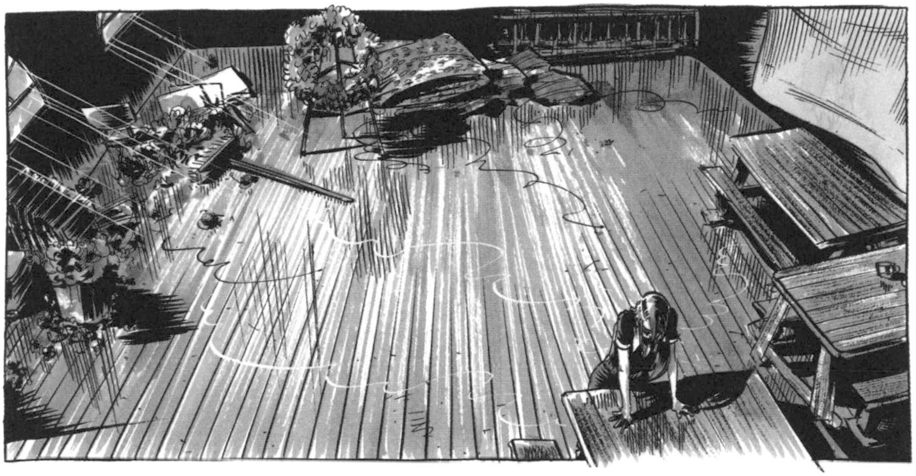

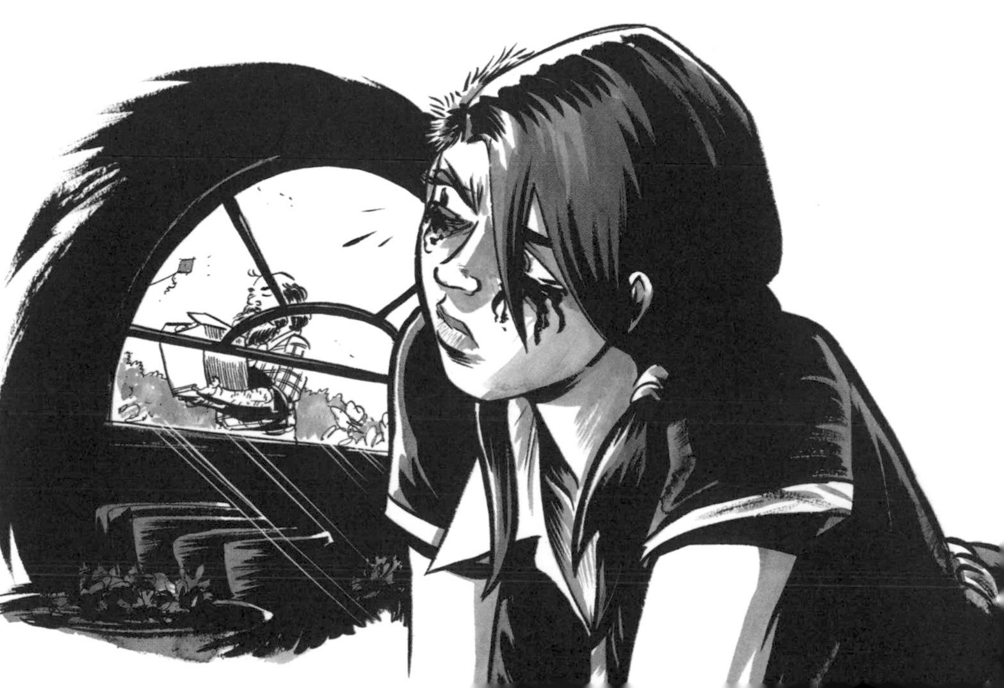

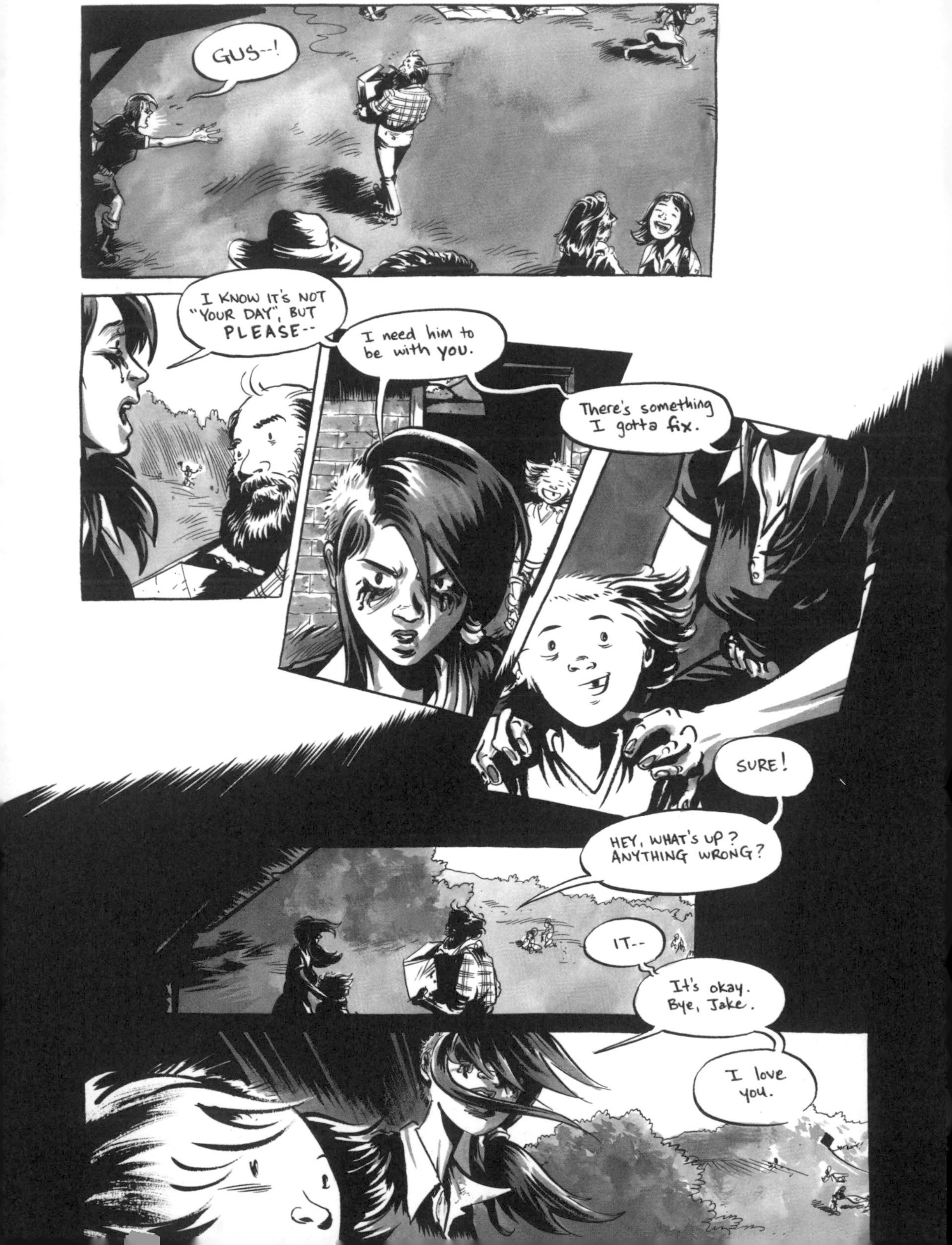
GUS--!
I KNOW IT'S NOT "YOUR DAY", BUT PLEASE--
I need him to be with you.
There's something I gotta fix.
SURE!
HEY, WHAT'S UP? ANYTHING WRONG?
IT--
It's okay. Bye, Jake.
I love you.

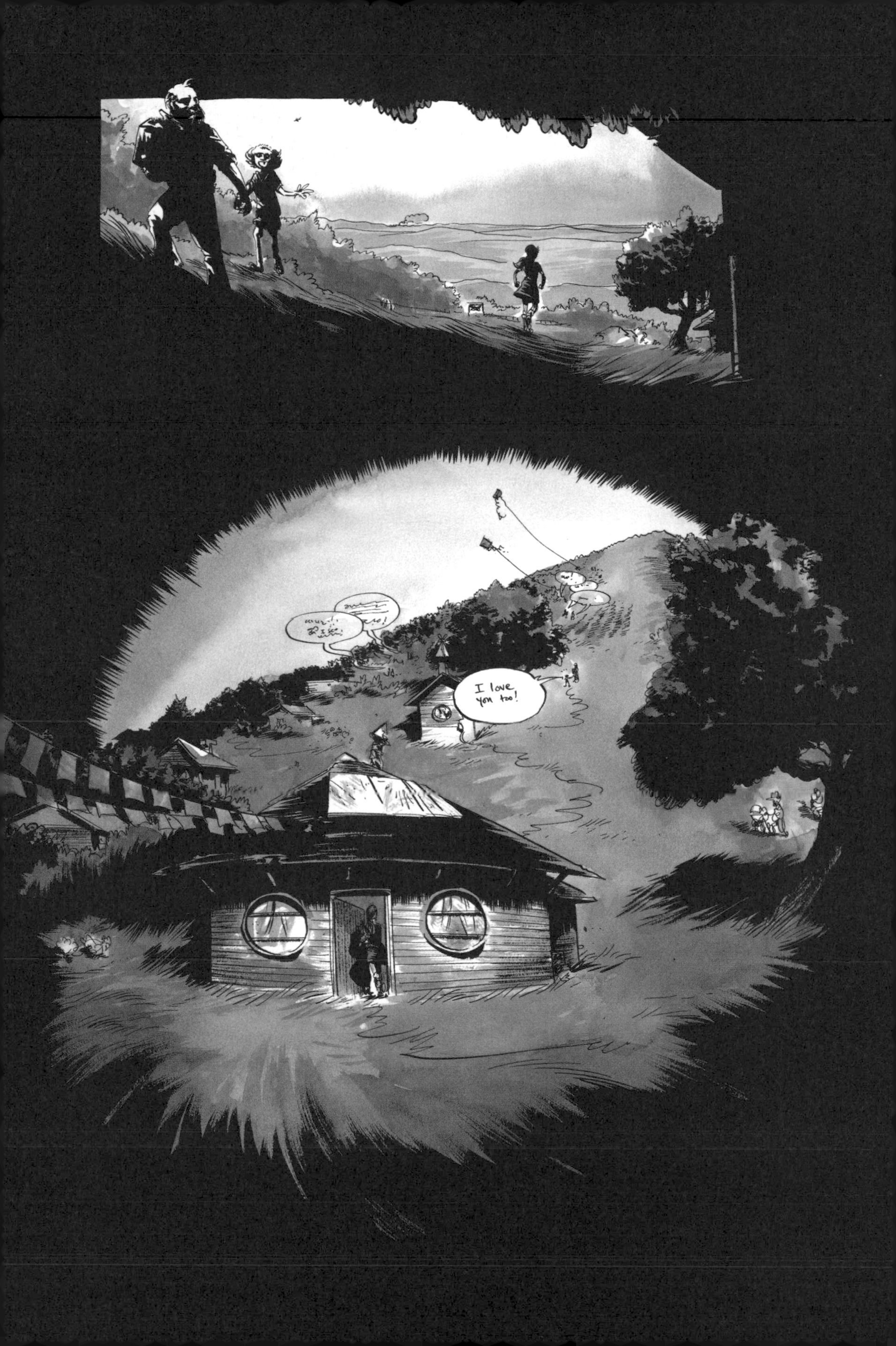
I love you too!

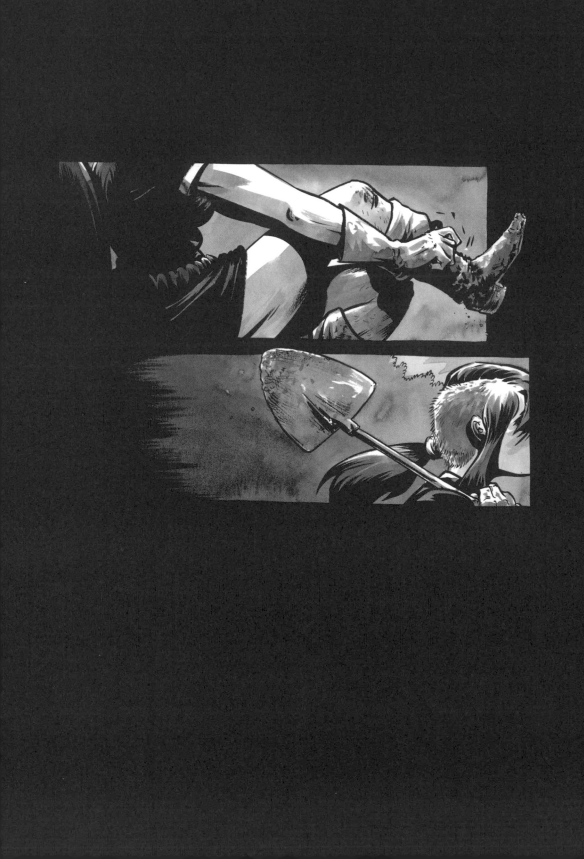

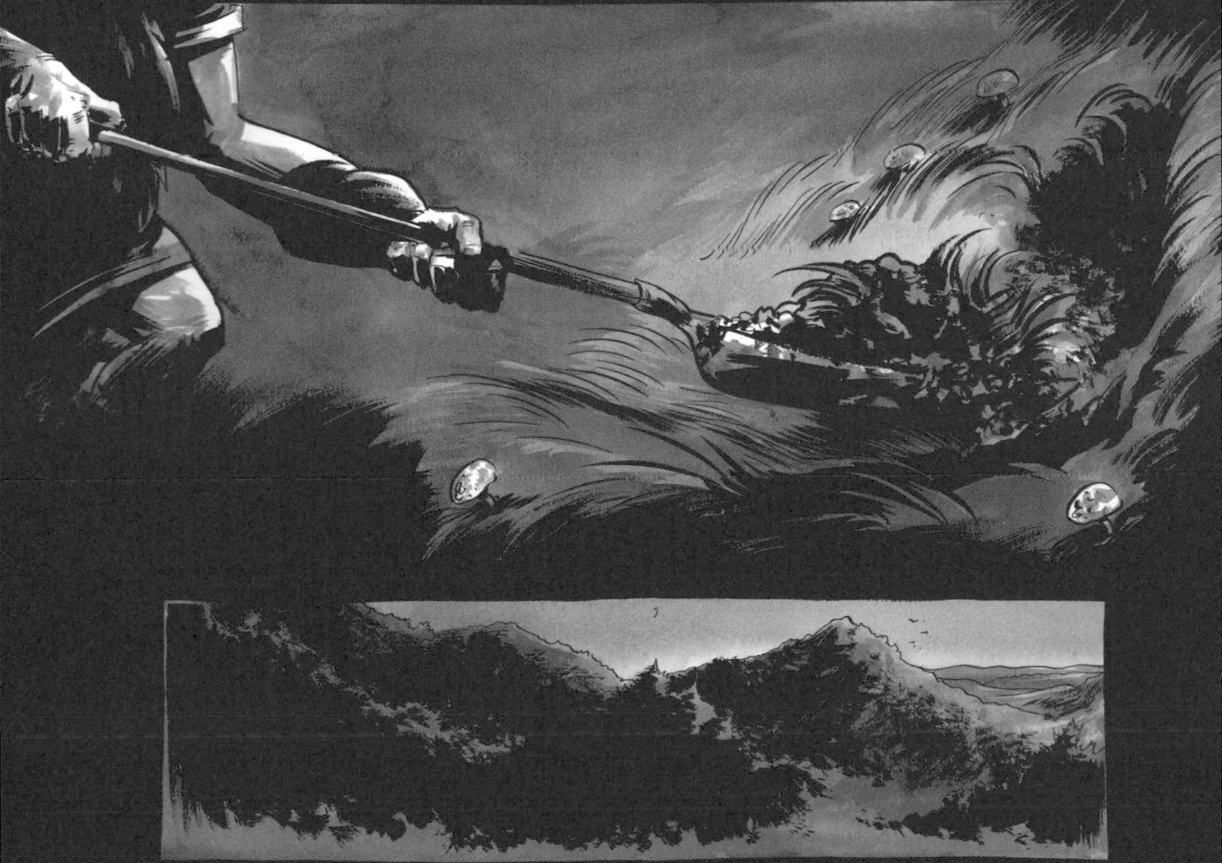

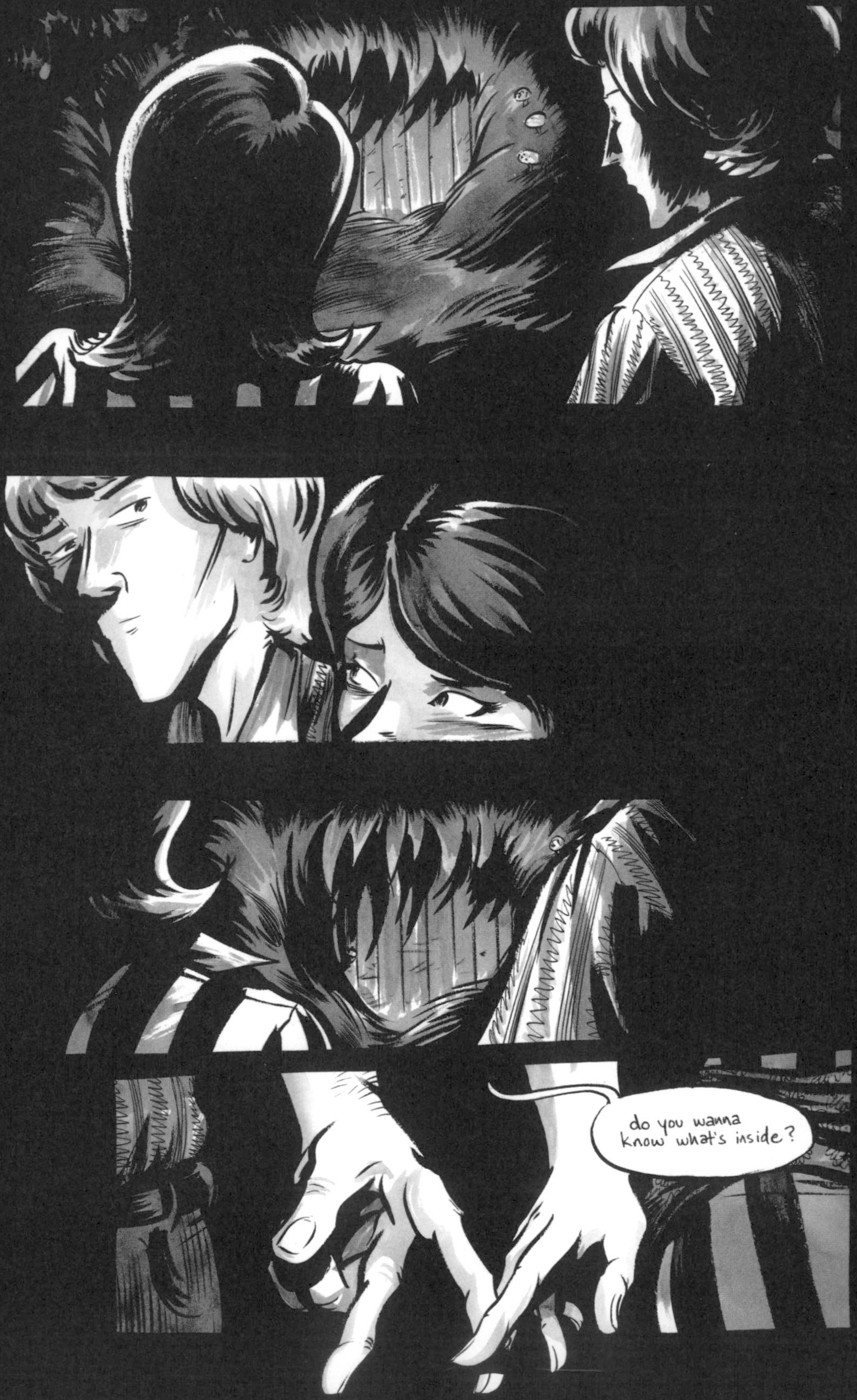
do you wanna know what's inside?

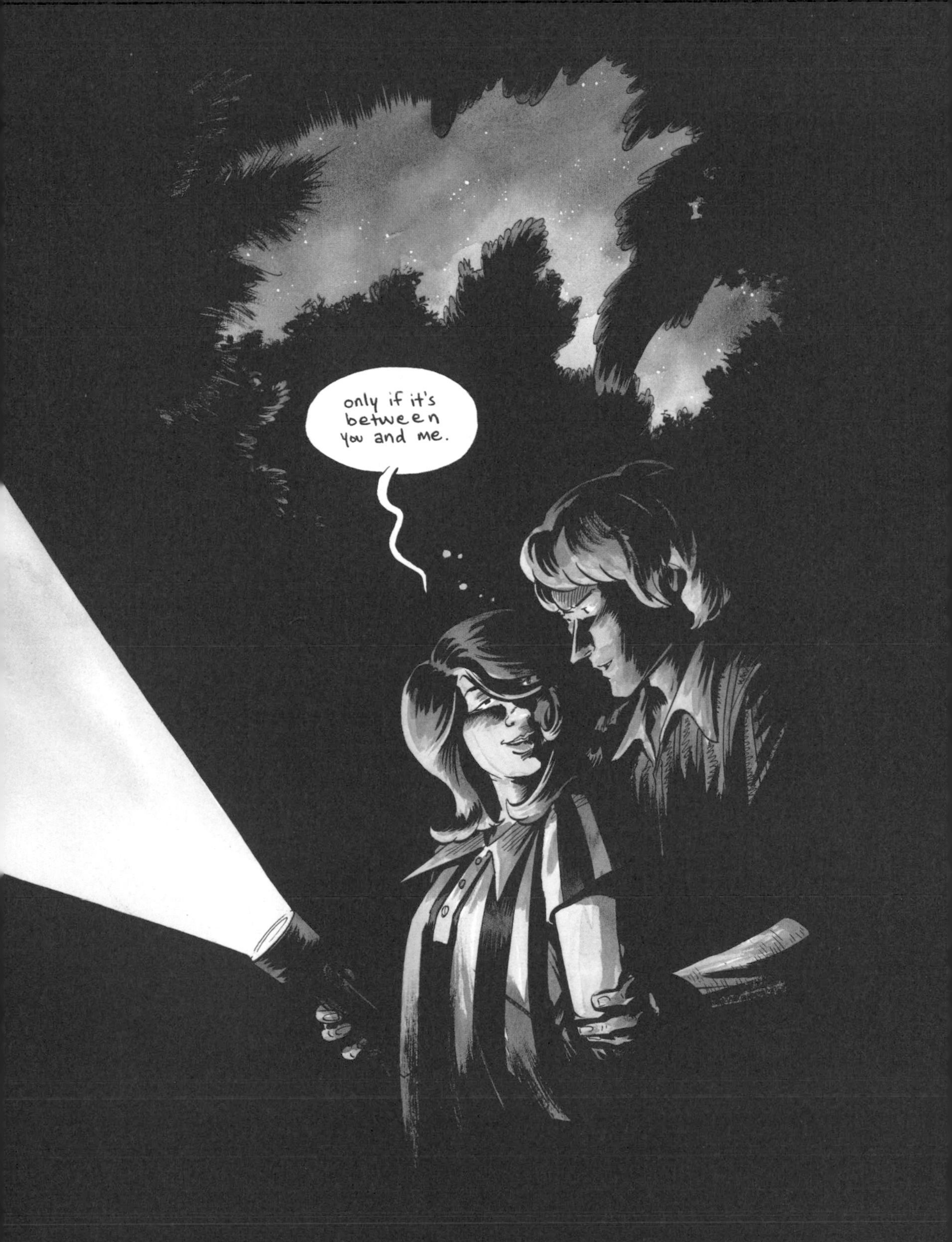
only if it's between you and me.

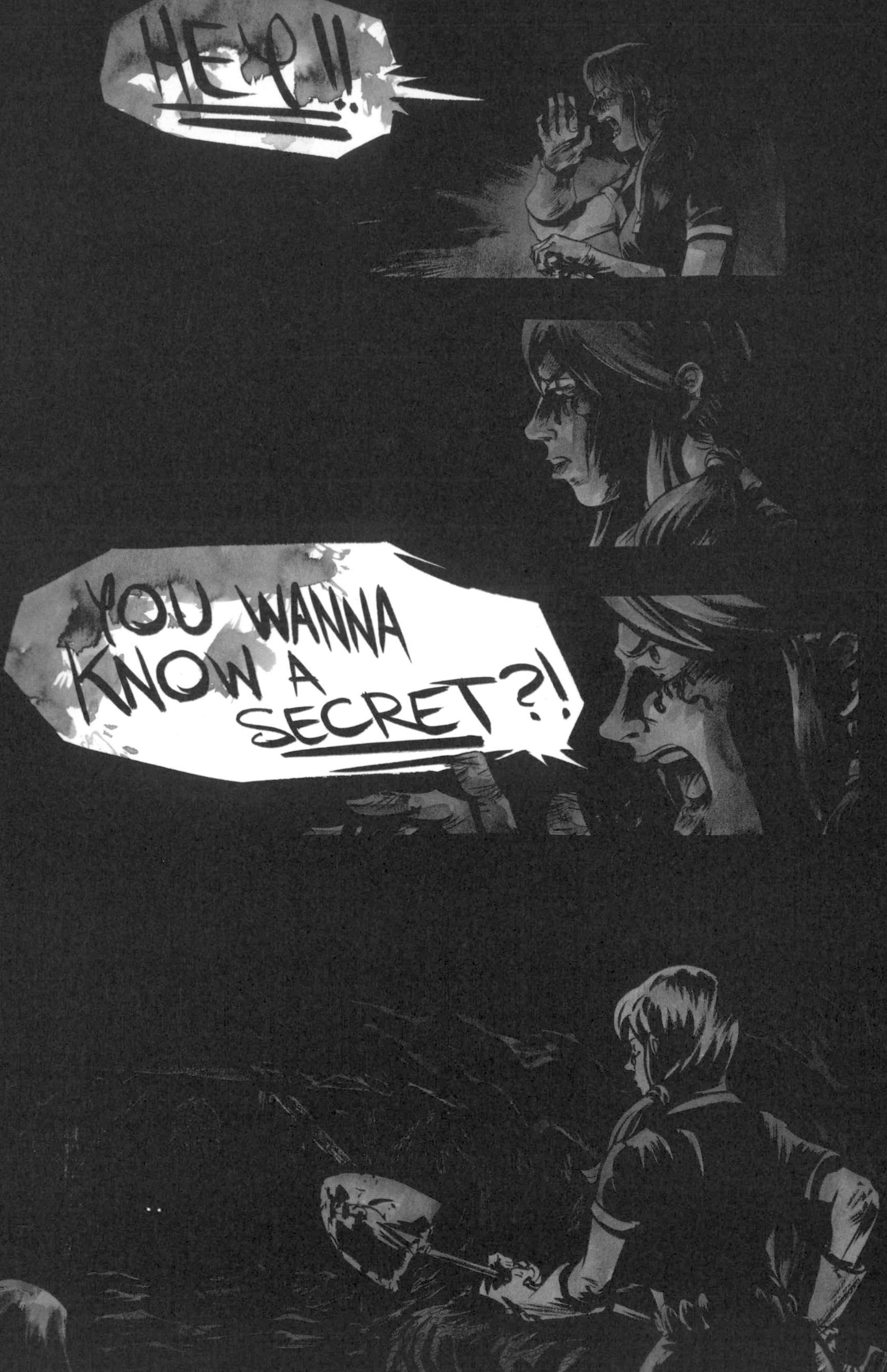
HEY!!
YOU WANNA KNOW A SECRET?!

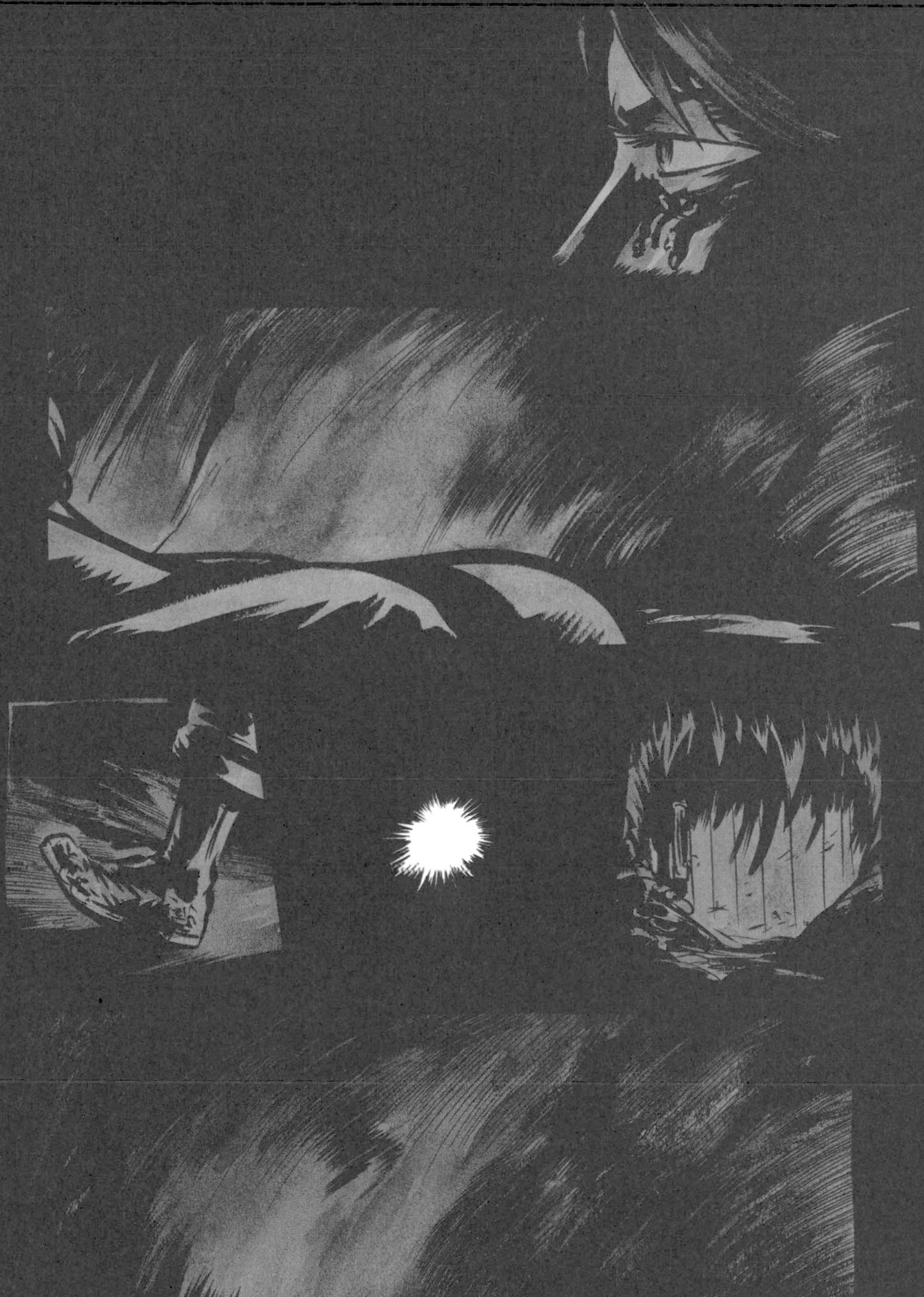

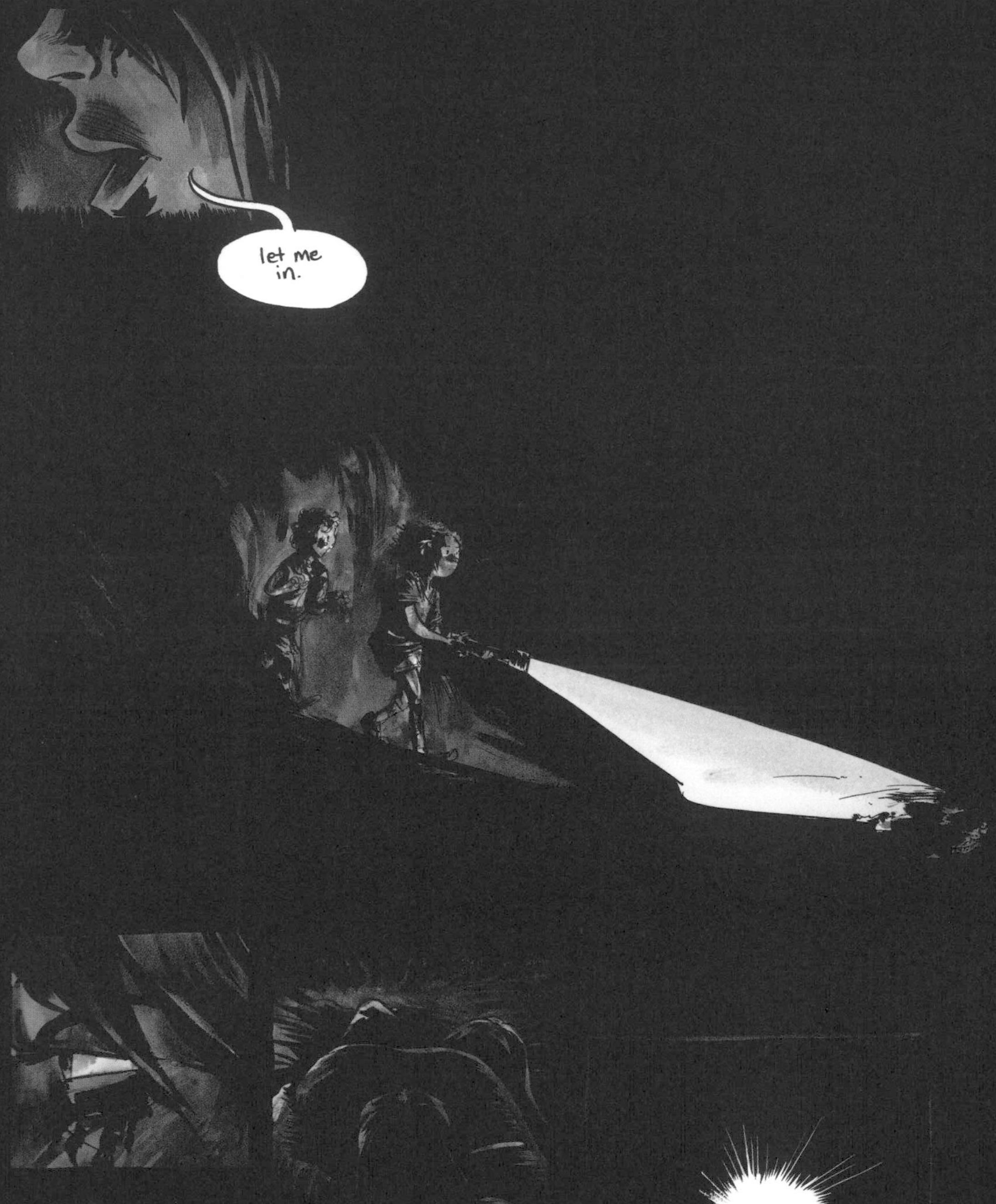
let me in.

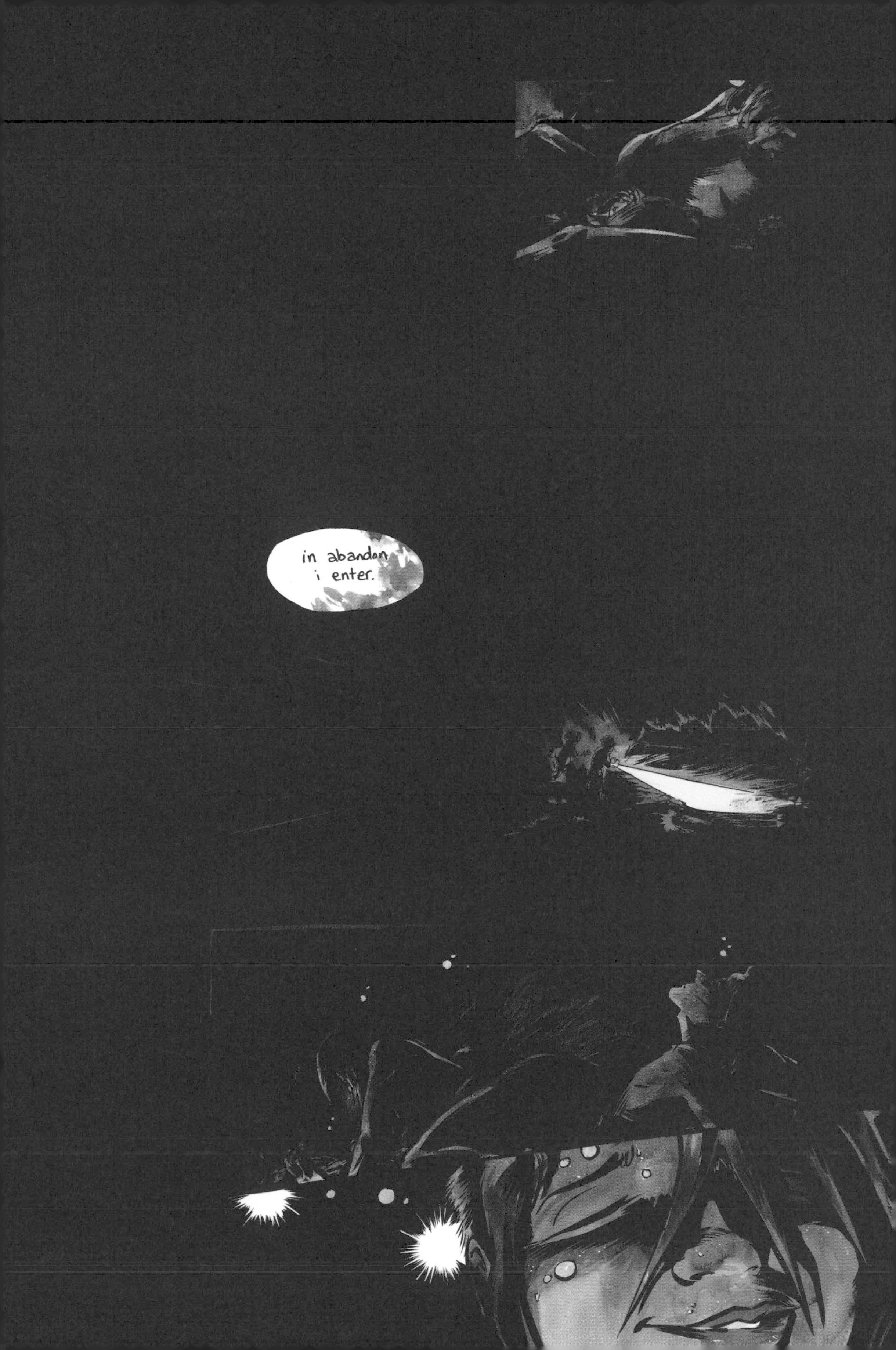
in abandon
i enter.

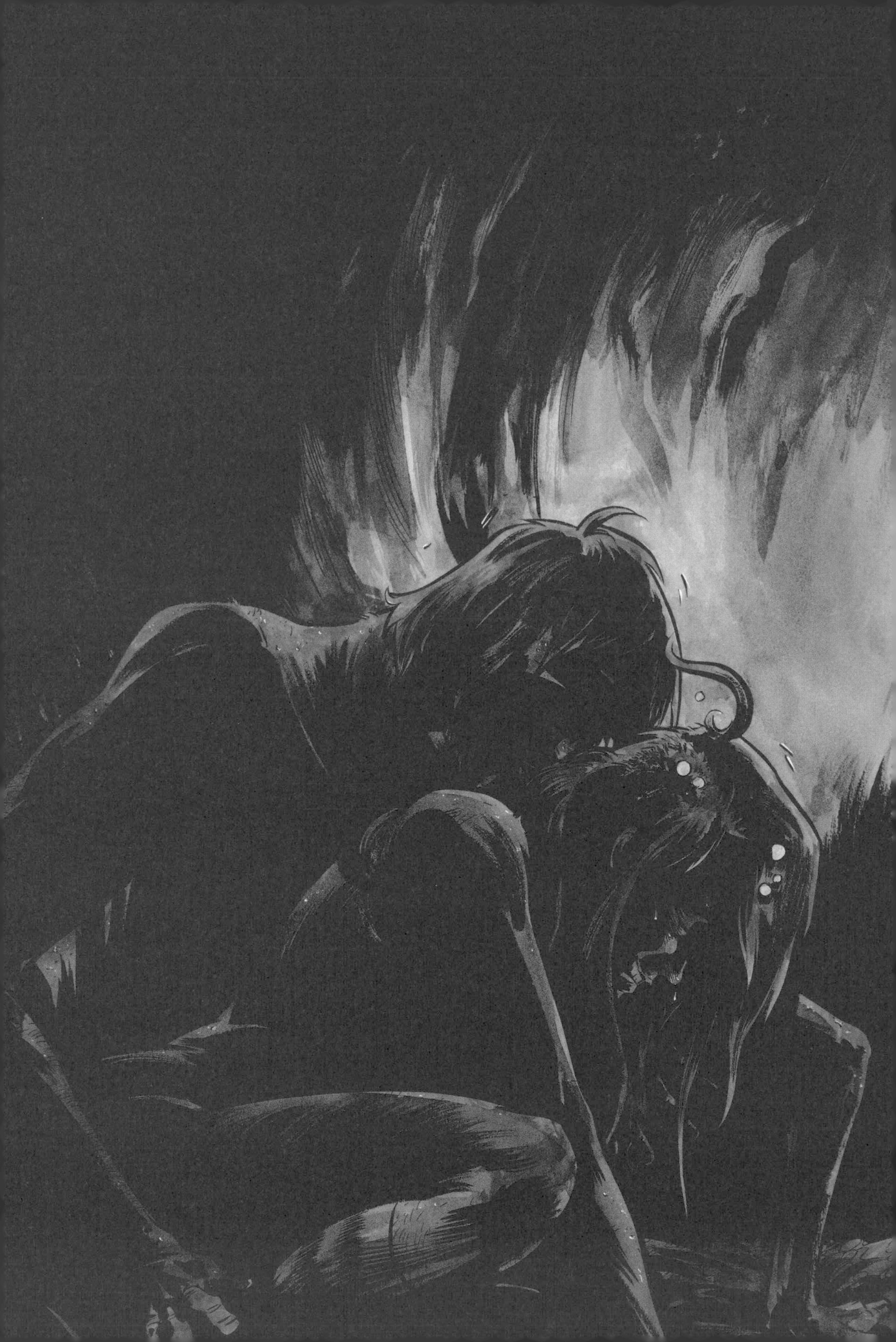

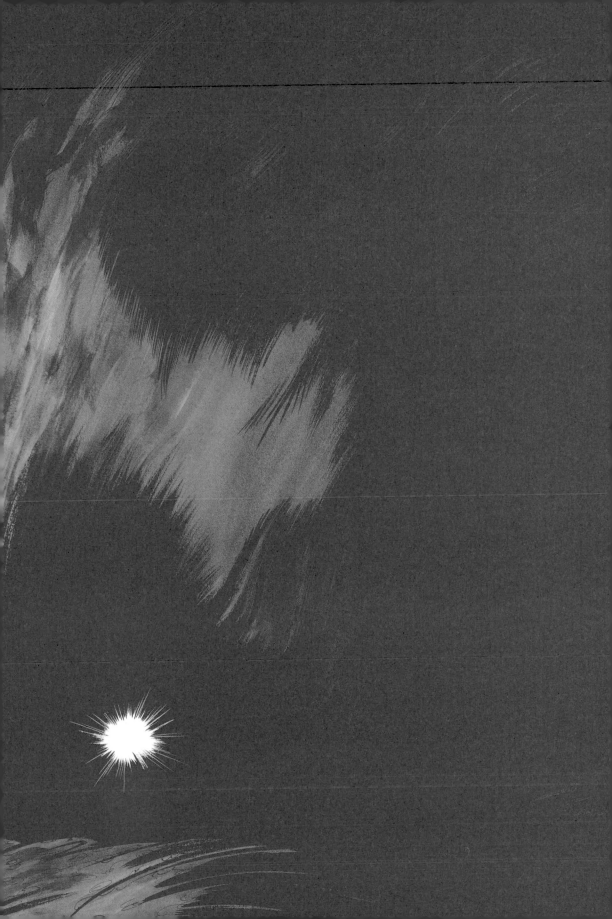

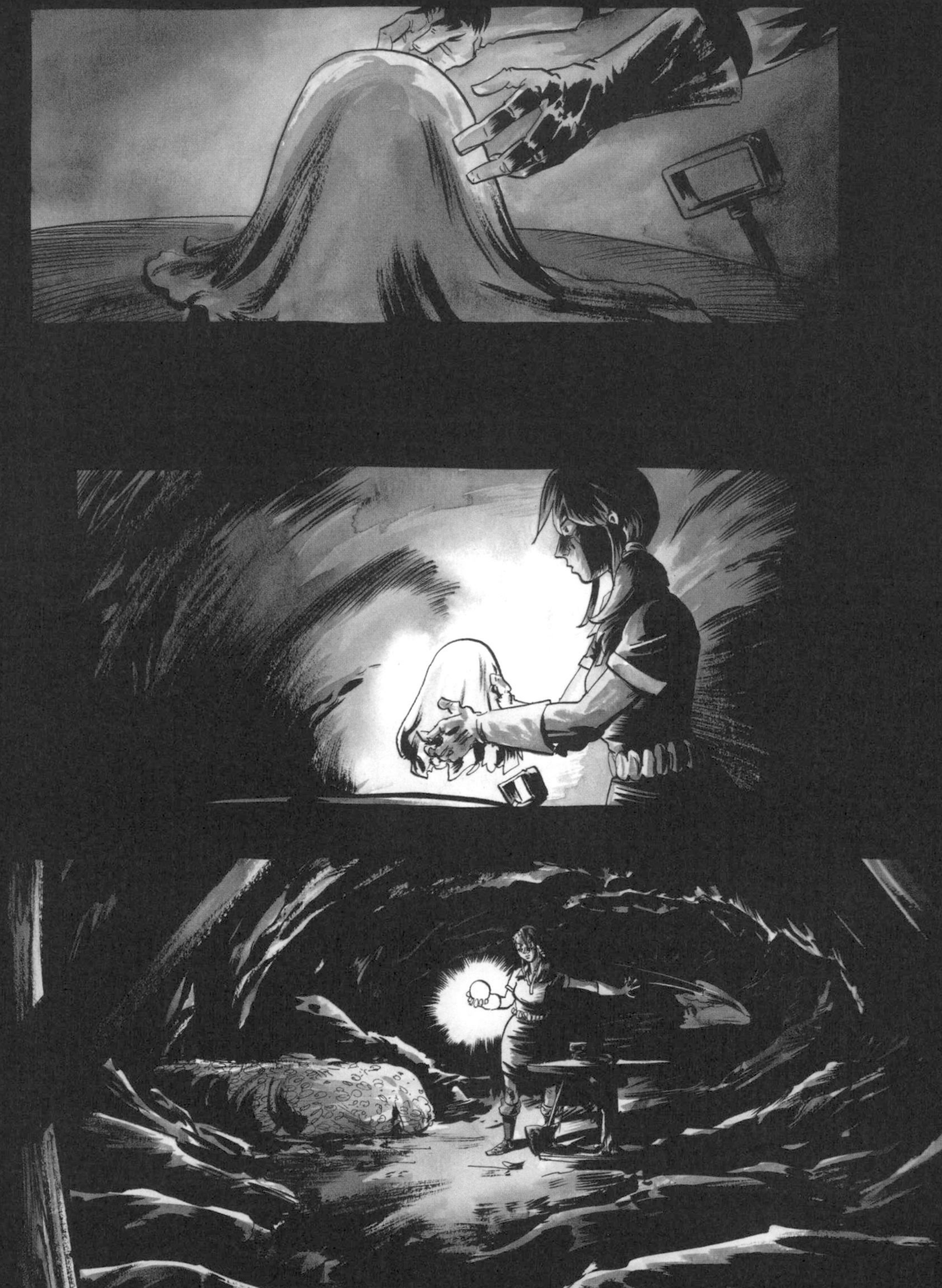

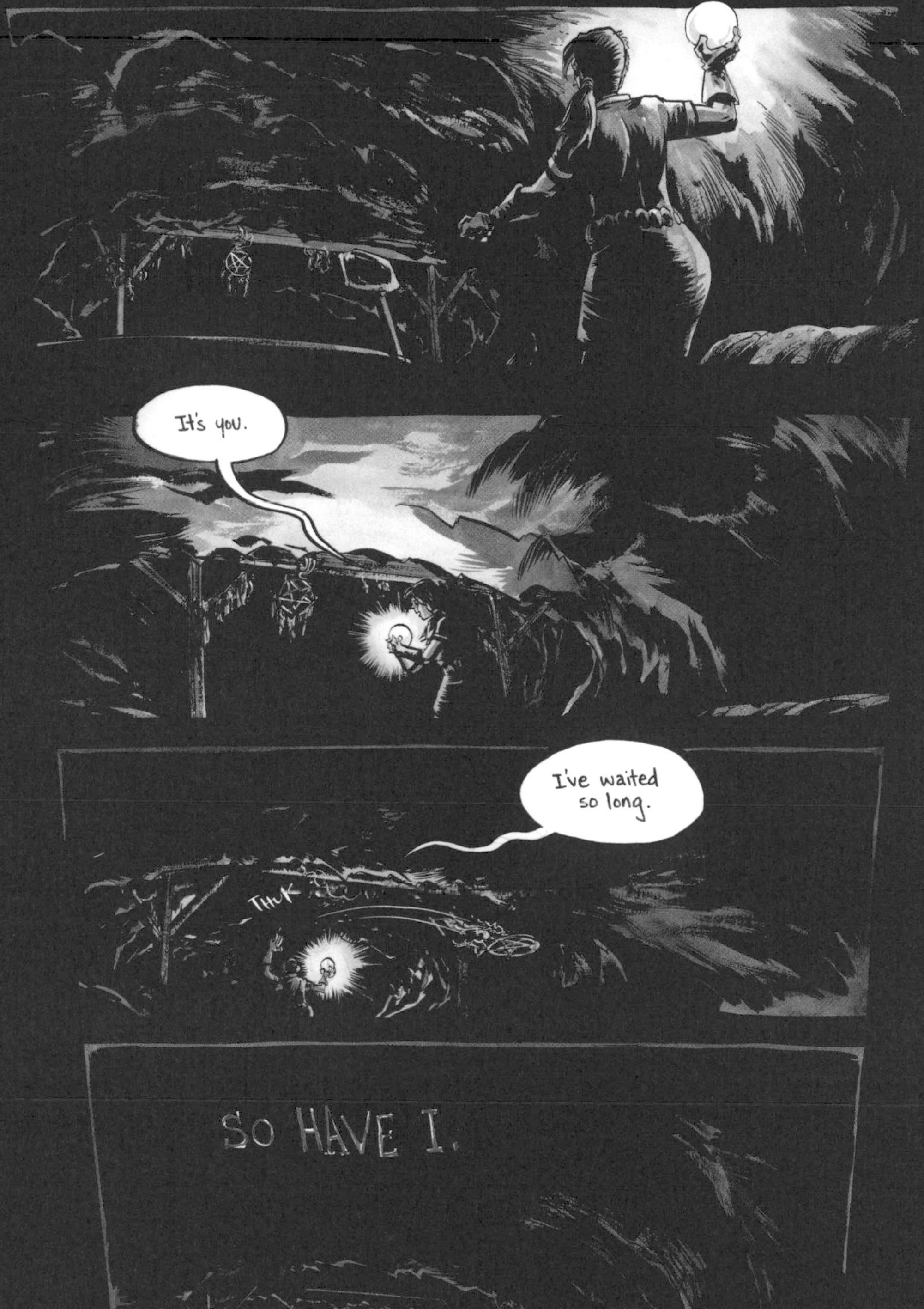
It's you.
I've waited so long.
THUK
SO HAVE I.

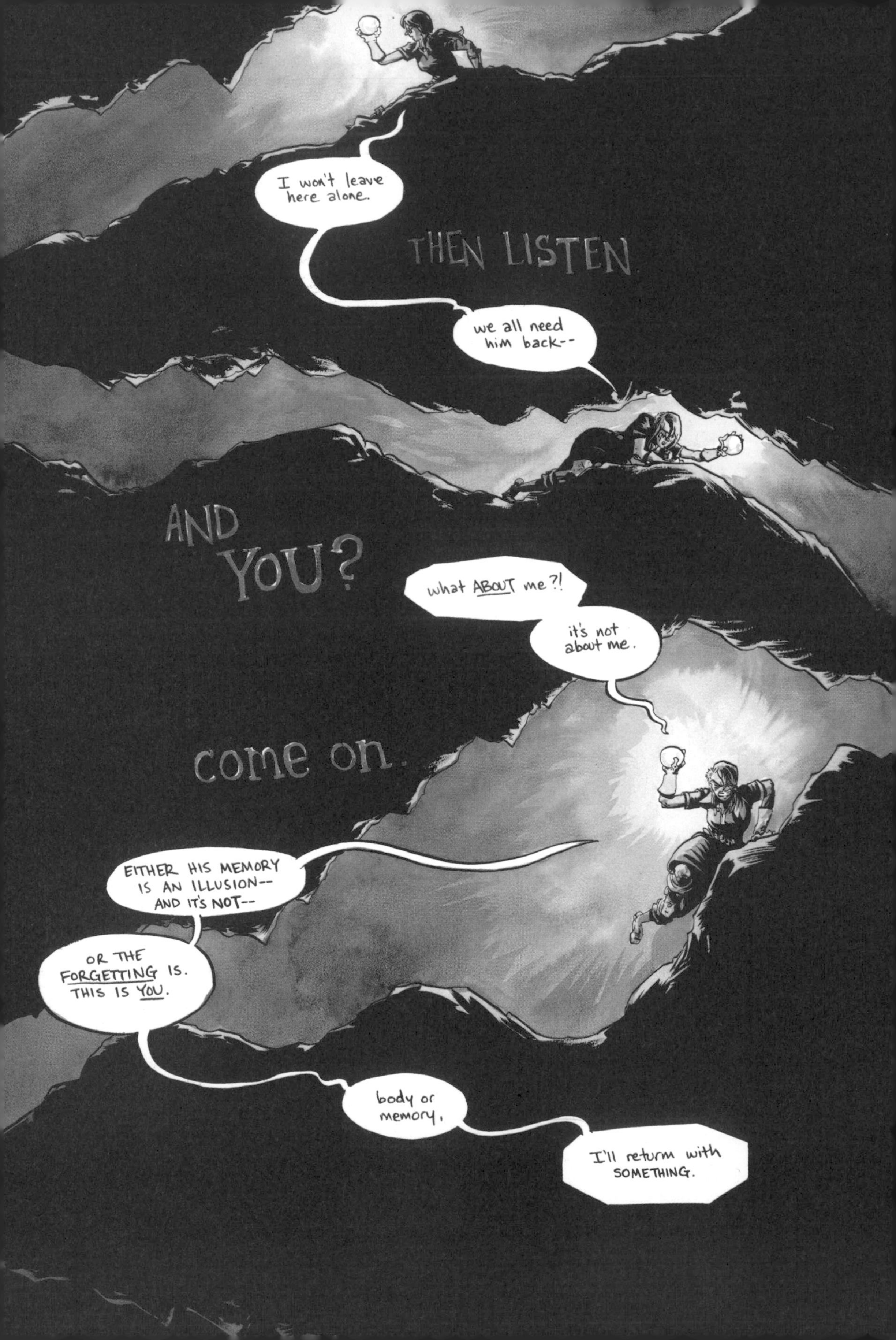
I won't leave here alone.
THEN LISTEN.
we all need him back--
AND YOU?
what ABOUT me?!
it's not about me.
come on.
EITHER HIS MEMORY IS AN ILLUSION-- AND IT'S NOT--
OR THE FORGETTING IS. THIS IS YOU.
body or memory,
I'll return with SOMETHING.

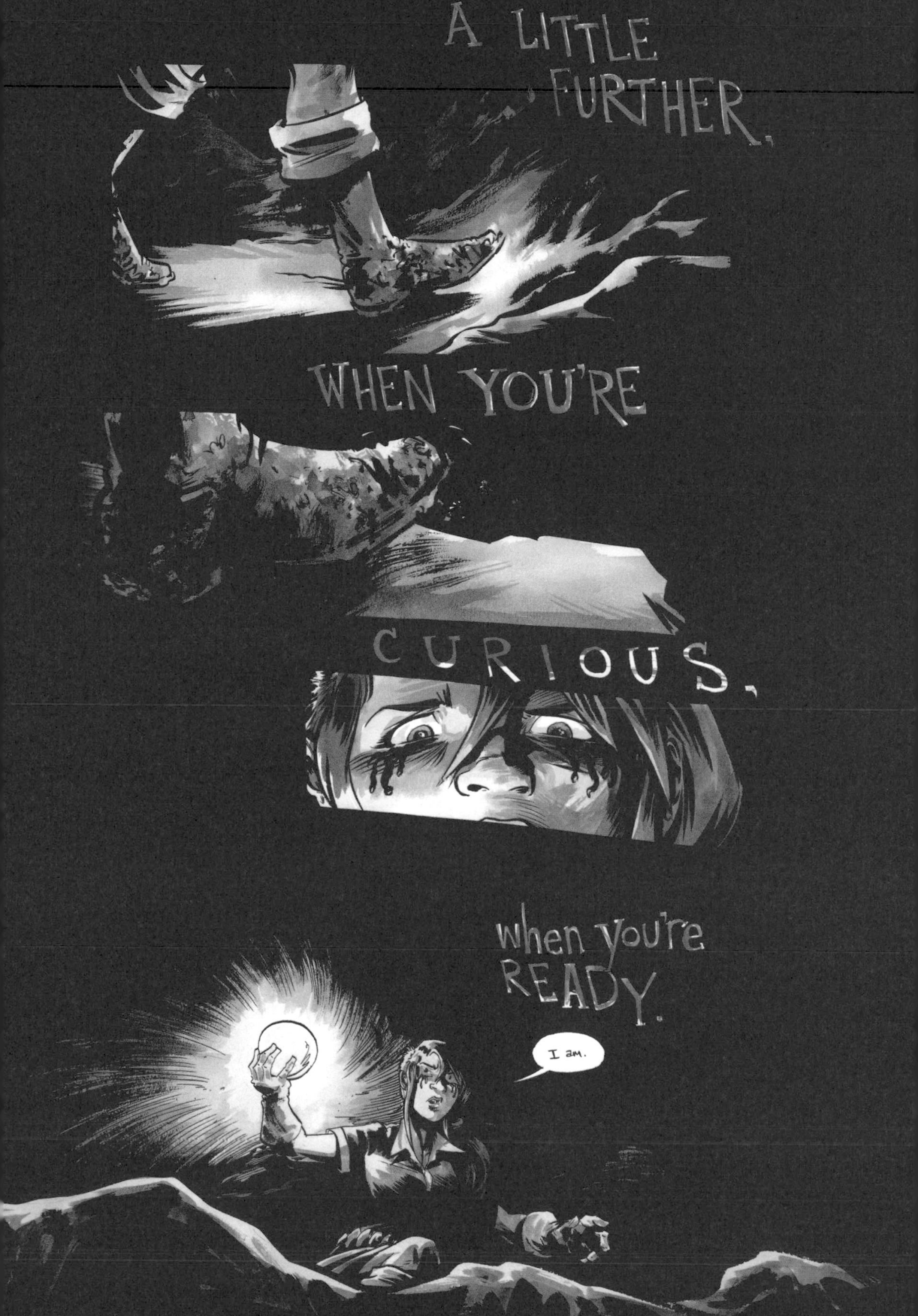
A LITTLE FURTHER,
WHEN YOU'RE
CURIOUS,
when you're READY.
I am.

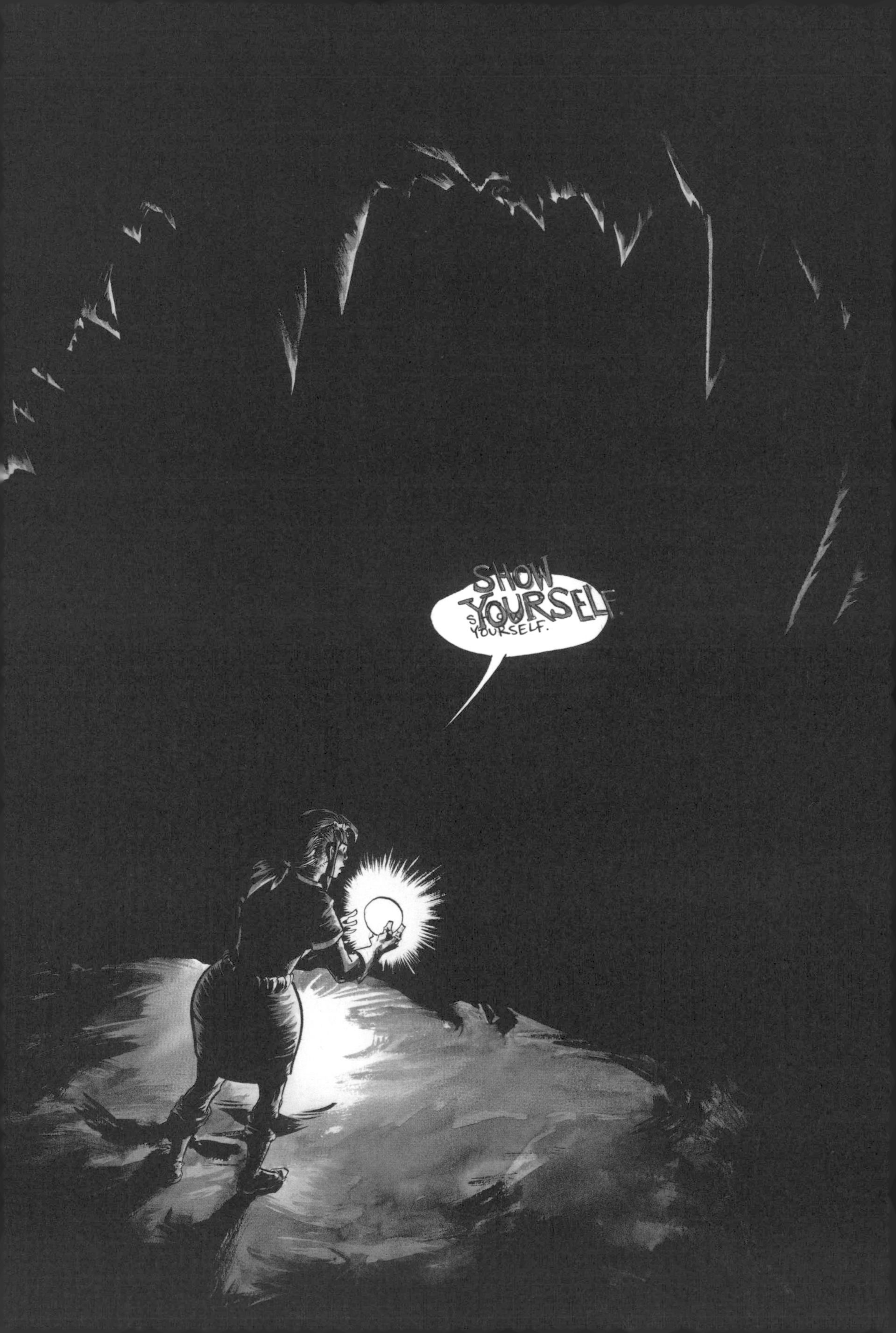
SHOW YOURSELF.

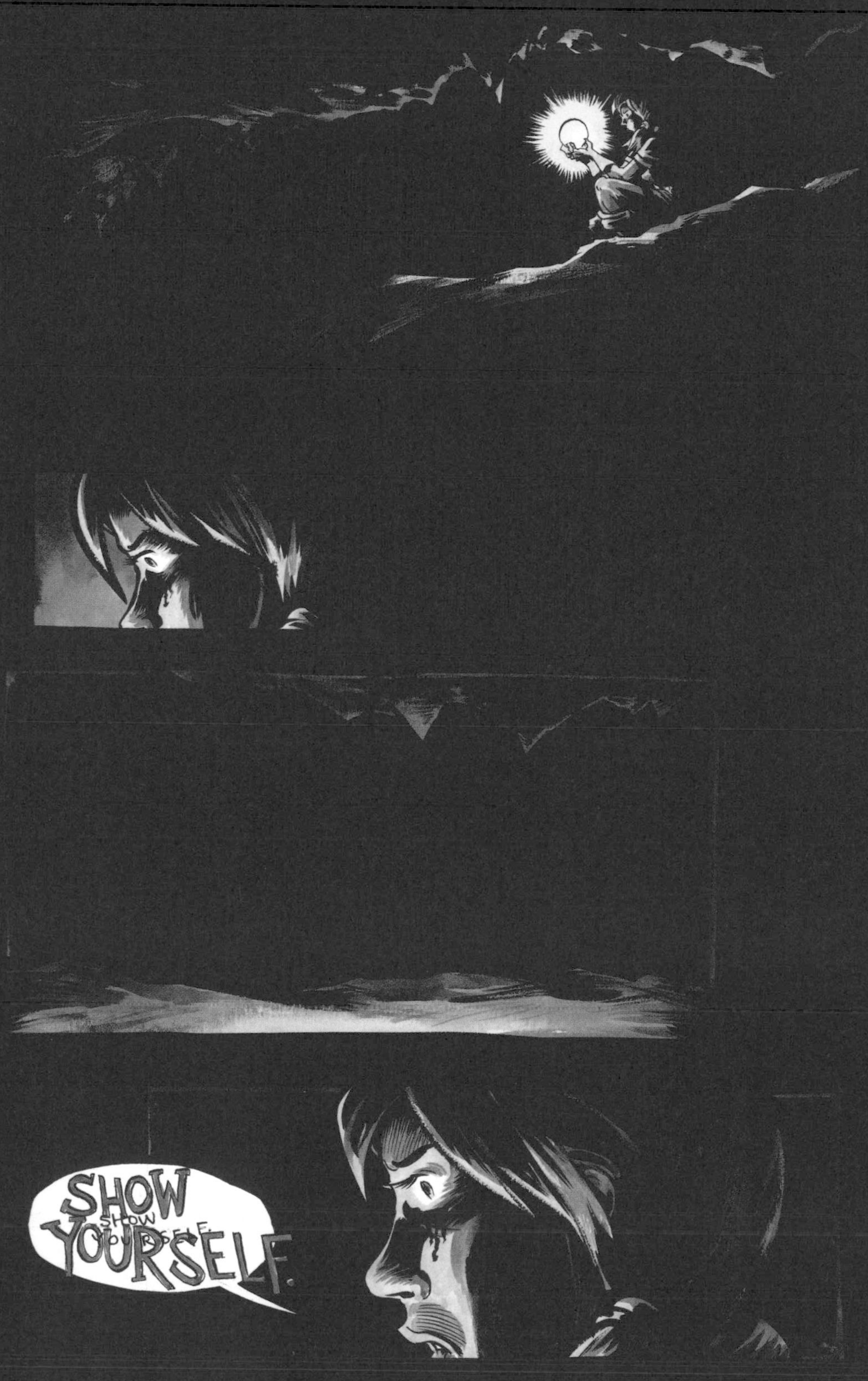
SHOW YOURSELF.

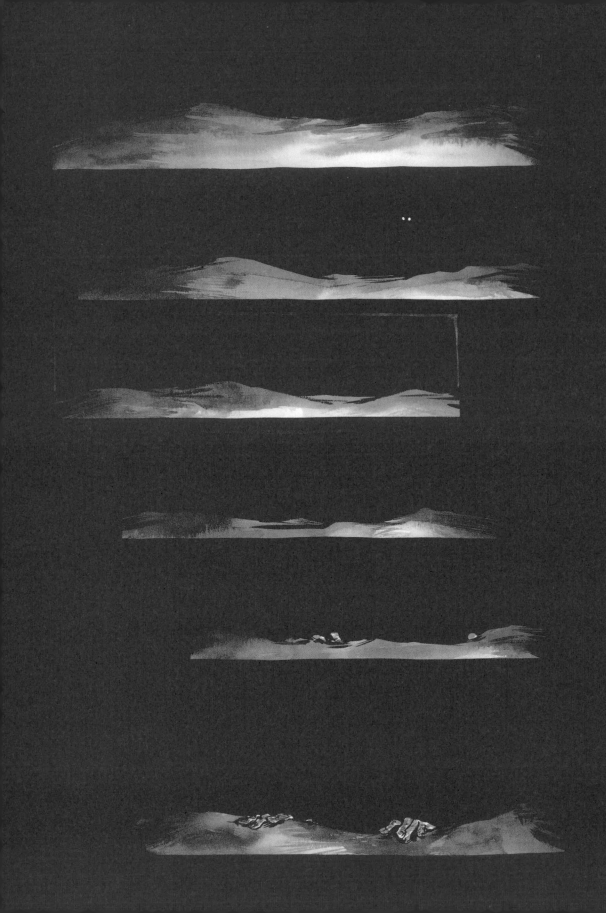

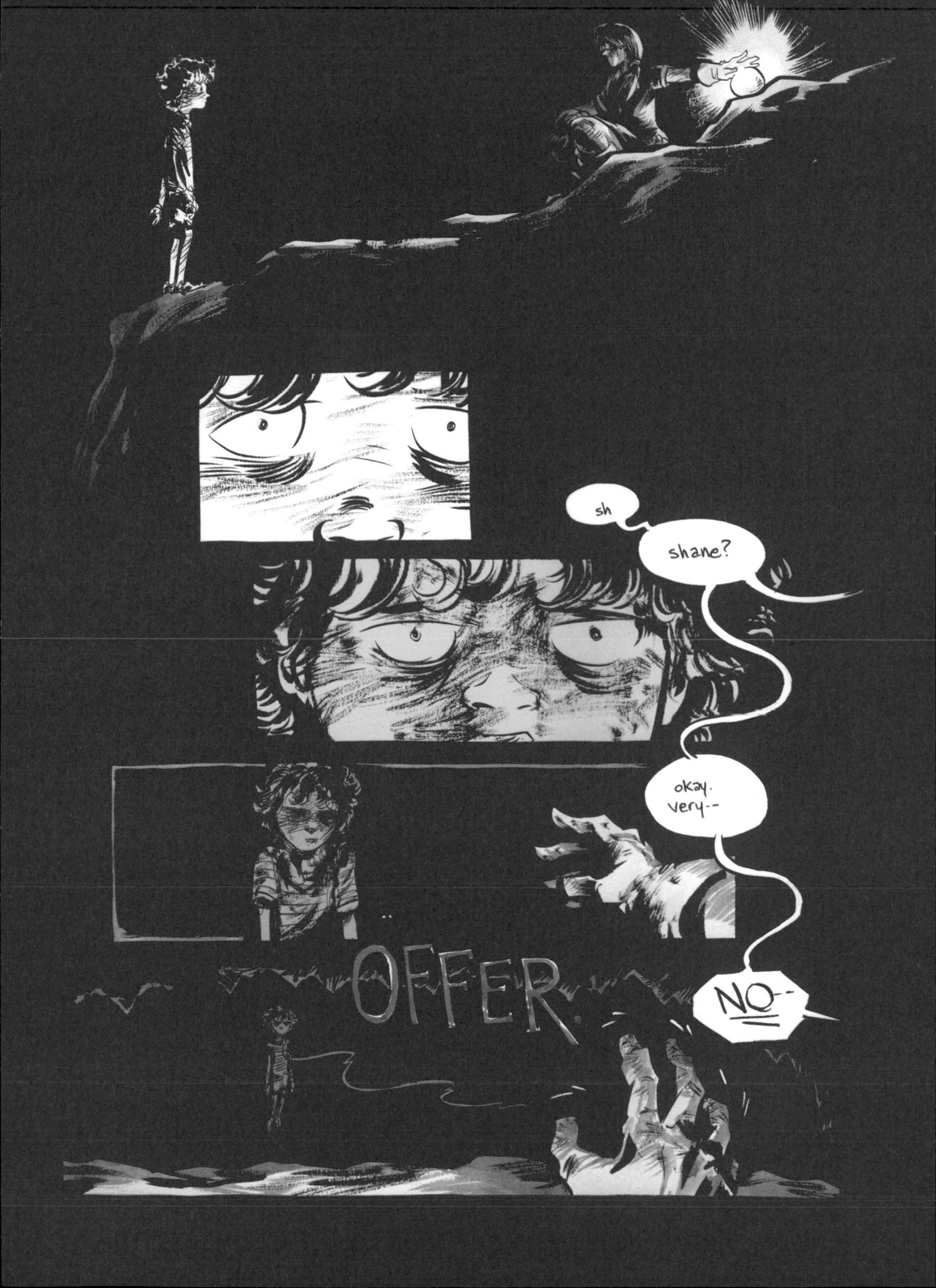
sh
shane?
okay.
very--
..
OFFER.
NO--

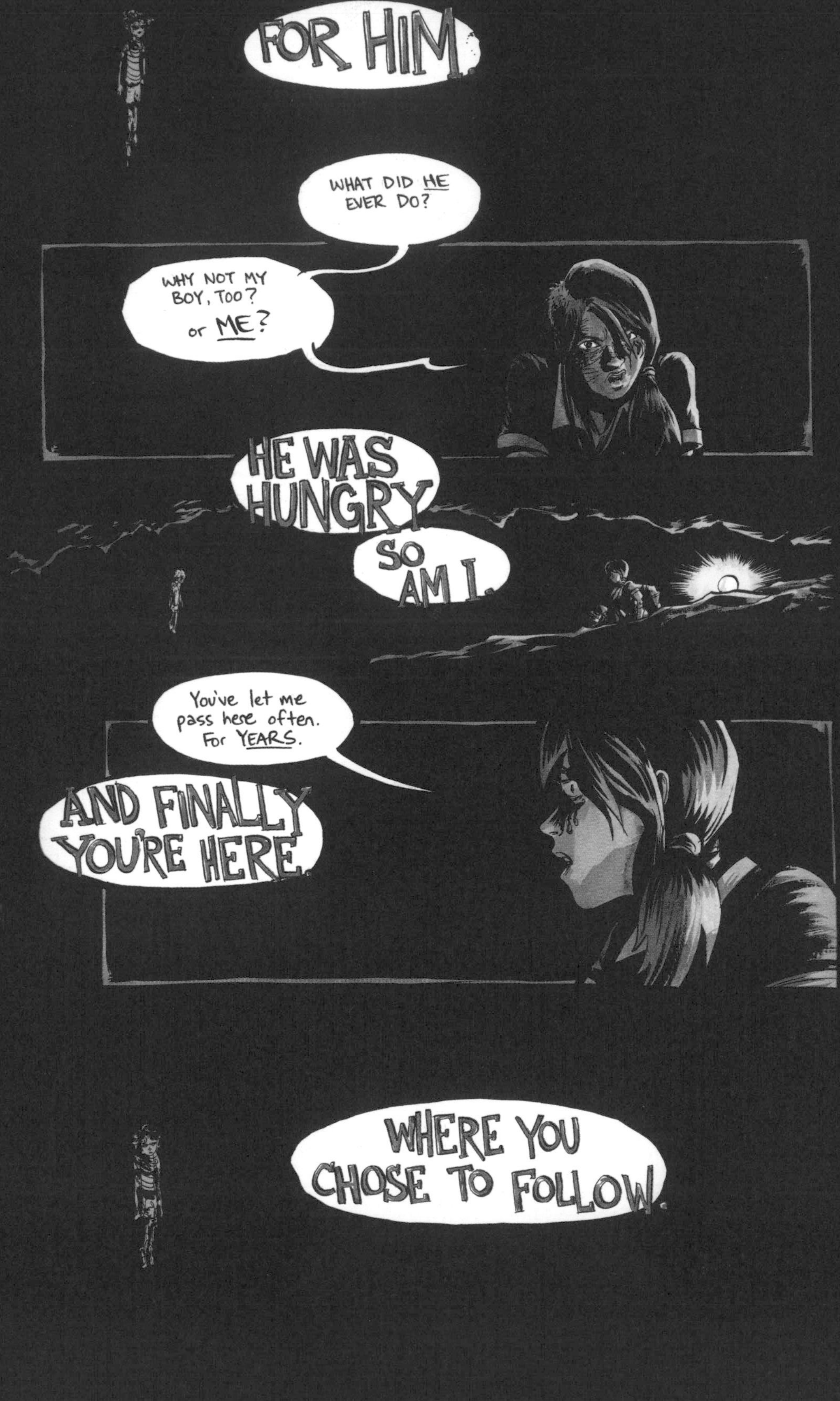
FOR HIM.
WHAT DID HE EVER DO?
WHY NOT MY BOY, TOO? or ME?
HE WAS HUNGRY.
SO AM I.
You've let me pass here often. For YEARS.
AND FINALLY YOU'RE HERE.
WHERE YOU CHOSE TO FOLLOW.

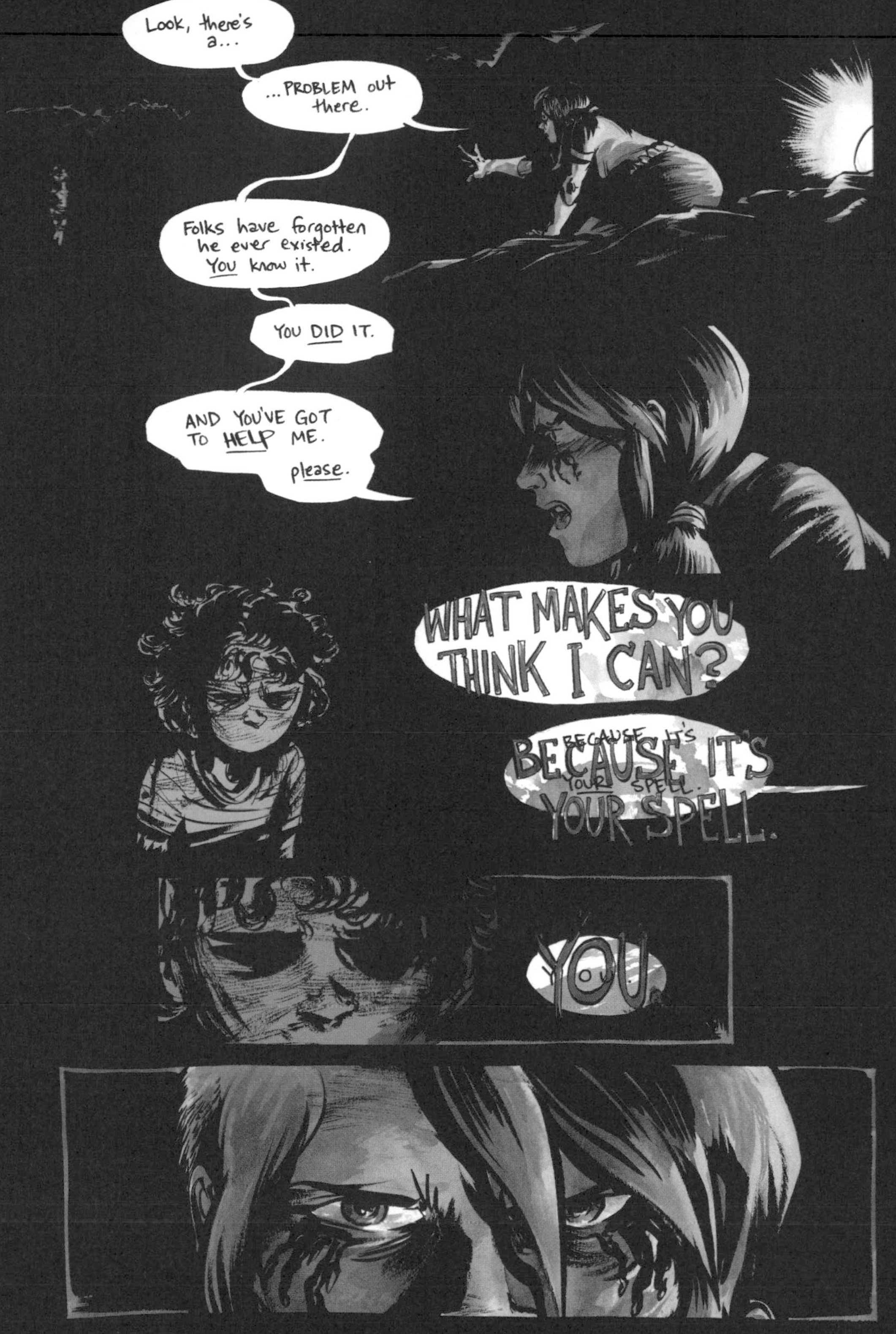

Look, there's a...
...PROBLEM out there.
Folks have forgotten he ever existed. YOU know it.
YOU DID IT.
AND YOU'VE GOT TO HELP ME.
please.
WHAT MAKES YOU THINK I CAN?
BECAUSE IT'S YOUR SPELL.
BECAUSE IT'S YOUR SPELL.
YOU.

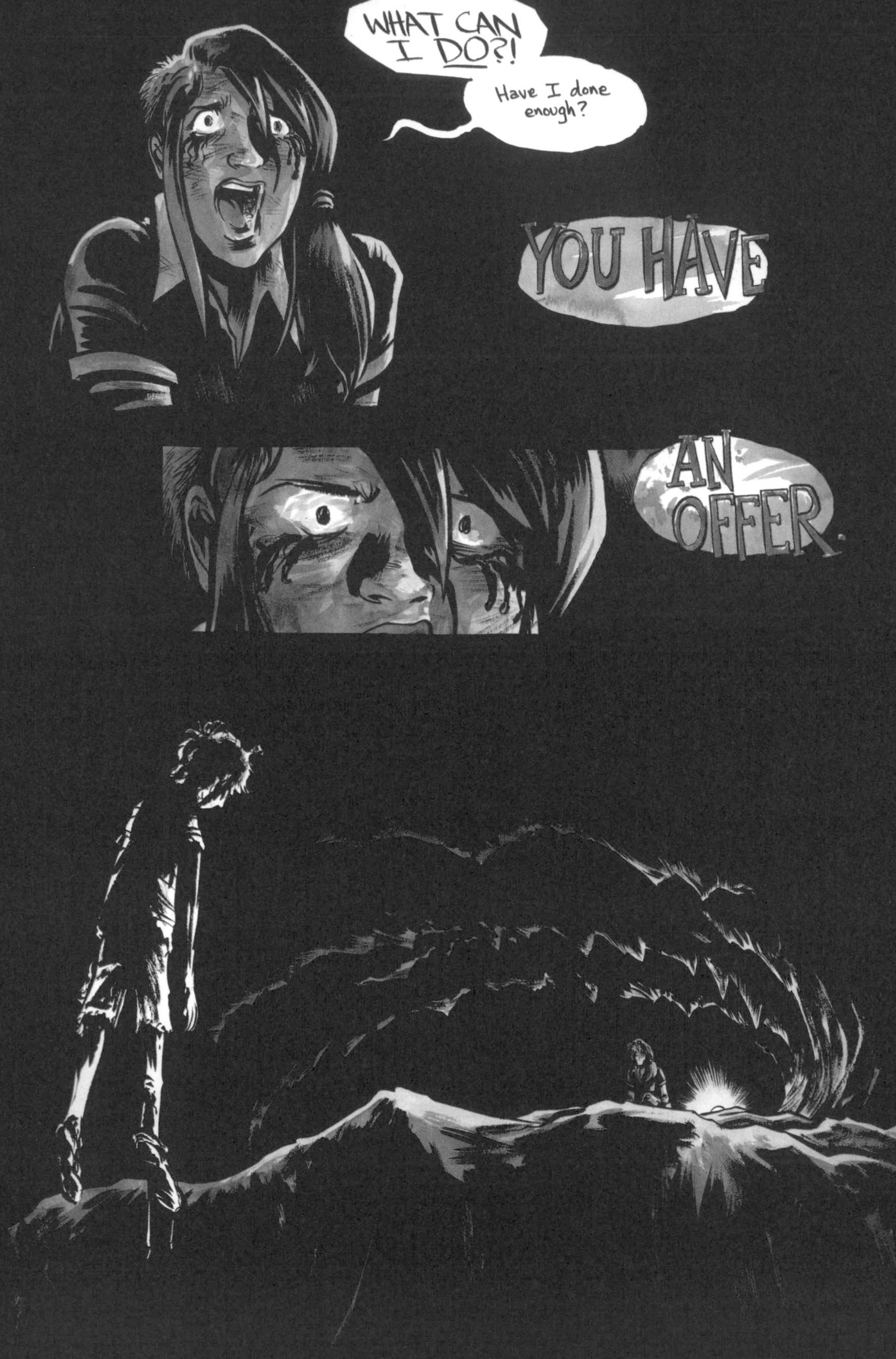
WHAT CAN I DO?!
Have I done enough?
YOU HAVE
AN OFFER.

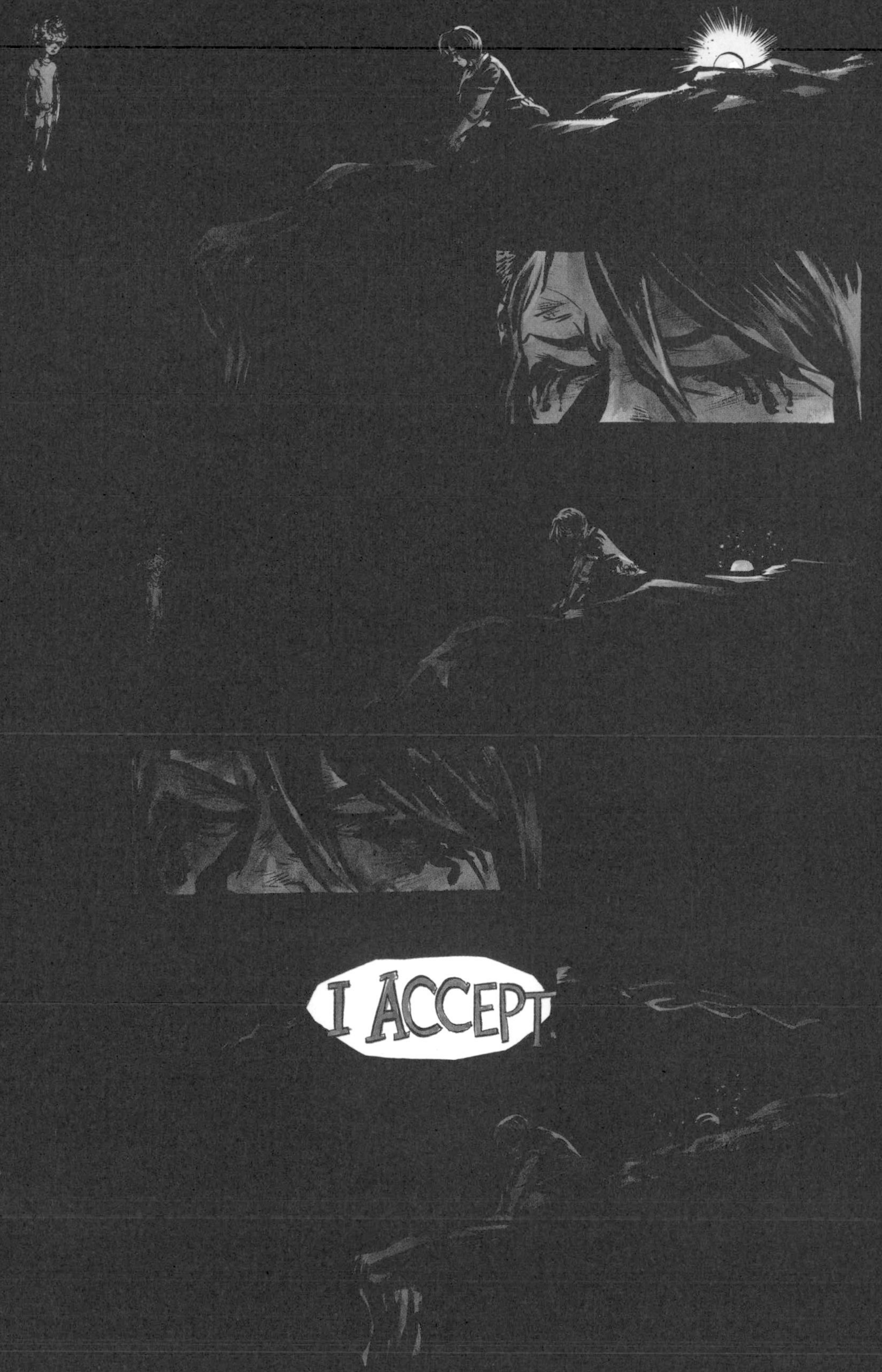
I ACCEPT

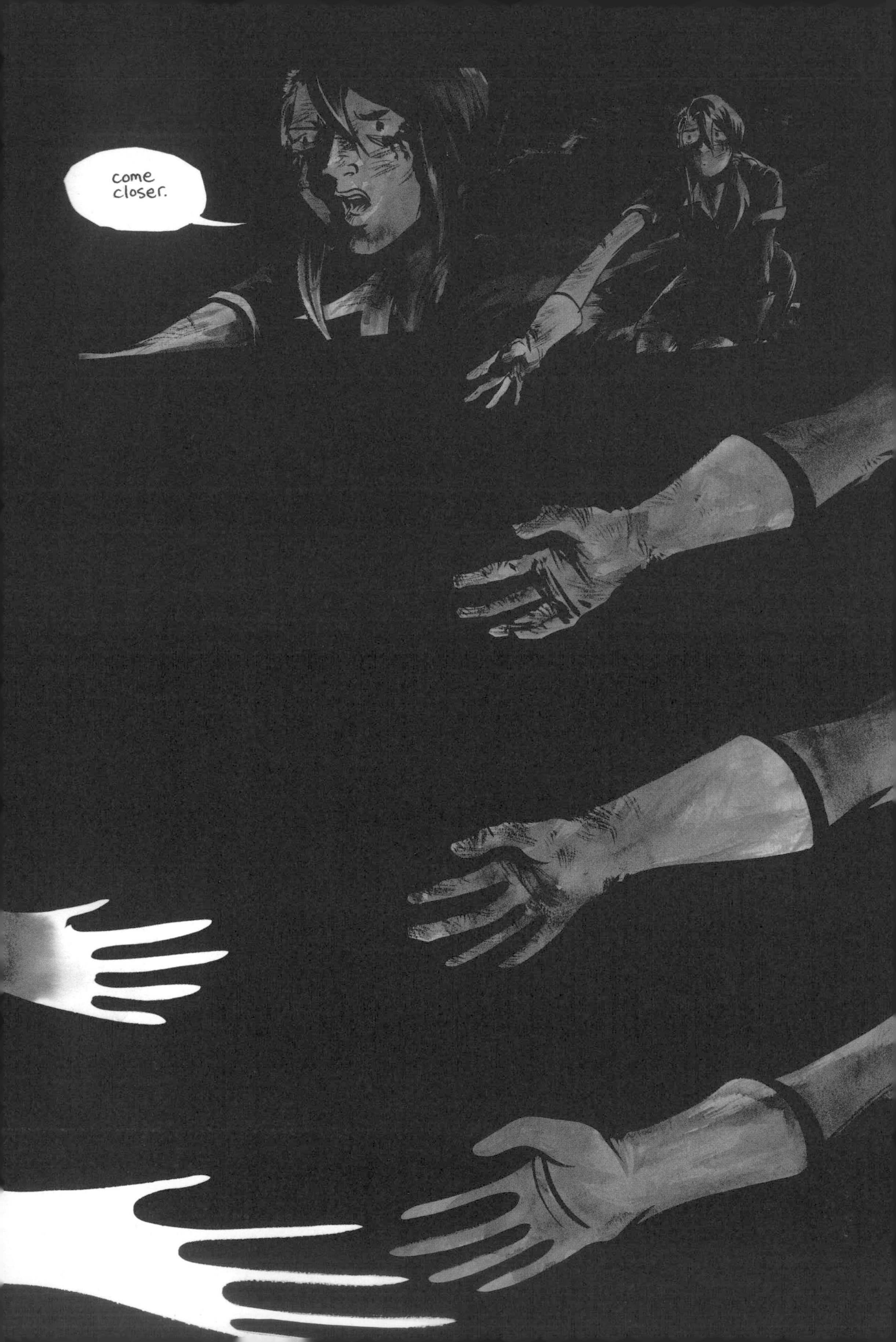
come closer.

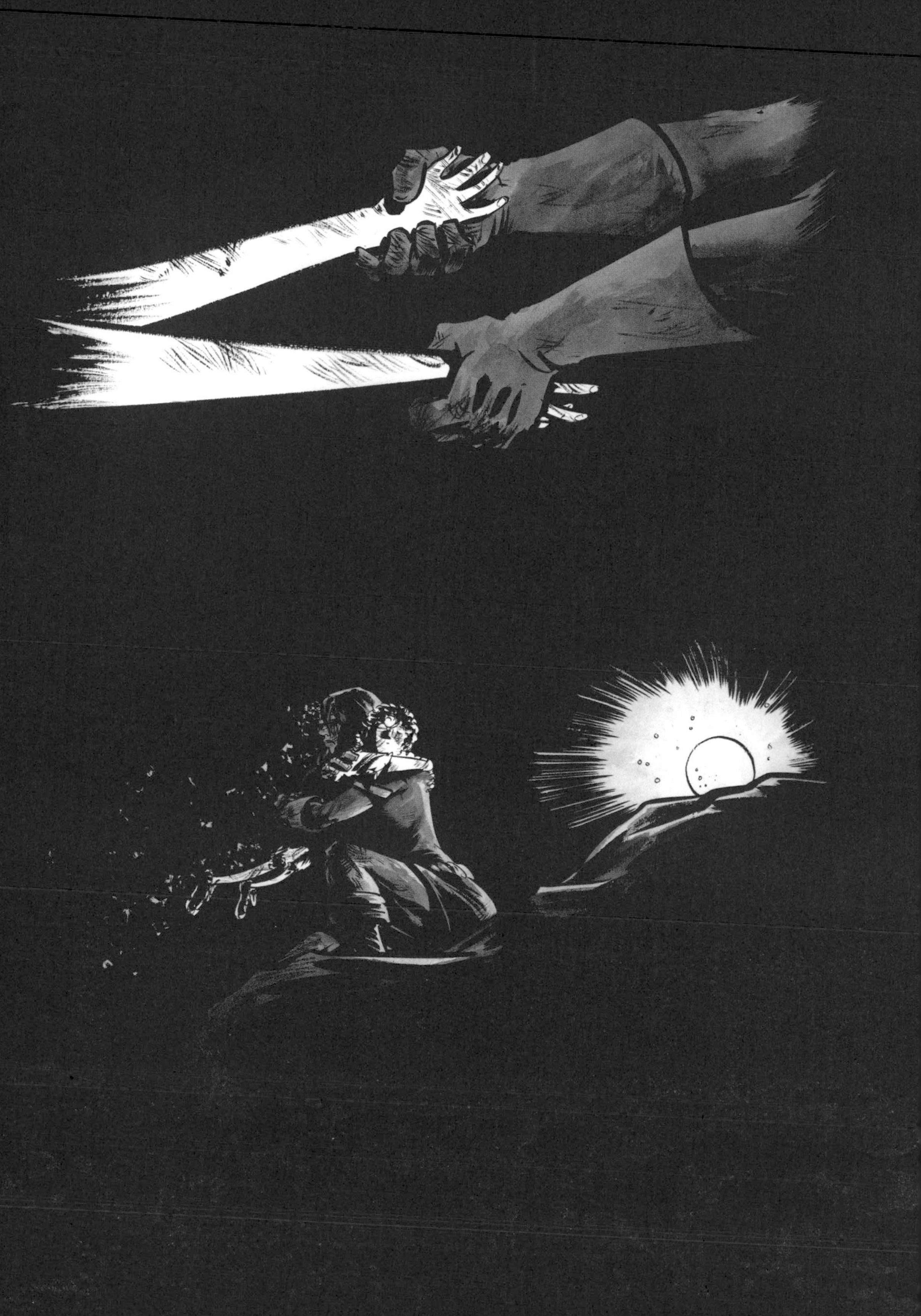

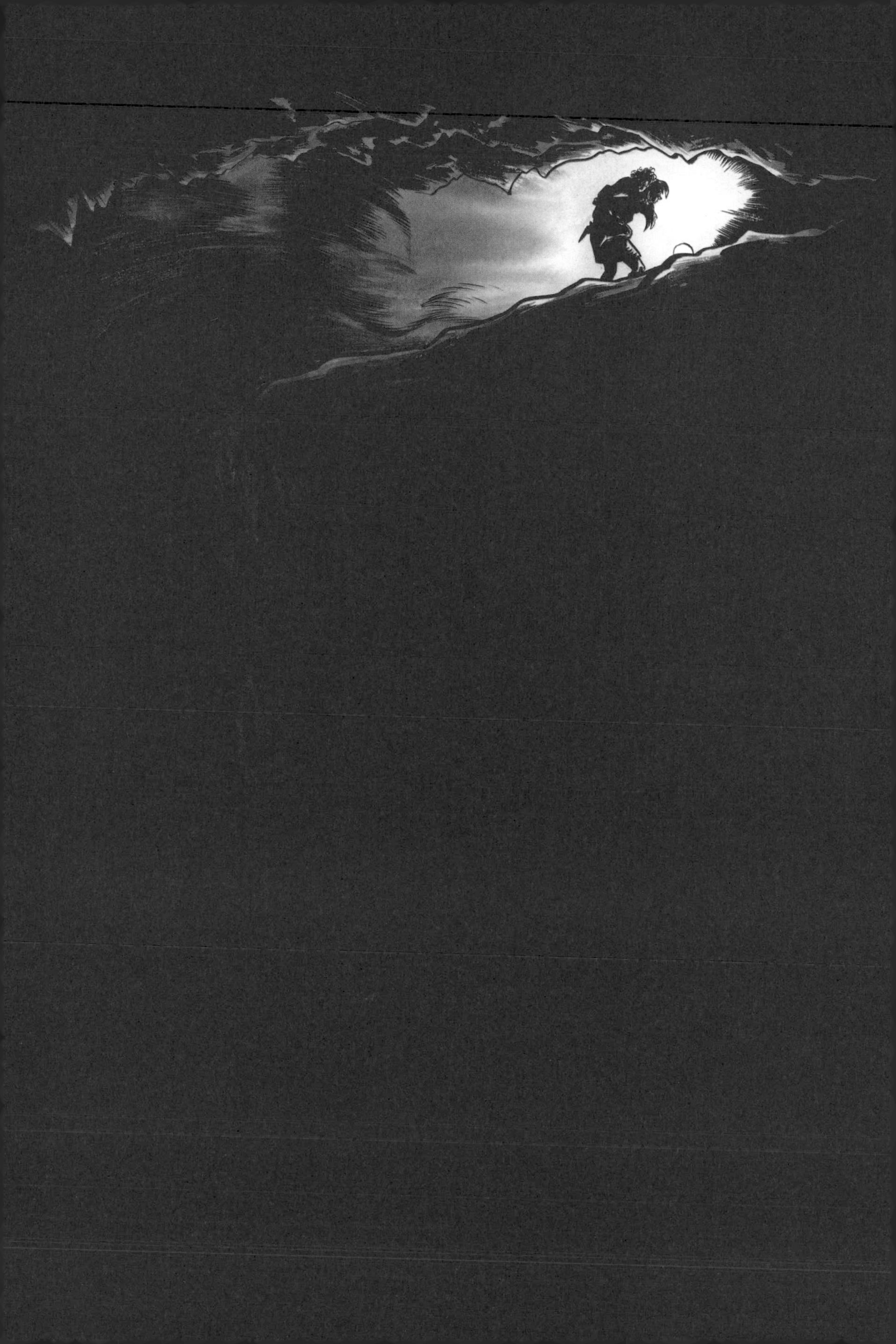

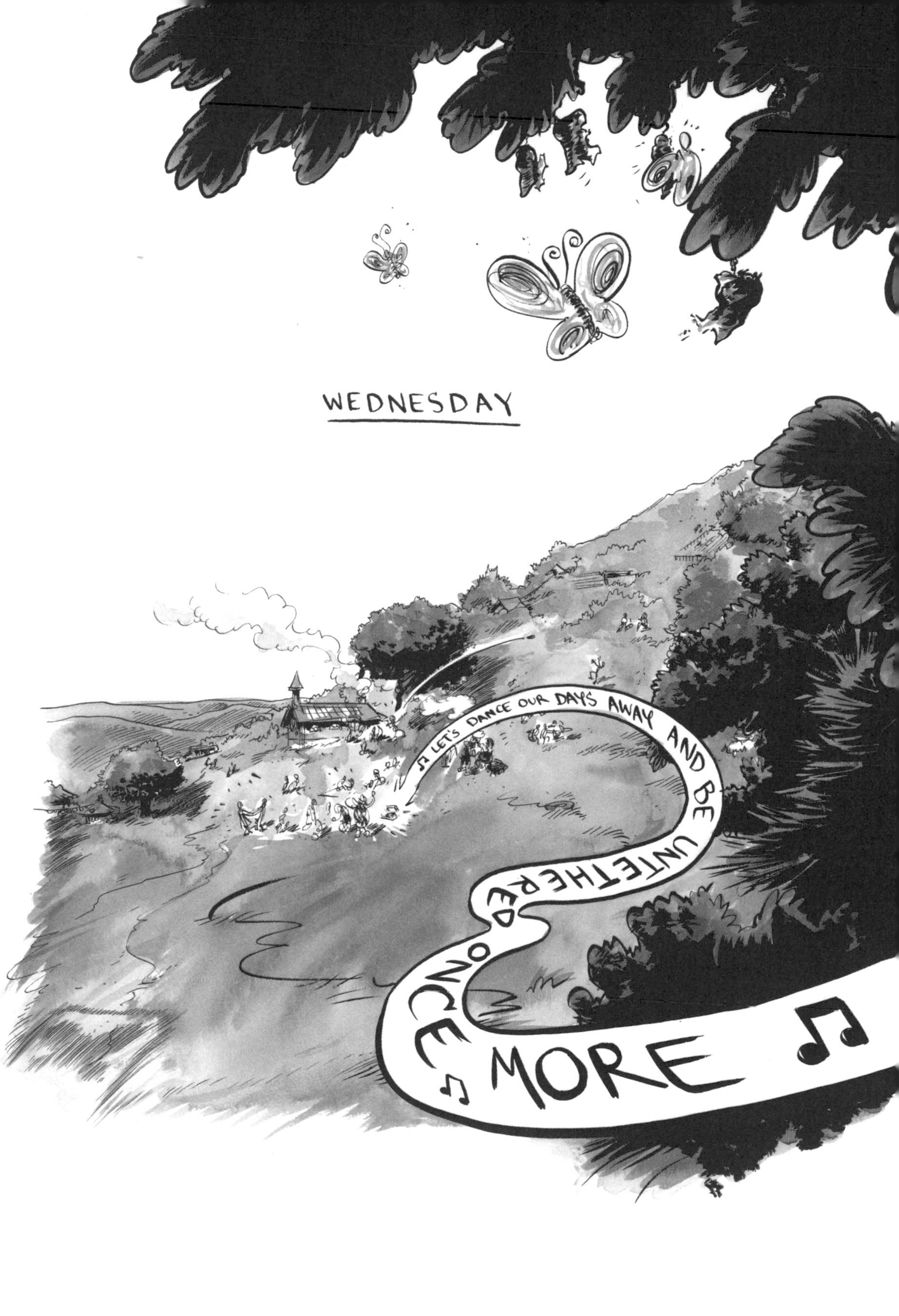
WEDNESDAY
♫ LET'S DANCE OUR DAYS AWAY AND BE UNTETHERED ONCE MORE ♫

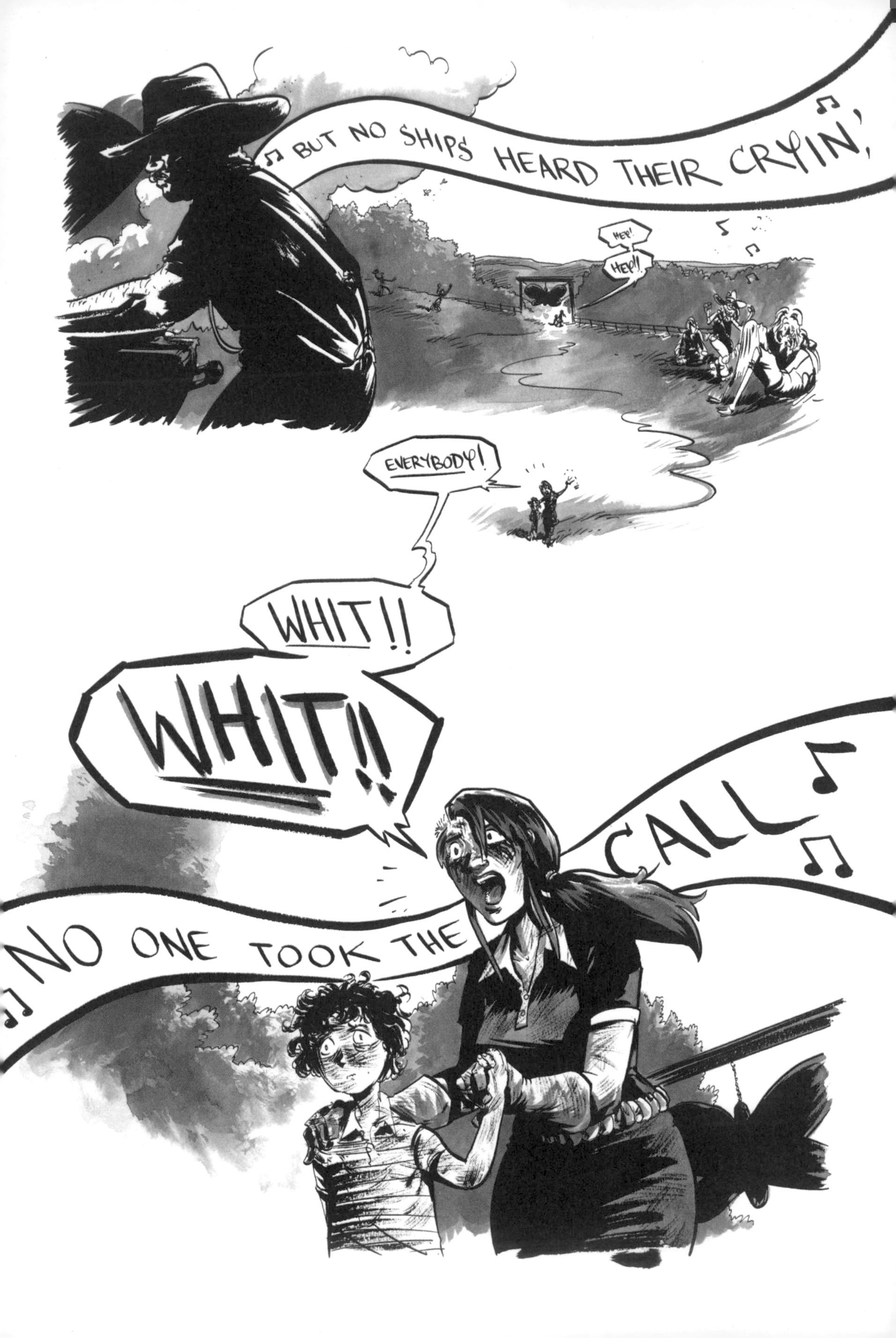
BUT NO SHIPS HEARD THEIR CRYIN',
HEP!
HEP!!
EVERYBODY!
WHIT!!
WHIT!!
NO ONE TOOK THE CALL

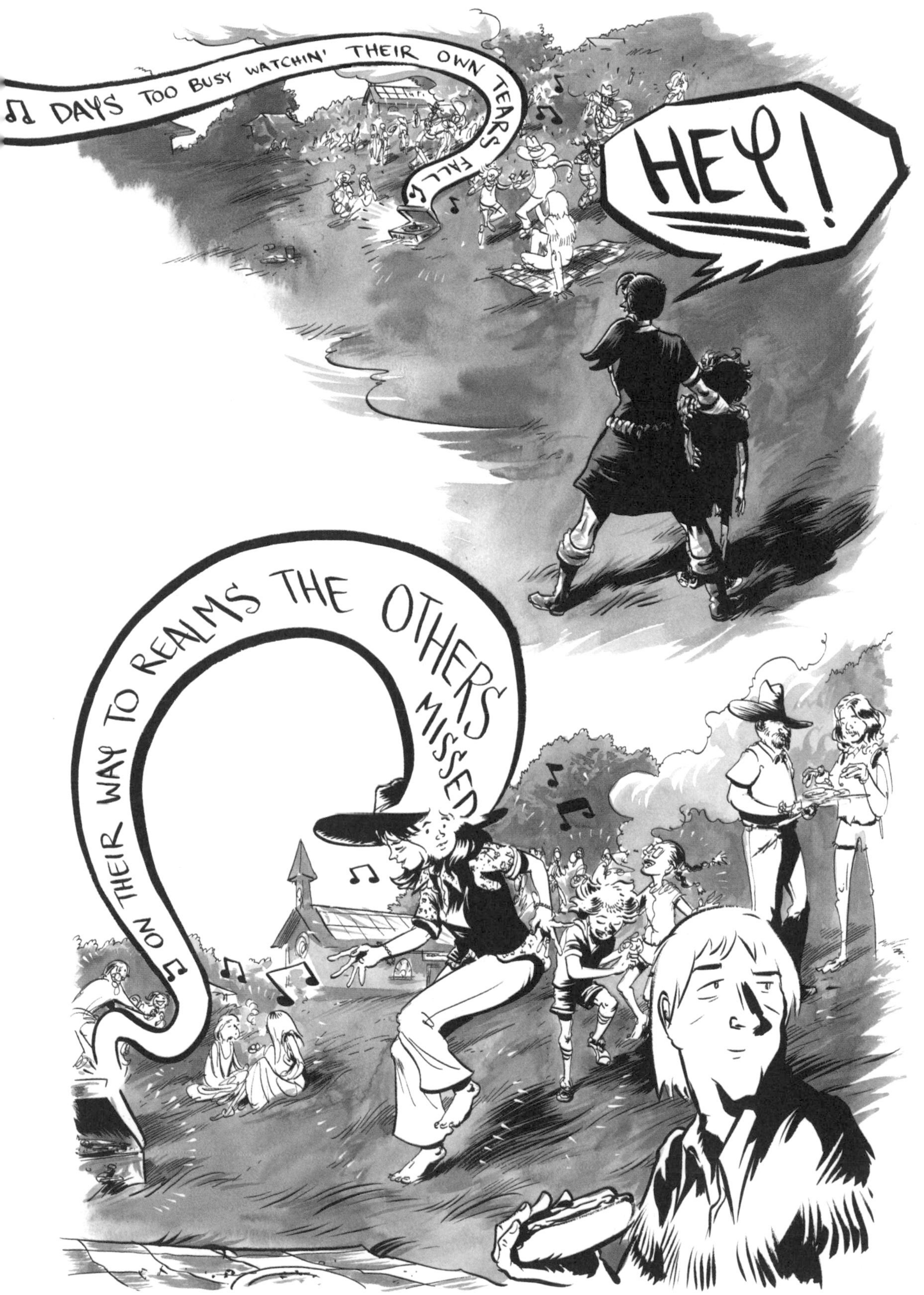
♫ DAYS TOO BUSY WATCHIN' THEIR OWN TEARS FALL ♫
HEY!
♫ ON THEIR WAY TO REALMS THE OTHERS MISSED

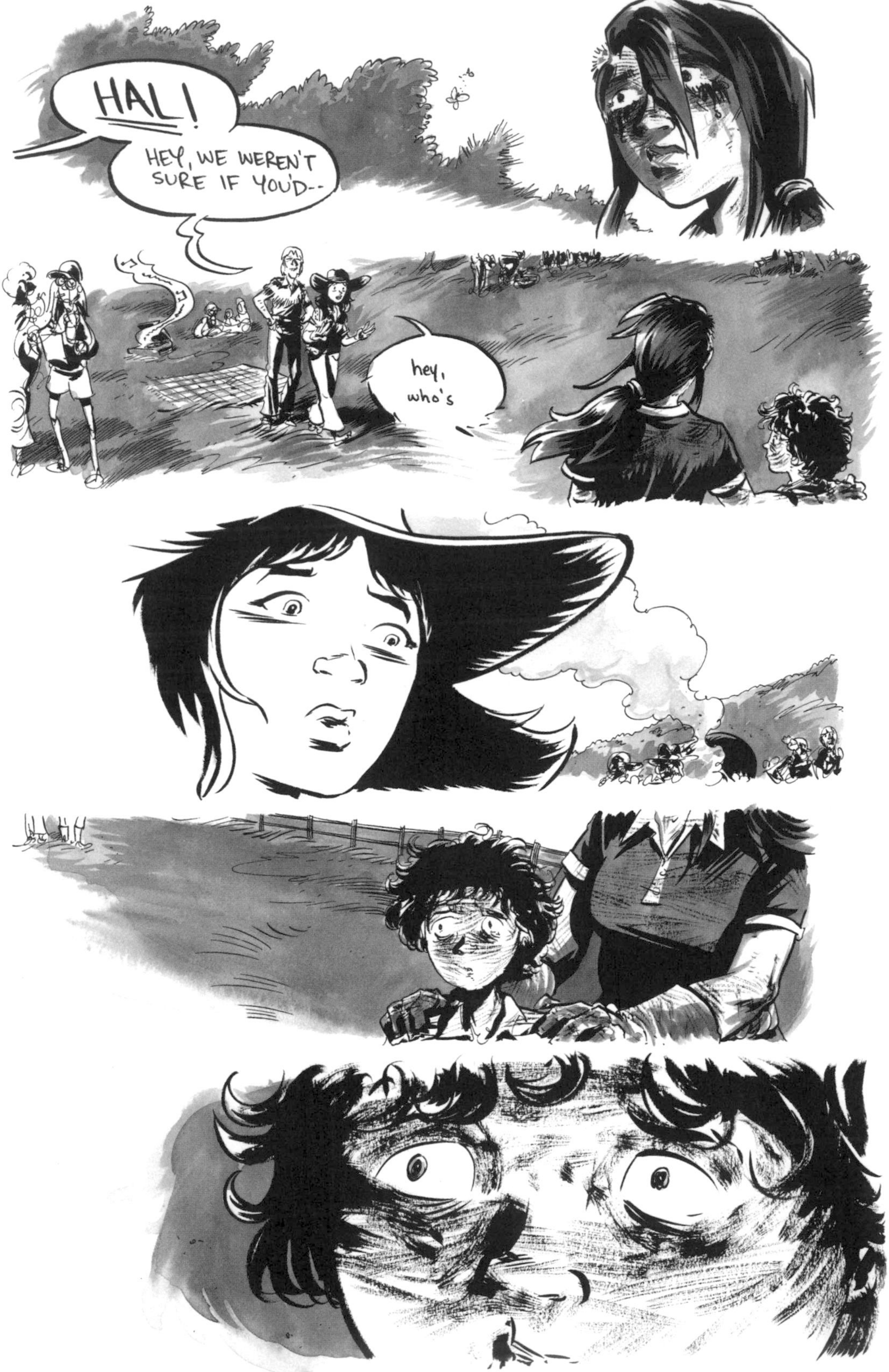
HAL!
HEY, WE WEREN'T SURE IF YOU'D--
hey, who's

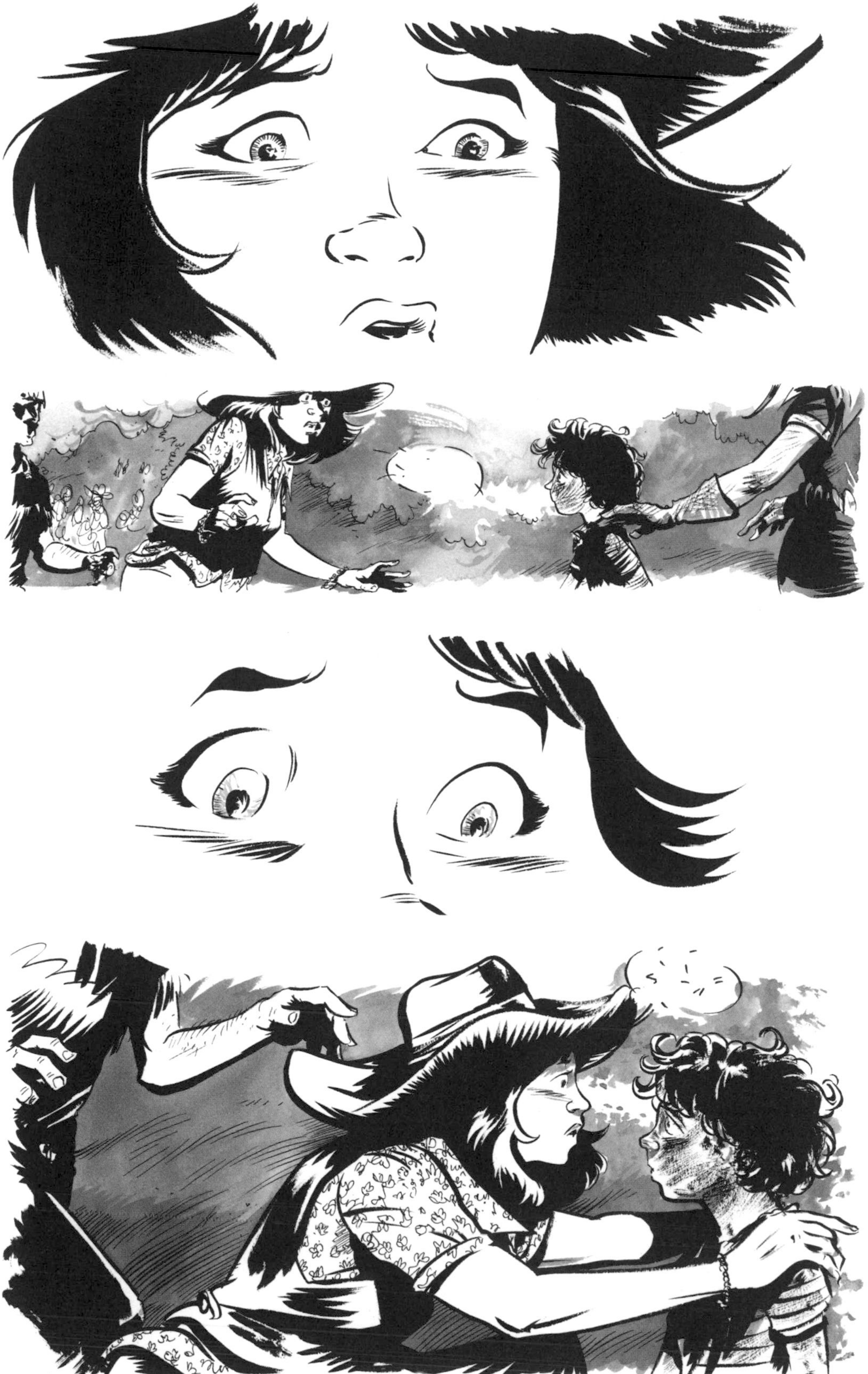

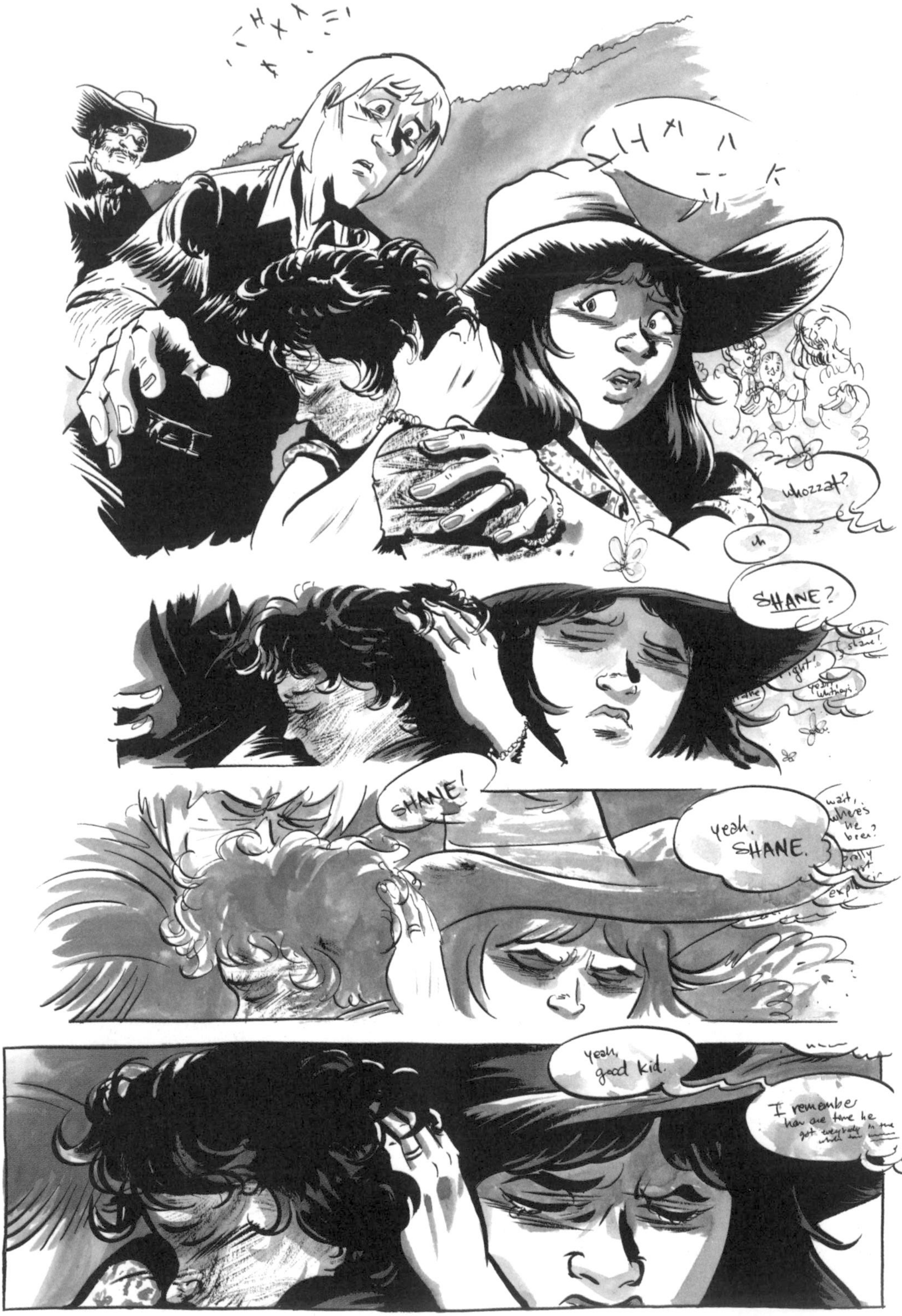
whozzat?
uh
SHANE?
SHANE!
yeah, SHANE.
yeah, good kid.
I remember

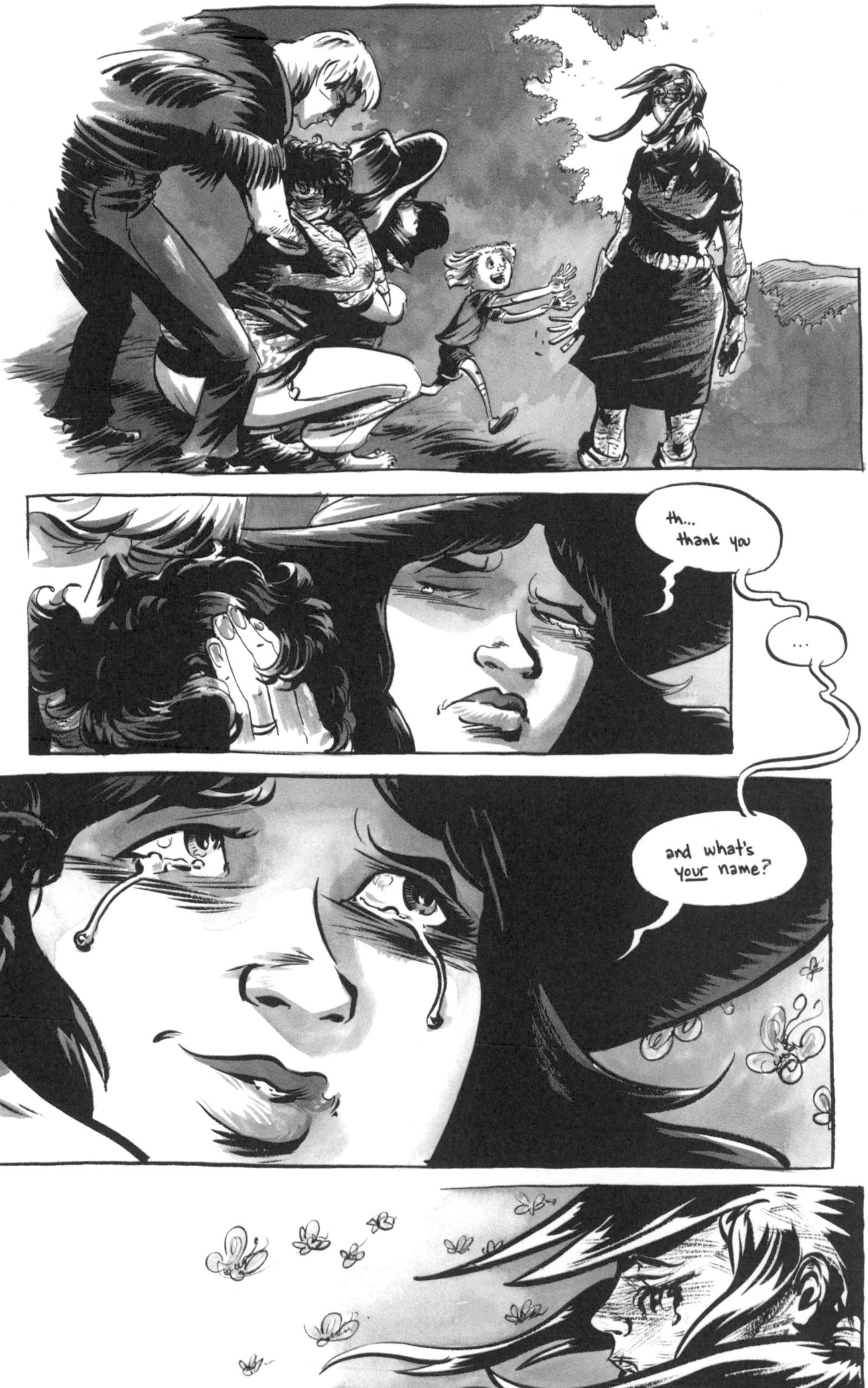
th... thank you
...
and what's your name?

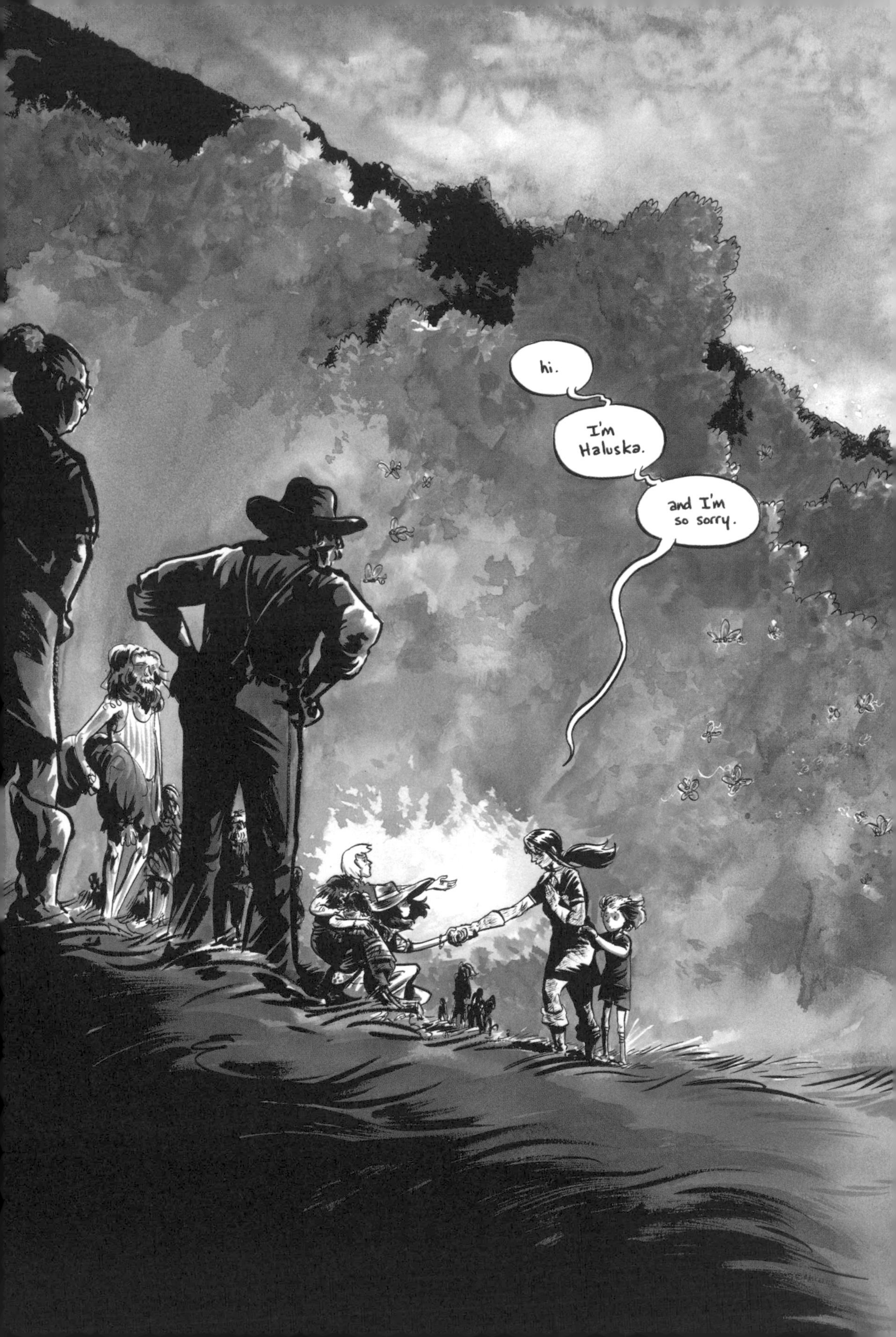
hi.
I'm Haluska.
and I'm so sorry.

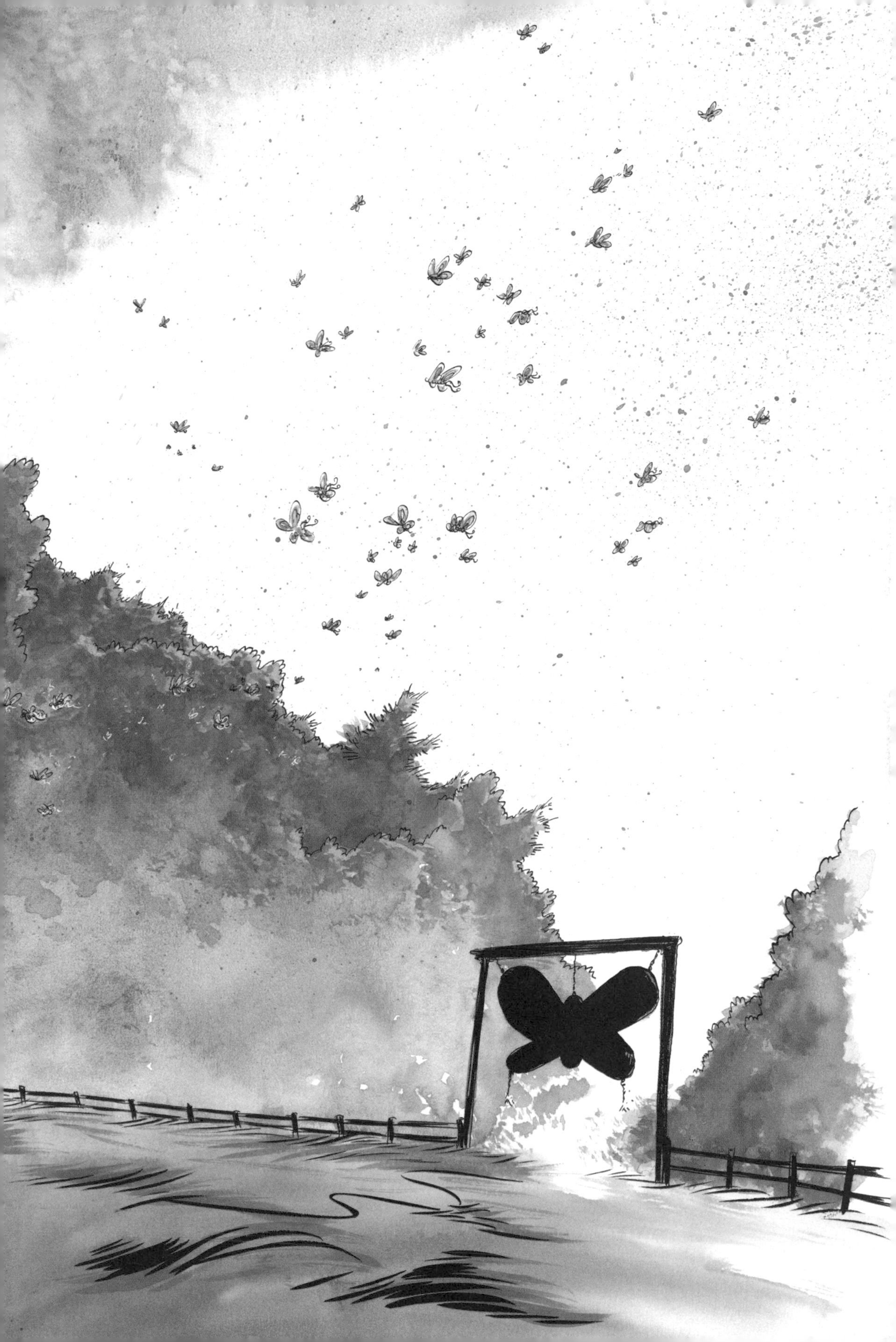

I FORGET HOW THE WORDS GO,

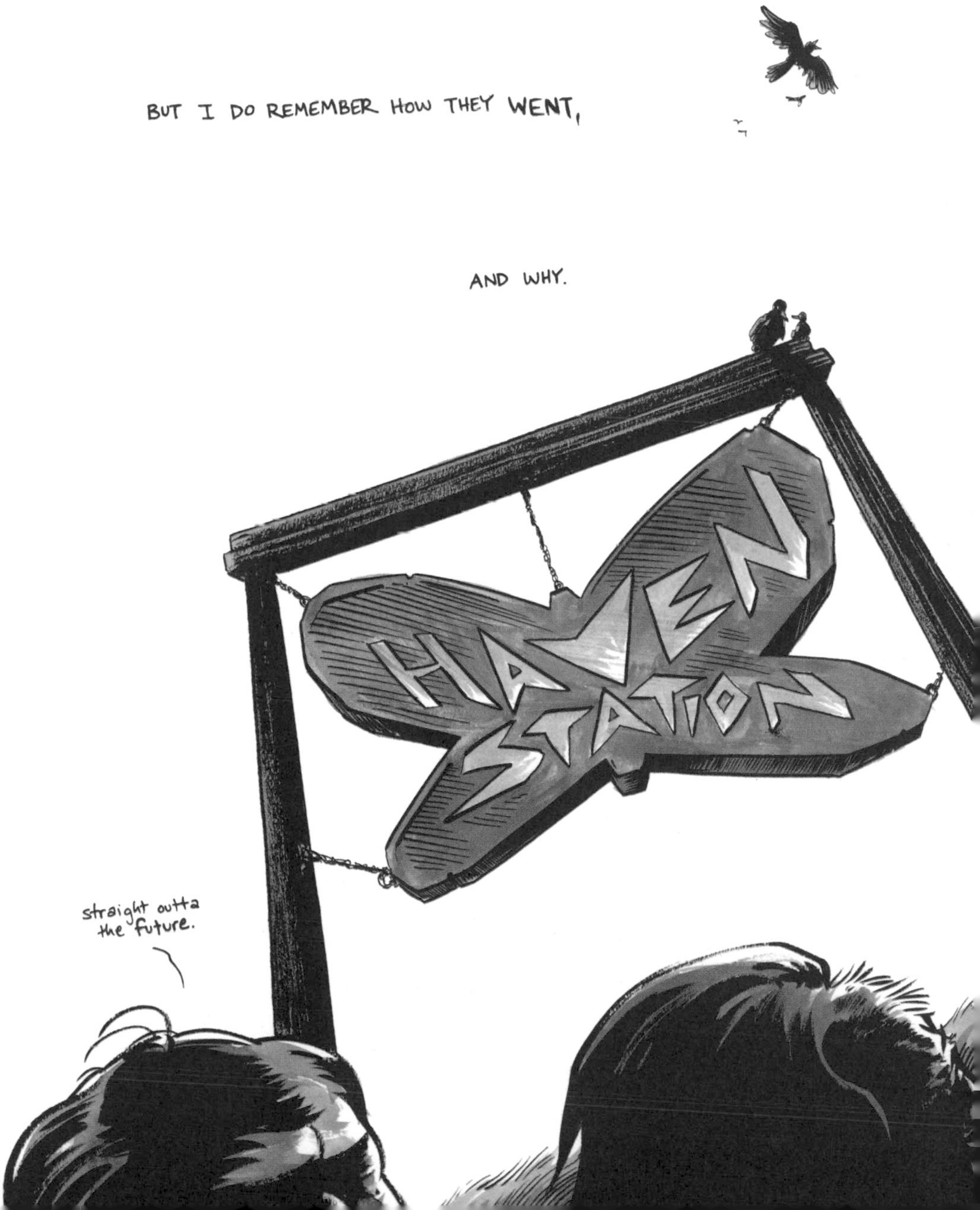

BUT I DO REMEMBER HOW THEY WENT,
AND WHY.
HAVEN STATION
straight outta the future.

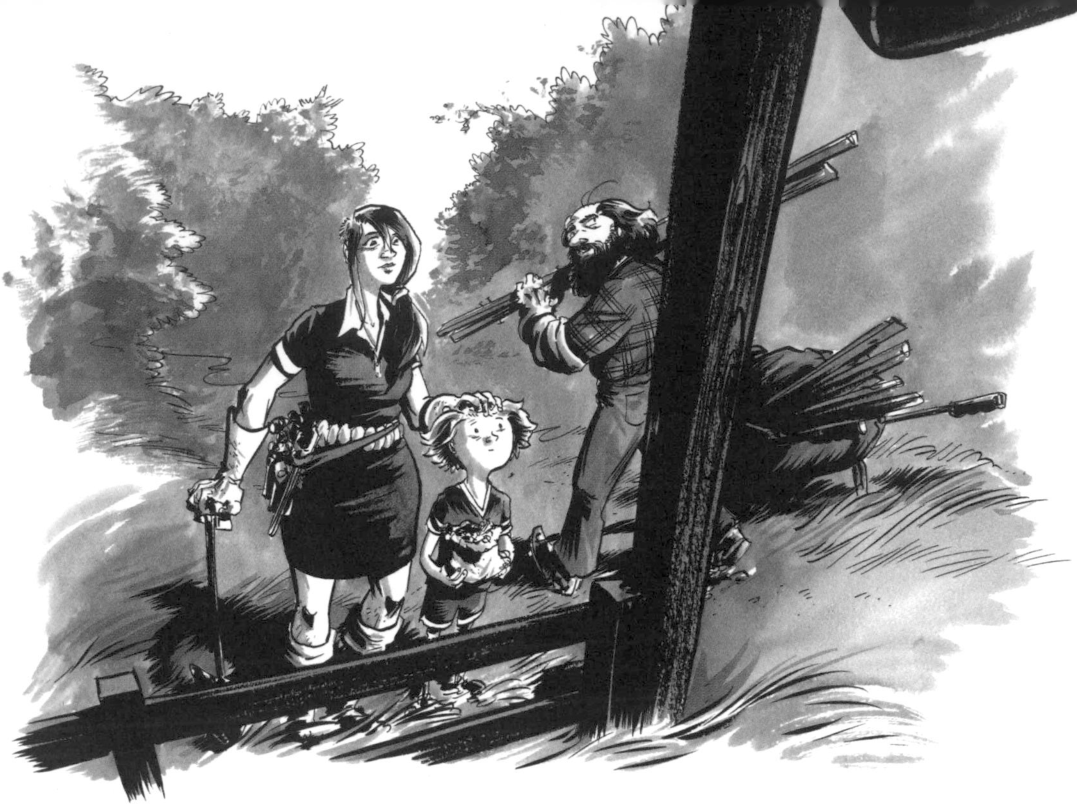

NEIGHBORS CATCH UP,

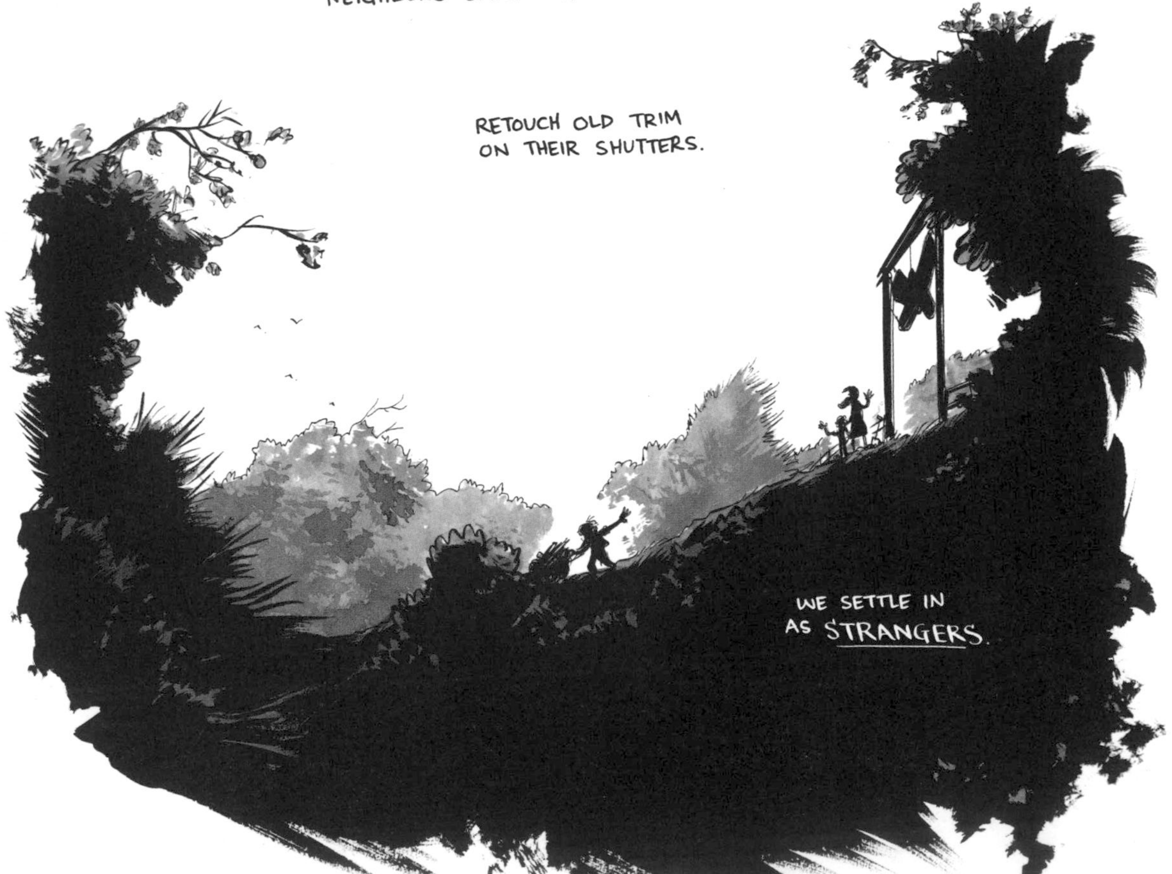
RETOUCH OLD TRIM ON THEIR SHUTTERS.
WE SETTLE IN AS STRANGERS.

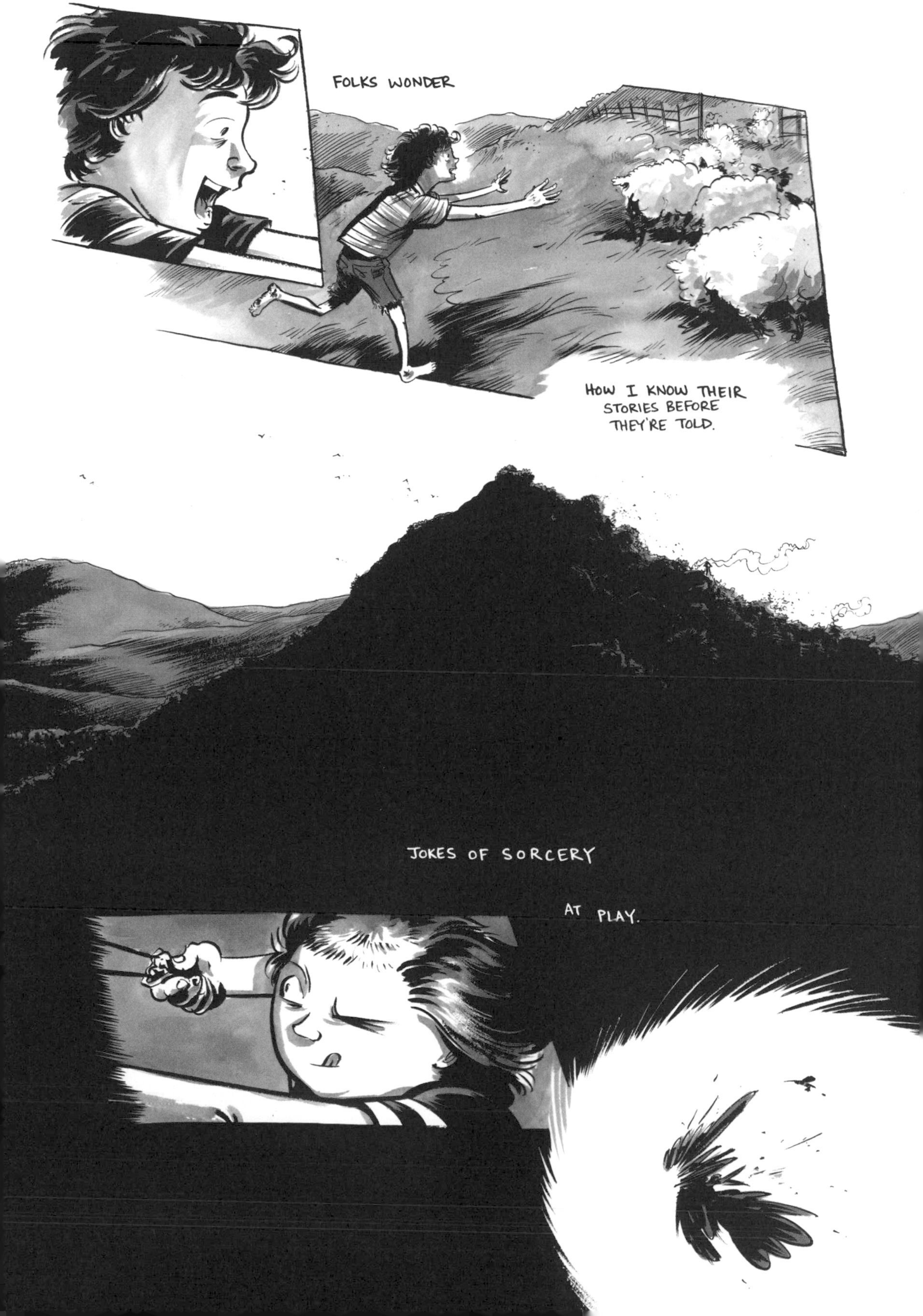
FOLKS WONDER
HOW I KNOW THEIR STORIES BEFORE THEY'RE TOLD.
JOKES OF SORCERY
AT PLAY.

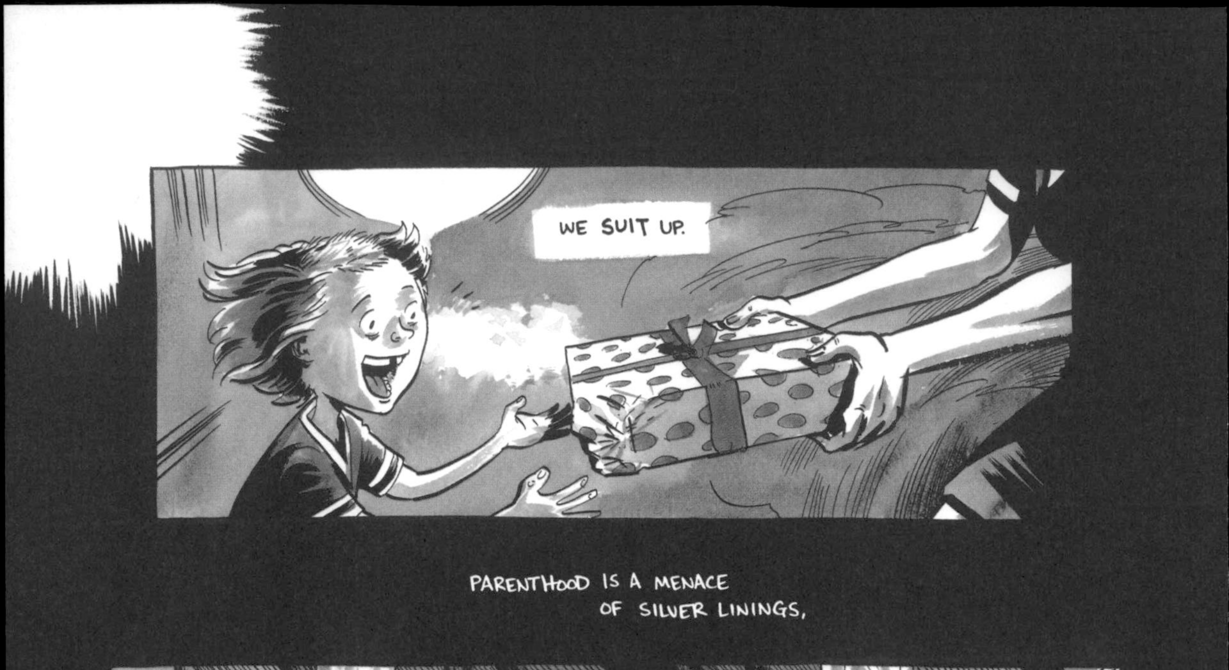
WE SUIT UP.

PARENTHOOD IS A MENACE
OF SILVER LININGS,

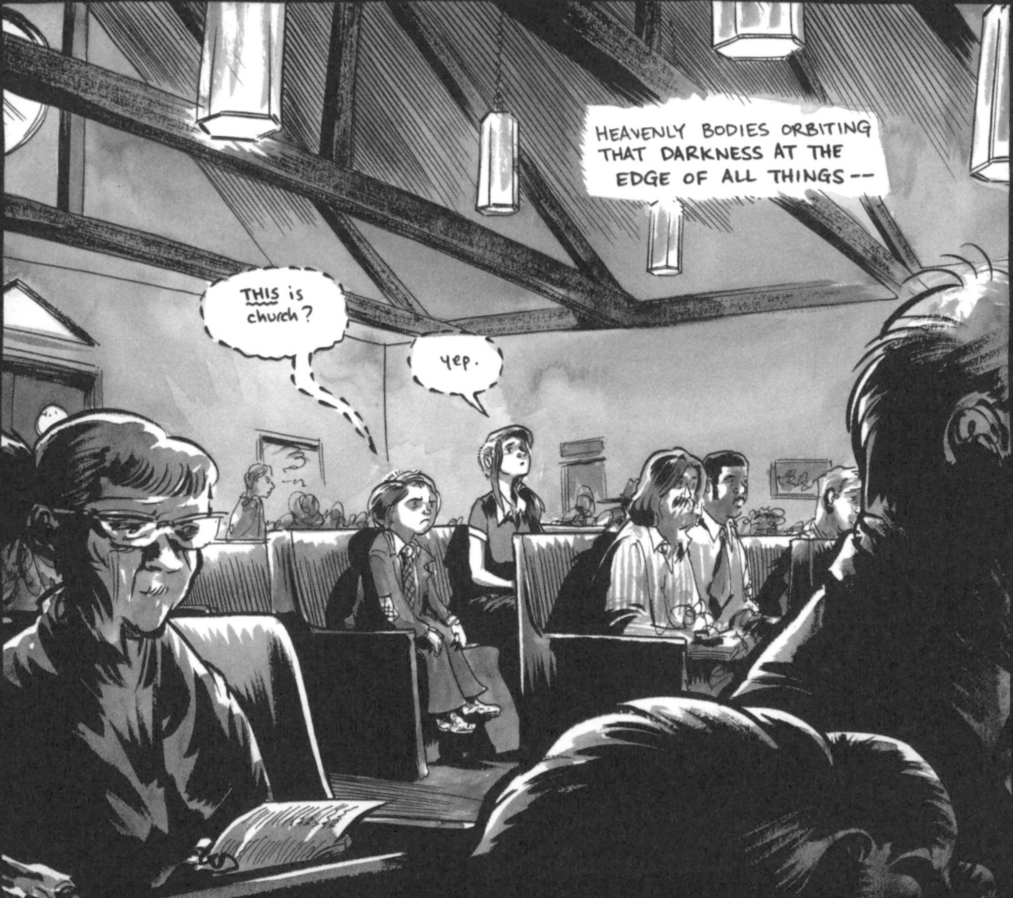
HEAVENLY BODIES ORBITING THAT DARKNESS AT THE EDGE OF ALL THINGS--
THIS is church?
yep.

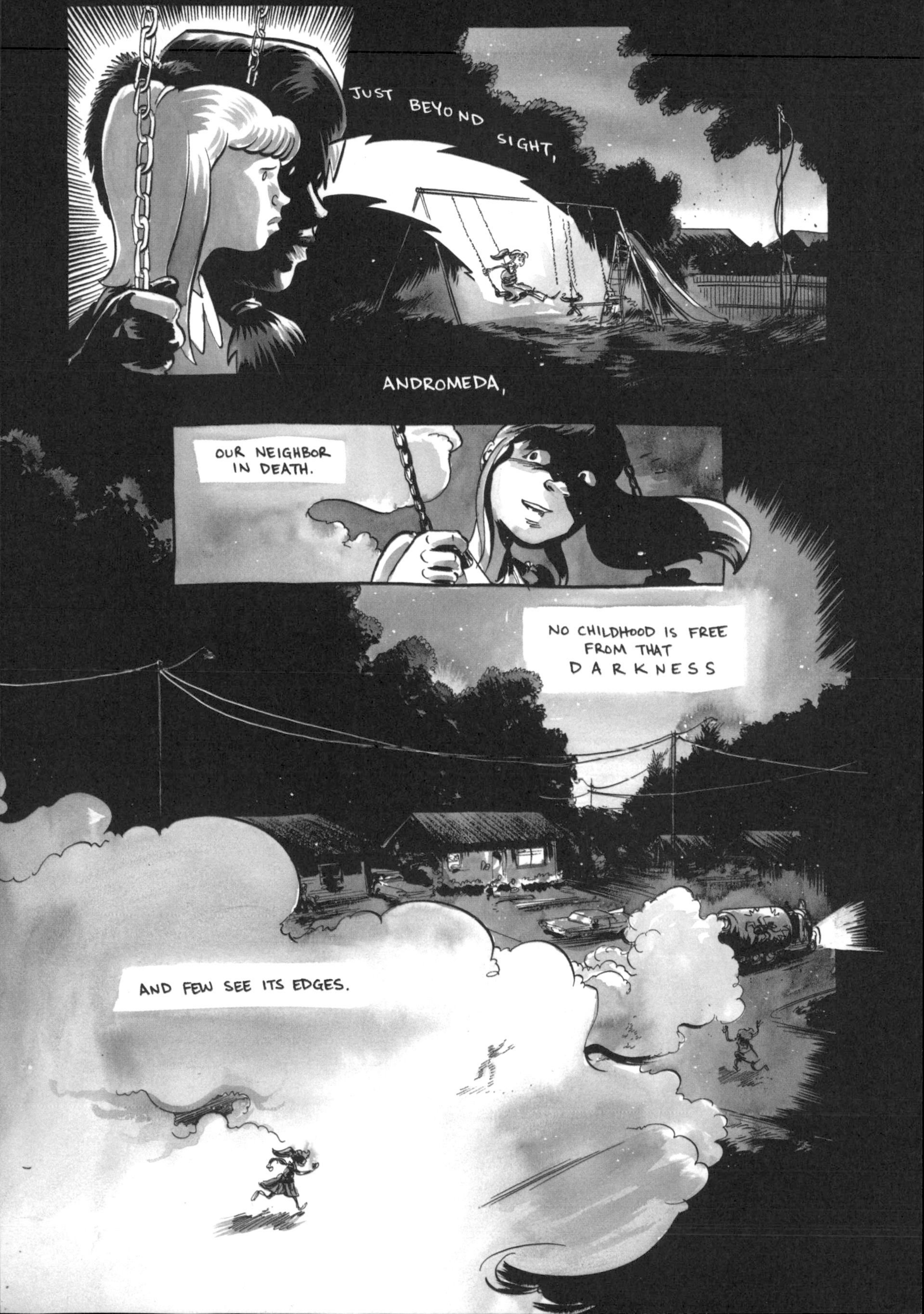

JUST BEYOND SIGHT,
ANDROMEDA,
OUR NEIGHBOR IN DEATH.
NO CHILDHOOD IS FREE FROM THAT DARKNESS
AND FEW SEE ITS EDGES.

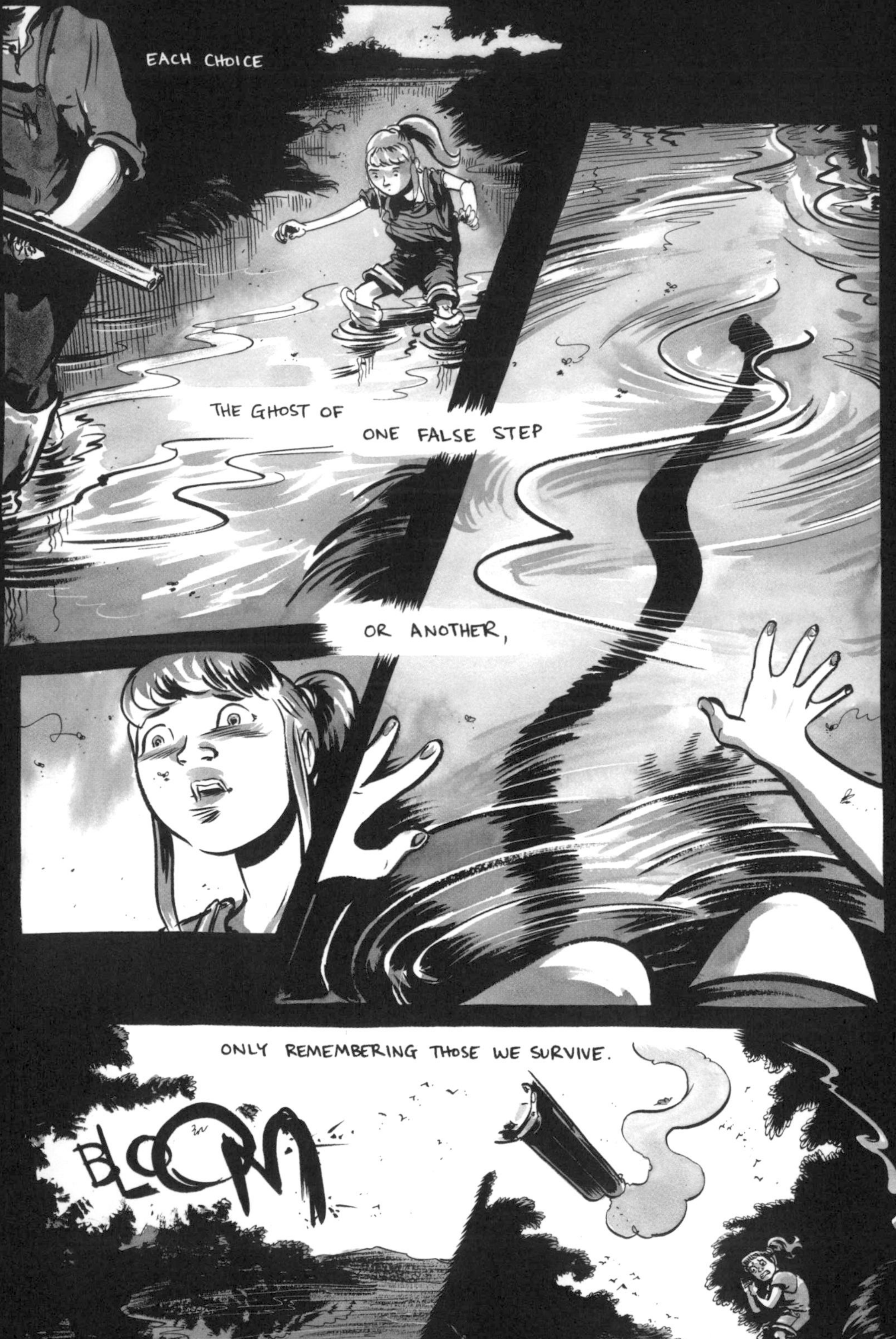
EACH CHOICE
THE GHOST OF
ONE FALSE STEP
OR ANOTHER,
ONLY REMEMBERING THOSE WE SURVIVE.
BLOOM

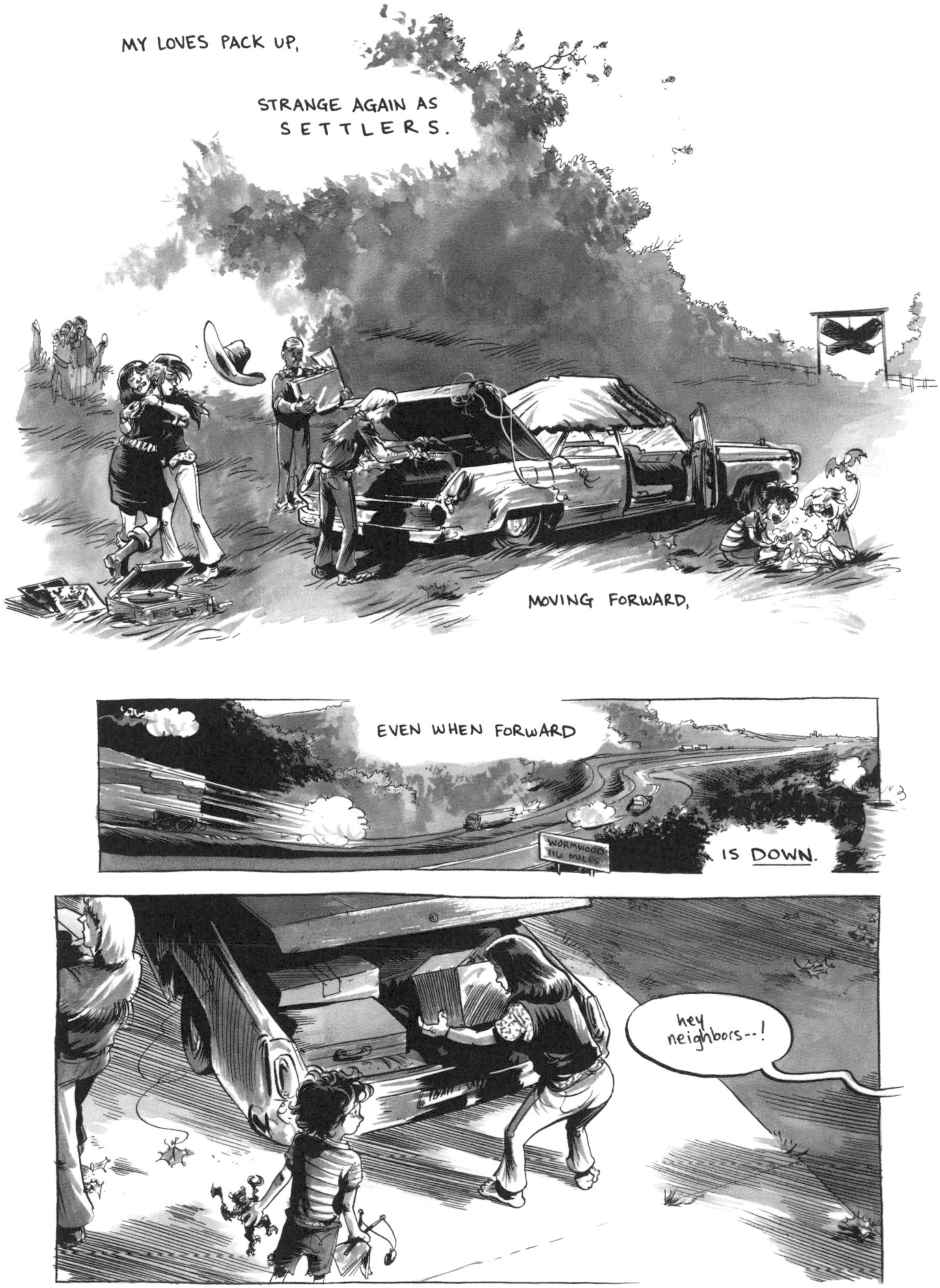
MY LOVES PACK UP,
STRANGE AGAIN AS SETTLERS.
MOVING FORWARD,
EVEN WHEN FORWARD
WORMWOOD 116 MILES
IS DOWN.
hey neighbors--!

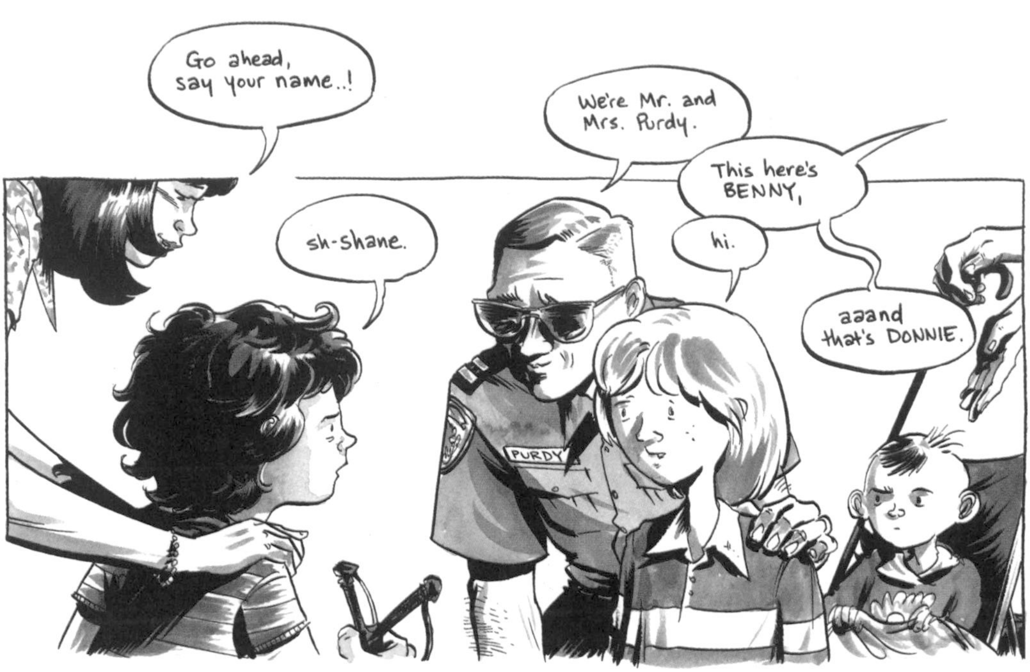
Go ahead, say your name..!
sh-shane.
We're Mr. and Mrs. Purdy.
This here's BENNY,
hi.
aaand that's DONNIE.

ONE STEP,

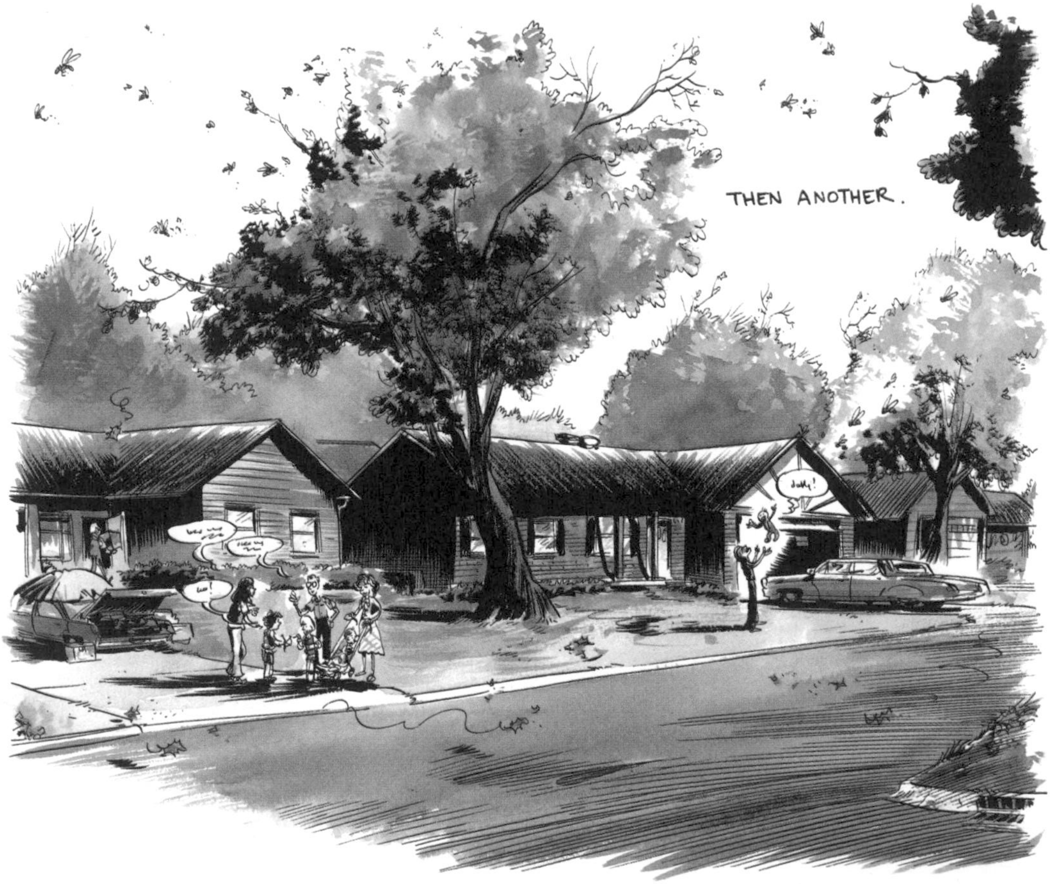
THEN ANOTHER.

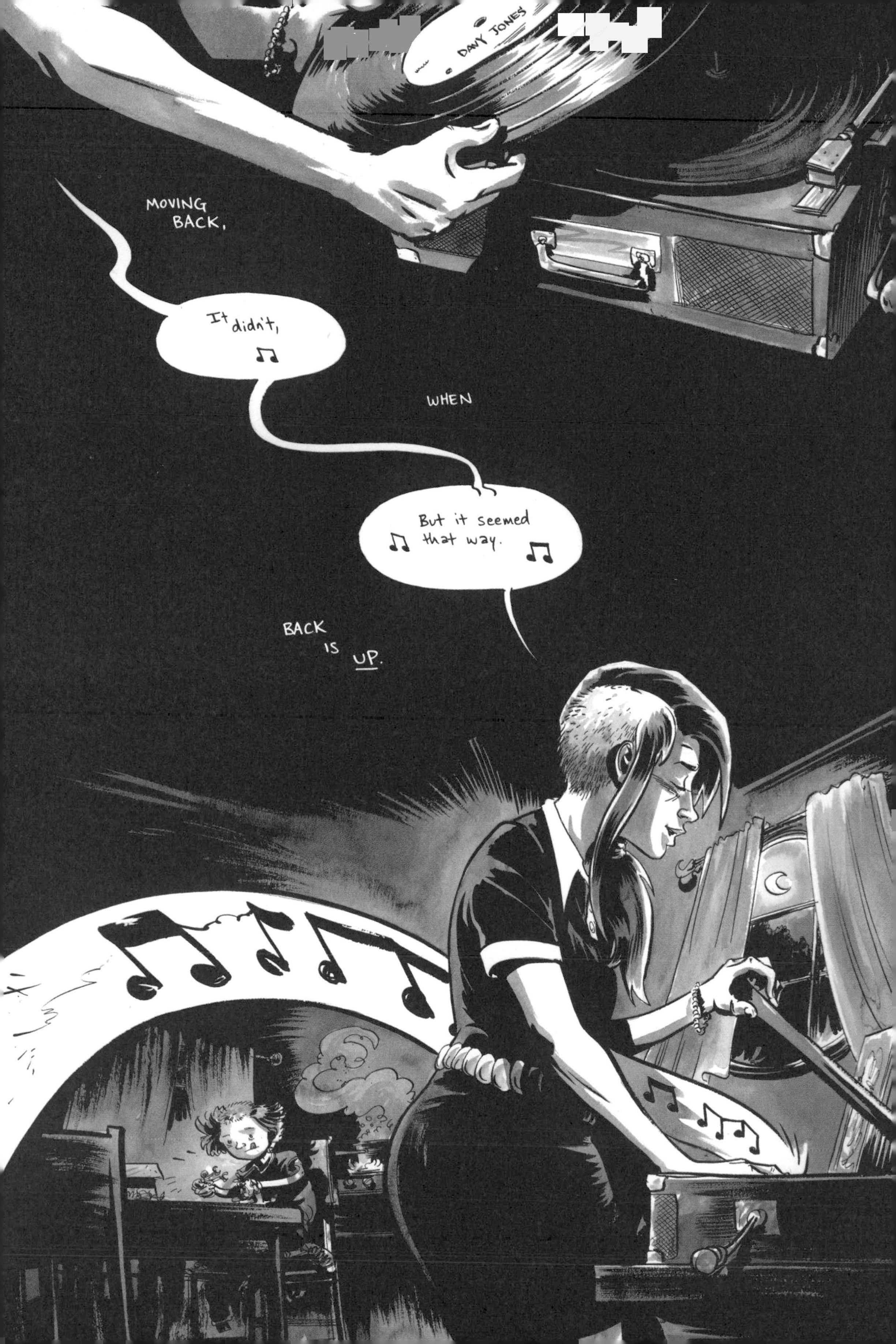
DAVY JONES
MOVING BACK,
It didn't,
WHEN
But it seemed that way.
BACK IS UP.

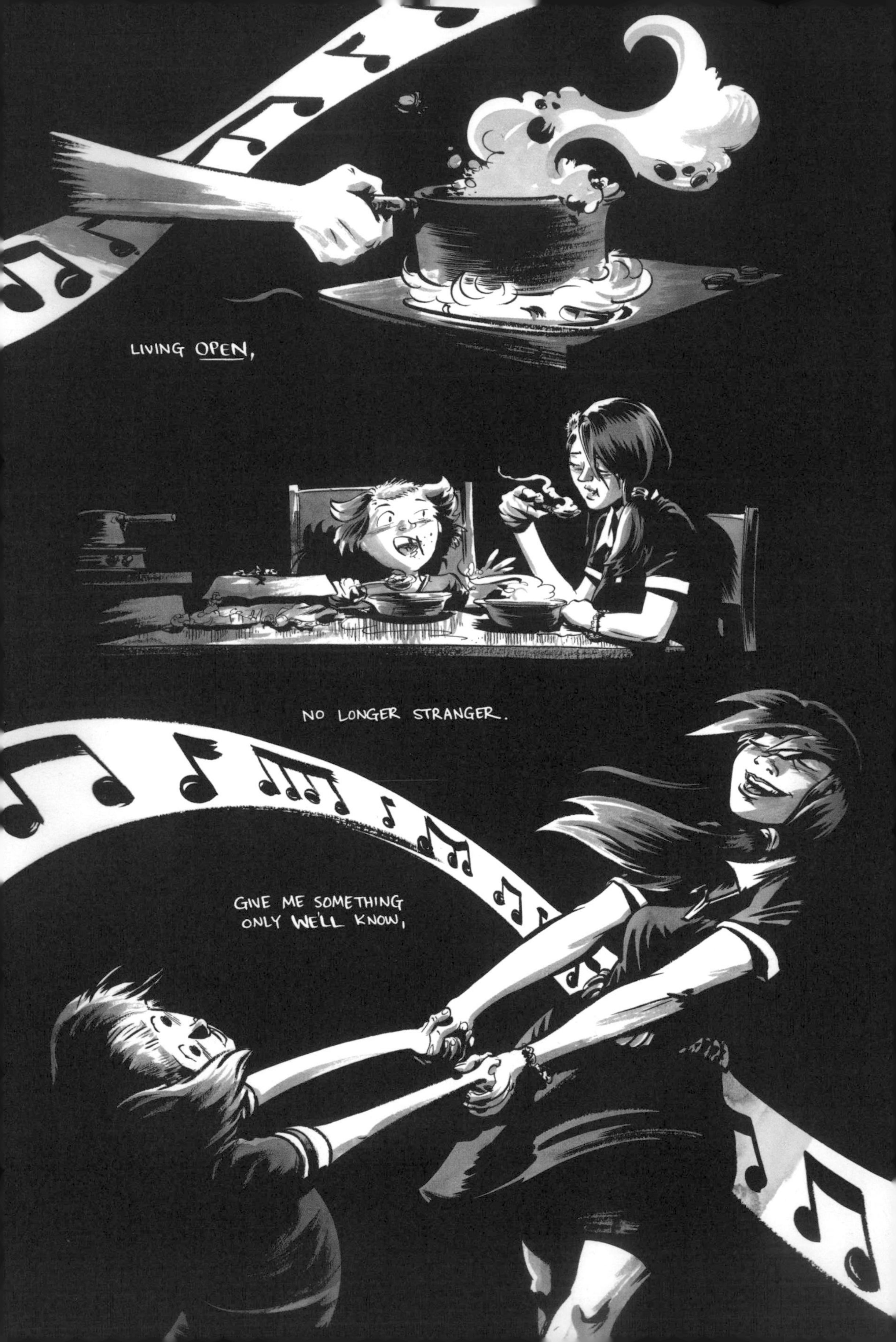
LIVING OPEN,
NO LONGER STRANGER.
GIVE ME SOMETHING ONLY WE'LL KNOW,

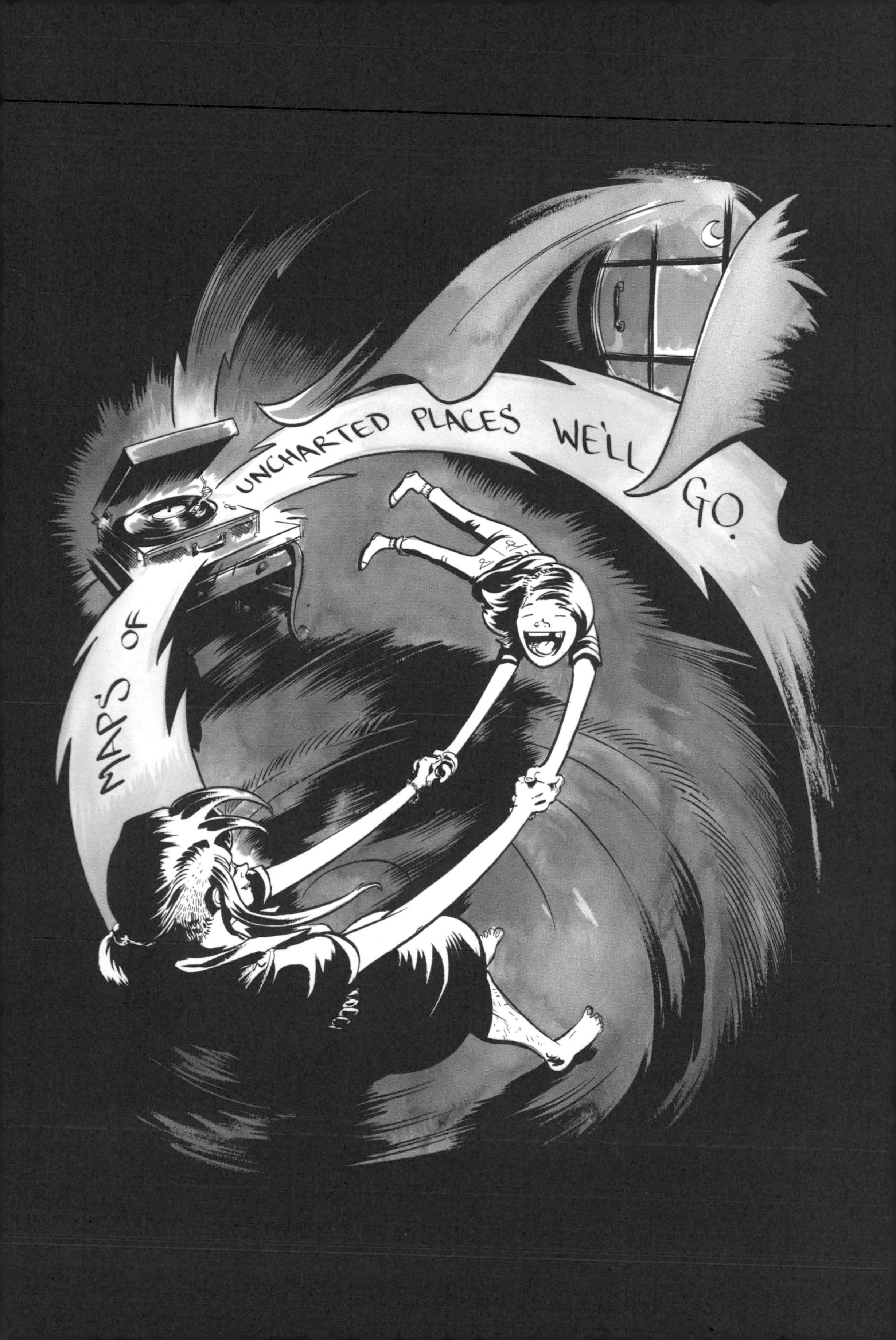
MAPS OF UNCHARTED PLACES WE'LL GO.

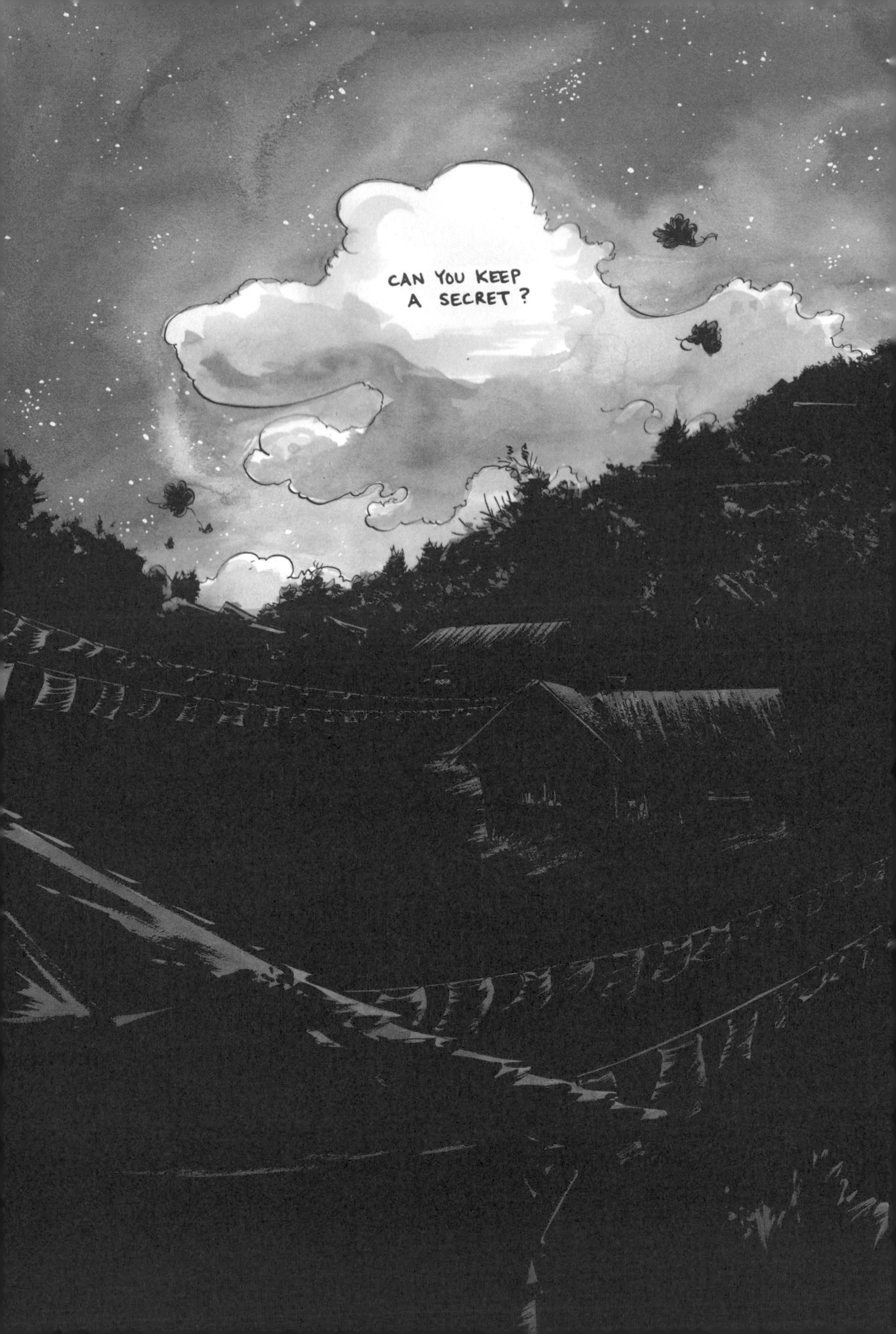
CAN YOU KEEP
A SECRET?

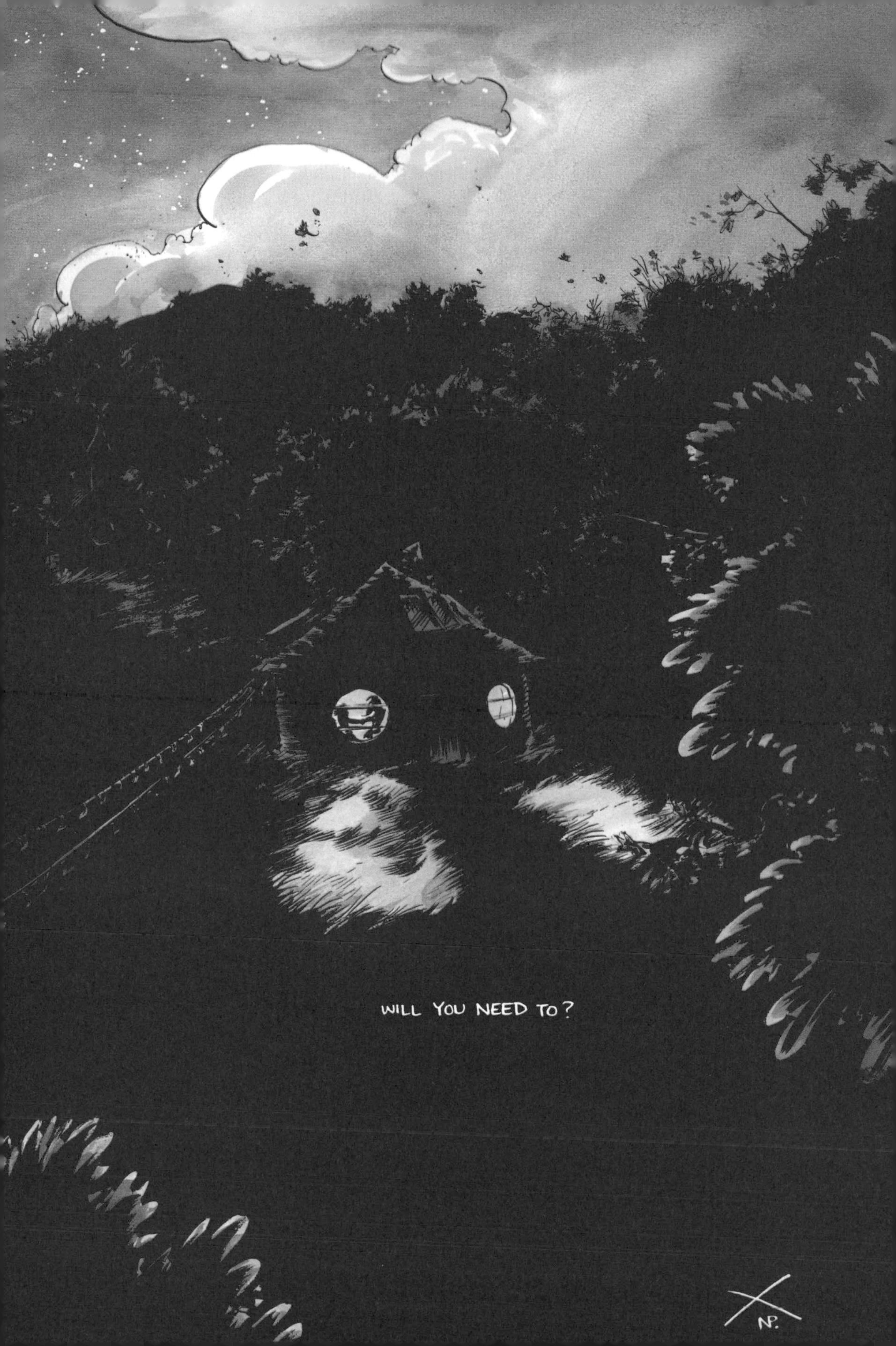
WILL YOU NEED TO?

DEDICATED TO
URSULA K. LeGUIN

THANK YOU:

♡ RACHEL, HARPER, EVERLY. ♡

MY PARENTS and PEYTON.

NATE WILSON and MIKE LIERLY, my OG collaborators on the earliest seeds leading to this story, from "The Porcelain Planet" to "OVOO" to "Cover".

CHRIS STAROS, LEIGH WALTON, CHRIS ROSS, and BRETT WARNOCK, supportive, engaging publishers/collaborators since day one.

ERIN TOBEY, ELI MILHOLLAND, MARALIE ARMSTRONG-RIAL, RYAN SEATON, ALAN SHORT, MARK LIERLY, and EMIL HEIPLE for raising each other-- and to the phantoms, lights, crafts, and little people we've seen.

FAT SHADOW (Dawn, Erin, Chris, Jeff), TIM SCOTT, and AMY OELSNER, for their likenesses and music.
My local comic shop VINTAGE PHOENIX.

CECIL CASTELLUCCI, KATIE SKELLY, VAN JENSEN, CAITLIN McGURK, KIM HIEFTJE, JEFF LEMIRE, ANDREW AYDIN, JOHN LEWIS, JONATHAN VANCE, TONIE JOY, ED PISKOR, PENINA GAL, BECKY CLOONAN, CLYDE PETERSEN, ANDREA ZOLLO, JILLIAN TAMAKI, AARON COMETBUS, MIRIAM LIBICKI, CT, MICHAEL HOERGER, PHOEBE GLOECKNER, JOEL GILL, DERF BACKDERF, ZAC BOONE, CHARLIE OLSEN, KATY NEW, ISSY MUELLER, NICOLE GEORGES, JOHN GREINER, JASON WHITE, MARLEY ZARCONE, ETHAN YOUNG.
Inspiration, love, good conversation.

IDW FOLKS past and present— MARION, ROZ, TED, GREG, CHRIS, DIRK, SARAH, JUSTIN, KAHLIL, MICHAEL, ROBBIE, and all !

Rest in peace, TRAVIS FRISTOE. We love you.

— REMAIN —
— OPEN —

NATE POWELL is the first cartoonist ever to win the National Book Award. Born in Little Rock, Arkansas in 1978, he began self-publishing at age 14 and graduated from School of Visual Arts in 2000.

His work includes MARCH, civil rights icon John Lewis' graphic memoir trilogy ; ANY EMPIRE, SWALLOW ME WHOLE, YOU DON'T SAY, THE SILENCE OF OUR FRIENDS, THE YEAR OF THE BEASTS, and Rick Riordan's THE LOST HERO.

Powell's work has recieved a Robert F. Kennedy Book Award, three Eisner Awards, two Ignatz Awards, the Michael L. Printz Award, the Walter Dean Myers Award, the Sibert Medal, multiple YALSA Great Graphic Novels For Teens selections, and has been a two-time finalist for the Los Angeles Times Book Prize. He has discussed his work at the United Nations, as well as on MSNBC's The Rachel Maddow Show and CNN.

He lives in Bloomington, Indiana, and is currently fighting alongside you to save the world.

www.seemybrotherdance.org

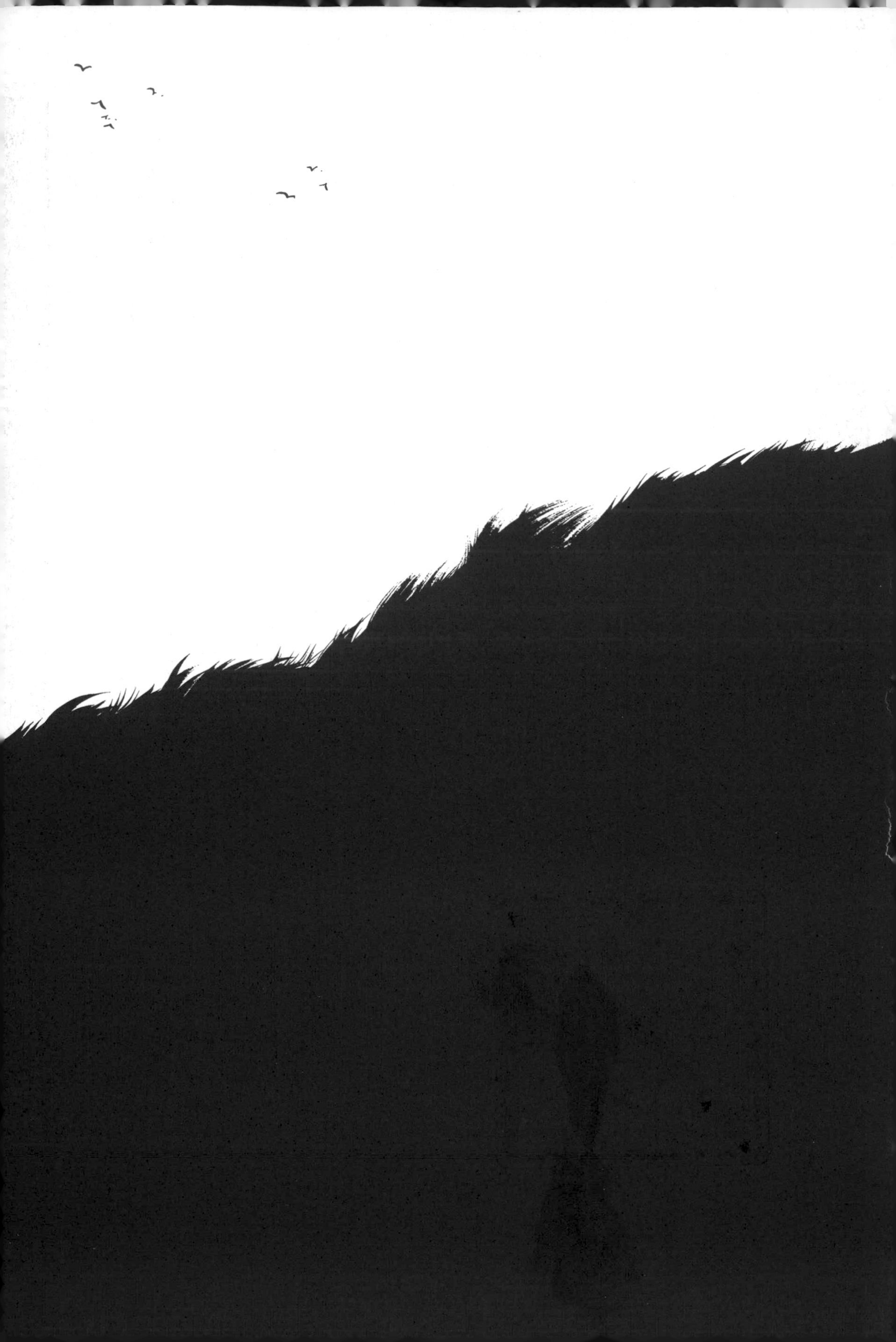